The Contribution of International and Supranational Courts to the Rule of Law

LEUVEN GLOBAL GOVERNANCE

Series Editor: Jan Wouters, *University of Leuven (KU Leuven), Belgium*

The Leuven Global Governance series comprises high-quality monographs and edited volumes dedicated to innovative research on global governance. The series focuses particularly on the following themes: European Union and global multilateral governance; trade and sustainable development; peace and security studies; human rights, democracy and the rule of law; space governance and comparative federalism. In full recognition of the complex issues involved, the series favours studies approaching global governance from a multidisciplinary, multi-level and multi-actor perspective.

Titles in the series include:

China, the European Union and Global Governance
Edited by Jan Wouters, Tanguy de Wilde, Pierre Defraigne and Jean-Christophe Defraigne

Private Standards and Global Governance
Legal and Economic Perspectives
Edited by Axel Marx, Miet Maertens, Johan F.M. Swinnen and Jan Wouters

The Governance of Climate Relations between Europe and Asia
Evidence from China and Vietnam as Key Emerging Economies
Edited by Hans Bruyninckx, Qi Ye, Nguyen Quang Thuan and David Belis

Indirect Expropriation in International Law
Sebastián López Escarcena

Global Governance and Democracy
A Multidisciplinary Analysis
Edited by Jan Wouters, Antoon Braeckman, Matthias Lievens and Emilie Bécault

The Contribution of International and Supranational Courts to the Rule of Law
Edited by Geert De Baere and Jan Wouters

Global Governance of Labor Rights
Assessing the Effectiveness of Transnational Public and Private Policy Initiatives
Edited by Axel Marx, Jan Wouters, Glenn Rayp and Laura Beke

Global Governance through Trade
EU Policies and Approaches
Edited by Jan Wouters, Axel Marx, Dylan Geraets and Bregt Natens

The Contribution of International and Supranational Courts to the Rule of Law

Edited by

Geert De Baere

Associate Professor, International Law and EU Law, Institute for European Law and Leuven Centre for Global Governance Studies, KU Leuven, Belgium

Jan Wouters

Full Professor, International Law and International Organizations, Jean Monnet Chair Ad Personam *EU and Global Governance, Director, Leuven Centre for Global Governance Studies and Institute for International Law, KU Leuven, Belgium*

LEUVEN GLOBAL GOVERNANCE

Edward Elgar
PUBLISHING

Cheltenham, UK • Northampton, MA, USA

Published by
Edward Elgar Publishing Limited
The Lypiatts
15 Lansdown Road
Cheltenham
Glos GL50 2JA
UK

Edward Elgar Publishing, Inc.
William Pratt House
9 Dewey Court
Northampton
Massachusetts 01060
USA

A catalogue record for this book
is available from the British Library

Library of Congress Control Number: 2015943172

This book is available electronically in the **Elgar**online
Law subject collection
DOI 10.4337/9781783476626

MIX
Paper from
responsible sources
FSC® C013056
FSC
www.fsc.org

ISBN 978 1 78347 661 9 (cased)
ISBN 978 1 78347 662 6 (eBook)

Typeset by Columns Design XML Ltd, Reading
Printed and bound in Great Britain by TJ International Ltd, Padstow

Contents

Contributors

Serge Brammertz is the Prosecutor of the International Criminal Tribunal for the former Yugoslavia (ICTY). In Belgium, he has served as Deputy to the Prosecutor-General at the Liège Court of Appeal, was in charge of coordinating investigations in the fields of international drug trafficking and trafficking of human beings as a national magistrate, and was later the Belgian federal chief prosecutor. He was Deputy Prosecutor of the International Criminal Court, in charge of the Investigations Division of the Office of the Prosecutor when the investigations of crimes committed in Uganda, the DRC and Darfur were initiated. In 2006–07 he headed the investigation by the UN International Independent Investigation Commission into the murder of the former Lebanese Prime Minister Rafik Hariri. He holds a law degree from the Université catholique de Louvain, a degree in criminology from the University of Liège and a PhD in international law from the Albert Ludwig University in Freiburg, Germany. He is currently also visiting professor at Strathmore law school, Nairobi, teaching international criminal law

Antônio Augusto Cançado Trindade has been a Judge at the International Court of Justice (ICJ) since 2009. He holds an LLM and PhD in International Law from the University of Cambridge. He is a Full Professor of Public International Law at the University of Brasilia and was a lecturer at the Hague Academy of International Law. He received honorary degrees at the Universidad Nacional Mayor de San Marcos, the Central University of Chile, the Catholic University of Peru, the American University of Paraguay and the National University of La Plata. He is a former President of the Inter-American Court of Human Rights and Executive Director of the Inter-American Institute of Human Rights. Since 2004, he has been a Member of the Curatorium of the Hague Academy of International Law.

Kenneth Chan joined the Leuven Centre for Global Governance Studies in December 2010 as PhD candidate in the research programme Global Governance and Democratic Government. His research focuses on the global peace and security governance track of the programme. He has a background in law, receiving an LLB (Hons.) from the University of

Auckland, New Zealand (2009) and read for his LLM (adv) in Public International Law at the University of Leiden (2010). He has interned at the ICTY on the Stanišić trial and the Coalition for the ICC, acting as an independent legal observer for the Lubanga and Katanga/Ngudjolo trials. His main interest is international criminal law.

Anna-Luise Chané joined the Leuven Centre for Global Governance Studies in August 2013 as a research fellow and PhD candidate on the FP7 research project 'Fostering Human Rights Among European Policies' (FRAME). She studied law at the University of Cologne and KU Leuven and passed her First and Second Juridical State Examination with distinction. She holds a Master of Laws degree from Harvard Law School, where she was an ERP Scholar of the German Ministry of Economy and Technology and the German National Academic Foundation. Anna-Luise completed internships with the Association of German Chambers of Commerce and Industry in Brussels and the Federal Ministry of Transport, Building and Urban Development. In addition she was a research assistant at the Chair for Public International Law, European Law, European and International Economic Law at the University of Cologne. As a law clerk, she worked for Cleary Gottlieb Steen & Hamilton LLP and served among others in the Consulate General in Los Angeles and in the Federal Ministry for Economic Cooperation and Development.

Barbara Concolino studied law at the University of Roma Tre where she graduated summa cum laude. She then continued her studies with a doctorate in International and EU Law (University of Teramo). During her doctoral studies, she also worked as a University Assistant at the Universities of Roma Tre and LUISS Guido Carli and as a Trainee Lawyer for the Avvocatura Generale dello Stato (State Legal Counsel). From 2008 to 2013, she worked as a Legal Adviser at the Iran-United States Claims Tribunal. She is currently working as a Senior Associate in the International Arbitration Department of Bonelli Erede Pappalardo in Milan. She has published articles on a number of subjects including arbitration, international law, EU law, terrorism and human rights. She was admitted to practice law in Italy in 2007.

Philippe Couvreur has been the Registrar of the International Court of Justice (ICJ) since 2000 (re-elected in 2007 and 2014). He studied law at the Faculties of Notre-Dame de la Paix (Namur), Université catholique de Louvain (where he also studied philosophy), King's College London and the Universidad complutense (Madrid). At the ICJ he has been Special Assistant in the offices of the Registrar and Deputy-Registrar, Secretary,

First Secretary and Principal Legal Secretary (Head of the Legal Department). He has been guest lecturer in public international law at the Law Faculty of the Université catholique de Louvain since 1997 and taught inter alia at the Law Faculty of the University of Ouagadougou (Burkina Faso) and at the Ecole des Hautes études commerciales Saint-Louis. He is a Corresponding Member of the Spanish Royal Academy of Moral and Political Sciences and member of various other learned societies, and is the author of numerous publications.

Geert De Baere is Associate Professor of International Law and EU Law at the Institute for European Law and the Leuven Centre for Global Governance Studies at KU Leuven. He studied law at the University of Antwerp (Cand. Iuris, 1999 and Lic. Iuris, 2002) and at King's College, Cambridge (LLM, 2003 and PhD, 2007). In 2005, he was a visiting research fellow at Columbia Law School's European Legal Studies Center, New York City. From 2007 to 2009, he worked as a référendaire in the chambers of Advocate General Sharpston at the Court of Justice of the EU, while being a postdoctoral research associate at the University of Antwerp. His publications include G De Baere, *Constitutional Principles of EU External Relations* (OUP, 2008), E Cloots, G De Baere, and S Sottiaux (eds), *Federalism in the EU* (Hart Publishing, 2012), and PJ Kuijper, J Wouters, F Hoffmeister, G De Baere, and T Ramopoulos, *The Law of EU External Relations: Cases, Materials, and Commentary on the EU as an International Legal Actor* (OUP, 2013).

Andreas Follesdal is Professor of Political Philosophy affiliated with the Department of Philosophy at the University of Tromsø. PhD 1991 in Philosophy, Harvard University. Director of the Norwegian Centre of Excellence PluriCourts for the Study of the Legitimate Roles of the Judiciary in the Global Order (2013–24). Principal Investigator, European Research Council Advanced Grant MultiRights 2011–16, on the legitimacy of multi-level human rights judiciary. Publishes on a variety of issues concerning Human Rights, Globalisation, Democracy, and Europeanisation. Fellow of The Norwegian Academy of Science and Letters.

Daniel Fransen is the Pre-Trial Judge of the Special Tribunal for Lebanon (STL). After working as a defence lawyer at the Brussels Bar from 1989 to 1993 and subsequently as a lawyer in the public service at the Société régionale du Port de Bruxelles (1994 to 1995), he entered the judiciary, where he served as an investigating judge at the Brussels District Court for more than ten years. He dealt with serious and organised financial and economic crimes before specialising in international humanitarian law and terrorism cases. Until his appointment as the Pre-Trial Judge of the STL, Judge Fransen was dean of the investigating judges specialising in terrorism in Belgium (2006 to 2009). He has written several publications on terrorism.

Philippe Gautier has been the Registrar of the International Tribunal for the Law of the Sea (ITLOS) since 2001. He was Deputy Registrar of the Tribunal from 1997 to 2001. He is also Professor at the Catholic University of Louvain (Louvain-la-Neuve). He began his career in the Belgian Ministry of Foreign Affairs (1984–97), where he served as Head of the Treaties Division (1995–97) and as Head of the Law of the Sea Office (1991–95). He is doctor of law and holds a master in philosophy from the Catholic University of Louvain (Louvain-la-Neuve) where he has been teaching since 1993. He is the author of numerous publications on the law of treaties, protection of the environment, the law of international organizations, settlement of international disputes, law of the sea and Antarctica.

Paul Lemmens has been a Judge at the European Court of Human Rights since 2012. He is also a Professor of Human Rights Law at KU Leuven. He studied law at the universities of Antwerp and Leuven and at Northwestern University (Chicago). In 1987 he obtained his PhD in Law at KU Leuven. He was a visiting professor of human rights law at Northwestern University (1999). Since 1994 he has been a judge, later a chamber president in the Council of State. Previously, he worked as an attorney at the Brussels Bar and was an auditor in the Council of State.

Koen Lenaerts is a Judge and the President of the Court of Justice of the European Union and Professor of EU Law at KU Leuven. He studied law at the Faculties of Notre-Dame de la Paix (Namur), KU Leuven and Harvard University, and obtained a PhD in Law in 1982 in Leuven. He was the founding director of the Institute for European Law of KU Leuven. From 1989 to 2003 he was Judge at the General Court of the European Union. Since 2003 he has been a Judge at the European Court of Justice. He was made an Honorary Master of the Bench of the Inner Temple, London, in 2010.

Peter Van den Bossche has been a Member of the Appellate Body of the World Trade Organization (WTO) since 2009 and currently serves as its Chair. He is also Professor of International Economic Law at Maastricht University and Visiting Professor at the College of Europe, Bruges, the World Trade Institute, Berne and the Faculty of Law of the University of Barcelona. He holds a Doctorate in Law from the European University Institute, Florence, an LL.M. from the University of Michigan Law School and a Master in Law from the University of Antwerp. Previously, he was Counsellor and subsequently Acting Director of the WTO Appellate Body Secretariat. From 1990 to 1992, he served as a référendaire of Advocate General Walter van Gerven at the European Court of Justice. He has published extensively in the field of international economic law. He is the author (with W. Zdouc) of *The Law and Policy of the World Trade Organization,* 3rd edition (Cambridge University Press, 2013).

Hans van Houtte is the President of the Iran-United States Claims Tribunal. He holds a degree in European Law, an LLM from Harvard and a diploma cum laude from the Hague Academy of International Law, and obtained a PhD in Law at KU Leuven. He is member of several learned societies, inter alia the *Institut de Droit International.* He taught arbitration, international business law, conflicts of law and public international law at KU Leuven. He has published extensively on international commercial law and arbitration and has been involved in international commercial arbitration since 1973. He has served as chairman, sole arbitrator and party-appointed arbitrator in over 150 commercial and investment arbitration proceedings under, among others, the rules of ICC, LCIA, ICSID, AAA, Uncitral, the European Development Fund, Cepani, the Netherlands Arbitration Institution.

Jan Wouters is Full Professor of International Law and International Organizations, Jean Monnet Chair *Ad Personam* EU and Global Governance, Director of the Leuven Centre for Global Governance Studies and of the Institute for International Law at KU Leuven, and Visiting Professor at the College of Europe (Bruges), SciencesPo (Paris) and Luiss University (Rome). He is a Member of the Royal Academy of Belgium for Sciences and Arts, is President of the United Nations Association Flanders Belgium, and practises law as *Of Counsel* at Linklaters, Brussels. He is Editor of the *International Encyclopaedia of Intergovernmental Organizations*, Deputy Director of the *Revue Belge de Droit International* and an editorial board member in ten international journals. He has published widely on international, EU, corporate and financial law. His recent books include *The European Union and Multilateral Governance* (2012), *International Prosecutors* (2012), *Informal International Lawmaking* (2012), *Private Standards and Global Governance* (2012), *China, the European Union and Global Governance* (2012), *The EU's Role in Global Governance* (2013), *National Human Rights Institutions in Europe* (2013), *The Law of EU External Relations* (2013) and *China, the EU and the Developing World* (2015). He is

Coordinator of a large-scale FP7 Programme FRAME, 'Fostering Human Rights Among European (External and Internal) Policies' and Holder of the InBev-Baillet Latour EU China Chair at KU Leuven.

Acknowledgements

The editors would like to express their gratitude to the Faculty of Law and the Leuven Centre for Global Governance Studies at the University of Leuven, who co-organized the 2013 Spring Lecture Series on 'the Contribution of International and Supranational Courts and Tribunals to the Rule of Law', which formed the basis for the present volume. Special thanks are also due to all the distinguished speakers, notably Serge Brammertz, Antônio Augusto Cançado Trindade, Philippe Couvreur, Franklin Dehousse, Daniel Fransen, Philippe Gautier, Paul Lemmens, Koen Lenaerts, Peter Van den Bossche, Christine Van den Wyngaert and Hans van Houtte.

The editors would also like to thank Nora Kao for her language and style editing.

Table of cases

COURT OF JUSTICE OF THE EUROPEAN UNION

EUROPEAN COURT OF HUMAN RIGHTS

GERMANY: DOMESTIC CASES

INTER-AMERICAN COURT OF HUMAN RIGHTS

INTERNATIONAL COURT OF JUSTICE

INTERNATIONAL CRIMINAL COURT

INTERNATIONAL CRIMINAL TRIBUNAL FOR RWANDA

INTERNATIONAL CRIMINAL TRIBUNAL FOR THE FORMER YUGOSLAVIA

INTERNATIONAL TRIBUNAL FOR THE LAW OF THE SEA

IRAN-US CLAIMS TRIBUNAL

NUREMBERG WAR CRIMES TRIBUNAL

PERMANENT COURT OF ARBITRATION

PERMANENT COURT OF INTERNATIONAL JUSTICE

SPAIN: DOMESTIC CASES

SPECIAL COURT FOR SIERRA LEONE

SPECIAL TRIBUNAL FOR LEBANON

TOKYO WAR CRIMES TRIBUNAL

UK: DOMESTIC CASES

US: DOMESTIC CASES

WTO DISPUTE SETTLEMENT UNDERSTANDING

Table of international instruments and legislation

PART I

Theoretical framework

1. Prologue: An overview of the contribution of international tribunals to the rule of law

Antônio Augusto Cançado Trindade

I. INTRODUCTION

The gradual realization – that we witness, and have the privilege to contribute to, nowadays – of the old ideal of justice at international level[1] has been revitalizing itself, in recent years, with the reassuring creation and operation of the multiple contemporary international tribunals. This is a theme, proper of our times, which has definitively assumed a prominent place in the international agenda of this second decade of the twenty-first century.[2] Since the visionary ideas and early writings of some decades ago,[3] it was necessary to wait for some further decades for

[1] For a general study, cf, eg J Allain, *A Century of International Adjudication – The Rule of Law and Its Limits* (The Hague, TMC Asser Press, 2000) 1–186; and cf J Vervliet, 'Peaceful Settlement of International Disputes and the History and Legacy of the 1899 and 1907 Hague Conventions' in *One Century Peace Palace, from Past to Present* (The Hague, Asser Press, 2013) 39–72; DJ Bederman, 'The Hague Peace Conferences of 1899 and 1907' in MW Janis (ed.), *International Courts for the Twenty-First Century* (Dordrecht, Nijhoff, 1992) 10–11; G Fouda, 'La justice internationale et le consentement des États' in K Koufa (ed.), *International Justice – Thesaurus Acroasium* (vol XXVI Thessaloniki, Sakkoulas Publs, 1997) 889–91, 896 and 900.

[2] Cf AA Cançado Trindade and D Spielmann, *A Century of International Justice / Rétrospective d'un siècle de justice internationale et perspectives d'avenir* (Oisterwijk, Wolf Publs, 2013) 1–44; AA Cançado Trindade and AC Alves Pereira, *O Direito Internacional e o Primado da Justiça* (Rio de Janeiro, Edit Renovar, 2014) 3–363.

[3] Such as the writings of BCJ Loder, André Mandelstam, Nicolas Politis, Jean Spiropoulos, Alejandro Álvarez, Raul Fernandes, Édouard Descamps, Albert de La Pradelle, René Cassin, James Brown Scott, Georges Scelle, Max Huber, Hersch Lauterpacht, John Humphrey, among others; cf AA Cançado Trindade,

the current developments in the realization of international justice to take place, not without difficulties, now enriching and enhancing international law.

It is a source of satisfaction to me to contribute, with this brief Prologue, to the present book *The Contribution of International and Supranational Courts to the Rule of Law* (eds Geert De Baere and Jan Wouters), a timely initiative of the Centre for Global Governance Studies of the Catholic University of Leuven. May I start by recalling that contemporary international tribunals have been contributing decisively to the consolidation of the expanded international jurisdiction, as well as to the assertion and consolidation of the international juridical personality and capacity of the human person, as subject, both active (before international human rights tribunals) and passive (before international criminal tribunals), of international law. They have, accordingly, granted access to international justice to a considerably greater number of *justiciables*, in the most distinct circumstances, all over the world.

II. THE EXPANSION OF INTERNATIONAL JURISDICTION

Nowadays, the international community fortunately counts on a wide range of international tribunals, adjudicating cases that take place not only at *inter-State* level, but also at *intra-State* level. This invites us to approach their work from the correct perspective of the *justiciables* themselves[4] and brings us closer to their common mission of securing the realization of international justice, either at *inter*-State or at *intra*-State level. From the standpoint of the needs of protection of the *justiciables*, each international tribunal has its importance, in a wider framework encompassing the most distinct situations to be adjudicated, in each respective domain of operation.

The present day multiplicity of international tribunals has widened the scope of judicial settlement,[5] particularly when those tribunals, in

---

The Access of Individuals to International Justice (Oxford, Oxford University Press, 2011) 7–11.

[4] AA Cançado Trindade, *Évolution du Droit international au droit des gens – L'accès des particuliers à la justice internationale: le regard d'un juge* (Paris, Pédone, 2008) 1–187.

[5] K Oellers-Frahm, 'Multiplication of International Courts and Tribunals and Conflicting Jurisdiction – Problems and Possible Solutions' (2001) 5 *Max-Planck Yearbook of United Nations Law*, 69, and cf 74–75.

resolving disputes lodged with them, also care to *say what the Law is* (*juris dictio*). Each international tribunal operates in the ambit of its own jurisdiction, but all undertake in harmony their *common mission* of imparting justice. Nowadays, even the settlement of disputes by the International Court of Justice (ICJ) itself, requires it at times to go beyond the inter-State dimension, as that settlement also comprises issues which pertain ultimately to the condition of individuals in international law.

Thus, in respect of situations concerning individuals or groups of individuals, reference can be made, eg to the *Nottebohm* case (1955) pertaining to double nationality; to the cases of the *Trial of Pakistani Prisoners of War* (1973), and of the *Hostages (US Diplomatic and Consular Staff) in Teheran* case (1980); to the case of the *Application of the Convention against Genocide* (1996 and 2007); to the case of the *Frontier Dispute between Burkina Faso and Mali* (1998); to the triad of cases concerning consular assistance – namely, the cases *Breard* (1998), the case *LaGrand* (Germany versus United States, 2001), the case *Avena and Others* (Mexico versus United States, 2004).

In respect of those cases, one cannot fail to reckon that one of their predominant elements has been precisely the concrete situation of the individuals directly affected, and not merely abstract issues of exclusive interest of the litigating States in their relations *inter se*. Moreover, one may further recall that, in the case of *Armed Activities in the Territory of Congo* (DR Congo versus Uganda, 2000), the ICJ was concerned with grave violations of human rights and of international humanitarian law; and the *Land and Maritime Boundary between Cameroon and Nigeria* (1996) was likewise concerned with the victims of armed clashes.

More recently, examples wherein the Court's concerns have had to go beyond the inter-State outlook have further increased in frequency. They include, the case on *Questions Relating to the Obligation to Prosecute or Extradite* (2009–13) pertaining to the principle of universal jurisdiction under the UN Convention against Torture, the case of *AS Diallo* (Guinea versus DR Congo, 2010) on detention and expulsion of a foreigner, the case of the *Jurisdictional Immunities of the State* (2010–12), the case of the *Application of the International Convention on the Elimination of All Forms of Racial Discrimination* (2011), and the case of the *Temple of Preah Vihear* (provisional measures, 2011).

The same can be said of the two last Advisory Opinions of the Court, on the *Declaration of Independence of Kosovo* (2010), and on a *Judgment of the ILO Administrative Tribunal upon a Complaint Filed against the IFAD* (2012), respectively. The artificiality of the exclusively inter-State outlook has thus often been made manifest, and increasingly so;

that outlook rests on a longstanding dogma of the past which has survived to date as a result of mental lethargy. Those more recent contentious cases, and requests for Advisory Opinions, lodged with the Court, have asked the latter, by reason of their subject-matter, to overcome that outlook.

Even if the mechanism of dispute settlement by the ICJ remains strictly or exclusively inter-State, the *substance* of those disputes or issues brought before the Court pertains also to the human person as the aforementioned cases and opinions clearly show. The truth is that the strictly inter-State outlook has an ideological content, is a product of its time, a time long past. In these more recent decisions (1999–2013), the ICJ has at times rightly endeavoured to overcome that outlook, so as to face the new challenges of our times, brought before it in the contentious cases and requests of Advisory Opinions it has been seized of.

The United Nations era has in effect been marked by the rise of multiple international tribunals. This is, in my perception, a reassuring phenomenon which has filled a gap which persisted in the international legal order. It has contributed to the access to justice at international level. The international procedural capacity of individuals has been exercised before international human rights tribunals, thanks to the system of international individual petitions:[6] the European Court of Human Rights (ECtHR), which celebrated its 60th anniversary in 2010, and the Inter-American Court of Human Rights (IACtHR), which celebrated its 30th anniversary in 2009, have more recently (in 2006) been followed by the African Court of Human and Peoples' Rights (AfCtHPR).[7]

Their contribution to the historical recovery of the position of the human person as subject of the law of nations (*droit des gens*) constitutes, in my understanding, the most important legacy of the international

[6] AA Cançado Trindade, *El Acceso Directo del Individuo a los Tribunales Internacionales de Derechos Humanos* (Bilbao, Universidad de Deusto, 2001) 34–5.

[7] Those three international human rights tribunals had their first joint meeting in December 2008. For an account of that meeting, held in Strasbourg on 08-09.12.2008, cf: AA Cançado Trindade, 'Quelques réflexions à l'occasion de la première Réunion des trois Cours régionales des droits de l'homme' (2009) 9 *Revista do Instituto Brasileiro de Direitos Humanos* 229–39; Ph Weckel, 'La justice internationale et le soixantième anniversaire de la Déclaration Universelle des Droits de l'Homme' (2009) 113 *Revue générale de droit international public* 5–17.

legal thinking of the last six and a half decades.[8] In their operation in the last decades, the ECtHR and the IACtHR have in effect set higher standards of State behaviour and have established some degree of control over the interposition of undue restrictions by States; they have thereby reassuringly enhanced the position of individuals as subjects of international law with full procedural capacity.

By correctly resolving basic procedural issues raised in some landmark cases,[9] both international tribunals have aptly made use of the techniques of public international law in order to strengthen their respective jurisdictions of protection of the human person, emancipated vis-à-vis her own State.[10] International human rights tribunals have drawn attention to the position of *centrality* of the victims, the *justiciables*. It should be kept in mind that the *corpus juris gentium* of the International Law of Human Rights is clearly *victim-oriented*. In this respect, it should not pass unnoticed that distinct trends of protection of the human person (International Law of Human Rights, International Humanitarian Law, International Law of Refugees, International Criminal Law) *converge*, rather than conflict with each other, at normative, hermeneutic and operational levels.[11]

Contemporary international criminal tribunals, for their part, saw the light of day in the 90s, bearing in mind the precedents of the Nuremberg and the Tokyo Tribunals of the post-World War II era. Ad hoc international criminal tribunals (for the Former Yugoslavia and for Rwanda)

---

[8] AA Cançado Trindade, *Évolution du Droit international au droit des gens …*, above n4 at 1–187; AA Cançado Trindade, *Le Droit international pour la personne humaine* (Paris, Pédone, 2012) 45–368.

[9] Eg the ECtHR's decisions in the cases of *Belilos* (1988), of *Loizidou* (preliminary objections, 1995), and of *Ilascu, Lesco, Ivantoc and Petrov-Popa* (2001), as well as, eg the IACtHR's decisions in the cases of the *Constitutional Tribunal* and of *Ivtcher Bronstein* (jurisdiction, 1999), as well as of *Hilaire, Benjamin and Constantine* (preliminary objection, 2001).

[10] AA Cançado Trindade, 'The Trans-Atlantic Perspective: The Contribution of the Work of the International Human Rights Tribunals to the Development of Public International Law' in *The European Convention on Human Rights at 50 – Human Rights Information Bulletin*, n 50 (Special Issue), Strasbourg, Council of Europe, 2000, 8–9; AA Cançado Trindade, 'The Merits of Coordination of International Courts on Human Rights' (2004) 2 *Journal of International Criminal Justice* 309–12.

[11] Cf AA Cançado Trindade, *Los Tribunales Internacionales Contemporáneos y la Humanización del Derecho Internacional* (Buenos Aires, Ed Ad-Hoc, 2013) 7–185; AA Cançado Trindade, *Derecho Internacional de los Derechos Humanos, Derecho Internacional de los Refugiados y Derecho Internacional Humanitario – Aproximaciones y Convergencias* (Geneva, ICRC, 2000) 1–66.

were established (in 1993 and 1994) by decision of the UN Security Council in the light of chapter VII of the UN Charter. They were followed by the permanent International Criminal Court (ICC) (Rome Statute of 1998) and by the so-called 'internationalized' or 'hybrid' or mixed international tribunals (for Sierra Leona, East Timor, Kosovo, Bosnia-Herzegovina, Cambodia and Lebanon).

Each of these tribunals has contributed, in its own way, to the determination of the accountability of those responsible for grave violations of human rights and of international humanitarian law. They afford yet another illustration of the rescue of the international legal personality (and responsibility) of individuals, but, ironically, first as *passive* subjects of international law (international criminal tribunals), and, only afterwards, as *active* subjects of international law (international human rights tribunals).

Such developments, due to a reaction of the conscience of humankind against acts of genocide, crimes against humanity, crimes against peace, grave violations of human rights and of international humanitarian law, give testimony of the expansion not only of international personality (and capacity) but also of international jurisdiction and of international responsibility. This is a notable feature of our times in this present era of international tribunals.

Due to the work of those international tribunals, the international community no longer accepts impunity for international crimes, for *grave* violations of human rights and of international humanitarian law. The determination of the international criminal responsibility of individuals by those tribunals is a reaction of contemporary international law to *grave* violations guided by fundamental principles and values shared by the international community as a whole.[12] There is no more room for impunity, with the present-day configuration of a true *droit au Droit*, of the persons victimized in any circumstances, including amid the most complete adversity.[13]

Their jurisprudential advances in recent years were unforeseeable, and even unthinkable, some decades ago.[14] International human rights tribunals have helped to awaken public conscience in respect of situations of

---

[12] S Zappalà, *La justice pénale internationale* (Paris, Montchrestien, 2007) 15, 19, 23, 29, 31, 34–5, 43, 135, 137 and 145–6.

[13] AA Cançado Trindade, *The Access of Individuals to International Justice*, above n3 at 196–8 and cf 132–191.

[14] As to the growing importance currently devoted to the theme, cf Y Beigbeder, *International Justice against Impunity – Progress and New Challenges* (Leiden, Nijhoff, 2005) 1–235.

utmost adversity or even defencelessness affecting individuals and of widespread violence victimizing vulnerable segments of the population.[15] They have, in effect, brought justice to those victimized, even in situations of systematic and generalized violence and mass atrocities. They have thus contributed, considerably and decisively, to the primacy of the *rule of law* at national and international levels, demonstrating that no one is above the law – neither the rulers, nor the ruled, nor the States themselves. International law applies directly to States, to international organizations, and to individuals.

III. THE CONTRIBUTION OF EXPANDED ADVISORY JURISDICTION TO THE RULE OF LAW

It was with the Permanent Court of International Justice (PCIJ) that, for the first time, an international tribunal was attributed the advisory function – surrounded as it was by much discussion. It was originally conceived to assist the Assembly and the Council of the League of Nations, but the PCIJ, making good use of this, ended up by assisting not only those organs but States as well. The advisory jurisdiction, as exercised by the PCIJ, contributed also to the progressive development of international law. While the PCIJ Statute enabled only the League Council and Assembly to request Advisory Opinions, the ICJ Statute enabled other United Nations organs (besides the General Assembly, the Security Council and ECOSOC) and specialized agencies and others to do so.

Advisory Opinions of the ICJ, for their part, have also contributed to the prevalence of the *rule of law* at national and international levels. Some of them have, likewise, contributed to the progressive development of international law (eg the ones on *Reparation for Injuries*, 1949; on *Namibia*, 1970; on *Immunity from Legal Process of a Special Rapporteur of the UN Commission on Human Rights*, 1999; among others). The same can be said of some of the Advisory Opinions of the IACtHR (eg the ones on the *Right to Information on Consular Assistance in the Framework of the Guarantees of the Due Process of Law*, 1999; on the

---

15 Cf as to the ECtHR, eg MD Goldhaber, *A People's History of the European Court of Human Rights* (New Brunswick/London, Rutgers University Press, 2009) 2, 11, 57, 123, 126–7, 149–51, 155–8 and 168; and, as to the IACtHR, eg AA Cançado Trindade, 'Die Entwicklung des interamerikanischen Systems zum Schutz der Menschenrechte' (2010) 70 *Zeitschrift für ausländisches öffentliches Recht und Völkerrecht* 629–99.

Juridical Condition and Human Rights of the Child, 2002; on the *Juridical Condition and Rights of Undocumented Migrants*, 2003).

With the operation of international tribunals (in the exercise of their advisory function and in the adjudication of contentious cases), there have gradually emerged two basic distinct conceptions of the exercise of the international judicial function: one – a strict one – whereby the tribunal has to limit itself to settle the dispute at issue and to handle its resolution of it to the contending parties (a form of transactional justice), addressing only what the parties had put before it; the other, a larger one – the one I sustain – whereby the tribunal has to go beyond that, and *say what the Law is* (*juris dictio*), thus contributing to the settlement of other like situations as well, and to the progressive development of international law. In the interpretation itself – or even in the search – of the applicable law, there is space for judicial creativity; each international tribunal is free to find the applicable law, independently of the arguments of the contending parties[16] (*juria novit curia*).

IV. THE RELEVANCE OF GENERAL PRINCIPLES OF LAW

May I move on to my next point: general principles of law, enlisted among the formal sources of international law (Article 38 of the ICJ Statute), encompass those found in all national legal systems (being thus ineluctably linked with the very foundations of Law) and likewise the general principles of international law. Such principles, in my own conception, inform and conform the norms and rules of international law, being a manifestation of the universal juridical conscience, the ultimate *material* source of all Law; in the evolving *jus gentium* of our times, basic considerations of humanity play a role of the utmost importance.[17]

International human rights tribunals and international criminal tribunals have ascribed great importance to general principles of law. Those principles have been reaffirmed time and time again and retain full

---

16 Cf M Cappelletti, *Juízes Legisladores?* (Porto Alegre/Brazil, SA Fabris Ed, 1993) 73–5 and 128–9; MO Hudson, *International Tribunals – Past and Future* (Washington DC, Carnegie Endowment for International Peace/Brookings Inst, 1944) 104–5.

17 AA Cançado Trindade, *International Law for Humankind – Towards a New Jus Gentium* (2nd rev ed, Leiden/The Hague, Nijhoff, 2013) 1–726.

validity in our time.[18] Legal positivism has always attempted, in vain, to minimize their role, but the truth is that, without those principles, there is no legal system at all, be it national or international. They give expression to the idea of an *objective justice*, paving the way to the application of the *universal* international law.

V. THE MOVE TOWARDS COMPULSORY JURISDICTION

In the present era of international tribunals there have been advances towards *compulsory* international jurisdiction, seeking to secure the primacy of the *jus necessarium* over the *jus voluntarium*. The present-day phenomenon of the multiplicity of international tribunals is indeed related to the move towards international compulsory jurisdiction.[19] As to the ICJ, the original purpose of the optional clause (Article 36(2) of the Statute) was to attract general acceptance so as to establish compulsory international jurisdiction, in the light of the principle of juridical equality of States; the subsequent practice of adding restrictions – at each State's free will – to the acceptance of the optional clause distorted the purpose originally propounded. But there is today renewed hope in the growing use of compromissory clauses, as jurisdictional basis in the *contentieux* before the ICJ;[20] for their consideration one is, in my view, to take into

---

[18] AA Cançado Trindade, 'Foundations of International Law: The Role and Importance of Its Basic Principles' in *XXX Curso de Derecho Internacional Organizado por el Comité Jurídico Interamericano* – OAS (2003) 359–415.

[19] Cf H Ascensio, 'La notion de juridiction internationale en question' in *La juridictionnalisation du droit international* (SFDI, Colloque de Lille de 2002, Paris, Pédone, 2003) 192–4; E McWhinney, *Judicial Settlement of International Disputes – Jurisdiction, Justiciability and Judicial Law-Making on the Contemporary International Court* (Dordrecht, Nijhoff, 1991) 13.

[20] Cf, in this sense, eg C Wilfred Jenks, *The Prospects of International Adjudication* (London/Dobbs Ferry NY, Stevens/Oceana, 1964) 110–11 and 115; JI Charney, 'Compromissory Clauses and the Jurisdiction of the International Court of Justice', (1987) 81 *American Journal of International Law* 859–61 and 883; CJ Tams, 'The Continued Relevance of Compromissory Clauses as a Source of ICJ Jurisdiction' in T Giegerich and UE Heinz (eds), *A Wiser Century? Judicial Dispute Settlement, Disarmament and the Laws of War 100 Years after the Second Hague Peace Conference* (Berlin, Duncker & Humblot, 2009) 464, 471, 480 and 487–9; AA Cançado Trindade, 'Towards Compulsory Jurisdiction: Contemporary International Tribunals and Developments in the International Rule of Law – Part II' in *XXXVIII Curso de Derecho Internacional Organizado por el Comité Jurídico Interamericano* – OAS (2012) 285–366.

account the respective conventions as a whole (including their object and purpose) in the path towards international compulsory jurisdiction.

The International Tribunal for the Law of the Sea (UNTLOS) counts on a *sui generis* mechanism (*supra*), opening four alternatives for dispute-settlement: if there is no agreement as to which one to select, arbitration applies. This provides another illustration that State discretion is not unlimited as in times past. The Court of Justice of the European Union (CJEU) provides yet another illustration of the move towards international compulsory jurisdiction, in the domain of regional or subregional integration, a domain in which there is a multiplicity of international tribunals nowadays (eg in Latin America and in Africa).

An international tribunal such as the CJEU has contributed considerably to the consolidation of the *autonomous* nature of EU law, to its effectiveness and to the specificity of Union Treaties, and to the identification of the essential characteristics of the EU legal order.[21] Among such characteristics stand its primacy over the law of member States, and the direct effect of several of its provisions, applicable alike to their nationals and to member States themselves.

VI. INTERNATIONAL TRIBUNALS, JURISPRUDENTIAL CROSS-FERTILIZATION AND THE RULE OF LAW

In our time, the more lucid international legal doctrine has at last discarded the empty euphemistic expressions used some years ago – such as so-called 'proliferation' of international tribunals, so-called 'fragmentation' of international law, so-called 'forum-shopping'. Such euphemisms sought in vain to divert attention to false issues of delimitation of competences, oblivious of the need to focus it on the imperative of an enlarged access to justice.

It has become clear today that contemporary international tribunals, rather than threatening the cohesion of international law, enrich and

---

21 Cf, eg PJG Kapteyn, 'The Role of the Court of Justice in the Development of the Community Legal Order' in F Salerno (ed), *Il Ruolo del Giudice Internazionale nell'Evoluzione del Diritto Internazionale e Comunitario – Atti del Convegno di Studi in Memoria di G Morelli* (Università di Reggio Calabria, 1993 – Padova, CEDAM, 1995) 161–2, 165–7 and 170–3. And cf recently, eg A von Bogdandy, *I Principi Fondamentali dell'Unione Europea – Un Contributo allo Sviluppo del Costituzionalismo Europeo* (Roma, Edit Scientifica, 2011) 63–137.

strengthen it, in asserting its aptitude to resolve disputes in distinct domains of international law, at both *inter*-State and *intra*-State levels. Contemporary international law has thereby become more responsive to the fulfilment of the basic needs of the international community, of human beings and of humankind as a whole, among which is that of the realization of justice. The expansion of international jurisdiction by the establishment of contemporary international tribunals is but a reflection of the way contemporary international law has evolved, no longer indifferent to human suffering, and of the current search for, and construction of, a *corpus juris gentium* for the international community guided by the *rule of law* in democratic societies and committed to the realization of justice.

In the performance of their common mission of imparting justice, contemporary international tribunals have begun to take into account each other's case law, and nowadays contribute to jurisprudential cross-fertilization. Jurisprudential cross-fertilization, ensuing therefrom, exerts a constructive function in the safeguard of the rights of the *justiciables*. It is thus to be expected that contemporary international tribunals remain increasingly aware of the case law of each other, in their continuing performance of their common mission of imparting justice in distinct domains of international law,[22] thus preserving its basic *unity*. This is to the benefit of the international community as a whole and of all the *justiciables*, all subjects of law around the world – States, international organizations and individuals alike.

VII. EFFECTS OF THE WORK OF INTERNATIONAL TRIBUNALS AND THE RULE OF LAW

In the present era of multiple international tribunals, the effects of their joint work can already be perceived. These effects have been, in my perception, first, their *law-making* endeavours, not only applying but also creating an *objective* law, beyond the will or consent of individual States, on the basis of the consciousness of human values; secondly, the acknowledgment of the fundamental importance of general principles of law; thirdly, the development of international legal procedure (with a blend of traditions of national legal systems around the world, and the acknowledgment of the importance for the *justiciables* of the holding of

---

22 Cf in general, eg G de Vergottini and JJ Pardini, *Au-delà du dialogue entre les Cours* (Paris, Dalloz, 2013) 39–138.

oral hearings); fourthly, the fostering of the *unity* of law, with the interactions between international law and domestic law; and fifthly, the aforementioned fostering of respect for the *rule of law* at national and international levels.

The assertion of an *objective* law, beyond the will of individual States, is a revival of jusnaturalist thinking. Judicial settlement of international disputes is needed as a guarantee against unilateral interpretation by a State of conventional obligations. After all, the basic foundations of international law emanate ultimately from the human conscience, from the universal juridical conscience, and not from the 'will' of individual States. The assertion of the *unity* of the law is intertwined with the *rule of law* at national and international levels, as access to justice takes place, and ought to be preserved, at both levels.

VIII. INTERACTIONS BETWEEN INTERNATIONAL AND DOMESTIC LAW: THE UNITY OF THE LAW

The work of contemporary international tribunals bears witness to the interactions between international and domestic law in their respective domains of operation. The realization of justice becomes a common goal, and a converging one, at the domestic and international legal orders. They both testify to the *unity of the Law* in the realization of justice, a sign of our times. It should not pass unnoticed that there have been occasions when international jurisdiction has come to the support of national jurisdiction so as to secure also within this latter the primacy of law (*préeminence du droit*, *rule of law*). In effect, the expansion of international jurisdiction (cf supra) has counted on the co-participation of national jurisdictions.[23]

After all, international law attributes international functions also to national tribunals.[24] These latter have a role to play also in the search of the primacy of the international *rule of law*.[25] Among international criminal tribunals, the ICC shows, inter alia, that the principle of

[23] Cf in general, eg Y Shany, *Regulating Jurisdictional Relations between National and International Courts* (Oxford, Oxford University Press, 2009) 1–200.

[24] Cf AA Cançado Trindade, *The Access of Individuals to International Justice*, above n3 at 76–112 (on the interaction between international law and domestic law in human rights protection).

[25] A Nollkaemper, *National Courts and the International Rule of Law* (Oxford, Oxford University Press, 2011) 1–304.

complementarity, for example, signals the call for a greater approximation, if not interaction, between the international and national jurisdictions. And it could not be otherwise, particularly in our times, when, with growing frequency, the most diverse matters are brought before judicial control at international level.[26]

There are significant illustrations, in certain situations of extreme adversity to human beings, of the international jurisdiction having even *preceded* national jurisdiction in the protection of the rights of the victimized and in the reparations due to them. For example, the determination, by the IACtHR, of the international responsibility of the respondent State for grave violations of human rights in the cases of the massacres of *Barrios Altos* and *La Cantuta* (Judgments of 2001[27] and 2006,[28] respectively), *preceded* the condemnation, by the Special Penal Chamber of the Peruvian Supreme Court (in 2007–10) of the former President of the Republic (A Fujimori).[29]

In those two cases, in addition to the paradigmatic case of the *Constitutional Tribunal* (IACtHR's Judgment of 2001) – pertaining to the destitution of three magistrates, later reincorporated into the Tribunal – the *international jurisdiction effectively intervened in defence of the national one*, decisively contributing to the restoration of the *État de Droit* (*rule of law*) – as it occurred – besides having safeguarded the rights of the victimized.[30] In the history of the relations – and

---

[26] T Koopmans, 'Judicialization' in N Colneric et al. (eds), *Une communauté de droit – Festschrift für G.C. Rodríguez Iglesias* (Berlin, Berliner Wissenschafts-Verlag (BWV), 2003) 51–7; G Ulfstein, 'The International Judiciary' in J Klabbers, A Peters and G Ulfstein (eds), *The Constitutionalization of International Law* (Oxford, Oxford University Press, 2011) [reed], 126–52.

[27] Judgments of 14.03.2001 (merits), 03.09.2001 (interpretation) and 30.11.2001 (reparations).

[28] Judgment of 29.11.2006 (merits and reparations).

[29] For a historical account, cf AA Cançado Trindade, *El Ejercicio de la Función Judicial Internacional – Memorias de la Corte Interamericana de Derechos Humanos* (3rd ed, Belo Horizonte/Brazil, Edit Del Rey, 2013) 42–5.

[30] Almost three years after the IACtHR's Judgment (of 31.01.2001) in the case of the *Constitutional Tribunal*, I sent a letter to this latter [*tribunal?*] (on 04.12.2003), as then President of the IACtHH, in which I expressed, inter alia, that:

> we can appreciate this Judgment of the IACtHR in historical perspective …, as a landmark one not only … [in the] inter-American system of protection of human rights. … [It] constitutes an unprecedented judicial decision also at world level. It has had repercussions not only in our region but also in other continents. It has marked a starting point of a remarkable and reassuring

interactions – between national and international jurisdictions, this trilogy of cases will surely keep on being studied by the present and future generations of internationalists and constitutionalists.

IX. THE UNITED NATIONS AND THE RULE OF LAW

The importance assumed by international tribunals in contemporary international law has been accompanied by a growing attention dispensed in recent years to the *rule of law* (*état de Droit/Estado de Derecho*) in the international agenda of the United Nations. In effect, by the time of the adoption of the document *World Summit Outcome*, at the end of the UN World Summit of 2005, there was a general awareness that the international and national dimensions of the *rule of law* were firmly intertwined, and that, accordingly, the enhancement of the rule of law at international level had a direct impact on the rule of law at national level.

The way was thus paved for the insertion of the matter in the agenda of the UN General Assembly, wherein it has been present ever since 2006 up to the present (mid-2014).[31] It has counted on the interventions, year after year, of an increasing number of member States engaged in contributing to the UN endeavours in the present domain. This is reassuring as it discloses a new consciousness of the pressing need to secure the enhancement of the rule of law at both national and international levels.[32]

The 2012 *Declaration of the High-Level Meeting of the General Assembly on the Rule of Law at the National and International Levels*, echoing the successive GA resolutions on the matter,[33] reiterated the key importance of the rule of law for the three main pillars of the United Nations, namely, international peace and security, human rights and development (preamble). It added that human rights, the rule of law and

---

approximation between the judicial power at national and international levels …

Text of the letter reproduced *in*: OAS, *Informe Anual de la Corte Interamericana de Derechos Humanos – 2003*, San José of Costa Rica, IACtHR, 2004, Annex LVII, 1459–60, and cf 1457–8.

[31] Cf GA resolutions 61/39, of 18.12.2006; 62/70, of 06.12.2007; 63/128, of 11.12.2008; 64/116, of 16.12.2009; 65/32, of 06.12.2010; 66/102, of 09.12.2011; 67/97, of 14.12.2012; and 68/116, of 16.12.2013.

[32] For a recent account, cf AA Cançado Trindade, *Direito das Organizações Internacionais* (6th ed, Belo Horizonte/Brazil, Edit Del Rey, 2014) 584–7.

[33] Cf above n31.

democracy are strongly interlinked and mutually reinforcing, belonging to 'the universal and indivisible core values and principles of the United Nations' (paras 5 and 7). It stressed 'the right of equal access to justice for all, including members of vulnerable groups' (para 14). It further acknowledged the value of the contribution of the work of the ICJ and other contemporary international tribunals for the promotion of the rule of law (paras 31–32).

X. CONCLUDING REMARKS

I have now come to my brief concluding remarks keeping in mind the lessons learned along a century of experience sedimented in the domain of international justice. It is high time, in my view, to turn and focus attention on the proper ways of achieving the *realization of justice*, rather than – as the legal profession is used to – being attentive only to strategies of litigation for the sake of it, making abstraction of human values. Likewise, it is high time to accompany consistently the ongoing expansion of international jurisdiction, and of international legal personality and capacity, as well as international responsibility, by drawing closer attention to *all* subjects of international law, not only States, but also international organizations, peoples and individuals.

Moving to another point, it is now time to accompany the expansion of international jurisdiction, also by fostering the dialogue and coordination between contemporary international tribunals. Endeavours of coordination already exist[34] but have been far from sufficient to date. There is nowadays a pressing need for greater dialogue and coordination of contemporary international tribunals in their common mission of imparting justice. At conceptual level, there is a pressing need of further jurisprudential developments in the matter of reparations, as well as provisional measures of protection, both still in their infancy.

---

34 Two meetings, open to all contemporary international tribunals, have taken place to date: the first one, on the occasion of the 50th anniversary of the Court of Justice of the European Communities (CJEC, now the Court of Justice of the European Union (CJEU)), was held in Luxembourg, on 03–04.12.2002; and the second meeting, to commemorate the centenary of the creation of the old Central-American Court of Justice, took place in Managua, on 04–05.10.2007; for an account of both meetings, in which I participated, cf AA Cançado Trindade, *Direito das Organizações Internacionais*, above n32 at 582–4 and 601–2.

The issue of compliance with judgments and decisions of international tribunals requires far greater attention and study on the part of international tribunals – some of them being currently engaged already in its careful consideration. Here, each international tribunal counts on a mechanism of its own; yet, all of them are susceptible to improvement. This issue pertains, as pointed out by the ECtHR in the case *Hornsby versus Greece* (Judgment of 19.03.1997) and by the IACtHR in the case of *Baena Ricardo and Others (270 Workers) versus Panama* (jurisdiction, Judgment of 28.11.2003) to the *rule of law* itself, so as to secure the proper administration of justice.

Only with the due compliance with the judgments of international tribunals will the rights at stake be effectively protected and will the realization of justice be achieved. Such faithful compliance with their judgments is a legitimate concern of all contemporary international tribunals. Access to justice *lato sensu* encompasses the full and faithful compliance with their Judgments[35]. This is a position of principle, in relation to an issue which pertains to the international *ordre public* and to the *rule of law* (*préeminence du droit*) at international and national levels.

Last but not least, the reassuring coexistence of multiple international tribunals has considerably enlarged the number of *justiciables*, in all parts of the world, even in situations of great adversity or vulnerability, if not defencelessness. The operation of international tribunals, in a harmonious and coordinated way, is essential to the gradual realization of the old ideal of international justice as well as to the constant renewal of faith and hope in the construction of a world with prevailing justice.

---

[35] For a general study of the matter, cf AA Cançado Trindade, *El Derecho de Acceso a la Justicia en Su Amplia Dimensión* (2nd ed, Santiago de Chile, Edit Librotecnia, 2012) 79–574.

2. The contribution of international and supranational courts to the rule of law: A framework for analysis

Geert De Baere, Anna-Luise Chané and Jan Wouters*

I. INTRODUCTION

Since the beginning of the 1990s, international adjudication has undergone dramatic changes. Not only has the quantity of international judicial bodies significantly increased, but today's international courts and tribunals[1] also wield considerably more power than their predecessors and adjudicate an ever-growing number of cases. Over the past two decades there has been a multiplication of bodies that match the criteria of an international court or tribunal, in the sense that they are: (1) permanent institutions; (2) composed of independent judges; (3) adjudicate disputes between two or more entities, at least one of which must be a State or an international organization;[2] and (4) render binding decisions; (5) on the basis of predetermined procedural and substantive rules of international law.[3] While up until the end of the Cold War only a handful of courts and

* The authors wish to thank Mr Nicolas Hachez for his helpful comments on an earlier draft of this chapter.

1 The terms 'international court' and 'international tribunal' are treated as essentially synonymous for the purposes of this chapter.

2 This also encompasses international criminal courts and tribunals. While states are not parties to the proceedings, an organ of the international court – the Prosecutor – brings cases against individuals.

3 Criteria used by the Project on International Courts and Tribunals (PiCT), see <http://www.pict-pcti.org/matrix/matrixhome.html> accessed 15 January 2015; see similar definition applied in Cesare PR Romano, 'A Taxonomy of International Rule of Law Institutions' (2011) 2 *Journal of International Dispute Settlement* 241, 261 et seq.

tribunals existed,[4] they have since been joined by a large number of general, specialized and regional courts and tribunals. Based on the above-mentioned criteria, more than 20 international courts currently active can be identified,[5] as well as a considerable number of bodies that

---

[4] Among them the International Court of Justice (ICJ), the European Court of Human Rights (ECtHR), the Inter-American Court of Human Rights (IACtHR), the Court of Justice of the EU (CJEU), the Court of Justice of the Benelux Economic Union (CJBEU) and the Andean Tribunal of Justice (ATJ). See also the epilogue to the present volume by Andreas Follesdal.

[5] This includes the ICJ, the International Tribunal for the Law of the Sea (ITLOS) and the Appellate Body of the World Trade Organization (WTO AB), the human rights courts (ECtHR, IACtHR, African Court of Human and Peoples' Rights (ACtHPR)), the economic integration courts in Europe (CJEU, CJBEU, Economic Court of the Commonwealth of Independent States, European Free Trade Association (EFTA) Court), in Africa (Organization for the Harmonization of Corporate Law in Africa Common Court of Justice and Arbitration, East African Community Court of Justice, Economic Community of West African States (ECOWAS) Court of Justice), in the Americas (ATJ, Caribbean Court of Justice, Mercosur Dispute Settlement System, Central American Court of Justice) and in Asia (ASEAN Enhanced Dispute Settlement Mechanism) as well as the International Criminal Court (ICC), and a large number of international administrative tribunals (AT) or boards (among the international organizations that have established an AT are the African Development Bank, the Arab League, the Asian Development Bank, the Council of Europe, the EU, the European Bank for Reconstruction and Development, the European Space Agency, the European Stability Mechanism, the Inter-American Development Bank, the International Labour Organization (ILO), the International Monetary Fund (IMF), the North Atlantic Treaty Organization (NATO), the Organisation for Economic Co-operation and Development (OECD), the Organization of American States (OAS), the World Bank and the UN (now UN Dispute Tribunal and UN Appeals Tribunal). The entries listed in this and the subsequent footnotes are based on the courts identified in the following works: Karen J Alter, *The New Terrain of International Law: Courts, Politics, Rights* (Princeton University Press, 2014) 72 et seq; Henry G Schermers and Niels M Blokker, *International Institutional Law: Unity within Diversity* (5th edn, Brill, 2011) 439 et seq, para 605 et seq; Romano, above n3 at 261 et seq; Ruth Mackenzie, Cesare PR Romano, Yuval Shany and Philippe Sands, *Manual on International Courts and Tribunals* (OUP, 2010); and William A Schabas, Solomon T Ebobrah, Carl Baudenbacher/ Michael-James Clifton, David D Caron, Christoph Schreuer and Chittharanjan F Amerasinghe in the section 'Orders and Families of International Adjudicative Bodies' of *The Oxford Handbook of International Adjudication* edited by Cesare PR Romano, Karen Alter and Yuval Shany (OUP, 2014); for more information see also the case law databases World Courts (<www.worldcourts.com/>) and WorldLII (<www.worldlii.org/int/cases/>), and the international court directory of the iCourts project (<http://jura.ku.dk/icourts/caselaw-finder/>).

are inactive or have a minimal caseload.[6] Extending the definition to include non-permanent adjudicative bodies, one can add a large number of ad hoc or hybrid criminal tribunals,[7] arbitral tribunals[8] and international claims tribunals.[9]

---

6 The categorization into active and inactive/less active courts varies, depending on the source. Courts that have been labelled as inactive or having a minimal caseload include eg the European Nuclear Energy Tribunal, the European Tribunal on State Immunity, the Judicial Tribunal of the Organization of Arab Petroleum Exporting Countries, the Court of Justice of the Economic Community of Central African States, the Judicial Organ of the Arab Maghreb Union, the Court of Justice of the African Economic Community, the Court of Justice of the West African Economic and Monetary Union, the Court of Justice of the Common Market for Eastern and Southern Africa, the Southern Africa Development Community Tribunal, the Court of Justice of the Central African Monetary Community, and the Court of Justice of the African Union; sources see above n5.

7 These notably include the International Criminal Tribunal for the Former Yugoslavia (ICTY), the International Criminal Tribunal for Rwanda (ICTR), and the UN Mechanism for International Criminal Tribunals (UNMICT), which will take over functions of the ICTY and the ICTR after the end of their mandate, the Special Court for Sierra Leone (and the Residual Special Court for Sierra Leone), the Special Tribunal for Lebanon, the Extraordinary Chambers in the Courts of Cambodia, the War Crimes Chamber of the Court of Bosnia and Herzegovina, and most recently the Extraordinary African Chambers (established 'within the Senegalese judicial system to prosecute those most responsible for crimes and serious violations of international law, international custom, and international conventions ratified by Chad and Senegal committed on the territory of Chad from 7 June 1982 to 01 December 1990' (see art I(1) of the Agreement Between the Government of the Republic of Senegal and the African Union on the Establishment of Extraordinary African Chambers Within the Senegalese Judicial System), in particular those committed during the administration of former president Hissène Habré).

8 It is impossible to provide an exhaustive list of all international arbitral tribunals. Among the more permanent bodies are eg the Permanent Court of Arbitration, the International Joint Commission, the Bank for International Settlements Arbitral Tribunal, the International Civil Aviation Organization Council, the International Centre for the Settlement of Investment Disputes, the Gulf Cooperation Council Commission for the Settlement of Disputes, the Court of Arbitration for Sport, the North American Commission on Environmental Cooperation, the North American Free Trade Agreement (NAFTA) Dispute Settlement System, the Organization for the Harmonization of Corporate Law in Africa Common Court of Justice and Arbitration and the World Intellectual Property Organization Arbitration and Mediation Center; sources see above n5.

9 Over the course of the nineteenth and twentieth century, almost 90 of these bodies were established (Romano, above n3 at 264). Today among others

Not only has the number of available tribunals increased, but also the number of cases on their dockets and consequently their judicial output. Alter counts 3,300 judicial decisions issued collectively by all international courts until 1989, and 34,000 judicial decisions in the period between 1990 and 2011.[10] This increase in judicial output is certainly tied to the establishment of new adjudicative bodies, several of which have been particularly active, for example the WTO Dispute Settlement System, which generated 188 panel reports and 110 appellate reports between 1995 and 2013.[11] But also pre-existing international courts have been utilized more frequently in the past decades. The International Court of Justice (ICJ), for example, has delivered 117 judgments since 1946, of which 66 alone were delivered since 1990.[12] This increased recourse to international adjudication has created a wealth of case law in many areas of international law.

In addition to this, the new generation of international courts frequently enjoys more power than their older counterparts and has taken on new roles, which indicate not only a quantitative but also a qualitative change in the international judiciary.[13] Whereas international courts were traditionally only mandated with dispute settlement between states, today they fulfil multiple functions, including the judicial review of acts and practices of domestic and international authorities, the prosecution of perpetrators of international crimes, the provision of authoritative interpretations and clarifications of the law, as well as the promotion of the development of international law.[14] Whereas the international judiciary

---

the Iran-United States Claims Tribunal (IUSCT), the Marshall Islands Nuclear Claims Tribunal, and the Eritrea-Ethiopia Claims Commission remain in existence, sources see above n5.

10 Alter only identifies two dozen international courts, see Karen Alter, 'The Multiplication of International Courts and Tribunals After the End of the Cold War', in Cesare PR Romano, Karen Alter, Yuval Shany (eds), *The Oxford Handbook of International Adjudication* (OUP, 2014) 65, 68.

11 See the chapter by Peter Van den Bossche in the present volume.

12 See the chapter by Philippe Couvreur in the present volume.

13 Alter, above n4 at 64; Jenny Martinez, 'Towards an International Judicial System' (2003) 56 *Stanford Law Review* 429, 438 et seq; Christopher J Borgen, 'Transnational Tribunals and the Transmission of Norms: The Hegemony of Process' (2007) 39 *George Washington International Law Review* 685, 686 et seq.

14 Armin von Bogdandy and Ingo Venzke, 'On the Functions of International Courts: An Appraisal in Light of Their Burgeoning Public Authority' (2012) Amsterdam Center for International Law, ACIL Research Paper No 2012/10, 2.

was traditionally dependent on the voluntary acceptance of its jurisdiction by the parties, several of the newer international courts have compulsory jurisdiction, and some older international courts have been granted compulsory jurisdiction through subsequent reforms.[15] Finally, international adjudication is no longer a state-only affair, with more and more courts either enabling individuals to submit their claims or holding them accountable for violations of international law.[16]

To say that these developments have attracted a lot of scholarly attention would be an understatement. Recent years have seen numerous studies mapping the new world of international courts,[17] analysing their roles and powers,[18] assessing their effectiveness,[19] and measuring their

---

[15] See eg Van den Bossche, above n11. See also part XV of UNCLOS, which provides for compulsory jurisdiction but leaves the state parties the choice of forum (ITLOS, ICJ, arbitration): see Philippe Gautier in the present volume. See Protocol No 11 to the Convention for the Protection of Human Rights and Fundamental Freedoms, restructuring the control machinery established thereby, adopted 11 May 1994, entered into force 1 November 1998, ETS No 5, which established the compulsory jurisdiction of the ECtHR. However, some courts have been unaffected by this development, as exemplified by the persistently low number of states which have accepted the compulsory jurisdiction of the ICJ under art 36(2) of the Statute of the International Court of Justice (ICJ Statute) (currently 71 declarations).

[16] Eg natural and legal persons may appear before the Seabed Disputes Chamber of the ITLOS (see Gautier, above n15); individuals may bring claims before the reformed ECtHR (see Paul Lemmens in the present volume); the international criminal tribunals, above n5, have the competence to prosecute individuals for international crimes.

[17] Romano, above n3.

[18] See for example iCourts, the Danish National Research Foundation's Centre of Excellence for International Courts, which was created in 2012 for the study of the role and impact of international courts, <http://jura.ku.dk/icourts/>; Dinah Shelton, 'Form, Function, and the Powers of International Courts' (2009) 9 *Chicago Journal of International Law* 537; Anna Spain, 'Examining the International Judicial Function: International Courts as Dispute Resolvers' (2011) 34 *Loyola of Los Angeles International and Comparative Law Review* 5; von Bogdandy and Venzke, above n14; Alter, above n5.

[19] Yuval Shany, *Assessing the Effectiveness of International Courts* (OUP, 2014) and 'Assessing the Effectiveness of International Courts: A Goal-Based Approach' (2012) 106 *American Journal of International Law* 225, see also 226 fn 5; Laurence R Helfer, 'The Effectiveness of International Adjudicators' in Cesare PR Romano, Karen Alter, Yuval Shany (eds), *The Oxford Handbook of International Adjudication* (OUP, 2014) 464.

legitimacy.[20] Several scholars and practitioners have voiced concerns about the 'proliferation' of international courts, in particular referring to potentially conflicting jurisdictions and the fragmentation of international law through contradictory judgments.[21] Nevertheless, the benefits of the increasing judicialization of the international order have also been highlighted,[22] and the scarcity of conflicts and contradictions has been emphasized.[23] Several studies suggest solutions, ranging from the avoidance of double proceedings to the establishment of a judicial dialogue

---

20 See for example the project PluriCourts at the University of Oslo, which studies the legitimacy of international courts and tribunals from an interdisciplinary perspective, <www.jus.uio.no/pluricourts/english/>; Tullio Treves, 'Aspects of Legitimacy of Decisions of International Courts and Tribunals' with comments by Rein Müllerson, in Rüdiger Wolfrum and Volker Röben (eds), *Legitimacy in International Law* (Springer, 2008) 169 et seq; Yuka Fukunaga, 'Civil Society and the Legitimacy of the WTO Dispute Settlement System' (2009) 34 *Brooklyn Journal of International Law* 85; Nienke Grossman, 'The Normative Legitimacy of International Courts' (2013) 86 *Temple Law Review* 61; Koen Lenaerts, 'How the ECJ Thinks: A Study on Judicial Legitimacy' (2013) 36 *Fordham International Law Journal* 1302; Geir Ulfstein, 'International Courts and Judges: Independence, Interaction and Legitimacy' (2014) 46 *NYU Journal of International Law and Policy* 849; see also the issue 'International Courts and the Quest for Legitimacy' (2013) 14:2 *Journal Theoretical Inquiries in Law*.

21 Gilbert Guillaume, 'The proliferation of international judicial bodies: The outlook for the international legal order', Speech to the Sixth Committee of the UN General Assembly, 27 October 2000 and Gilbert Guillaume, 'Advantages and Risks of Proliferation: A Blueprint for Action' (2004) 2 *Journal of International Criminal Justice* 300; Thomas Buergenthal, 'Proliferation of International Courts and Tribunals: Is it Good or Bad? (2001) 14 *Leiden Journal of International Law*, 267, 272 et seq; J G Merrills, 'The Mosaic of International Dispute Settlement Procedures: Complementary or Contradictory?' (2007) 54 *Netherlands International Law Review* 361.

22 See Antônio Augusto Cançado Trindade in the present volume.

23 Chester Brown, *A Common Law of International Adjudication* (OUP, 2007); Jonathan I Charney, 'The Impact on the International Legal System of the Growth of International Courts and Tribunals' (1993) 31 NYU *Journal of International Law and Politics* 697; Buergenthal, above n21 at 271 et seq; Martti Koskenniemi and Päivi Leino, 'Fragmentation of International Law? Postmodern Anxieties' (2002) 15 *Leiden Journal of International Law* 553; Fausto Pocar, 'The Proliferation of International Criminal Courts and Tribunals: A Necessity in the Current International Community' (2004) 2 *Journal of International Criminal Justice* 304; Rosalyn Higgins, 'The ICJ, the United Nations System, and the rule of law', speech delivered at the London School of Economics, 13 November 2006 and Rosalyn Higgins, 'A Babel of Judicial Voices? Ruminations from the Bench' (2006) 55 *International and Comparative Law Quarterly* 791.

among international judges.[24] Nevertheless, knowledge gaps remain. In particular, there is still a lack of understanding of the functioning of international courts and of their contribution to the rule of law at the international, regional and domestic levels.

Almost in parallel to the expansion of international adjudication, the concept of the rule of law has taken centre stage. Possibly fuelled by the political changes after the end of the Cold War, the rule of law has turned into a 'panacea for the ills of countries in transition'.[25] It has developed into a leitmotiv in international relations and is being referred to in countless policy documents, in various contexts. Having so far eluded a clear-cut definition, the rule of law has been employed flexibly, and is open to a variety of interpretations.[26] The 2012 UN General Assembly (UNGA) *Declaration of the High-level Meeting of the General Assembly on the Rule of Law at the National and International Levels* ('the 2012 Declaration')[27] illustrates the different facets associated with the rule of law, ranging from terrorism, to corruption, organized crime, development and conflict prevention, to name but a few. This elasticity may be

---

[24] Karin Oellers-Frahm, 'Multiplication of International Courts and Tribunals and Conflicting Jurisdiction – Problems and Possible Solutions' (2001) 5 *Max Planck Yearbook of United Nations Law* 67; Merrills, above n21; Nele Matz-Lück, 'Promoting the Unity of International Law: Standard-Setting by International Tribunals' in Doris König, Peter-Tobias Stoll, Volker Röben and Nele Matz-Lück (eds), *International Law Today: New Challenges and the Need for Reform?* (Springer, 2008) 99; Nikolaos Lavranos, 'Regulating Competing Jurisdictions Among International Courts and Tribunals' (2008) 68 *Zeitschrift für ausländisches öffentliches Recht und Völkerrecht* 575; Suzannah Linton and Firew Kebede Tiba, 'The International Judge in an Age of Multiple International Courts and Tribunals' (2009) 9 *Chicago Journal of International Law* 407; Joost Pauwelyn and Luiz Eduardo Salles, 'Forum Shopping Before International Tribunals: (Real) Concerns, (Im)Possible Solutions' (2009) 42 *Cornell International Law Journal* 77; see also the address by Judge Schwebel to the Plenary session of the UN General Assembly on 26 October 1999, where he argued in favour of enabling international courts and tribunals to request advisory opinions from the ICJ.

[25] Thomas Carothers, 'The Rule of Law Revival' (1998) 77 *Foreign Affairs* 95.

[26] See Jeremy Waldron, 'The Rule of Law and the Importance of Procedure', in James E Fleming (ed.) *Getting to the Rule of Law* (NYU Press, 2011) 3, 4 et seq, on the gap between formal conceptions of the term in legal philosophy, and its actual use outside the field.

[27] UNGA Res 67/1 (24 September 2012) UN Doc A/RES/67/1.

expedient at the policy level,[28] but its implications for the rule of law remain uncertain, particularly as regards its translation from the domestic to the international level.[29]

The present volume aims to make a contribution to the ongoing academic debate by taking a closer look at the actual functioning and work of a set of international and supranational courts and tribunals and by analysing their contribution to the rule of law at the international, regional and domestic levels. Due to their large number, an exhaustive coverage of international and supranational judicial bodies currently in existence would clearly exceed the scope of this volume. Therefore, based on Romano's 'taxonomy' of international adjudicative bodies, a sample of courts was selected, illustrating the spectrum of international and supranational courts: a state-only court with general jurisdiction (ICJ), two state-only courts with specialized jurisdiction (International Tribunal for the Law of the Sea, Appellate Body of the World Trade Organization), a court of a regional integration organization (Court of Justice of the European Union), a human rights court (European Court of Human Rights), as well as a permanent, an ad hoc and a hybrid international criminal court (International Criminal Court, International Criminal Tribunal for the Former Yugoslavia, Special Tribunal for Lebanon respectively). In addition, attention will be paid to the Iran-United States Claims Tribunal (IUSCT), as an example of an international claims and compensations body that has made a considerable contribution to international arbitration law. Such a selection – although aiming for a certain degree of representativeness – necessarily has its weaknesses. This volume therefore does not claim to be comprehensive. It should be considered as a preliminary contribution, laying the basis for future larger studies of the international judiciary. The authors of the chapters are primarily judges, prosecutors and registrars of the respective bodies, which provides for unique insights and a large spectrum of opinions and expertise. Most of them were part of the lecture series on 'the Contribution of International and Supranational Courts and Tribunals to the Rule of Law', co-organized by the Faculty of Law and the Leuven Centre for Global Governance Studies at the University of Leuven in the Spring of 2013.

By way of introduction, this chapter first provides a brief historical overview of the multiplication of international courts and tribunals (II),

---

[28] Philip Alston, 'The concept of the rule of law and the way it has been dealt with at the international level', lecture held at the EIUC Venice Academy of Human Rights 2014 – 'Judicial Legitimacy and the Rule of Law', 9 July 2014.

[29] See below, section IV(B).

and clarifies the distinction between supranational and international bodies (III). In the light of the indeterminacy of the concept of the rule of law, the present chapter then provides an exploration of its possible conceptions (IV). Subsequently, the chapter places the international judiciary in its political context and analyses the institutional safeguards of the courts' independence and impartiality (V). Finally, the chapter provides a preliminary comparative analysis of the many ways in which international courts may arguably strengthen the rule of law (VI) and concludes by taking a closer look at the remaining challenges that the international judiciary faces today (VII).

II. THE MULTIPLICATION OF INTERNATIONAL COURTS AND TRIBUNALS

While international adjudication in the form of arbitration dates back at least to Roman times, it was only in the late nineteenth century that the idea of a permanent international court took shape.[30] A standing body was considered to have several advantages, among them increased effectiveness, due to its ready availability, as well as the contribution that its case law would make to the development of international law. Proposals towards a standing international court were submitted at the First Hague Peace Conference (1899).[31] Ultimately, however, the delegates could only agree on the creation of the Permanent Court of Arbitration (PCA), which famously is neither a court, nor permanent but only acts as a secretariat that facilitates arbitration between its Members.[32] The Second Hague Peace Conference (1907) reached an agreement on the creation of a Permanent Prize Court, but the body never came into being. Nevertheless, the conference did sow the seeds for the later foundation of a permanent judicial body.[33]

---

30 Mary Ellen O'Connell and Lenore VanderZee, 'The History of International Adjudication' in Cesare PR Romano, Karen Alter, Yuval Shany (eds), *The Oxford Handbook of International Adjudication* (OUP, 2014) 40.

31 Ibid. at 47.

32 Jan Wouters, 'De proliferatie van internationale rechtscolleges: goed of slecht?' in Bart Raymaekers and Gerd van Riel (eds), *De horizonten van weten en kunnen. Lessen voor de eenentwintigste eeuw* (Vol 8, Universitaire Pers Leuven, 2002) 123.

33 See Geert De Baere and Alex Mills, 'TMC Asser and Public and Private International Law: The Life and Legacy of "a Practical Legal Statesman"' (2011) 42 *Netherlands Yearbook of International Law* 28–9.

It was only after the end of the First World War that a permanent international court with general jurisdiction was finally established. The Permanent Court of International Justice (PCIJ) (1922–46) did not have compulsory jurisdiction over the Member States of the League of Nations, but members could voluntarily accept the jurisdiction of the Court. Although operating in the conflict-ridden interwar era, the PCIJ's body of case law has been widely recognized for its valuable contribution to international law, which still serves as a reference point for international courts today.[34] The PCIJ established the role of a permanent adjudicative body at the international level and to that extent introduced the rule of law to international relations.[35]

Its reputation unscathed by the war,[36] the PCIJ was considered a success and its institutional and legal framework were therefore left

---

[34] See eg PCIJ, *The case of the S.S. 'Lotus' (France v Turkey)* PCIJ Rep Series A No 10, p 18, where the PCIJ held:

> International law governs relations between independent States. The rules of law binding upon States therefore emanate from their own free will as expressed in conventions or by usages generally accepted as expressing principles of law and established in order to regulate the relations between these co-existing independent communities or with a view to the achievement of common aims. Restrictions upon the independence of States cannot therefore be presumed.

This constitutes the so-called '*Lotus* principle', according to which in international law everything that is not subject to a specific prohibition is permitted. The continued validity of the principle was challenged by the question in ICJ, *Legality of the Threat or Use of Nuclear Weapons*, Advisory Opinion, ICJ Reports 1996, p 226: 'Is the threat or use of nuclear weapons in any circumstance permitted under international law?' However, the ICJ held that 'the argument concerning the legal conclusions to be drawn from the use of the word "permitted", and the questions of burden of proof to which it was said to give rise, are without particular significance for the disposition of the issues before the Court' (at 239, para 22). See Martti Koskenniemi, 'Case Analysis: Faith, Identity, and the Killing of the Innocent: International Lawyers and Nuclear Weapons' (1997) 10 *Leiden Journal of International Law* 139–40; see also the Declaration of Judge Simma in ICJ, *Accordance with International Law of the Unilateral Declaration of Independence in Respect of Kosovo*, Advisory Opinion, ICJ Reports 2010, p 403, criticizing the ICJ's upholding of the *Lotus* principle. On the contribution of the PCIJ to international law see Ole Spiermann, *International Legal Argument in the Permanent Court of International Justice* (CUP, 2005); and Christian Tams, Malgosia Fitzmaurice (eds), *Legacies of the Permanent Court of International Justice* (Brill, 2013).

[35] Wouters, above n32 at 4.

[36] O'Connell and VanderZee, above n30 at 56.

largely untouched when the ICJ was created as its successor. At the same time, the International Military Tribunals of Nuremberg (1945–46) and Tokyo (1946–48) laid the groundwork for international criminal adjudication.[37] But the end of the Second World War also heralded a shift of attention from the global to the regional level. On the European continent, the post-war years witnessed an increased move towards the promotion of economic integration, human rights and the rule of law. The Court of Justice of the European Coal and Steel Communities (now Court of Justice of the European Union, CJEU)[38] was established in 1952, the European Court of Human Rights (ECtHR) followed in 1958. On the American continent the Inter-American Commission on Human Rights was founded in 1959, joined in 1979 by the Inter-American Court of Human Rights.

However, during the Cold War, the multiplication of international courts and tribunals slowed down. The changing political landscape after the collapse of the East-West dichotomy created the 'permissive environment' needed for the establishment of an increasing number of international courts and tribunals.[39] Since the 1990s, international courts have sprung up in almost all corners of the world, covering a wide range of legal areas. The majority have a jurisdiction *ratione territoriae* limited to a specific region.[40] However, with the Appellate Body of the World Trade Organization (WTO AB, 1994), the International Tribunal for the Law of

---

37 See for more detail Luc Reydams and Jan Wouters, 'The Politics of Establishing International Criminal Tribunals' in Luc Reydams, Jan Wouters and Cedric Ryngaert (eds), *International Prosecutors* (OUP, 2012) 6.

38 Under the first para of art 19(1) of the Treaty on European Union (TEU) (Consolidated version of the Treaty on European Union [2012] OJ C326/13), the institution of the Court of Justice of the EU (CJEU) encompasses the Court of Justice (ECJ), the General Court (EGC) and specialized courts (at present, the EU Civil Service Tribunal).

39 Alter, above n10 at 75; Martinez, above n13 at 437. On the impact of the end of the Cold War on the development of international law more generally, see James Crawford and Sarah Nouwen (eds), *Select Proceedings of the European Society of International Law, Volume 3, 2010* (Hart, 2012).

40 This includes for example the ICTY and the ICTR, which were established by the UN Security Council to prosecute perpetrators of international crimes 'in the territory of the former Yugoslavia' and 'in the territory of Rwanda and [...] neighboring states' (the latter applies *ratione personae* only to Rwandan citizens), see Statute of the International Criminal Tribunal for the Former Yugoslavia, UNSC Res 827 (1993) UN Doc S/RES/827 (ICTY Statute) art 1, and Statute of the International Tribunal for Rwanda, UNSC Res 955 (1994) UN Doc S/Res/955 (ICTR Statute) art 1.

the Sea (ITLOS, 1996) and the International Criminal Court (ICC, 2002), three specialized international courts with a global reach were created.[41]

Nevertheless, it would be an oversimplification to regard the development of the international judiciary as a 'linear story of successes'.[42] Scholarship traditionally focuses on those adjudicative bodies that have actually successfully taken up their work, thereby risking to detract from the fact that a large number of bodies exist only on paper or have fallen into a state of dormancy. Romano rightly observes that '[f]or every contemporary thriving body, there are at least twice as many that failed to set sail, or got caught in the doldrums, or even sunk after launch'.[43] Examples include the European Nuclear Energy Tribunal,[44] the European Tribunal on State Immunity,[45] the Judicial Tribunal of the Organization of Arab Petroleum Exporting Countries (OAPEC),[46] the Court of Justice of

---

41 There are calls for additional specialized international tribunals, for example in the areas of international human rights law, environmental law or investment law. See Julia Kozma, Manfred Nowak and Martin Scheinin, 'A World Court of Human Rights – Consolidated Draft Statute and Commentary', May 2010, <www.eui.eu/Documents/DepartmentsCentres/Law/Professors/Scheinin/ConsolidatedWorldCourtStatute.pdf>; ICE Coalition – Creating the International Court for the Environment, <http://icecoalition.com>; Michael Goldhaber, 'Wanted: A World Investment Court' (2004) 3 *Transnational Dispute Settlement*.

42 Cesare PR Romano, 'Trial and Error in International Judicialization' in Cesare PR Romano, Karen Alter, Yuval Shany (eds), *The Oxford Handbook of International Adjudication* (OUP, 2014) 112.

43 Ibid.

44 The Convention on the Establishment of a Security Control in the Field of Nuclear Energy and the Protocol on the Tribunal established by the Convention were adopted in 1957 and entered into force in 1959. However, so far the court has received no cases. OECD Nuclear Energy Agency, 'European Nuclear Energy Tribunal' <https://www.oecd-nea.org/law/european-nuclear-tribunal.html>.

45 The European Tribunal on State Immunity was inaugurated in 1985 but has not received a case yet. See Schermers and Blokker, above n5 at 457 et seq, para 633.

46 The Judicial Tribunal of the Organization of Arab Petroleum Exporting Countries (OAPEC) was established by a Protocol signed in 1978, which entered into force in 1980, see <www.oapecorg.org/Home/About-Us/Organizational-Structure/Council-of-Ministers/Judicial-Tribunal>. At the time of writing, it had only received two cases and it is widely regarded as dormant. See Romano, above n42 at 117 et seq; Mackenzie, Romano, Shany and Sands, above n5 at 250.

the Economic Community of Central African States (ECCAS),[47] the Judicial Organ of the Arab Maghreb Union[48] and the Court of Justice of the African Economic Community.[49] Not much attention has been paid to these unsuccessful attempts towards international judicialization and more research is needed to analyse the underlying factors that determine the success or failure of an international court, and ultimately to create a coherent and inclusive theoretical framework.

Similarly, the conclusion that judicialization has occurred evenly would be premature, both in terms of geographic and thematic scope.[50] All but five of the currently existing international courts have a jurisdiction *ratione territoriae* limited to a specific region and not all regions of the world are evenly judicialized. In particular, the Asian-Pacific and the Arab regions remain blank spots on the map of international adjudication. In terms of thematic coverage, judicialization has occurred mostly in the areas of human rights, international criminal law, trade, intellectual property, property and investment.[51] Cases in other areas such as defence or the environment rarely reach an international tribunal and have so far not seen the creation of any specialized court.[52] And even those areas that appear prima facie highly judicialized may have gaps with regard to certain issues. While, for example, the competence of international human rights courts to deal with civil and political rights is

---

47 The Court was created by the Treaty Establishing the Economic Community of Central African States (adopted 18 October 1983, entered into force 18 December 1984), see art 16 et seq. It is not yet operational, see <www.ceeac-eccas.org/index.php/fr/a-propos-de-la-ceeac/organes-de-la-ceeac>.

48 The Judicial Organ was founded in 1989: see art 13 of the Treaty Establishing the Arab Maghreb Union (adopted 17 February 1989, entered into force 1 July 1989). It holds regular meetings but there are no public records of cases received so far, see <www.aict-ctia.org/courts_subreg/amu/amu_home.html>.

49 The Court of Justice of the African Economic Community (AEC) was established by the Treaty Establishing the African Economic Community (adopted 3 June 1991, entered into force 12 May 1994) art 18 et seq. It is considered to be dormant. See Romano, above n42 at 113.

50 Ulfstein, above n20 at 849.

51 Cesare PR Romano, 'The Shadow Zones of International Judicialization' in Cesare PR Romano, Karen Alter, Yuval Shany (eds), *The Oxford Handbook of International Adjudication* (OUP, 2014) 104.

52 Ibid. at 105.

widely accepted, the justiciability of economic, social and cultural rights continues to be contested.[53]

III. SUPRANATIONALISM AND INTERNATIONALISM

The title of the volume suggests that a distinction can be made between international and supranational courts. But what exactly are the characteristics that set a supranational court apart from its international counterpart, and where to draw the line? The terms are often used interchangeably, which may be due to the fact that there is currently no single definition of supranationalism. Various scholars have identified different characteristics which they associate with supranational organizations. Schermers and Blokker, for example, propose the following basic indicators:

1) The organization has the power to take decisions that are binding on the Member States.
2) The organs taking these decisions are not entirely dependent on the cooperation of all Member States (for example composed of independent individuals, decision-making by majority vote).
3) The organization has the power to adopt rules that directly bind the inhabitants of the Member States.
4) The organization has the power to enforce its decisions, even if only through the help of an organ of the Member States.
5) The organization enjoys some financial autonomy.
6) No unilateral withdrawal from the organization is possible. The organization cannot be dissolved without the collaboration of it is own organs.[54]

---

[53] Aoife Nolan, Bruce Porter and Malcolm Langford, 'The Justiciability of Social and Economic Rights: An Updated Appraisal' (2007) NYU Centre for Human Rights and Global Justice Working Paper Series, No 15, 1 et seq; Michael J Dennis and David P Stewart, 'Justiciability of Economic, Social, and Cultural Rights: Should There Be an International Complaints Mechanism to Adjudicate the Rights to Food, Water, Housing, and Health?' (2004) 98 *American Journal of International Law* 462.

[54] Schermers and Blokker, above n5 at 56 et seq, para 61; see also José E Alvarez, *International Organizations as Law-makers* (OUP 2005) 16; Jan Klabbers, *An Introduction to International Institutional Law* (2nd edn, CUP, 2009) 24 et seq.

While these indicators are primarily tailored to fit rule-making organizations, they can also to a large extent be applied to judicial bodies. There is currently no organization that fulfils all of the criteria, but many match the description to various degrees. It is therefore important to consider the 'international' or 'supranational' character of a court not as an absolute value, but as a sliding scale, on which some courts are located further on the side of supranationalism, and others less so.

The different degrees of supranationalism are apparent already with regard to the first criterion. All international courts and tribunals have the power to take decisions that are binding on the Member States. For most, however, this power exists only under the condition that the respective members have voluntarily accepted the jurisdiction of the judicial body. It might therefore be argued that judicial bodies such as the WTO AB, the ECtHR and the CJEU, which have compulsory jurisdiction over their members, are more supranational in this respect than others such as the ICJ, for which jurisdiction is optional.

With respect to the second criterion, all courts and tribunals covered in this volume can issue their judgments, decisions, opinions or reports without the cooperation of their Member States. They are composed of independent judges whose freedom from external – particularly political – pressures is safeguarded by various institutional means.[55] With regard to the broader political framework, however, a certain degree of political influence cannot be entirely ruled out. States retain certain means of control through their political leverage, which may be stronger or weaker, depending on the level of competition and the degree of policy diversity between the Member States. The degree of dependence may therefore impact on the internationalism or supranationalism of a court. Benvenisti and Downs, for example, consider the ICJ to be a more dependent court, due to the strong scrutiny exercised by the Permanent Members of the UN Security Council, and the ECtHR to be a more independent court, due to the high degree of competition between the Member States of the Council of Europe.[56] This would support the assumption of a more pronounced supranational character of the latter, in contrast to the former.

Furthermore, supranational institutions have the power to make rules that directly bind the inhabitants of the Member States. Again, some courts fulfil this criterion to a higher degree than others. State-only courts, such as the ICJ, the WTO AB and the ITLOS, only have

---

[55] See below, section V.

[56] Eyal Benvenisti and George W Downs, 'Prospects for the Increased Independence of International Tribunals' (2011) 12 *German Law Journal* 1057, 1060 et seq, 1073 et seq.

jurisdiction over cases between states.[57] Their decisions formally only bind the parties to the dispute, although in reality they may have indirect consequences for the inhabitants of a Member State and/or the cases may largely be driven by private parties.[58] Other courts appear to be more supranational in this respect. This includes in particular the international criminal courts, which decide on the international criminal responsibility of individuals.[59]

The last three criteria of Schermers' definition of supranationalism are less frequently matched by international courts and tribunals. In particular, in contrast to national courts, international courts are generally not backed by a reliable enforcement procedure carried out by independent authorities. Reference can be made to Article 94 of the UN Charter, an option hardly ever used, which allows the party of a judgment delivered by the ICJ to have recourse to the UN Security Council if the other party fails to meet the obligations of the judgment.[60] Reference should also be made to the WTO Dispute Settlement System, which aims to ensure compliance with the outcome of cases by allowing for compensation and retaliation. Particularly the latter – self-enforcement by the Member State – is a means of exercising significant political and economic pressure on the other party, at least in cases of relative economic equality.[61] Nevertheless, the enforcement mechanism for ECJ judgments is unusually strong for international law. The European Commission is responsible for ensuring that an ECJ judgment finding an infringement of EU law[62] is complied with. If the Commission considers that the Member State concerned has not taken the necessary measures to comply with the judgment of the ECJ, it may bring the case before the Court. In doing so, it is to specify the amount of the lump sum or penalty payment to be paid by the Member State concerned which it considers appropriate in the circumstances.[63] Furthermore, if a national court fails to comply with its

---

[57] Note, however, that the WTO Dispute Settlement System also has jurisdiction over the EU.

[58] Eg in the framework of the WTO Dispute Settlement System, see Van den Bossche, above n11.

[59] Michael Zürn, 'From Interdependence to Globalization', in Walter Carlsnaes, Thomas Risse and Beth A Simmons (eds), *Handbook of International Relations* (Sage Publications, 2007) 247.

[60] See Couvreur, above n12.

[61] See Van den Bossche, above n11.

[62] See subsection VI(B) below.

[63] Art 260(2) TFEU. See Koen Lenaerts, Ignace Maselis and Kathleen Gutman (Janek Tomasz Nowak ed.), *EU Procedural Law* (OUP, 2014) 208–14.

obligation to follow an ECJ judgment giving a preliminary ruling,[64] infringement proceedings may be brought against that Member State.[65]

In addition, international courts generally do not enjoy financial autonomy – on the contrary, they are largely dependent on the financing through the Member States.[66] Some courts have found themselves to be in comfortable positions, such as the ICTY and the ICTR, which are funded from the UN peacekeeping budget and consequently enjoy comparative financial security.[67] Other courts, such as the Special Tribunal for Lebanon (STL), have to rely wholly or partially on voluntary contributions.[68]

Finally, the Member States formally retain the power to withdraw from an international court or tribunal, to dissolve it or to change its mandate. While this may indicate that the states ultimately remain above the courts, withdrawal will mean in many cases that the state will also have to withdraw altogether from the international organization in which the court is embedded. The costs of leaving, for example, the WTO, the EU or the Council of Europe will in most cases be too high to consider withdrawal from the respective judicial bodies as a valid option. Dissolving or renegotiating necessitates political consensus on the part of all Member States, which will often be impossible to achieve. Although the Member States remain the masters of the international instrument that constituted the international court, their power may exist rather in theory than in practice – depending on the individual benefits and the political framework of the respective court.

While a clear-cut distinction between international and supranational courts is therefore impossible, they can be situated on a sliding scale from internationalism to supranationalism, based on the extent to which they match the abovementioned criteria. Some scholars have doubted the usefulness of the concept of supranationalism;[69] others have rejected it

---

64 Art 267 TFEU. See subsections VI(B) and VI(D) below.

65 Arts 258–260 TFEU. See Lenaerts, Maselis and Gutman, above n63 at 244; and see subsection VI(B) below.

66 Alain Pellet, 'The Anatomy of Courts and Tribunals' (2008) 7 *The Law and Practice of International Courts and Tribunals* 275, 286.

67 Romano, above n3 at 273.

68 See Agreement between the United Nations and the Lebanese Republic on the establishment of a Special Tribunal for Lebanon (adopted 22 January 2007 and 6 February 2007, entered into force 10 June 2007) (STL Agreement) art 5, according to which 51 per cent of the budget is to be borne by voluntary contributions of states and 49 per cent of the budget by the Lebanese Government.

69 Klabbers, above n54 at 24.

altogether.[70] Nevertheless, while the concept is ill-suited to characterize an international organization *in toto*, it arguably has some value in highlighting particular characteristics in a certain body that indicate the extent to which it can validly be considered to be *supra* its Member States.

IV. THE CONCEPT OF THE RULE OF LAW

A. Point of Departure

The rule of law has been variously described as an 'essentially contested concept',[71] a 'bit of ruling class chatter',[72] or a 'hurrah word',[73] and indeed 'remains contested across both time and geography'.[74] This book acknowledges those contestations and contradictions, but nevertheless takes as a point of departure for its enquiry the link between the national and international judiciary and the rule of law as highlighted in the 2012 Declaration.[75] There, the UNGA recognized that the rule of law applies to all states equally, and to international organizations, including the United Nations and its principal organs, and that respect for, and promotion of, the rule of law and justice should guide all of their

70 See Schermers and Blokker, above n5 at 57, para 62, fn 236 for references to critical authors.

71 Jeremy Waldron, 'Is the Rule of Law an Essentially Contested Concept (In Florida)?' (2002) 21 *Law and Philosophy* 137–64, referring to Richard Fallon, '"The Rule of Law" as a Concept in Constitutional Discourse' (1997) 97 *Columbia L Rev* 6, citing Walter Bryce Gallie, 'Essentially Contested Concepts' (1955–56) 56 *Proceedings of the Aristotelian Society* 167.

72 Judith Shklar, 'Political Theory and the Rule of Law' in Alan Hutchinson and Patrick Monahan (eds), *The Rule of Law: Ideal or Ideology* (Carswell, 1987) 1: 'It would not be very difficult to show that the phrase "the Rule of Law" has become meaningless thanks to ideological abuse and general over-use … No intellectual effort need therefore be wasted on this bit of ruling-class chatter.'

73 Stéphane Beaulac, 'The Rule of Law in International Law Today' in Gianluigi Palombella and Neil Walker (eds), *Relocating the Rule of Law* (Hart Publishing, 2009) 222–3, who argues that 'the rule of law' is a formulation of 'Hurrah!' words, ie words that provoke a positive emotion as used by Charles Kay Ogden and Ivor Armstrong Richards, *The Meaning of Meaning: A Study of the Influence of Language upon Thought and of the Science of Symbolism* (Harcourt Brace Jovanovich, 1923).

74 Simon Chesterman, 'An International Rule of Law?' (2008) 56 *AJCL* 340.

75 UN Doc A/RES/67/1.

activities and accord predictability and legitimacy to their actions.[76] The 2012 Declaration affirms that the independence of the judicial system, together with its impartiality and integrity, is an essential prerequisite for upholding the rule of law and ensuring that there is no discrimination in the administration of justice, and emphasizes the right of equal access to justice for all, including members of vulnerable groups.[77] The 2012 Declaration also commits to ensuring that impunity is not tolerated for genocide, war crimes and crimes against humanity or for violations of international humanitarian law and gross violations of human rights law, and that such violations are properly investigated and appropriately sanctioned, including by bringing the perpetrators of any crimes to justice, through national mechanisms or, where appropriate, regional or international mechanisms, and explicitly recognizes the role of the ICC in a multilateral system that aims to end impunity and establish the rule of law.[78] Finally, the 2012 Declaration also recognizes the positive contribution of the ICJ, the principal judicial organ of the United Nations, including in adjudicating disputes among states, and the value of its work for the promotion of the rule of law, and indeed the contributions of the ITLOS, as well as other international courts and tribunals, in advancing the rule of law at the international and national levels.[79] The 2012 Declaration served as a conceptual point of departure for this book – as it did for the lecture series on which the book is based – providing a platform from which the individual authors developed a plurality of conceptions of the rule of law as espoused by them or their institutions.

This chapter and this book proceed on the working assumption that, at its most basic, the rule of law can arguably be described as a principle that all individuals and entities, including states and international organizations, are to be subject to and accountable to the law.[80] That implies the subjection of individuals and all levels of public power in the national

---

[76] Ibid., para 2.

[77] Ibid., paras 13–14.

[78] Ibid., paras 22–23.

[79] Ibid., paras 31–32.

[80] That core aspect is expressed cogently and concisely in Thomas Fuller's phrase 'Be you never so high, the Law is above you': Thomas Fuller, *Gnomologia: Adagies and Proverbs; Wise Sentences and Witty Sayings, Ancient and Modern, Foreign and British* (Barker and Bettesworth and Hitch, 1732) sentence no 943, quoted by Lord Denning MR in *Gouriet v Union of Post Office Workers* [1977] QB 729, 762, and by Tom Bingham, *The Rule of Law* (Allen Lane, 2010) 4. See further Geert De Baere, 'European Integration and the Rule of Law in Foreign Policy' in Julie Dickson and Pavlos Eleftheriadis (eds), *Philosophical Foundations of European Union Law* (OUP, 2012) 354–83, arguing that that

and international realm to legal constraints with a view to guaranteeing the equal protection of all individuals against arbitrary or unlawful use of power.[81] That also entails a number of minimal characteristics, such as that law must be prospective, public, general, clear, stable, certain and applied to everyone equally according to its terms.[82] As Follesdal notes,[83] at least part of the justification of those characteristics can be based on two interests of individuals: our interest in non-domination, that is the 'protection from the arbitrary use of political authority and coercive power',[84] and in predictability, that is 'our ability to make longer term plans in pursuit of our various interests with some expectation of success – in particular, to be able to rely on general compliance with legal rules'.[85] That leaves room for various more or less formal or substantive conceptions of the rule of law that are more or less expansive in what they encompass.

A notable maximalist or substantive conception of the rule of law was put forward by UN Secretary-General Kofi Annan in his 2004 report *The rule of law and transitional justice in conflict and post-conflict societies*:[86]

---

principle as applied to public authorities, particularly those involved in foreign policy, is the cornerstone of European integration.

[81] Compare the similar conception in Chesterman, above n74 at 342; and James Crawford, 'Chance, Order, Change: The Course of International Law. General Course on Public International Law' (2013) 265 *Collected Courses of The Hague Academy of International Law* 271.

[82] Brian Tamanaha, 'A Concise Guide to the Rule of Law' in Palombella and Walker (eds), *Relocating the Rule of Law*, above n73 at 3. See also the eight desiderata in Lon Fuller, *The Morality of Law* (Revised edn, Yale UP, 1969) 38–9; the eight desiderata in John Finnis, *Natural Law and Natural Rights* (2nd edn, OUP, 2011) 270–1; and the eight principles in Joseph Raz, *The Authority of Law* (2nd edn, OUP, 2009) 214–19; and compare the definition of the rule of law in Friedrich Von Hayek, *The Road to Serfdom* (Routledge, 1944) 54. See also the somewhat different list of features 'arguably necessary if the international legal system can be said to be governed by the rule of law' in Crawford, above n81 at 253.

[83] See Follesdal, above n4.

[84] P Pettit, *Republicanism: A Theory of Freedom and Government* (Clarendon Press, 1997).

[85] See Raz, above n82.

[86] UN Security Council, *The rule of law and transitional justice in conflict and post-conflict societies. Report of the Secretary-General* (UN Doc S/2004/616) para 6.

> The 'rule of law' is a concept at the very heart of the Organization's mission. It refers to a principle of governance in which all persons, institutions and entities, public and private, including the State itself, are accountable to laws that are publicly promulgated, equally enforced and independently adjudicated, and which are consistent with international human rights norms and standards. It requires, as well, measures to ensure adherence to the principles of supremacy of law, equality before the law, accountability to the law, fairness in the application of the law, separation of powers, participation in decision-making, legal certainty, avoidance of arbitrariness and procedural and legal transparency.

As Crawford notes, these precepts were articulated in the context of an international organization with international legal personality and a mandate to support domestic transitional justice. They arguably require adaptation before they can be applied to the system of international law as a whole.[87] Moreover, even at the UN level, contrasting conceptions of the rule of law exist, notably on whether human rights are included in the rule of law, or alternatively, whether they are a necessary complement of the rule of law, but not included in it. As pointed out by Follesdal,[88] the latter is what the 2012 Declaration appears to suggest. There, the Heads of State and Government, and heads of delegation reaffirm, 'that human rights, the rule of law and democracy are interlinked and mutually reinforcing and that they belong to the universal and indivisible core values and principles of the United Nations'.[89]

They also express their conviction:

> … that the advancement of the rule of law at the national and international levels is essential for sustained and inclusive economic growth, sustainable development, the eradication of poverty and hunger and the full realization of all human rights and fundamental freedoms, including the right to development, all of which in turn reinforce the rule of law … .[90]

Finally, the Heads of State and Government, and heads of delegation emphasize:

> … the importance of continuing our consideration and promotion of the rule of law in all its aspects, and to that end we decide to pursue our work in the General Assembly to develop further the linkages between the rule of law and

---

87 Crawford, above n81 at 262.
88 Follesdal, above n4.
89 UN Doc A/RES/67/1, para 5.
90 Ibid., para 7.

> the three main pillars of the United Nations: peace and security, human rights and development … .[91]

This chapter is not intended as a further examination of the merits or demerits of formal or substantive rule of law conceptions[92] or of more or less comprehensive conceptions including or not the respect for human rights. It aims to do no more than set out an analytical framework to assess the contribution of international and supranational courts to the rule of law at international, regional, and domestic levels, while leaving room for various institutional and individual conceptions in that regard.

B. The Rule of Law in the International Legal Order

The rule of law (or its equivalents in other languages) was originally developed to be applied to and within states,[93] as a glance at the names of the equivalent (though not entirely identical) concepts in a number of other languages makes clear.[94] Does the origin of the rule of law in a national context imply that it is, as Crawford asks, 'still extraneous to the real hard business of international law, like an accidental tourist at a diplomatic conference?'[95] That is clearly not a forgone conclusion. In fact, the 'domestic' origin does not seem to stand in the way of the application of the rule of law, in its core meaning, to other entities, both at national and international levels.[96] Arguably, there can be no clear-cut distinction between the state and other public or quasi-public bodies from the perspective of the elimination of arbitrary power.[97] As the ICJ put it

---

[91] Ibid., para 41.

[92] See further Paul Craig, 'Formal and Substantive Conceptions of the Rule of Law: An Analytical Framework' (1997) *PL* 467–87; an eminent example of the former is Raz, above n82, and of the latter Ronald Dworkin, *A Matter of Principle* (Harvard UP, 1985) 11–12. See specifically with respect to the international level: Hans Corell, 'A Challenge to the United Nations and the World: Developing the Rule of law' (2004) 18 *Temple International and Comparative Law Journal* 391, 393.

[93] The phrase 'rule of law' itself originates from Albert Venn Dicey, *Introduction to the Study of the Law of the Constitution* (6th edn, Macmillan, 1902).

[94] Eg *Rechtsstaat, Etat de droit, Stato di diritto, Estado de derecho.*

[95] Crawford, above n81 at 257.

[96] See in that sense UN General Assembly and Security Council, *Uniting our strengths: Enhancing United Nations support for the rule of law. Report of the Secretary-General* (UN Doc A/61/636–S/2006/980).

[97] See Trevor Allan, *Constitutional Justice: a Liberal Theory of the Rule of Law* (OUP, 2001) 11.

in *ELSI*: 'Arbitrariness is not so much something opposed to a rule of law, as something opposed to the rule of law.'[98]

That said, the manner in which the rule of law is applied to international institutions and the international legal order in general needs to take into account the fact that, compared to most states, the international legal order has a varying but generally weaker degree of institutionalization, lacks a centralized and hierarchical structure, and is hence organized along horizontal rather than vertical lines.[99] That also implies the correlative need for many decisions to be taken by consensus, if at all.[100] As will be seen, the absence of a central legislature in the international legal order also impacts on the role and the operation of international and supranational courts.[101]

Furthermore, account must be taken of the divergent meanings given to the equivalent concepts in various systems, especially as failing to take account of local traditions may be a major stumbling block in promoting the rule of law.[102] Much like with respect to human rights, a consensus on the rule of law cannot be achieved by ignoring pre-existing traditions, but by different groups, within their own heritage, 'travelling different routes to the same goal'.[103] The importance of that diversity is also acknowledged by the UN, notably in the 2008 Report of the Secretary General and in the 2012 Declaration. In his 2008 Report, the Secretary-General argued that in fulfilling its responsibilities, the UN must work towards achieving appropriate application at the international level of the Organization's understanding of the principle of the rule of law. However, efforts to do so 'must be based on commonly agreed values', which are to be drawn from existing commitments in the UN, the Declaration on Principles of International Law concerning Friendly Relations and

---

[98] ICJ, *Elettronica Sicula SpA (ELSI)*, Judgment, ICJ Reports 1989, 76, para 128, referring to what it had held in the *Asylum case*, when it spoke of 'arbitrary action' being 'substituted for the rule of law' (ICJ, *Asylum*, Judgment, ICJ Reports 1950, p 284).

[99] Jan Wouters and Matthieu Burnay, 'The International Rule of Law: European and Asian Perspectives' (2013) *Revue belge de droit international* 299, 300.

[100] Crawford, above n81 at 261.

[101] See subsection IV(C) and section VII below.

[102] Rosa Ehrenreich Brooks, 'The New Imperialism: Violence, Norms and the "Rule of Law"' (2003) 101 *Michigan Law Review* 2275, 2322.

[103] Charles Taylor, 'Conditions for an Unforced Consensus on Human Rights' in Joanne Bauer and Daniel Bell (eds), *The East Asian Challenge for Human Rights* (CUP, 1999) 144.

Cooperation among States,[104] the 2005 World Summit Outcome Document[105] and multilateral treaties.[106] In the 2012 Declaration, the Heads of State and Government, and heads of delegation recognized 'the progress made by countries in advancing the rule of law as an integral part of their national strategies', and 'that there are common features founded on international norms and standards which are reflected in a broad diversity of national experiences in the area of the rule of law', stressing 'the importance of promoting the sharing of national practices and of inclusive dialogue'.[107] International law does not exist to exhort or enforce a homogenous set of values at all costs, but in large areas allows states to be different. As Vaughan Lowe put it: 'International law deals in polyphony, not in plainsong.'[108]

International law constrains the unlimited exercise of power by states through subjecting their behaviour to a set of rules. That not only makes their behaviour compatible with similar behaviour of other states and actors in international law, but also makes it more predictable and hence creates opportunities for individuals to act freely and autonomously.[109] Rules establish expectations for individuals. If the bases of these rules and claims are unsure, 'so are the boundaries of men's liberties'.[110] In that sense, too extensive a conferral of discretion upon public authorities may invite the judgement that the regime in question is a marginal instance of a legal ordering. If discretion is too broadly conferred, individuals will have to guide their conduct by prediction of official

---

104 UN General Assembly, *Declaration on Principles of International Law Concerning Friendly Relations and Co-operation among States in Accordance with the Charter of the United Nations* (UN Doc A/RES/25/2625).

105 UN General Assembly, *2005 World Summit Outcome* (UN Doc A/RES/60/1).

106 UN General Assembly, *Strengthening and coordinating United Nations rule of law activities. Report of the Secretary-General* (UN Doc A/63/226) paras 24–5.

107 Ibid., para 10.

108 Vaughan Lowe, 'The Function of Litigation in International Society' (2012) 61 *International and Comparative Law Quarterly* 221.

109 This is arguably the '*raison d'être* of the rule of law': Jeremy Waldron, 'The Rule of International Law' (2008) 30 *Harvard J of L & Public Policy* 17. See also Amanda Perreau-Saussine, 'Immanuel Kant on International Law' in Samantha Besson and John Tasioulas (eds), *The Philosophy of International Law* (OUP, 2010) 55, noting that for Kant, 'the closer a state approaches perpetual peace with its potential enemies, the more secure citizens' juridical freedom will be'. See also De Baere, above n80 at 358.

110 John Rawls, *A Theory of Justice* (Revised edn, Belknap, 1999) 207.

behaviour, rather than by legal rules. This also means that the rule of law implies independence of the power of others, and is not content with mere predictability in action by public authorities: 'even when we are fully under the power of the unconstrained will of our governors, the exercise of that power may be highly predictable'.[111] That is true of all public authorities, from the local to the international level, even if international organizations do not as a rule aim at the monopoly of the use of force in a specific territorial circumscription.[112] Nevertheless, the risk of discretionary competences that are too broad in scope is often higher in the international action of states, which is traditionally the domain of the executive, with often little involvement of the legislature or the judiciary. For example, an international rule of precedence such as Article 103 of the UN Charter, which provides that in case of conflict obligations under the Charter prevail over obligations under any other international agreement, can have the effect not of limiting the discretionary power of an essentially executive organ such as the Security Council, but of expanding it at the expense of rule of law constraints, democratic accountability, and the rights of individuals.[113] The peace and security powers given to or asserted by the UN Security Council and the unusual relationship to other legal regimes due to Article 103 of the UN Charter may lead to questioning whether the UN may properly be said to embody the rule of law in a meaningful way.[114] In short, there exists an inherent contradiction between the rule of law and the notion of a purely administrative or discretionary act that determines a citizen's fate without recourse to legal safeguards,[115] and such acts are arguably more common in international action than in internal action.

---

111 Nigel Simmonds, *Law as a Moral Idea* (OUP, 2007) 90, but also 46 and 98.

112 Alan Buchanan and Robert Keohane, 'The Legitimacy of Global Governance Institutions' (2006) 20 *Ethics and International Affairs* 406.

113 Jean Cohen, *Globalization and Sovereignty. Rethinking Legality, Legitimacy, and Constitutionalism* (CUP, 2012) 291. The tension between the obligations under art 103 UN Charter and the rule of law at the level of the EU was famously the subject of the *Kadi* litigation before the EU courts: see the EGC judgments in *Kadi v Council and Commission*, T-315/01, EU:T:2005:332 and *Kadi v Commission*, T-85/09, EU:T:2010:418; and the ECJ judgments in *Kadi and Al Barakaat International Foundation v Council and Commission*, C-402/05 P and C-415/05 P, EU:C:2008:461 and *Commission, Council and UK v Kadi*, C-584/10 P, C-593/10 P and C-595/10 P, EU:C:2013:518. See Koen Lenaerts in the present volume; and further De Baere, above n80 at 374–83.

114 Chesterman, above n74 at 354.

115 Allan, above n97 at 174.

Clearly therefore, an individual's liberties are as much at stake when the state acts externally as when it acts internally. Indeed, many more individuals may be affected by the state's external action than by its internal action. Moreover, lawless state action in the international realm may entail lawless state action at home, as abuses in the government's treatment of others abroad can creep back in and insinuate themselves into domestic state practice, infecting and contaminating the culture of legality at home. As Waldron put it: the 'governmental character of the nation-state does not evaporate when we move up a level to the international realm'.[116] Furthermore, the strong global interdependence causes individuals and groups often to be affected more readily by the actions of other states than by those of the state in which they live or of which they are nationals. However, the existing international legal order, subdivided as it is into sovereign and equal states, does not allow individuals to be included in decision-making processes that cover competences of other states or political communities, but the outcome of which will nevertheless affect their life and wellbeing.[117]

Governments should therefore proceed on the basis that they are to act both internally and externally in accordance with law in all of their operations, and thus subject themselves to constraint by law so that citizens can enjoy freedom under law.[118] That idea is reflected in Article 14 of the Draft Declaration on Rights and Duties of States:[119]

---

[116] Jeremy Waldron, 'Are Sovereigns Entitled to the Benefit of the International Rule of Law?' (2011) 22 *Eur J Intl L* 341–2. See Mark Reiff, 'The Attack on Liberalism' in Michael Freeman and Ross Harrison (eds), *Law and Philosophy* (OUP, 2007) 181–3. See also De Baere, above n80 at 358–9.

[117] Ronald Dworkin, 'A New Philosophy for International Law' (2013) 41 *Philosophy and Public Affairs* 18 and 28–9. Nevertheless, a distribution of decision-making authority based purely on who is affected by a specific decision would lead to complex procedural difficulties and problems of interaction and overlap: see eg Andreas Follesdal, 'Subsidiarity and the Global Order' in Michelle Evans and Augusto Zimmermann (eds), *Global Perspectives on Subsidiarity* (Springer, 2014) 214–15; and see with respect to the EU, Nick Barber, 'The Limited Modesty of Subsidiarity' (2005) 11 *ELJ* 317; Alexia Herwig, 'Federalism, the EU and International Law: On the Possible (and Necessary) Role of Subsidiarity in Legitimate Multilevel Trade Governance' in Elke Cloots, Geert De Baere and Stefan Sottiaux (eds), *Federalism in the European Union* (Hart Publishing, 2012) 68.

[118] Waldron, above n116 at 340, arguing also that the government's own freedom of action is not an intrinsic value as it is for individual citizens.

[119] Draft Declaration on Rights and Duties of States, 1949 *YB Int'l L Comm'n* 178. On the relationship between sovereignty and the rule of law, see eg John Rawls, *Lectures in the History of Political Philosophy* (Belknap Press,

> Every State has the duty to conduct its relations with other States in accordance with international law and with the principle that the sovereignty of each State is subject to the supremacy of international law.

Depending on the sources of rule of law constraints and the public authorities to which they apply, a distinction could in that regard be drawn between an external and an internal aspect of the rule of law.[120] The sources of *external* rule of law constraints are legal orders that include but are broader in scope than the legal order whose public authorities they are meant to constrain; for example, constraints on states imposed by an international organization of which they are a member, but equally constraints on international organizations imposed by general international law. The sources of *internal* rule of law constraints are the legal orders themselves whose public authorities are to be constrained; for example, constraints imposed by the internal law of those states or international organizations. In both cases, those constraints can pertain to public authority action within the legal order; that is, internal or (for states) domestic policy, and public authority action outside the legal order; that is, external or (for states) foreign policy. An example of an external rule of law constraint on foreign policy is the prohibition on the threat or use of force in international relations contained in Article 2(4) of the UN Charter. An example of an external rule of law constraint on internal or domestic policy is the right not to be subjected to torture as guaranteed by Article 3 of the European Convention on Human Rights (ECHR). An example of an internal rule of law constraint on external or foreign policy would be the possibility for courts to review the compliance of an international agreement with internal constitutional principles. An example of an internal rule of law constraint on internal or domestic policy would be the possibility for courts to review the legality of police action by a state on its own territory. As will be explored further below,[121] by assessing the compliance by public authorities with international law constraints, international and supranational courts can contribute to internal rule of law constraints within the organizations of which they are an organ (internal compliance assessment), as well as to

2007) 86; and Pavlos Eleftheriadis, 'Law and Sovereignty' (2010) 29 *Law and Philosophy* 535–69. Further: Sir Neil MacCormick, *Questioning Sovereignty: Law, State, and Practical Reason* (OUP, 1999); Katrin Flikschuh, 'Kant's Sovereignty Dilemma: A Contemporary Analysis' (2010) 18 *The Journal of Political Philosophy* 469–93.

120 De Baere, above n80 at 355.

121 See section VI(B) below.

the external rule of law constraints on states subject to their jurisdiction (external compliance assessment). In turn, those external rule of law constraints imposed by international and supranational courts may contribute to the internal rule of law constraints on states imposed by their own courts or administrations.

For states, rule of law constraints may be regarded as limiting their freedom of action.[122] It has been often argued that in an unpredictable world states must not be constrained by rules that prevent them from acting quickly and decisively.[123] States may well take the view that they can only allow themselves to be so constrained if the behaviour of other international actors can be predicted because it is governed by rules. That is arguably why foreign policy has frequently been claimed to escape any grasp of law.[124] On the internal level, it is often held that the penetration of law into foreign policy should be kept to a minimum: the executive must have its hands free to react to international developments quickly and effectively, without interference from the legislature or the judiciary.[125] On the international level, a similar attitude has sometimes led to the rejection of the legal character of international law,[126] or the downplaying of its significance.[127]

---

122 De Baere, above n80 at 359–60.

123 See eg notably James Madison, Alexander Hamilton and John Jay, *The Federalist Papers* (J & A McLean, 1788) XXIII and XLI.

124 See Thomas Franck, *Political Questions/Judicial Answers: Does the Rule of Law Apply to Foreign Affairs?* (Princeton UP, 1992) 49, reviewed in Anne-Marie Slaughter, 'Are Foreign Affairs Different?' (1993) 106 *Harvard L Rev* 1980–2008; and see Alter, above n5 at 3.

125 See Franck, above n124 at 3–4, who refers to:

> a constitutional theory, still asserted by many lawyers and judges, that foreign affairs are *different* from all other matters of state in some crucial fashion … Carried to its logical extreme, this doctrine holds that the political authorities are suit-proof as long as they purport to act in pursuance of their 'foreign-affairs' power.

126 Famously John Austin, *The Province of Jurisprudence Determined* (Wilfrid Rumble (ed.) CUP, 1832/1995) 20 *et passim*, also classifying constitutional law as 'positive morality merely': at 216 *et passim*. But see Thomas Franck, *Fairness in International Law and Institutions* (Clarendon Press, 1995) 6, arguing that international law has entered a 'post-ontological era', enabling international lawyers to 'undertake critical assessment' of their subject, instead of continuously having to defend its existence. See James Brierly, *The Law of Nations: An Introduction to the International Law of Peace* (4th edn, Clarendon Press, 1949) 73.

127 Eg Herbert Hart, *The Concept of Law* (2nd edn, OUP, 1994) 198, remarking that law in the international system has been confined to matters that do not 'affect "vital" issues'.

Conversely, international law can nevertheless often also be actively used by states to achieve particular objectives that they find difficult to achieve using purely internal means.[128] It can, for example, be used to entrench rules that are not easily subject to entrenchment by ordinary statute.[129] Indeed, politicians may even use international courts or other independent dispute settlement organs instead of bilateral negotiations so as to avoid the political costs of negotiating a deal that may be not as attractive to their constituents as other options.[130] Moreover, states often do regard themselves bound by certain constraints regardless of whether other international actors are so constrained. For example, many states would hold themselves bound by an obligation not to torture prisoners, regardless of whether other states or international actors are under the same obligation.[131]

Crucially, international courts provide an important method for states to bind themselves without the danger of facing an 'unbound' opponent. Conferring jurisdiction, especially compulsory jurisdiction, to an international court is a tool for states to bind other states and to create the background conditions for the law to be implemented and respected by all parties.[132] In other words, accepting the jurisdiction of international courts makes the mutual commitments between states credible, which may provide an incentive for their creation.[133] In addition, while under a contract-based conception of international obligations, the breach by one party of its obligations releases or modifies the obligations of the other party, international law has arguably seen a shift toward expectations of

---

128 De Baere, above n80 at 360.

129 For example, bilateral investment treaties (BITs) can resolve the problem that a state cannot make a commitment to an investor under national law, because it may be unable securely to bind itself domestically: Alex Mills, 'The Public-Private Dualities of International Investment Law and Arbitration' in Chester Brown and Kate Miles (eds), *Evolution in Investment Treaty Law and Arbitration* (CUP, 2011) 97.

130 Benedict Kingsbury, 'International Courts: Uneven Judicialisation in Global Order' in James Crawford and Martti Koskenniemi (eds), *The Cambridge Companion to International Law* (CUP, 2012) 216.

131 A liberal state may, for example, take the view that resorting to torture would undermine the basis of the proper constitutional relationship between state and citizen: see Allan, above n97 at 83–4. Further: Jeremy Waldron, *Torture, Terror, and Trade-Offs: Philosophy for the White House* (OUP, 2010).

132 Alter, above n5 at 10–11

133 Kingsbury, above n130 at 217.

compliance grounded in the rule of law, regardless of what other parties may be doing. That shift is most visible in the operation of international courts.[134]

C. The Rule of Law and International Courts

As noted by Waldron, principles (such as the rule of law) 'cannot conduct distributions by themselves: they must be administered by working institutions', and 'to the extent that the avoidance of injustice is a moral imperative, the establishment of coordinating institutions is a moral imperative'.[135] The establishment of international and supranational courts is to be understood against that background.[136]

The possibility of access to an independent judiciary and of judicial review is an essential aspect in many understandings of the rule of law.[137] The judiciary's crucial role of preventing discrepancy between the law as declared and as administered,[138] ensuring that legal rules prevail over power in the settlement of disputes,[139] and rendering the law clearer, more predictable, and more coherent, makes international and supranational courts a logical focal point for a discussion of the rule of law at the international, regional and national levels.[140]

---

[134] Alter, above n5 at 18–19.

[135] Jeremy Waldron, 'Special Ties and Natural Duties' (1993) 22 *Philosophy & Public Affairs* 15 and 28. See Pavlos Eleftheriadis, *Legal Rights* (OUP, 2008) 56, arguing that the creation of legal institutions is a matter of a special moral duty and that the successful function of law is therefore a distinct moral requirement.

[136] See De Baere, above n80 at 362, arguing that the establishment of the EU and its institutions and the rule of law as the cornerstone of that project of European integration are to be understood against that same background.

[137] On the merits and demerits of judicial review in constitutional systems, see eg Jeremy Waldron, 'The Core of the Case against Judicial Review' (2006) 115 *Yale LJ* 1346–406; Richard Fallon, 'The Core of an Uneasy Case *For* Judicial Review' (2008) *Harvard L Rev* 1693–763; Mark Tushnet, 'How Different are Waldron's and Fallon's Core Cases For and Against Judicial Review?' (2010) 30 *OJLS* 49–70. See also John Rawls, *Political Liberalism* (Expanded edn, Columbia UP, 2005) 339.

[138] Fuller, above n82 at 81; see Jeremy Waldron, 'The Concept and the Rule of Law' (2008) 121 43 *Georgia L Rev 1*, 20, arguing that absent the existence and operation of the sort of institutions we call courts, something should not be regarded as a legal system. See also Allan, above n97 at 43.

[139] Nicolas Hachez, 'What Elements of the Rule of Law Can be Put to Use at International Level?' (2013) *Revue belge de droit international* 307, 311.

[140] See De Baere, above n80 at 367–8.

For Hans Kelsen, the judicial process is the foundation of each legal organization and every community of law, and the introduction of a judicial organ with compulsory jurisdiction is the turning point in the transition from a decentralized legal order to a more centralized and more effective legal order.[141] In the international legal order, that process is still in its infancy, as judicial dispute settlement remains an exception to the rule of autonomous interpretation by states of their international obligations and free choice of means of peaceful dispute settlement.[142] Indeed, Grotius felt perfectly comfortable putting forward the idea of an international legal order based on rights, duties, and rules of conduct, but without courts.[143] Nevertheless, as Alter has powerfully demonstrated, international courts play an ever-increasing central role in the debate about the meaning of international law and about what respect for the rule of law by governments entails. Their contribution rests in their independent ability to state what the law is, point out violations, indicate remedies, and increase the credibility of the consequences of non-compliance with international rules. They further effectuate change by working with actors in various guises and combinations that for various reasons want to see international law respected.[144]

International courts and tribunals adjudicate disputes not on the basis of political discretion, but on the basis of previously established rules.[145] They thus contribute to a situation in which not physical force and the arbitrariness and oppressiveness of power contests but a system of rules is the manner in which disputes are to be settled, thereby representing the normative ideal of the rule of law.[146] Nevertheless, international courts not only settle disputes, but especially in the absence of an international legislature, also contribute to the development of the law.[147] Indeed,

---

[141] Hans Kelsen, *Peace Through Law* (The University of North Carolina Press, 1944) 73. See Charles Leben, 'Hans Kelsen and the Advancement of International Law' (1998) 9 *EJIL* 287, 291–2. Further: Jochen von Bernstorff, *The Public International Law Theory of Hans Kelsen: Believing in Universal Law* (CUP, 2010) 191–224.

[142] See art 33 UN Charter. Further Andreas Paulus, 'International Adjudication' in Besson and Tasioulas above n109 at 207.

[143] As pointed out by Kingsbury, above n130 at 203, referring to Hugo Grotius, *De jure belli ac pacis* (1625).

[144] Alter, above n5 at 4–5 and 28.

[145] Paulus, above n142 at 217–19.

[146] Hachez, above n139 at 308.

[147] Lowe, above n108 at 212–14.

dispute settlement may currently no longer be the task most often given to an international court, nor its most often performed function.[148]

The diversity of the contexts in which the rule of law at international level operates mentioned above also has clear consequences for the operation of courts. While domestic courts work against the background of a shared minimum set of common values, such commonality is often very thin in the international legal order. International courts and tribunals are therefore faced with a fraught balancing act between different legal and moral systems.[149] Indeed, the key difference between national and international law in that regard may be that the latter must compete with domestic rule of law conceptions. Governments may therefore try to justify their disregard for decisions of international courts and tribunals by arguing that they are inconsistent with the domestic conception of the rule of law.[150] Moreover, and partly as a consequence, the difficulties for international courts and tribunals start at the level of sources, which are notoriously more difficult to identify than in domestic legal systems. In the absence of an international legislator, a consequence of what Dworkin described as the 'unmitigated Westphalian system',[151] international judges must find the law before being able to apply it.[152] The political context within which international courts and tribunals operate is therefore of crucial importance in order to understand their functioning.

V. INDEPENDENCE AND IMPARTIALITY

International courts and tribunals do not exist in a vacuum. They operate in a politico-legal framework formed by international institutions and Member States. It is particularly the relationship with the latter that has raised concerns. Why would states voluntarily create international adjudicative bodies and submit to their jurisdiction? What means of control do they retain? Different models have been applied to capture this phenomenon.[153] Proponents of the Principal–Agent theory, for example, posit that courts and tribunals are mere agents of their Member States,

---

[148] Alter, above n5 at 12–13. See section VI below.
[149] Paulus, above n142 at 213.
[150] Alter, above n5 at 8 and 20.
[151] Dworkin, above n117 at 27.
[152] Donald Regan, 'International Adjudication: A Response to Paulus – Courts, Custom, Treaties, Regimes, and the WTO' in Besson and Tasioulas above n109 at 227–9.
[153] See for an overview Ulfstein, above n20 at 850 et seq.

susceptible to political sanctions and threats thereof. The Member States can renegotiate the mandate of the courts or threaten to do so in order to ensure compliance with their own preferences. Others see courts as trustees of their Member States – independent but nevertheless subject to political influence.[154] In particular, Member States might use 'rhetorical politics' to impact on a court's reasoning, they may delegitimize a court, or disband it altogether. Whereas Posner and Yoo consider the fragmentation of international courts as a consequence and proof of the states' desire to retain control,[155] Slaughter and Helfer argue that international courts only enjoy 'constrained independence', meaning that they are formally independent but in fact controlled by their Member States through a 'range of structural, political, and discursive mechanisms'.[156] Regardless of the label, it appears that a certain degree of political influence may often exist and should not be ignored.

This political influence risks undermining the contribution of international courts and tribunals to the rule of law. Independence and impartiality are the basic criteria for any court and tribunal that aspires to enjoy even a minimal degree of legitimacy, respect and confidence and to fulfil effectively the various roles with which it has been mandated.[157] They are the *sine qua non* for any judicial contribution to the rule of law.[158] Courts must be free from any form of external pressure – be it from the parties of the case, the states parties to the instrument establishing the court, the country hosting the seat of the court, or the international organization of which the court forms a part (independence). Judges need to base their decisions on the relevant facts and the

---

[154] Karen J Alter, 'Agents or Trustees? International Courts in their Political Context' (2008) 14 *European Journal of International Relations* 33.

[155] Eric A Posner and John C Yoo, 'Judicial Independence in International Tribunals' (2005) 93 *California Law Review* 1, 73.

[156] Laurence R Helfer and Anne-Marie Slaughter, 'Why States Create International Tribunals: A Response to Professors Posner and Yoo' (2005) 93 *California Law Review* 899, 902.

[157] Gilbert Guillaume, 'De l'indépendance des membres de la cour internationale de justice' in *Boutros Boutros-Ghali Amicorum Discipulorumque Liber: Paix, Développement, Démocratie* (Vol 1, Bruylant, 1998) 475; Gleider I Hernández, 'Impartiality and Bias at the International Court of Justice (2012) 1 *Cambridge Journal of International and Comparative Law* 183; Benvenisti and Downs, above n56 at 1057.

[158] Theodor Meron, 'Judicial Independence and Impartiality in International Criminal Tribunals' (2005) 99 *American Journal of International Law* 359; Lon Fuller, 'Adjudication and the Rule of Law' (1960) 54 *Proceedings of the American Society of International Law* 1, 2; Shelton, above n18 at 545.

applicable law, rather than on their own preferences (impartiality).[159] These criteria constitute basic requirements for a court's effective contribution to the rule of law.

Independence and impartiality are values that need to be internalized by international judges and they must constantly guide their actions on the court. They need to 'reign the spirits and the hearts' of the judiciary.[160] In addition, the institutional framework of the international adjudicative bodies needs to provide sufficient room for the exercise of the judicial function in line with these values, which particularly means that judges must be shielded from any form of external pressure. All of the statutes and rules of procedures of the courts covered in this volume contain safeguards to ensure the independence and impartiality of the respective judicial body. They provide for appointment procedures designed to ensure the independence of the judges from external influences, list the independence of the candidate as one of the basic eligibility criteria, they contain provisions on incompatibility, on the nationality of the judges, on their privileges and immunities, on their irremovability and remuneration, on the secrecy of deliberations and votes and lastly on the terms of office. The following subsections give a brief comparative overview of these formal safeguards.

A. Eligibility Criteria

The independence and impartiality of the candidate is an eligibility criterion that can be found in the governing texts of all courts and tribunals covered in this volume. Judges and Advocates General of the CJEU 'shall be chosen from persons whose independence is beyond doubt',[161] the judges of the ICC and ICTY must distinguish themselves by their 'impartiality and integrity',[162] the ICJ is to be 'composed of a body of independent judges'[163] and the judges of the ITLOS are required

---

159 Hernández, above n157 at 184, 188 et seq.

160 Ibid. For a critical view of the independence of international judges, see Vitalius Tumonis, 'Adjudication Fallacies: The Role of International Courts in Interstate Dispute Settlement' (2014) 31 *Wisconsin International Law Journal* 35, 44 et seq.

161 Art 19(2), second subpara TEU and Arts 253–254 and 257 of the Treaty on the Functioning of the European Union (TFEU) (Consolidated Version of the Treaty on the Functioning of the European Union [2012] OJ C326/47).

162 Art 36(3)(a) Rome Statute of the International Criminal Court (adopted 17 July 1998, entered into force 1 July 2002) (ICC Statute), and art 13 ICTY Statute, respectively.

163 Art 2 ICJ Statute.

to enjoy the 'highest reputation for fairness and integrity'.[164] The Statute of the Special Tribunal for Lebanon is even more explicit on this issue. It provides not only that the judges be persons of 'impartiality and integrity', but also that they must be 'independent in the performance of their functions and shall not accept or seek instructions from any Government or any other source'.[165] With respect to the ECtHR, Article 21(1) ECHR does not explicitly list the independence or impartiality of the judges as an eligibility criterion, and only refers to their 'high moral character'. Nevertheless, Article 21(3) ECHR obliges judges to refrain from 'any activity which is incompatible with their independence [or] impartiality'. Finally, the Members of the WTO AB are required by the Rules of Conduct to be 'independent and impartial' and to 'avoid direct or indirect conflicts of interest'.[166] All of these provisions are kept in general terms and do not specify what these criteria imply. More detailed guidance is usually provided in the subsequent provisions of the governing texts. Nevertheless, the consistent inclusion of independence and impartiality in the eligibility criteria underlines their fundamental value for the international judiciary and ensures their central importance for the election process.

B. Appointment Procedure

The appointment procedures for most courts and tribunals covered in this volume are designed in order to avoid undue dominance by one state or group of states. Safeguards include the establishment of independent national nomination bodies or panels, the involvement of multiple organs in the election process, and the requirement of a high quorum. Candidates for the ICJ, for example, need to be nominated by the PCA national groups, a group of up to four individuals, which are appointed by the parties of the PCA to serve as potential arbitrators.[167] In theory, the PCA

---

164 Art 2(1) Statute of the International Tribunal for the Law of the Sea, Annex VI of the United Nations Convention on the Law of the Sea (adopted 10 December 1982, entered into force 16 November 1994) (ITLOS Statute).

165 Art 9(1) Statute of the Special Tribunal for Lebanon, UNSC Res 1757 (2007) UN Doc S/RES/1757 (STL Statute).

166 Section II(1) Rules of Conduct for the Understanding on Rules and Procedures Governing the Settlement of Disputes, WTO Doc WT/DSB/RC/1.

167 Art 4(2) ICJ Statute. Note, that the PCA national groups also play an important role in the ICC nomination process, where candidates must be nominated either '[b]y the procedure for the nomination of candidates for appointment to the highest judicial offices in the State in question' or in line with the ICJ nomination procedure: art 36(4) ICC Statute.

national groups are supposed to be independent from their national governments.[168] However, in practice it is not uncommon to find active government officials among them,[169] and it has been argued that the majority of these groups are in fact 'extensions of their governments'.[170] The CJEU and the ECtHR both have the safeguard of an independent nominations commission, which assesses the suitability of the candidates and delivers an opinion to the Member States before they proceed with the appointment. The panel for the CJEU is composed of former members of the CJEU or the General Court, members of national supreme courts, and 'lawyers of recognised competence'.[171] The composition of the ECtHR Advisory Panel is similar, but allows for the appointment of former judges of international courts more generally. These non-state selection committees may be more efficient in curtailing national influence on the nomination process.[172]

While judges of the ECtHR are selected by a simple majority in the Parliamentary Assembly of the Council of Europe,[173] the ICC Statute requires a two-thirds majority of the states parties present and voting,[174] similar to the ITLOS Statute, where the quorum is a 'two-thirds majority of the States Parties present and voting, provided that such majority includes a majority of the States Parties'.[175] ICJ judges need to be elected in both the UN Security Council and the UN General Assembly, by an

---

168 Ruth Mackenzie, Kate Malleson, Penny Martin and Philippe Sands, *Selecting International Judges: Principle, Process, and Politics* (OUP, 2010) 69 et seq.

169 Ibid. at 70.

170 Davis R Robinson, 'The Role of Politics in the Election and the Work of Judges of the International Court of Justice' (2003) 97 *American Society of International Law Proceedings* 277, 279; see also Mackenzie, Malleson, Martin and Sands, above n168 at 145.

171 Art 255 TFEU.

172 Resolution CM/Res(2010)26 on the establishment of an Advisory Panel of Experts on Candidates for Election as Judge to the European Court of Human Rights (adopted 10 November 2010). For an analysis of the politicization of the appointment process at the ECtHR before the establishment of the Advisory Panel see Erik Voeten, 'The Politics of International Judicial Appointments: Evidence from the European Court of Human Rights' (2007) 61 *International Organization* 669.

173 Art 22 Convention for the Protection of Human Rights and Fundamental Freedoms, adopted on 4 November 1950, entered into force on 3 September 1953, ETS 5; 213 UNTS 221 (ECHR).

174 Art 36(6)(a) ICC Statute.

175 Art 4(4) ITLOS Statute.

absolute majority in both organs.[176] The involvement of both organs is also required by the ICTY Statute. Here, the UN Security Council creates a list of candidates based on nominations of the UN Member States and observers, from which the UN General Assembly will then elect the permanent judges with an 'absolute majority of the votes of the States Members of the United Nations and of the non-member States maintaining permanent observer missions at United Nations Headquarters'.[177] Rather than by a majority vote, the judges of the CJEU are appointed 'by common accord' of all EU Member States.[178] The only appointment procedure not involving elections is the one of the Special Tribunal for Lebanon, where the judges are appointed by the UN Secretary General[179] following consultations with the Lebanese Government and the recommendation of a selection panel.[180] Lastly, the independence and impartiality of the members of the IUSCT is safeguarded by a procedure that reflects its character as a bilateral claims tribunal. Each government appoints one-third of the members; the remaining third is selected by mutual agreement by the state-appointed members.[181] While the selection process thus differs from court to court, most procedures display distinct democratic features and a strong merit-based approach. In all cases, the appointment procedure is designed in a way that aims to prohibit the dominance of one state or a group of states. However, whether these safeguards always achieve the intended results remains contested. Some have concluded that the election processes make it impossible for any state to exercise undue influence.[182] Others have recognized the efforts 'on paper … to reduce the effect of raw politics on the election process' while pointing out the 'reality of power politics', which ensures for example at the ICJ that the permanent members of the UN Security Council always have a national on the bench.[183]

---

[176] Art 10(1) ICJ Statute.

[177] Art 13 bis(1) ICTY Statute.

[178] Art 253 TFEU.

[179] Art 2(5)(a)–(b) STL Agreement; art 9(3) STL Statute.

[180] Art 2(5)(c)–(d) STL Agreement.

[181] Art III(1) Declaration of the Government of the Democratic and Popular Republic of Algeria Concerning the Settlement of Claims by the Government of the United States of America and the Government of the Islamic Republic of Iran (19 January 1981).

[182] Alter, above n154 at 46; for a careful assessment of the ICJ appointment process see Robert Kolb, *The International Court of Justice* (Hart, 2013) 140, who states that politicization cannot always be excluded but concludes that the system has 'overall … proved itself'.

[183] Robinson, above n170 at 278 et seq.

C. Incompatibility

The governing texts of most of the tribunals covered by this volume contain specific provisions on incompatibilities. Absolute incompatibility thereby refers to functions that are incompatible with the position of a judge per se, while relative incompatibility refers to the ability of a judge to hear a particular case.

The strictest rule is contained in the ICJ Statute which prohibits judges from exercising 'any political or administrative function, or engage in any other occupation of a professional nature'[184] or to 'act as agent, counsel or advocate in any case'.[185] The corresponding provision in the PCIJ Statute had been interpreted more leniently, as the Court's limited workload often allowed judges to pursue other activities on the side. An activity was not permissible 'if it interfered, even lightly or only potentially, with a judge's independence or impartiality', the mere semblance of incompatibility being sufficient to assume impermissibility.[186] The increased workload of the ICJ has restricted the possibility of judges to engage in additional activities, which today leaves occasional appointments as an arbitrator or academic work as the only two options generally accepted by the ICJ.[187] In a similar manner, the Statute of the CJEU provides that '[t]he Judges may not hold any political or administrative office', and that they 'may not engage in any occupation, whether gainful or not, unless exemption is exceptionally granted by the Council, acting by a simple majority'.[188]

The ECHR makes the nexus between the absolute incompatibility of activities and the requirements of independence and impartiality more explicitly. It generally provides in Article 21(3) that '[d]uring their term of office the judges shall not engage in any activity which is incompatible with their independence, impartiality or with the demands of a full-time office ... '. [189] Judges need to be transparent about their activities outside

---

[184] Art 16(1) ICJ Statute.

[185] Art 17(1) ICJ Statute. For more detail see Kolb, above n182 at 133–4; Guillaume, above n157 at 475.

[186] Kolb, above n182 at 133.

[187] Ibid. at 134.

[188] Art 4 Protocol (No 3) on the Statute of the Court of Justice of the European Union [2012] OJ C 326/210 (CJEU Statute). Pursuant to art 8, the same rules apply to the Advocates General.

[189] See also Rule 4 of the Rules of Procedure of the Court, which provides that judges shall not 'engage in any political or administrative activity or any professional activity which is incompatible with their independence or impartiality or with the demands of a full-time office'.

the court and any disagreements are to be decided by the plenary. Similarly, the ITLOS Statute provides that no member of the tribunal may exercise 'any political or administrative function', 'associate actively with or be financially interested' in enterprises who explore, exploit or otherwise commercially use the sea or the seabed' or 'act as agent, counsel or advocate in any case'.[190]

The ICC Statute not only prohibits the judges of the ICC from any 'activity which is likely to interfere with their judicial functions or to affect confidence in their independence', it also prohibits any other 'occupation of a professional nature'.[191] Conversely, persons serving on the WTO AB may engage in other professional activities, provided that they are 'unaffiliated with any government' and do 'not participate in the consideration of any disputes that would create a direct or indirect conflict of interest'.[192]

Most instruments also contain provisions on relative incompatibility in order to avoid conflicts of interest in specific cases. Incompatibilities are usually assumed if the judge (1) has personal interests in the case (for example family or professional ties with the parties), (2) has previously been involved in the case (for example as an agent, advocate, adviser or judge on another tribunal), (3) pursues political, administrative or professional activities incompatible with his independence and impartiality, or (4) publicly expressed his opinion on the case.[193]

D. Nationality

Several instruments contain provisions governing the situation where a judge and a party share the same nationality. The ICJ Statute and the ITLOS Statute, for example, explicitly provide that the judges/members of the nationality of any party retain their right to hear the case.[194] In these cases, the other party may choose an ad hoc judge to sit on the respective case. Ad hoc judges may also be appointed in cases where

---

190 Art 7 ITLOS Statute.

191 Art 40 ICC Statute.

192 Art 17 Understanding on Rules and Procedures Governing the Settlement of Disputes, Annex 2 of the Agreement establishing the World Trade Organization (signed 15 April 1994, entered into force 1 January 1995) (WTO DSU).

193 See eg rule 28 ECtHR Rules of Court (1 July 2014); art 41(2)(a) ICC Statute; art 17(2) ICJ Statute; art 8 ITLOS Statute; rule 25 Rules of Procedure and Evidence of the Special Tribunal for Lebanon (adopted 20 March 2009, in the version of 3 April 2014); see also arts 9–12 IUSCT Rules of Procedure (3 May 1983).

194 Art 31 ICJ Statute; art 17(1) ITLOS Statute.

neither of the parties has a judge of its own nationality on the bench. The possibility to appoint ad hoc judges therefore aims to bring relevant expertise to the bench and to increase the court's legitimacy, while also ensuring equality between the parties.[195] However, both the Rules of the Procedure of the ECtHR and of the ITLOS stipulate that the presidency may not be exercised by a national of any party in a given case.[196] Even though studies have found little evidence for the assumption that judges are generally more favourable towards the positions of their home country,[197] these rules contribute to the external perception of an impartial and balanced body, in line with the maxim that 'justice must not only be done, but be seen to be done'.[198] Nationality continues to play an important role with regard to the composition of the bench, as evidenced by the efforts to ensure a geographic balance, but also by the insistence of the permanent members of the UN Security Council to each have a national on the ICJ.[199]

E. Privileges and Immunities

An essential safeguard for the independence of a judge is the granting of privileges and immunities, which guarantees the judge the necessary freedom to fulfil his functions. In particular, it avoids pressure through politically motivated prosecutions. Most governing texts of the courts and tribunals in this volume contain provisions in this respect.[200] While the majority of these provisions only grant immunity during the exercise of the judicial function, the CJEU Statute and the ICC Statute also grant

---

195 Kolb, above n182 at 118 et seq; Leigh Swigart, 'The "National Judge": Some Reflections on Diversity in International Courts and Tribunals' (2010) 42 *McGeorge Law Review* 223, 227 et seq.

196 Rule 24(5)(c) ECtHR Rules of Court; art 16 ITLOS Rules of the Tribunal (17 March 2009).

197 This applies in the first line to permanent judges. Ad hoc judges have evidenced a tendency to vote in favour of the country that appointed them. See Guillaume, above n157 at 486 fn 8 for references to studies on the link between nationality and independence; see also Hernández, above n157 at 185.

198 Kolb, above n182 at 133.

199 See subsection V(B) above.

200 See art 3 CJEU Statute, which pursuant to art 8 also applies to Advocates General; art 51 ECHR; art 48 ICC Statute; art 19 ICJ Statute; art 30 ICTY Statute; art 10 ITLOS Statute; art 11 STL Agreement.

immunity after a judge has left the court with respect to legal proceedings on any acts performed in the judicial capacity.[201]

F. Irremovibility

Another essential tool to ensure the independence of the judges is their irremovibility from the bench during the period of their mandate. As, for example, the ICJ Statute provides: 'No member of the Court can be dismissed unless, in the unanimous opinion of the other members, he has ceased to fulfil the required conditions.'[202] Similar provisions can be found for example in the statutes of the CJEU, the ECtHR, the ICC and the ITLOS.[203] They are intended to serve as safeguards against political interference with the work of the court through the threat of dismissal of its members.

G. Remuneration

A similar motivation underlies a provision that can be found in statutes of several courts covered in this volume. In order to limit the scope of potential political pressure that may be exercised on the judges, these provisions stipulate that the salaries, allowances and compensation of the judges may not be decreased during their term of office.[204] Judges can therefore not be threatened with financial sanctions in order to ensure a certain voting behaviour.

H. Secrecy of Deliberations and Voting

It has been argued that 'in all judicial activity, the secrecy of deliberations serves as an essential guarantee of the judge's independence'.[205] However, this principle is interpreted differently across the various legal cultures of the world. Whereas judicial deliberations and votes are

---

201 Art 3 CJEU Statute, which pursuant to art 8 also applies to Advocates General; art 48(2) ICC Statute.

202 Art 18 ICJ Statute.

203 Art 6 CJEU Statute, which pursuant to art 8 also applies to Advocates General (unanimity of Judges and Advocates General required); art 23(4) ECHR (two-thirds majority of the other judges required); art 46 ICC Statute (two-thirds majority of the states parties following a recommendation adopted by two-thirds of the other judges); art 9 ITLOS Statute (unanimity of the other members of the Tribunal required).

204 See eg art 49 ICC Statute; art 32(5) ICJ Statute; art 18(5) ITLOS Statute.

205 Guillaume, above n157 at 484.

usually confidential in the continental European tradition, common law countries are more familiar with the disclosure of the votes and the publication of separate (dissenting and concurring) opinions. The practice at the level of the international judiciary is uneven. Nevertheless, there are certain commonalities.

All governing texts of the courts and tribunals covered in this volume protect the confidentiality of the judges' deliberations, which 'shall take place in private and remain secret'.[206] Most courts and tribunals also protect the secrecy of voting. The ICJ and ITLOS form an exception in this respect. Article 125(1)(l) of the ITLOS Rules states that the judgment shall contain 'the number and names of the judges constituting the majority and those constituting the minority, on each operative provision'. The ICJ Statute was originally silent on this issue. Until 1978, the ICJ rejected the publication of the voting behaviour, considering such a practice to be 'against the Statute itself'.[207] At the same time, however, judges were free to deliver separate opinions (dissenting or concurring), thus rendering the attempt to ensure secrecy rather futile. In 1978, the ICJ's Rules of Procedure were amended and now list 'the number and names of the judges constituting the majority' among the elements that need to be contained in a judgment.[208] The same issue can be observed with regard to most other international courts and tribunals. While for example the ECtHR, the three criminal courts and the IUSCT do not provide the names of the judges voting in favour or against a decision, they all permit the publication of separate opinions, thus allowing for inferences to be drawn on the voting behaviour.[209] The CJEU is the only court that maintains the principle of 'apparent unanimity' in line with the domestic legal traditions of its founding Member States:[210] deliberations and votes are kept secret, and no separate opinions are published. Aside

---

206 Art 54(3)ICJ Statute; see also art 35 CJEU Statute; rule 22 ECtHR Rules of Court; art 74(4) ICC Statute; rule 29, 87 ICTY Rules of Procedure and Evidence; note to art 31 IUSCT Rules of Procedure; art 42(1) ITLOS Rules of the Tribunal; rule 43, 148 STL Rules of Procedure and Evidence; arts 14, 17 WTO DSU.

207 Guillaume, above n157 at 485.

208 Art 95 ICJ Rules of Court; see also art 107 ICJ Rules of Court for Advisory Opinions.

209 Rule 74(1)(k) and 74(2) ECtHR Rules of Court; art 74(5) ICC Statute; art 23(2) ICTY Statute; art 32 IUSCT Rules of Procedure; art 23 STL Statute.

210 Rosa Raffaelli, 'Dissenting Opinions in the Supreme Courts of the Member States', Study for the European Parliament, Directorate General for Internal Policies, Policy Department C: Citizens' Rights and Constitutional Affairs, PE 462.470, 2012, 33.

from domestic legal traditions, fear of individual judges either always defending their home state's position or, conversely, declining to do so and consequently being refused an additional term by their home Member State, as well as the concern that dissenting opinions may undermine the authority of the Court, are often cited as the main reasons why allowing separate opinions was not considered apposite.[211] Finally, the WTO Dispute Settlement System aims for a compromise approach. Panel or AB members may publish separate opinions, but they must be anonymous.[212] However, critics have argued that this attempt to safeguard the independence of the panel or AB members is in practice not very effective, given that the name of the dissenter will often be easily identified by those familiar with the case.[213]

The picture is therefore mixed, ranging from complete confidentiality of the judges' deliberations and votes to disclosure of voting behaviour and publication of separate opinions. This can have implications for the degree of outside pressure that a judge may receive or perceive.

I. Term of Office

Schermers and Blokker identify the length of the term of office as a safeguard for judicial independence in the sense that a longer term equals more independence.[214] In contrast to judges on national courts, international judges are as a rule not appointed for life or until retirement but for limited periods of time, and may or may not be reappointed, depending on the institutional framework. This practice was established with the first international courts and tribunals in the beginning of the

---

211 See Geert De Baere, 'Aboli bibelot d'inanite´ sonore?' (2008) 33 *EL Rev* 935; further: Anthony Arnull, *The European Union and its Court of Justice* (2nd edn OUP, 2006) 11.

212 Arts 14 and 17 WTO DSU. Separate opinions in the WTO Dispute Settlement System are very rare. See for example Meredith Kolsky Lewis, 'The Lack of Dissent in WTO Dispute Settlement' (2006) 9 *Journal of International Economic Law* 895. See also <www.wto.org/english/res_e/booksp_e/analytic_index_e/dsu_06_e.htm#article14> for a list of individual opinions in panel reports and <www.wto.org/english/res_e/booksp_e/analytic_index_e/dsu_07_e.htm> for a list of concurring and separate opinions in the WTO AB reports (until 30 September 2011). For a recent noteworthy example, see the dissenting opinion in *China – Measures Related to the Exportation of Rare Earths, Tungsten and Molybdenum – Reports of the Panel*, WT/DS432/R.

213 Raffaelli, above n210 at 33.

214 Schermers and Blokker, above n5 at 486 et seq, para 683.

twentieth century[215] and maintained in the Statute of the PCIJ. The Advisory Committee of Jurists, which drafted the PCIJ's Statute, considered a proposal by Sweden to appoint the judges of the PCIJ for life but opted for a term of nine years with the possibility of re-election instead. It reasoned that the term should be long enough to create an 'esprit de corps', that re-election should be possible in order to reward 'faithful and efficient service' but that judges should not be appointed for life in order to preserve the possibility to replace those judges who 'failed to justify their election'.[216] With the exception of the IUSCT,[217] the courts and tribunals covered in this volume all follow this model. The length of the terms of office range from nine years (ICJ, ITLOS, ECtHR and ICC) to six (CJEU), four (WTO AB, ICTY) and three years (Special Tribunal for Lebanon).[218] Re-election is permitted by all courts except for the ECtHR and the ICC. The WTO AB limits the number of re-elections to one.

This practice appears to have been widely accepted. It should however not be overlooked that the fixed-term mandates of judges and the possibility of re-election may negatively impact on the independence and impartiality of judges. First, the opportunity of re-election can create incentives for judges to avoid decisions that might run contrary to the positions of influential Member States.[219] The mere existence of such incentive can be enough to cast doubt on their independence and impartiality, even if it does not in fact influence the motivation of the judge. Second, the re-election process provides a possibility for states to sanction unwelcome actions and thus to exercise political pressure.[220]

It would therefore arguably be more conducive to the independence and impartiality of the judges if international courts and tribunals opted

---

[215] This includes established and proposed courts, namely the Central American Court of Justice (five years, re-election possible), International Prize Court (six years), Court of Arbitral Justice (12 years, re-election possible), see John Dugard in Andreas Zimmermann, Karin Oellers-Frahm, Christian Tomuschat and Christian J Tams (eds), *The Statute of the International Court of Justice: A Commentary* (2nd ed, OUP, 2012) art 13 no 2.

[216] Ibid.

[217] IUSCT members are appointed for 'the course of the arbitral proceedings', but provision is made for their challenge and/or replacement pursuant to arts 9–13 IUSCT Rules of Procedure.

[218] Art 253 TFEU (six years); art 23 ECtHR (nine years); art 36(9)(a) ICC Statute (nine years); art 13 ICJ Statute (nine years); art 13bis (3) ICTY Statute (four years); art 5(1) ITLOS Statute (nine years); art 9(3) STL Statute (three years); art 17(2) WTO DSU (four years).

[219] Meron, above n158 at 362.

[220] Kolb, above n182 at 112.

for non-renewable long-term mandates instead of the current practice.[221] The solution adopted in the ECtHR could be considered a best practice in that regard.

J. Interim Conclusions

The courts and tribunals covered in this volume have been equipped with a range of safeguards against most forms of political interference. Nevertheless, it is doubtful whether these formal institutional rules can ever be sufficient. In the end, the Member States retain control over the delegated powers of the international court or tribunal and they can sanction the judicial body by renegotiating the foundational instrument on which the court or tribunal is based – even if that may only be a 'nuclear option'.[222] It is therefore important always to consider the broader politico-legal context in which international courts and tribunals operate. Besides all formal safeguards and the personal integrity of the judges, a high degree of intra- and interstate political competition between the courts' States, as well as a high degree of discrepancy in their policies remains the most important safeguard of a court's independence.[223] It is beyond the scope of this chapter to assess the various political forces that influence the different courts and tribunals covered in this volume. Nevertheless, the broader politico-legal framework must not be overlooked when dealing with the question of international judicial independence.

VI. AN OVERVIEW OF THE CONTRIBUTION OF INTERNATIONAL AND SUPRANATIONAL COURTS TO THE RULE OF LAW

This chapter adopted as a working assumption that, at its most basic, the rule of law can be described as a principle that all individuals and entities, including states and international organizations, are to be subject to and accountable to the law. That implies the subjection of individuals and all levels of public power in the national and international realm to

---

[221] See also Meron, above n158 at 362.

[222] Alter, above n154 at 44; see for example the case of the Southern African Development Community (SADC) Tribunal which was sanctioned, first by a blockade of the elections of judges, then by a restriction of its jurisdiction: Romano, above n42 at 123.

[223] See Benvenisti and Downs, above n56 at 1059.

legal constraints with a view to guaranteeing the equal protection of all individuals against the arbitrary or unlawful use of power.[224]

As explored above, international courts no longer solely fulfil the role of dispute settlers, but have taken on new functions.[225] Alter lists criminal enforcement and infringement proceedings, dispute resolution as well as administrative and constitutional review as the four ideal types of judicial functions. Von Bogdandy and Venzke additionally consider the international judiciary to have a law-making function,[226] while Shelton adds the provision of 'legal advice'.[227] Arguably, therefore, international and supranational courts can contribute to the rule of law through dispute settlement (VI(A)) and compliance assessment (VI(B)), the tackling of impunity (VI(C)), as well as through the clarification and development of international law (VI(D)). These (partially overlapping) functions may be considered direct contributions. Indirectly, international courts may, by fulfilling these functions, contribute to the socialization of states to the concept of the rule of law at the international level and to its growing importance in international relations.[228]

A. Dispute Settlement

Dispute settlement is the traditional domain of international courts and also the role that most of the international courts and tribunals covered in this volume have been allocated by their Member States. By peacefully settling disputes on the basis of law, the adjudicator ideally takes away sources of tension between the parties and ensures that it is not political or economic power that decides over the outcome of a dispute, but the law ('right over might'), thereby avoiding arbitrariness and contributing to the equal protection of individuals.

Dispute settlement is the core competence of the ICJ, the ITLOS, the WTO Dispute Settlement System and the IUSCT. The ICJ is explicitly mandated with the settlement of disputes,[229] and has at the time of

---

[224] See subsection IV(A) above.

[225] On the various roles and objectives of international courts see also Follesdal, above n4.

[226] Von Bogdandy and Venzke, above n14 at 9 et seq.

[227] Shelton, above n18 at 539.

[228] Buergenthal, above n21 at 271 et seq.

[229] Art 38(1) ICJ Statute. See also the affirmation in ICJ, *LaGrand (Germany v United States of America)*, Provisional Measures, Order of 3 March 1999, ICJ Reports 1999, p 9, para 25.

writing rendered 117 judgments,[230] the majority of which since the 1990s. Similarly, the ITLOS has been tasked to 'deal with disputes arising out of the Convention'.[231] So far, 22 contentious cases have been submitted to the Tribunal. However, both courts have received far fewer cases than the WTO Dispute Settlement System, which – with 188 panel reports and 110 appellate reports – is the most prolific state-to-state dispute settlement body.[232] The 'prompt settlement' of disputes is the principal objective of the WTO Dispute Settlement System and considered 'essential to the functioning of the WTO'.[233] Conversely, the IUSCT does not only have jurisdiction over state-to-state disputes (contractual claims of the United States and Iran against each other) but also over claims of nationals of either state against the other. It has received a total of 3,953 claims of which only 16 remain on the tribunal's docket today.

The increasing recourse to international dispute settlement might suggest that these international courts and tribunals enjoy legitimacy and inspire the necessary confidence that motivates parties to turn towards them for fair and just dispute settlement.[234] The settlement of disputes by legal means can in itself be considered an important contribution to the rule of law. However, critics point to the fact that only a small percentage of international disputes make it onto the docket of an international court or tribunal,[235] particularly if the case touches upon politically sensitive issues.[236] It has, for example, been argued that the ICJ has so far mostly dealt with rather uncontroversial cases on boundary delimitations and treaty interpretation.[237] The majority of international disputes never make it to a judge's desk. Furthermore, it has been pointed out that dispute settlement before an international court or tribunal requires money and expertise, and may thus not be accessible to poorer countries.[238] In

---

230 See Couvreur, above n12.

231 See Gautier, above n15.

232 See Van den Bossche, above n11.

233 Ibid.

234 See also section V above.

235 José E Alvarez, 'The New Dispute Settlers: (Half) Truths and Consequences' (2003) 38 *Texas International Law Journal* 405, 411 et seq.

236 Tumonis, above n160 at 40.

237 Ibid. See eg the *Nicaragua* case, in which the United States withdrew its acceptance of the ICJ's jurisdiction out of dissatisfaction with the Court: ICJ, *Military and Paramilitary Activities in and against Nicaragua (Nicaragua v United States of America)*, Jurisdiction and Admissibility, Judgment, ICJ Reports 1984, p 392.

238 Ibid 47.

particular, the judicialization of the WTO as opposed to the GATT regime and the disappearance of developing countries from the Dispute Settlement System's docket has been cited as illustrating the increasing hurdles these countries face.[239] However, this is countered by Van den Bossche, who not only sees no disparity in terms of numbers between developed and developing countries in the WTO Dispute Settlement System[240] but also refers to the Advisory Centre on WTO Law (ACWL), which provides low cost or pro bono legal services to developing country WTO Members.[241]

Through dispute settlement – their oldest and most uncontroversial[242] function – international courts and tribunals make a significant contribution to the rule of law. Nevertheless, other functions, such as the clarification of international law and compliance assessment, may in the meantime have come to rival it in terms of importance.

B. Compliance Assessment

As mentioned above, compliance assessment is a primary tool to subject public power to the constraints of international law and to protect the rights of individuals. External compliance assessment entails the control exercised by international courts and tribunals over the acts of domestic authorities. Internal compliance assessment involves the judicial control over the acts of the international organization of which they are organs. In that sense this chapter uses the term 'compliance assessment' flexibly, encompassing Alter's categories of 'enforcement', 'administrative review' and 'constitutional review',[243] in line with von Bogdandy's and Venzke's concept of 'controlling and legitimating public authority'.[244] Compliance assessment can thus be exercised by every international court and tribunal mandated to rule on the compliance of a public authority with international law. It can be exercised to different degrees: external compliance assessment is generally limited to declaring an action by public authorities non-compliant with international law or to awarding remedies, while internal compliance assessment may imply the authority to invalidate the non-compliant act.

---

239 Ibid 47 et seq.

240 See Van den Bossche, above n11.

241 Ibid.

242 The 'functional myopia' of scholarship to focus entirely or predominantly on dispute settlement is addressed in von Bogdandy and Venzke, above n14 at 3.

243 Alter, above n18.

244 Von Bogdandy and Venzke, above n14 at 11 et seq.

Illustrative of external compliance assessment are the powers exercised by the ECtHR, the WTO Dispute Settlement System and the CJEU, when they review the compliance of domestic authorities with the ECHR, WTO Law or EU law. The ECtHR has been created to 'ensure the observance of the engagements undertaken by the High Contracting Parties in the Convention and the Protocols thereto'.[245] Where it receives applications from states parties[246] or individuals[247] alleging a breach of the applicable law, the Court may decide on whether or not a violation exists, and authorize remedies. Similarly, the WTO Dispute Settlement System receives applications from other WTO Members alleging violations of the WTO Agreements. The CJEU has jurisdiction with respect to actions brought against a Member State for its failure to fulfil its obligations under the Treaties pursuant to Articles 258–60 TFEU ('infringement proceedings'), as well as with respect to preliminary ruling procedures in relation to the interpretation of Union law under Article 267 TFEU, which indirectly concern the compatibility of national law with Union law. None of these bodies has the competence to invalidate a non-compliant domestic law.[248]

Illustrative of internal compliance assessment is the judicial review by the CJEU of acts or failures to act of the Union institutions.[249] In that

---

[245] Art 19 ECHR.

[246] Art 33 ECHR.

[247] Art 34 ECHR.

[248] Eg as regards the CJEU, see with respect to infringement proceedings ECJ, Opinion of Advocate General Reischl in *France v UK*, 141/78, EU:C:1979:202, p 2946; and with respect to references for a preliminary ruling ECJ, judgment in *Essent Belgium*, C-204/12 to C-208/12, EU:C:2014:2192, para 51, recalling settled case law holding that:

> although the Court does not, in a reference for a preliminary ruling, have jurisdiction to give a ruling on the compatibility of a national measure with EU law, it does have jurisdiction to supply the national court with a ruling on the interpretation of EU law so as to enable that court to determine whether such compatibility exists in order to decide the case before it.

See also ECJ, judgment in *Ministero delle Finanze v IN.CO.GE.'90 and Others*, C-10/97 to C-22/97, EU:C:1998:498, para 21, holding that it could not be inferred from ECJ, judgment in *Amministrazione delle finanze dello Stato v Simmenthal*, 106/77, EU:C:1978:49, 'that the incompatibility with Community law of a subsequently adopted rule of national law has the effect of rendering that rule of national law non-existent. Faced with such a situation, the national court is, however, obliged to disapply that rule …'.

[249] The CJEU can exercise that review through the action for annulment under art 263 TFEU; the action for failure to act under art 265 TFEU; the

regard, the Court held in *Les Verts* that the Community, now the Union, is 'based on the rule of law, inasmuch as neither its Member States nor its institutions can avoid a review of the question whether the measures adopted by them are in conformity with the basic constitutional charter, the Treaty'.[250] Nevertheless, international courts or tribunals typically lack jurisdiction to adjudicate issues concerning the conduct of the organizations of which they are a part.[251] The WTO AB is a clear example of that phenomenon.[252] Furthermore, it remains contested whether the ICJ has any jurisdiction to review the legality of UN Security Council resolutions.[253] The issue was raised in the context of the *Lockerbie* case, which was withdrawn before the ICJ could render its final decision on the matter.[254]

While the contributions of the international judiciary to the rule of law are remarkable in this respect, it is also apparent that the rule of law is still weaker at the international level than at the regional and national level. There is a considerably lower degree of judicial control exercised over the activities of international actors, resulting in a comparatively weaker system of checks and balances.

---

objection of illegality under art 277 TFEU; preliminary rulings on the validity of Union acts under art 267 TFEU; the action for damages against the Union under arts 268 and 340(2) TFEU; and the application for an opinion on the compatibility of an international agreement to be concluded by the Union with the provisions of the Treaties under art 218(11) TFEU.

[250] ECJ, judgment in *Parti écologiste 'Les Verts' v European Parliament*, 294/83, EU:C:1986:166, para 23. See further Lenaerts, above n113.

[251] Kingsbury, above n130 at 211.

[252] Ibid.

[253] Higgins, above n23.

[254] See nevertheless the dissenting opinion of President Schwebel in ICJ, *Questions of Interpretation and Application of the 1971 Montreal Convention arising from the Aerial Incident at Lockerbie (Libyan Arab Jamahiriya v United States of America)*, Preliminary Objections, Judgment, ICJ Reports 1998, p 115, concluding from the *travaux préparatoires* (especially the episode of the failed Belgian proposal to introduce a limited possibility of review by the ICJ) that the ICJ was not and was not meant to be invested with a power of judicial review of decisions of the Security Council (dissenting opinion of President Schwebel, 171). Further: Bernd Martenczuk, 'The Security Council, the International Court and Judicial Review: What Lessons from Lockerbie?' (1999) 10 *European Journal of International Law* 517.

C. Tackling Impunity

As argued above, the rule of law requires that legal constraints bind not only all levels of public power but also individuals. Consequently, individuals who violate international norms that prohibit gross human rights violations, need to be held accountable for their actions. In this respect, the international criminal tribunals have contributed to the rule of law by 'reassert[ing] the vital truth that every person, at every level of seniority and influence, is subject to [the] law'.[255] Since its establishment, the ICTY has indicted 161 people for serious violations of international humanitarian law committed in the territory of the former Yugoslavia, of which 141 were either sentenced, acquitted, referred or had their proceedings terminated in another way.[256] The ICC currently conducts proceedings on 21 cases resulting from nine situations (Central African Republic I and II, Côte d'Ivoire, Darfur (Sudan), Democratic Republic of the Congo, Kenya, Libya, Mali and Uganda).[257]

These numbers, although illustrative of the courts' high workload, are vanishingly small when compared to the number of international crimes committed around the globe. The currently existing international criminal judicial bodies not only lack the jurisdiction but also the resources to address them. They are ill equipped to make more than a marginal contribution to ending impunity. Instead, they need to strengthen domestic accountability mechanisms[258] and be selective about their cases. As Brammertz explains, the ICTY adopted a combined 'top down' and 'bottom up' approach – targeting lower-level perpetrators in the start-up phase of the tribunal and moving onto more high-level perpetrators once the tribunal's expertise and its political support had increased.[259] In addition, a balance needed to be found between comprehensive indictments, which would cover all crimes a perpetrator was believed to be responsible for, and practical considerations, particularly concerning the duration of the trial.[260]

The contribution of international criminal courts and tribunals to tackling impunity – though important in those cases that actually make it

---

[255] See Serge Brammertz in the present volume.

[256] ICTY, 'Key Figures of the Cases', available at <http://www.icty.org/sections/TheCases/KeyFiguresoftheCases>.

[257] ICC, 'Report of the International Criminal Court on its activities in 2013/14' (18 September 2014) UN Doc A/69/321.

[258] See Chan and Wouters in the present volume.

[259] See Brammertz, above n255.

[260] Ibid.

on to the docket – must for the time being remain limited. At the same time, the focus on international criminal law as it is now also points to some of the remaining gaps in the rule of law at the international level. First, to the present day, only individuals are subject to the constraints of criminal law at the international level. Other international actors, such as multinational corporations, do not fall under the jurisdiction *ratione personae* of any international criminal court. Second, with the exception of EU law and international criminal law, international law as a rule does not contain binding obligations for other than state actors. This has been considered unsatisfactory in particular with regard to human rights law, in light of widespread human rights abuses by natural and legal persons. Domestic instruments have often proved insufficient to hold accountable perpetrators who operate globally, and flexibly move across borders.[261]

Ending impunity consequently remains an elusive goal, despite the considerable merits of the international criminal judiciary. The subjection of individuals and legal persons to legal constraints is still an area where the international rule of law evidences considerable weaknesses.

D. Clarification and Development of International Law

The concept of the rule of law implies the existence of a set of legal constraints that guides and binds the behaviour of all individuals and all levels of public power. The legal rules need to be sufficiently clear in order to provide a reliable and predictable framework. In this respect, international courts and tribunals make an important contribution to the rule of law through their interpretation and clarification of international law. This contribution goes beyond the cases that are submitted to the courts and affects international law as a whole.

The ICJ, as the only universal international court with general jurisdiction, plays a central role in this respect. Its interpretations enjoy the highest respect and are frequently referred to in the case law of other courts and tribunals.[262] As Couvreur has stated, 'its jurisprudence indisputably contributes to the establishment of a body of "precedents"

---

[261] Jan Wouters and Anna-Luise Chané, 'Multinational Corporations in International Law' in Math Noortmann, August Reinisch and Cedric Ryngaert (eds), *Non-State Actors in International Law* (Hart, 2015).

[262] Charney, above n23 at 699, 705. For a recent example, see ECJ, judgment in *Oberto and O'Leary*, C-464/13 and C-465/13, EU:C:2015:163, para 61, holding that 'as is clear from the case-law of the International Court of Justice, the subsequent practice followed in the application of a treaty may override the clear terms of that treaty if that practice reflects the parties' agreement (ICJ, *Case*

regarding questions of general international law, the authority and significance of which extend far beyond the parties to a particular dispute'.[263] It therefore plays a unifying role in international law, contributing to the coherence of this body of law and of the case law of other international judicial bodies. Areas in which the ICJ has particularly contributed to the clarification of international law include the law of state responsibility and the law of immunity.[264]

Article 3(2) DSU explicitly provides for the WTO Dispute Settlement System to be 'a central element in providing security and predictability to the multilateral trading system'. As the panel in *United States – Sections 301–310 of the Trade Act of 1974* held: 'The security and predictability in question are of "the multilateral trading system". The multilateral trading system is, per force, composed not only of States but also, indeed mostly, of individual economic operators. The lack of security and predictability affects mostly these individual operators.'[265] To that end, the Dispute Settlement System is mandated to 'clarify the existing provisions of those agreements in accordance with customary rules of interpretation of public international law'.[266] Unlike other international courts and tribunals, the WTO Dispute Settlement System follows a primarily textual interpretation approach, giving central importance to the wording of the agreements. As Article 3(2) and 19(2) DSU provide, the WTO panels and AB may not 'add to or diminish the rights and obligations provided in the covered agreements'. In that regard, Van den Bossche argues that the high respect enjoyed by the WTO AB today is 'to a large extent due to the Appellate Body's choice for, and consistent application of, a "text first" approach to interpretation'.[267]

In the field of international criminal law, the ICTY has made a significant contribution through its interpretation and clarification of the nascent legal regime, in particular concerning the modes of liability and

concerning the Temple of Preah Vihear (Cambodia v *Thailand)*, judgment of 15 June 1962, ICJ Reports 1962, p 6)'.

263 See Couvreur, above n12. For a more critical assessment see Koskenniemi and Leino, above n23 at 576.

264 See Couvreur, above n12.

265 WTO DSB Panel Report, *United States – Sections 301–310 of the Trade Act of 1974*, WT/DS152/R, adopted 22 December 1999, para 7.76

266 Art 3(2) WTO DSU.

267 See Van den Bossche, above n11. See further Isabelle Van Damme, *Treaty Interpretation by the WTO Appellate Body* (OUP, 2009); and Isabelle Van Damme, 'The Function of Interpretation in the WTO' (2010) 21 *European Journal of International Law* 605–48.

elements of crime under customary international law.[268] Its decisions have informed later case law by other international criminal tribunals and have strengthened legal certainty in international criminal law.

As a human rights court, the ECtHR sees its role not only in the provision of individual justice but also in the clarification of general human rights standards for the Member States of the Council of Europe. It has stated that 'its judgments serve not only to decide those cases brought before it but, more generally, to elucidate, safeguard and develop the rules instituted by the Convention, thereby contributing to the observance by the States of the engagements undertaken by them as Contracting Parties'.[269] The contribution of the ECtHR thus helps to clarify and strengthen the human rights system in Europe and ideally to decrease the need for judicial remedies.

While international courts and tribunals contribute to the growing body of precedents on international law with every decision rendered, some courts have additionally been provided with specific – non-contentious – procedures focused solely on providing legal interpretation. Two examples are illustrative in that regard.[270]

First, Article 96(a) of the UN Charter provides that the UN General Assembly and the UN Security Council may request the ICJ 'to give an advisory opinion on any legal question'. Article 96(b) UN Charter additionally grants that possibility to 'other organs of the United Nations and specialized agencies' if authorized by the UN General Assembly, provided they request clarification on legal questions 'arising within the scope of their activities'. The ICJ thus has the opportunity and competence to provide legal guidance to the UN, and consequently to strengthen the rule of law in the activities of the organization. Although they are not legally binding, advisory opinions enjoy a high degree of authority due to the Court's standing. However, they have also caused some controversy in the past, when an issue was perceived to be contentious and the advisory proceedings were seen as a 'back door' in order to circumvent the lack of jurisdiction. So far, the ICJ has rendered 27 advisory opinions on a diversity of issues ranging from the accession of Member States to the UN and the legality of the threat or use of nuclear weapons to the construction of a wall in the Occupied Palestinian

---

[268] See Brammertz, above n255.

[269] ECtHR, *Ireland v United Kingdom* (1978) Series A no 25, para 154; ECtHR, *Guzzardi v Italy* (1980) Series A no 39, para 86; ECtHR, *Karner v Austria* ECHR 2003-IX, para 26; ECtHR, *Konstantin Markin v Russia* ECHR 2012-III, para 89.

[270] See also Cançado Trindade, above n23.

Territory and the unilateral declaration of independence by Kosovo. Advisory proceedings are also foreseen in the ITLOS, either by the Seabed Disputes Chamber[271] or by the Tribunal, if this is provided for in an international agreement.[272] The Seabed Disputes Chamber delivered an advisory opinion on 1 February 2011,[273] and the Tribunal received its first request for an advisory opinion on 28 March 2013 from the Sub-Regional Fisheries Commission.[274]

Second, under Article 218(11) TFEU, the European Parliament, the Council of the EU, the European Commission or an EU Member State may obtain the opinion of the ECJ as to whether an envisaged international agreement is compatible with the provisions of the TEU and the TFEU. That provision has the aim of 'forestalling complications which would result from legal disputes concerning the compatibility with the Treaties of international agreements binding upon the EU'.[275] Where the opinion of the Court is adverse, the international agreement envisaged may not enter into force unless it is amended or the Treaties are revised. Furthermore, pursuant to Article 267 TFEU, the ECJ has jurisdiction to give preliminary rulings concerning the interpretation of the Treaties and of acts of the various Union institutions, bodies, offices, or agencies. That mechanism aims to avoid divergences in the interpretation of EU law by national courts. Article 267 TFEU confers on national courts the power and, in certain circumstances, an obligation, to make a reference to the ECJ once the national court considers that a case pending before it raises issues involving an interpretation or assessment of the validity of provisions of EU law.[276] The ECJ has emphasized that the system, established by Article 267 TFEU with a view to ensuring that EU law is interpreted uniformly throughout the Member States, establishes direct cooperation between the ECJ and the national courts by means of a procedure that is completely independent of any initiative by the parties. In that regard, the system of references for a preliminary ruling is based

---

271 Art 191 UNCLOS.

272 Art 21 UNCLOS; art 138 ITLOS Rules of the Tribunal.

273 ITLOS Seabed Disputes Chamber, *Responsibilities and obligations of States sponsoring persons and entities with respect to activities in the Area (no 17) (Request for Advisory Opinion submitted to the Seabed Disputes Chamber)* (Advisory Opinion of 1 February 2011, ITLOS Reports 2011).

274 ITLOS, *Request for an advisory opinion submitted by the Sub-Regional Fisheries Commission (SRFC) (no 21)*. The progress of the proceedings can be followed on <www.itlos.org/en/affaires/role-des-affaires/affaire-no-21/>.

275 See ECJ, Opinion 2/13, *Accession of the EU to the ECHR*, EU:C:2014:2454, para 145.

276 See ECJ, judgment in *Kelly*, C-104/10, EU:C:2011:506, paras 60–61.

on a dialogue between one court and another, the initiation of which depends entirely on the national court's assessment as to whether a reference is appropriate and necessary.[277] Nevertheless, in its much-anticipated judgment in *Gauweiler* on the legality of certain decisions of the Governing Council of the European Central Bank (ECB) on a number of technical features regarding the Eurosystem's outright monetary transactions in secondary sovereign bond markets (which also constitutes the first-ever reference by the *Bundesverfassungsgericht* (German Constitutional Court)), the ECJ recalled that 'it does not have jurisdiction to give a ruling where the court making the reference is not bound by the Court's interpretation. Indeed, the Court does not have jurisdiction to provide, in preliminary ruling proceedings, answers which are purely advisory.'[278]

The clarification of international law goes hand in hand with its development. Whereas some scholars have identified law-making as one of the functions of international courts and tribunals,[279] others do not go that far.[280] But even without crossing the threshold to actual law-making, courts can 'thicken'[281] international law by creating a body of precedents that impacts not only on subsequent judicial decisions but also on political discussions about the content and scope of the law. The ICJ, for example, although generally considered to be one of the more restrained courts, has created a body of case law that has shaped and developed international law far beyond the scope of the disputes that were actually submitted to it.[282] Couvreur refers by way of example to the ICJ's decisions on the Vienna Convention on the Law of Treaties.[283] Other authors similarly highlight the various ways in which international courts and tribunals have shaped international law, starting with the considerable contributions by the IUSCT to the rules of international arbitration and the issues of nationality, attribution and expropriation in international law, as well as by the ITLOS with its case law on functional protection, precise allocation of damages, the protection of procedural rights in

---

[277] Ibid, paras 62–63.

[278] ECJ, judgment in *Gauweiler and Others*, C-62/14, EU:C:2015:400, para 12, referring to that effect to its judgment in *Kleinwort Benson*, C-346/93, EU:C:1995:85, paras 23 and 24.

[279] Von Bogdandy and Venzke, above n14 at 9 et seq.

[280] Eg Couvreur, above n12.

[281] Von Bogdandy and Venzke, above n14 at 9.

[282] See Couvreur, above n12.

[283] UN Doc A/Conf.39/27; 1155 UNTS 331; 8 ILM 679 (1969); 63 AJIL 875 (1969).

environmental cases and the delimitation of the continental shelf beyond 200 nautical miles. With regard to the CJEU, Lenaerts states that it 'had to create new norms that would supplement and complete the legal order established by the Treaty, aligning it with both public international law and the fundamental constitutional tenets common to its Member States' in order to ensure the legitimacy of the EU legal order.[284] Finally, the ECtHR considers the ECHR as a 'living instrument' and applies an evolutive interpretation, aiming to render its rights 'practical and effective'.[285]

Critics who measure the contribution of the international judiciary to the rule of law only based on the number and the nature of the disputes settled overlook that the courts' impact transcends the individual case and affects the international legal order as a whole. Despite the fact that judgments are binding only *inter partes*, and despite the lack of a rule of precedent in international law, judicial decisions contribute to shaping the standards of the entire international legal system.[286] The importance that lies in the clarification and development of international law for the promotion of the rule of law must not be underestimated.

VII. CONCLUSION

The past two and a half decades have seen an unprecedented multiplication of international adjudicative bodies, which enjoy increasing powers and deal with an ever-growing number of cases. Despite concerns about the possible negative consequences for the unity of international law, this development has to be welcomed from a rule of law perspective. International courts and tribunals settle disputes peacefully by legal means, assess the compliance of public power with international legal constraints, tackle impunity and contribute to the clarification and development of international law. All of their functions are aimed towards promoting and strengthening the rule of law.

While there can therefore be no doubt about the important contribution of the international judiciary to the rule of law, attention needs to be drawn to the remaining challenges.

The multiplication of international tribunals has widened the range of possibilities for states to settle their disputes peacefully by legal means, to obtain legitimation through compliance assessment by an independent

[284] See Lenaerts, above n113.
[285] See Lemmens, above n16.
[286] Matz-Lück, above n24 at 109.

body, and to combat impunity for the most serious crimes. This, and the significant contributions of every individual court and tribunal, are to be welcomed from a rule of law perspective. However, the unstructured and non-hierarchical growth of the international judicial system has also raised concerns with regard to the potential impact on the coherence of international law.[287] Scholars and practitioners fear that the fragmentation of the institutional framework might translate into a fragmentation of the legal framework. Competing jurisdictions, parallel proceedings, conflicting decisions and forum shopping might threaten not only the rule of law and the legitimacy of the international legal order but risk that 'the very essence of a normative system of law will be lost'.[288] These concerns abounded particularly in the late 1990s and early 2000s, when they were prominently taken up by two successive ICJ presidents and triggered a wealth of scholarship. Today, it would seem that these potential problems largely did not materialize.[289] In fact, open contradictions in the case law of different international courts – as often illustrated with the saga of the *Nicaragua*, *Tadic* and *Genocide* cases – have remained a rare exception.[290] This corresponds to the observation already made by Charney in the late 1990s, that in the 'core areas of international law, the different international tribunals of the late twentieth century do share relatively coherent views'.[291] An important role in the avoidance of conflicts between the various tribunals can be attributed to the emergence of a transnational judicial dialogue – between international courts and tribunals and between international and domestic courts.[292] Indeed, Brown has

---

287 On the risks for the integrity of international law see for example Luis Barrionuevo Arrévalo, 'The Multiplication of International Jurisdictions and the Integrity of International Law' (2008) 15 *ILSA Journal of International and Comparative Law* 49, 53 et seq. See also Follesdal, above n4.

288 Charney, above n23 at 699.

289 See also Cançado Trindade, above n23. See also the ILC Report on Fragmentation, United Nations, *Fragmentation of International Law: Difficulties Arising from the Diversification and Expansion of International Law, Report of the Study Group of the International Law Commission* (2006) UN Doc A/CN.4/L.682.

290 Pierre-Marie Dupuy and Jorge E Viñuales, 'The Challenge of "Proliferation": An Anatomy of the Debate' in Cesare PR Romano, Karen Alter and Yuval Shany (eds), *The Oxford Handbook of International Adjudication* (OUP, 2014) 135, 146.

291 Charney, above n23 at 699.

292 See Cançado Trindade, above n23; Anne-Marie Slaughter, 'Judicial Globalization' (2000) 40 *Virginia Journal of International Law* 1103; Francis G Jacobs, 'Judicial Dialogue and the Cross-Fertilization of Legal Systems: The

argued that there is an increasing commonality in the practice of international courts to the application of rules concerning issues of procedure and remedies, and that this represents the emergence of a common law of international adjudication. This suggests that international courts can develop common approaches to the challenges that they face in the age of proliferation. It also suggests that international courts do not generally operate as self-contained regimes, but rather that they regard themselves as forming part of a community of international courts, which has positive implications for the development of the international legal system.[293] Furthermore, although international law does not have rules on precedent or *stare decisis*, courts tend to rely on their own prior decisions and have frequently adopted a deferential approach to decisions rendered by other institutions. The judgments and advisory opinions of the ICJ notably enjoy a high degree of authority and are often cited in the case law of other tribunals. Consequently, the fragmentation of international law through international adjudication causes less alarm today than it did two decades ago. Nevertheless, frictions remain and need to be addressed. Some have argued for the creation of an international 'supreme court' or urged the ICJ to take up this role. However, this solution appears not only politically and practically unfeasible, but would also take away the benefits of an international judiciary with many voices, areas of expertise and backgrounds.[294] Instead, it is the task of every single international judge to recognize his role in the wider system and realize the responsibility that this entails. Today, judicial dialogue is still ad hoc and unpredictable, and rather unevenly exercised across the range of judicial bodies. The ICJ, for example, remains a relatively self-contained body, which rarely relies on decisions other than its own. In sum, judges cannot live in 'splendid isolation'[295] but must be aware of the competences and case law of other

European Court of Justice' (2003) 38 *Texas International Law Journal* 547; Yonatan Lupu and Erik Voeten, 'Precedent in International Courts: A Network Analysis of Case Citations by the European Court of Human Rights' (2011) 42 *British Journal of Political Science* 413; Marc Jacob, 'Precedents: Lawmaking Through International Adjudication' (2011) 12 *German Law Journal* 1005; Anthony Arnull, 'Judicial Dialogue in the European Union', in Julie Dickson and Pavlos Eleftheriadis (eds), *Philosophical Foundations of European Union Law* (OUP, 2012) 109.

293 Brown, above n23.

294 See Charney, above n23 at 698.

295 Linton and Tiba, above n24 at 418.

institutions and maintain an open dialogue.[296] Courts and tribunals need to enter into such an open dialogue with their international, supranational and domestic counterparts in order to avoid the potential negative facets of the institutional mosaic, in particular concerning competing jurisdictions and conflicting decisions. This dialogue can be informal, particularly through reference and deference to the decisions of other courts and tribunals, but it can also be formalized through regular visits and exchanges between the different courts.

A second point of concern – and a 'more disturbing element' to some[297] – is the institutional design of most international courts, which continues to rely on state consent in order to establish jurisdiction. While compulsory jurisdiction is exercised by a number of courts, many important courts, including the ICJ, do not figure among them. This lack of compulsory jurisdiction has received considerably less attention than the issue of fragmentation, although its negative impact on the rule of law is arguably far more severe. A system in which all levels of public power are equally subjected to legal constraints does not square with a judicial system that can fulfil its functions only upon the agreement of the parties. Compulsory jurisdiction is in need of strengthening at the international level and reforms for those international courts and tribunals that still operate on a voluntary basis ought to be considered as a matter of urgency. At the same time, the capacities of the international adjudicative bodies must be enhanced through adequate financing and staffing, thereby allowing the international judiciary to maintain reasonably short timeframes for their proceedings while also respecting aspects of procedural fairness.

Lastly, the expanding caseload of international courts and tribunals is both a blessing and a curse. While on the one hand the increased recourse to adjudicative bodies strengthens the rule of law, on the other it creates capacity problems for the judiciary. Short on resources and staff, many courts face a considerable backlog of pending cases, leading to increasingly long proceedings. In line with the maxim 'justice delayed is justice denied', this situation weakens the rule of law. Several courts and tribunals have recognized the need for action and have taken measures, ranging from 'practice directions' for parties and judges at the ICJ[298] to the increased use of the single-judge procedure at the ECtHR.[299] While these steps may be successful in reducing the backlog, they can also have

---

[296] Buergenthal, above n21 at 274.
[297] Higgins, above n23.
[298] See Couvreur, above n12.
[299] See Lemmens, above n16.

negative effects on courts' procedural fairness and consequently on the rule of law. The ECtHR, for example, managed to reduce the number of cases on its docket from more than 160,000 in 2011 to less than 100,000 in 2014.[300] This significant decrease was largely due to the strong reliance on the new competence of single judges to declare cases inadmissible 'where such a decision can be taken without further examination'.[301] Single judge decisions are not only not published, they are also 'no longer than a one-page letter stating the formal ground for rejection without further reasoning or argumentation'.[302] There can be considerable doubts on the fairness of a judicial procedure that in many cases makes it difficult for the applicant to understand the grounds on which the decision was taken and severely limits the possibility for internal and external control. Not only will the authority of such a decision be weaker, it may also negatively impact on the legitimacy of the court or tribunal, which should strive to reconcile efficiency with procedural fairness. Only if both factors are ensured can the judiciary effectively contribute to the rule of law.

Finding answers to these challenges will be essential for the further strengthening of the international judiciary's contribution to the rule of law.

What is more, international courts and tribunals are by no means a panacea for all the problems facing the international community. As Lon Fuller put it: 'the most we can expect of constitutions and courts is that they save us from the abyss; they cannot be expected to lay out very many compulsory steps toward truly significant accomplishment'.[303] Furthermore, notwithstanding the crucial role of adjudication in the

---

300 ECHR, Press conference President Dean Spielmann 30 January 2014, <www.echr.coe.int/Documents/Speech_20140130_Spielmann_JY_PC_ENG.pdf>.

301 Art 27 ECHR.

302 Janneke Gerards, 'Inadmissibility Decisions of the European Court of Human Rights: A Critique of the Lack of Reasoning' (2014) *Human Rights Law Review* 1, 6.

303 Fuller, above n82 at 44. See the similar sentiment expressed by Secretary-General Dag Hammarskjöld with respect to the UN:

> It has been said that the United Nations was not created in order to bring us heaven, but in order to save us from hell. I think that sums up as well as anything I have heard both the essential role of the United Nations and the attitude of mind that we should bring to its support

United Nations, *Address by Secretary-General Dag Hammarskjöld at University of California Convocation, Berkeley, California, Thursday, May 13, 1954, at 10:00 A.M. (Pacific Coast Time)* (UN Doc SG/382).

international legal order, judicial settlement may have unintended effects on the development of the law. Notably, there exists a tension between the retrospective analysis of the rights and duties of states involved in litigation needed for the settlement of disputes on the one hand, and the prospective effect of the principles emerging from the judicial decision that may govern future conduct on the other. The absence of an international legislature implies that judicial pronouncements are not easily overturned, and a judicial decision may prematurely restrict the development of the law in areas that are in flux.[304] Finally, bringing issues such as the permissibility of the killing of innocents by nuclear weapons within the realm of judicial reasoning may detract from the relevant moral standard and leave the prohibition in a weakened state.[305]

The imperfect but important contribution of international courts consists in convincing other actors in international law of a more rigorous application of the rule of law at all levels. That arguably implies making international law 'a better example of a legal system',[306] thereby conforming to a greater extent with what may be the real purpose of international law and of the rule of law in the international realm: not the protection of sovereign states, but the protection of the populations committed to their charge.[307] States are indeed not ends in themselves, but instruments for the wellbeing of human individuals, who are ends in

---

304 See Lowe, above n108 at 209–222.

305 Koskenniemi, above n34 at 140, 152–153 and 161, arguing that the ICJ should not have been asked the question of the permissibility of nuclear weapons in *Legality of the Threat or Use of Nuclear Weapons,* above n34, and that the Court's silence was beneficial 'inasmuch as it, and it only, could leave room for the workings of the moral impulse, the irrational non-foundational appeal against the killing of the innocent' (at 153).

306 Waldron, above n138 at 46–7. See also Simmonds, above n111 at 5, 46, 99, proposing an archetypal concept of law: to count as 'law', a regime or system must approximate to the archetype to some degree. That archetype can be reached to varying degrees, which implies that it also serves as a guiding ideal 'to which legal systems ought to strive to conform more closely', and social practices therefore 'count as instances of law only when they partially embody an idea that they can never fully realize'; see also Rawls, above n110 at 207, arguing that the precepts of justice associated with the rule of law 'are those that would be followed by any system of rules which perfectly embodied the idea of a legal system'; and Kelsen, above n141 at ix, describing the approach to the aim of world peace as 'one of slow and steady perfection of the international legal order'.

307 See Koskenniemi, above n34 at 145, suggesting that arguably 'the law's purpose is to protect the innocent', adding that 'it is hard to see a more basic purpose for it in a system that excludes reference to personal virtue'.

themselves.[308] International and supranational courts infuse predictability and security in the international legal order, creating space for the liberty of individuals and groups. Such liberty as independence from the power of others, including public authorities, can only be realized by that form of moral association called 'the rule of law'.[309]

---

308 Waldron, above n109 at 24 building on Immanuel Kant, *Groundwork of the Metaphysics of Morals* (Mary Gregor (ed) CUP, 1785/1999) 78–9.

309 Simmonds, above n111 at 152, describing it as 'a common good that is intrinsic to law's nature'. See also De Baere, above n80 at 382–3, with respect to the rule of law as the cornerstone of European integration.

PART II

Global courts and tribunals

3. The International Court of Justice

Philippe Couvreur*

'The term "rule of law" is more easily invoked than understood'![1]

It raises a number of questions of principle to which we should briefly give our attention.

It might indeed be said that assessing the contribution of the International Court of Justice (the Court or the ICJ) to the rule of law requires us to understand what is covered by that expression, to try to propose a definition for it, and to be able to establish its practical and legal scope. However, the extent of such questions would lead me beyond the bounds of the present contribution. I shall therefore confine myself, by way of introduction, to making three short series of remarks on the general subject of the rule of law and the issues that it raises, before turning to the question of the contribution of the International Court of Justice in that respect.

> (1) In the first place, the rule of law is a concept specific to the constitutional organization of the State, the expression having been developed in England. It was an English writer, AV Dicey, at the end of the nineteenth century, who drew on his observation of the legal and political system in the United Kingdom to set forth the characteristics and a first theory of the rule of law.

In the way that it was developed, the expression 'the rule of law' ties in with concepts that had taken shape elsewhere in Europe, continuing the strides forward in ideas and political philosophy that were made in the Enlightenment. The notion which comes principally to mind is that of the *Rechtsstaat*, developed in Germany from the first half of the nineteenth century onwards, and taken up later, in France, in the theories of the *Etat de droit*.

---

* The opinions expressed are of a strictly personal nature.

[1] Sir Arthur Watts, 'The International Rule of Law' (1993) 36 *German Yearbook of International Law* 15–45 at 15.

These various expressions – rule of law, *Rechtstaat* and *Etat de droit* – were thus each born out of a particular historical, social and political context. They also bear on a specifically constitutional set of issues: the public authorities being made subject to the law, the guaranteeing of individual rights and freedoms, and a certain separation of legal powers and functions among the political institutions of each State.

It nonetheless remains difficult, beyond a general and intuitive understanding of the expression 'rule of law', to define that concept accurately and to draw specific legal conclusions from it. That is of course essentially a question for theorists of constitutional law, and one that would require a comparative law approach. Here, therefore, I would merely point to the continuing debates as to the existence of a common conception of the rule of law, beyond the various specific national and constitutional features of each State.

Whatever the outcome of these theoretical questions, it is clear that the rule of law has been recognized explicitly in numerous international instruments adopted since 1945.

I should like to make a second introductory comment in that respect.

> (2) The expression 'rule of law' has acquired an incontrovertible legal value, at international level, with the developments in international organizations, the international recognition of human rights, and the establishment of mechanisms to provide international guarantees and protection for individuals against infringements of their fundamental rights by States.

The idea thus conceived of a common principle of the rule of law has of course emerged in a regional context, and on the European continent in particular. Mention is generally made of the reference thereto in the preamble of the Statute of the Council of Europe in 1949 or in the preamble of the European Convention for the Protection of Human Rights and Fundamental Freedoms (1950). In the former text, the governments that founded the Council of Europe reaffirmed 'their devotion to the spiritual and moral values which are the common heritage of their peoples and the true source of individual freedom, political liberty and *the rule of law*, principles which form the basis of all genuine democracy'.[2] In the European Convention adopted in 1950, the European

---

[2] In the French version: 'inébranlablement attachés aux valeurs spirituelles et morales qui sont le patrimoine commun de leurs peuples et qui sont à l'origine des principes de liberté individuelle, de liberté politique et de *prééminence du droit*, sur lesquels se fonde toute démocratie véritable'.

governments likewise recognized their 'common heritage of political traditions, ideals, freedom and *the rule of law*'.[3]

Beyond the European context, in the Universal Declaration of Human Rights, adopted on 9 December 1948, reference was similarly made to the rule of law: the UN General Assembly asserted that 'it is essential, if man is not to be compelled to have recourse, as a last resort, to rebellion against tyranny and oppression, that human rights should be protected by *the rule of law*'.[4]

These general affirmations have obviously given rise to countless legal instances which it would be impossible to synthesize into a few words here. Let us simply note that, in this context, the rule of law can be taken as the common denominator of democratic political regimes which respect fundamental individual rights and freedoms, and which provide effective legal guarantees.

While it is therefore possible to see in the rule of law a principle of international law, enshrined or in the process of being enshrined in positive international law, the expression remains essentially connected to a set of rules concerning the internal organization of the State, democracy and respect for human rights.

While naturally having the same object as the notion that has been derived from theories of constitutional law, namely a certain form of internal organization of the State, the development of the rule of law at international level nonetheless points to a broader or more general significance, which can be transposed in some respects to international legal relations. The translation of the term into French, for example in the official documents of the United Nations, is particularly illuminating in this regard. It is not merely a question of guaranteeing the *Etat de droit* under the auspices of the rule of law, as applied to the internal organization of a State.[5] It is also a matter of guaranteeing an '*état de droit*',[6] '*la*

---

[3] In the French version: 'animés d'un même esprit et possédant un patrimoine commun d'idéal et de traditions politiques, de respect de la liberté et de *prééminence du droit*'.

[4] In the French version: 'il est essentiel que les droits de l'homme soient protégés par *un régime de droit* pour que l'homme ne soit pas contraint, en suprême recours, à la révolte contre la tyrannie et l'oppression'.

[5] The *Dictionnaire de droit public international* defines the *Etat de droit* in this sense as a 'State whose internal organization is governed by law and justice', J. Salmon (ed.), Bruylant, 2001, 456.

[6] This is the official typography finally used in United Nations documents in French for the translation of 'rule of law'.

prééminence du droit'[7] or '*le règne de la loi*',[8] according to the various translations that have been provided for the expression 'the rule of law'. It is in this sense that the expression has been taken up very widely in the UN during the last decade, on the basis, crucially, of it being established that reference can be made to the rule of law at both national and *international* level.

That brings me to my third set of introductory comments.

> (3) Any notion, in becoming more widespread, loses something of its substance and its precision. Referring to 'the rule of law at national and international level' does nothing to reduce, in that respect, the number of questions that can be brought to the jurist's mind by the simple expression 'the rule of law'.

It was under that heading that the rule of law was recently the object of a particularly solemn act of recognition, in the Declaration of the High-level Meeting of the General Assembly on the Rule of Law at the National and International Levels, adopted on 24 September 2012 (A/RES/67/1). The impressive series of points addressed by this Declaration, in no fewer than 42 paragraphs, reflects the sheer diversity of the subjects covered, ranging from preventing corruption or terrorism to economic development and extending to the elimination of poverty and hunger, while taking in the combating of impunity for genocide and other international crimes.

What was new about this Declaration, however, was the solemn affirmation of the international dimension of the rule of law, and the commitment to 'an international order based on the rule of law' (para 1). The rule of law thus applies 'to all States equally, and to international

---

7 See the examples given above.

8 An author has pointed out that this was the translation chosen in the jurisprudence of the International Court of Justice (O Corten, Rapport général, in *L'Etat de droit en droit international*, Brussels colloquium, Paris, Pedone, 2009, p 12). Cf *Asylum (Colombia/Peru)*, Judgment, ICJ Reports 1950 284, the French text being authoritative ('En principe donc, l'asile ne peut être opposé à l'action de la justice. Il n'y a d'exception à ce principe que si, sous le couvert de la justice, l'arbitraire se substitue au règne de la loi [arbitrary action is substituted for the rule of law].' In a celebrated dictum, the Court observed, the English text being authoritative: 'Arbitrariness is not so much something opposed to a rule of law, as something opposed to the rule of law'/'L'arbitraire n'est pas tant ce qui s'oppose à une règle de droit que ce qui s'oppose au règne de la loi', *Elettronica Sicula SpA (Elsi),* Judgment, ICJ Reports 1989, 76, para 128.

organizations, including the United Nations and its principal organs, and … respect for and promotion of the rule of law and justice should guide all of their activities and accord predictability and legitimacy to their actions' (para 2).

However, it does not provide a definition which is any more precise of what is to be understood by 'the rule of law'. In very general terms, the authors of the Declaration:

- reaffirm, in the preamble, the 'fundamental importance [of the rule of law] for political dialogue and cooperation among all States and for the further development of the three main pillars upon which the United Nations is built: international peace and security, human rights and development';
- and agree that '[their] collective response to the challenges and opportunities arising from the many complex political, social and economic transformations before us must be guided by the rule of law, as it is the foundation of friendly and equitable relations between States and the basis on which just and fair societies are built'.

The rule of law at international level, in a context such as this, can be given two interpretations.

On the one hand, it can be a general expression covering essentially the requirement of universal compliance with international law, in accordance with the purpose and principles of the United Nations. In this sense, asserting the international dimension of the rule of law cannot be said to represent something new in the field of positive international law. For example, the Declaration on Principles of International Law concerning Friendly Relations and Co-operation among States in accordance with the Charter of the United Nations, adopted in 1970 (resolution 2625, 24 October 1970), affirmed 'the paramount importance of the Charter of the United Nations in the promotion of the rule of law among nations'.[9] And in the same vein, the Declaration on the Rule of Law, adopted in 2012, points to existing and well-established rules to uphold the sovereign equality of all States, to respect their territorial integrity, to prohibit the threat or use of force in any manner inconsistent with the purposes and principles of the United Nations, and to uphold the resolution of international disputes by peaceful means (paras 3–4).

---

[9] Preamble, fourth recital: 'l'importance de la Charte des Nations Unies pour favoriser le règne du droit parmi les nations'.

On the other hand, the affirmation of the rule of law in international legal relations could encompass a transformation of the international legal order itself, and the application in that context of 'constitutional' principles which have been developed in domestic legal orders. But we should not underestimate the limitations, if not the risks, which are attached to a sudden transposition to international level of concepts that are essentially tied to the legal forms of the modern State. In an international society which remains principally composed of sovereign States, the rule of law naturally cannot correspond in every way to what is generally understood by that term in a State which has a constitution, separation of powers and binding judicial controls that are intended to ensure, in the face of the powers of the public authorities, respect for the law and for the fundamental rights and freedoms of individuals. Nor can the United Nations constitute a type of legal structure comparable to a State; as the International Court of Justice has found, while:

> [i]t is at present the supreme type of international organization, … [t]hat is not the same thing as saying that [the Organization] is a State, which it certainly is not … Still less is it the same thing as saying that it is a 'super-State', whatever that expression may mean.[10]

Consequently, the content of the rule of law, at international level, appears to be extremely open. Either it relates to certain legal principles affirmed *de lege ferenda*, which would point to a radical transformation of positive law – in this context, for example, one might think of the introduction of a systematic form of judicial control of the acts and decisions of the organs of the United Nations. Or the rule of law relates to, and underlines the importance of, certain 'values' which guide the rules of positive international law whose development is beyond dispute: hence the Declaration of 2012 reaffirms that 'human rights, the rule of law and democracy are interlinked and mutually reinforcing and that they belong to the universal and indivisible core values and principles of the United Nations' (para 5).

The very broad nature of the concept of the rule of law could undoubtedly lead to the topic of 'the contribution of the ICJ to the rule of law' becoming excessively diluted. As the Court has said, in response to a

---

[10] *Reparation for Injuries Suffered in the Service of the United Nations*, Advisory Opinion, ICJ Reports 1949, 179.

questionnaire drawn up by the Secretariat (with a view to preparing an inventory of the activities of the United Nations in the area of the rule of law):

> everything [the Court] does is aimed at promoting the rule of law: it hands down judgments and gives advisory opinions in accordance with its Statute [thereby contributing to the promotion and clarification of international law].[11]

Assessing the contribution of the ICJ to the rule of law would thus involve a review of the Court's whole history and body of work.

Faced with the breadth of such open questions, and in keeping with the emphasis placed by the editors of the present book on the role of the various international courts, I shall therefore confine my remarks to two aspects:

- first, I shall endeavour to show in what respects the ICJ's contribution is a special and significant one, compared with other international courts and tribunals; and
- secondly, I shall focus as far as possible on certain cases settled recently by the Court, in so far as they may have given rise to developments in jurisprudence relating to the general concept of the rule of law.

I shall therefore consider, in the first part of the present contribution, the particular nature of the ICJ as the principal judicial organ of the United Nations, and the essential role which it is therefore called upon to play in the promotion of the rule of law.[12]

In the second part, I shall then deal with the particular scope of the Court's jurisprudence, in terms of the promotion of the rule of law at international level.

---

11 *Report of the International Court of Justice (1 August 2007–31 July 2008)*, p6, para 22. [http://www.icj-cij.org/court/en/reports/report_2007-2008.pdf].

12 As the Court points out in this respect, in each of its annual reports: 'it should be kept in mind that the Court, as a court of justice and, moreover, the principal judicial organ of the United Nations, occupies a special position', ibid.

I. THE PRINCIPAL JUDICIAL ORGAN OF THE UNITED NATIONS: STATUS AND FUNCTIONS OF THE INTERNATIONAL COURT OF JUSTICE IN THE PROMOTION OF THE RULE OF LAW AT THE INTERNATIONAL LEVEL

By the mere fact of its existence, the International Court of Justice can certainly be seen as an essential element of the rule of law at international level. A former President of the Court, Judge Higgins, saw it as 'personify[ing]' 'the rule of law'.[13]

It is needless to say, however, that the attributes of the Court are very different from those of a national court. Rooted in arbitral practice, its jurisdiction is always based on the consent of the disputant States and the specific characteristics of the international disputes which are brought before it cannot be disregarded where its composition and the organization of its procedure are concerned. It also has characteristics distinguishing it from the various international courts and tribunals that have been created in recent decades.

The Court's special contribution to the rule of law lies in 'its character, both as a principal organ of the United Nations and as a judicial body'.[14] As a principal organ of the UN, the Court enjoys not only a unique legitimacy and universality at the international level, but, in addition, it participates effectively in achieving the purposes and principles of the UN (A). Moreover, as a judicial body, its manner of operating meets needs which are inherent to its task of settling disputes judicially and certainly fundamental with regard to the requirements of the rule of law (B).

I shall examine these two aspects in turn.

A. The Unique Nature of the ICJ as a Principal Organ of the UN

The International Court of Justice represents the final stage in a long process in the history of international justice: the creation of a permanent

---

[13] 'The ICJ and the Rule of Law', Speech by HE Judge Rosalyn Higgins, President of the International Court of Justice, at the United Nations University, 11 April 2007. [http://archive.unu.edu/hq/library/Collection/PDF_files/Higgins_speech.pdf], at 4.

[14] *Judgment No 2867 of the Administrative Tribunal of the International Labour Organization upon a complaint filed against the International Fund for Agricultural Development,* Advisory Opinion, ICJ Reports 2012, 25, para 33.

court with general jurisdiction and universal reach, tasked with administering justice between States.

I shall not revisit here the origins of the ICJ, in particular the establishment of its predecessor, the Permanent Court of International Justice (Permanent Court or PCIJ). Nonetheless, it must be borne in mind that the Statute of the present Court was based on the Statute of the Permanent Court (Art 92 of the Charter), and that many of the solutions adopted in 1945 were taken up thanks to the success of the first permanent international court in the days of the League of Nations. Even earlier, the experience of arbitration between States also had a profound influence on the establishment of the Hague Court.

Rather, I wish first to focus briefly on the novel nature of an international court directly engaged in achieving the purposes and principles of the UN, the first universal political organization. The Court's necessarily close links with the UN, of which it is a principal organ, confer on it a unique legitimacy and unique responsibilities.

1. Composition

It should be noted first of all that the Court, as an organ of the UN, is open to all Members of the UN, which are *ipso facto* parties to its Statute (Art 93 of the UN Charter (the 'Charter') and Article 35 of the Statute of the Court (the 'Statute')). Consequently, 193 Member States of the UN today recognize the Court and its authority as an organ for the judicial settlement of disputes. This means that the composition of the Court reflects, as far as possible, the composition of the organization, while preserving its nature as a 'body of independent judges, elected regardless of their nationality' and ensuring that the Members of the Court have the outstanding skills and competence required for the performance of their duties (Art 2 of the Statute).

The Court thus consists of 15 judges of different nationalities, the only judges in the world to be elected by both the General Assembly and the Security Council. According to Article 9 of the Statute of the Court, the judges must, as a whole, represent 'the main forms of civilization and of the principal legal systems of the world'. This unique composition is ensured by a method of election designed to meet both the principle of equality between all Members of the Organization through the participation of the General Assembly and also the particular responsibilities of the Security Council under the Charter.

This compromise between these different requirements is expressed in practice in the distribution of membership of the Court among the principal regions of the globe. Today this distribution is as follows: Africa, three; Latin America and the Caribbean, two; Asia, three; Western

Europe and other States, five; and Eastern Europe, two. This distribution is comparable to that of membership of the Security Council. Although there is no entitlement to membership on the part of any country, the Court has always included judges of the nationality of the permanent members of the Security Council.

This composition and the requirements it reflects also have implications for the proper functioning of the Court and its working methods. I shall come back to this a little later.

2. Consensual jurisdiction

Furthermore, the Court's role falls naturally within the primary aims of the UN since it provides one of the means for the peaceful settlement of international disputes, thereby contributing to the objective of maintaining international peace and security.

As such, the ICJ is undoubtedly the preferred forum for the settlement of disputes between States concerning any point of international law. This is expressly recognized in the Charter of the UN, which provides in particular that the Security Council, in the exercise of its powers with respect to the peaceful settlement of disputes which are likely to endanger international peace and security, 'should … take into consideration that legal disputes should as a general rule be referred by the parties to the International Court of Justice' (Art 36, para 3).

The General Assembly has on many occasions recalled the fundamental principles contained in this regard in the Charter: with the 1982 Manila Declaration,[15] the Assembly recalled the terms of Article 33 of the Charter putting particular emphasis on judicial settlement. It specified in particular that recourse to judicial settlement of legal disputes, particularly referral to the ICJ, should not be considered an unfriendly act between States. Moreover, in its 1988 Declaration on the Prevention and Removal of Disputes and Situations Which May Threaten International Peace and Security,[16] the General Assembly underlined the role of the Security Council and its duty to cooperate more closely with the Court. The text referred in particular to the need for the Security Council to

[15] Manila Declaration on the Peaceful Settlement of International Disputes, 15 November 1982, A/RES/37/10.

[16] Declaration on the Prevention and Removal of Disputes and Situations Which May Threaten International Peace and Security and on the Role of the United Nations in this Field, 5 December 1988, A/RES/43/51.

make more frequent use of the advisory procedure for the purposes of clarifying legal issues;[17] I shall return to this a little later.

In addition to the opportunities afforded to the UN Member States by the ICJ as a forum for the judicial settlement of disputes, particular reference must also be made to the support provided to the Court by its position within the UN. The existence of guarantees concerning the implementation of judgments is, in any legal system, a key element in the rule of law. In this connection, the second paragraph of Article 94 of the Charter provides that:

> [i]f any party to a case fails to perform the obligations incumbent upon it under a judgment rendered by the Court, the other party may have recourse to the Security Council, which may, if it deems necessary, make recommendations or decide upon measures to be taken to give effect to the judgment.

While this mechanism does not of course confer safeguards comparable to those which may exist within a centralized system of recourse to public law enforcement authorities, it nonetheless reflects the importance attached to the role played by the ICJ and to the implementation of its decisions. I would also point out that, fortunately, the implementation of the Court's decisions, which are binding on the parties to a case, has throughout the Court's history only very exceptionally given rise to problems.

The Court's unique position within the UN, and more broadly within the international legal order, should not be allowed to conceal the continuing limitations of the judicial settlement of disputes in international law.

I will not here revisit at length the familiar question of the compulsory jurisdiction of the ICJ, which has been widely debated since the first attempts to create a permanent international court in the twentieth century. The system that was eventually adopted in 1920, and retained in 1945 in the Statute of the present Court, leaves States free to consent to the compulsory jurisdiction of the Court to settle their disputes whether with regard to a particular case, by means of a special agreement to that effect, to a category of disputes concerning the interpretation and

---

[17] 'The Security Council, if it is appropriate for promoting the prevention and removal of disputes or situations, should, at an early stage, consider making use of the provisions of the Charter concerning the possibility of requesting the International Court of Justice to give an advisory opinion on any legal question', para 15. The Declaration on the Rule of Law (2012) simply 'recall[s] the ability of the relevant organs of the United Nations to request advisory opinions from the International Court of Justice', para 31.

application of a treaty, by means of a compromissory clause or, lastly, to all legal disputes, by a declaration made under Article 36, paragraph 2, of the Statute recognizing the jurisdiction of the Court 'as compulsory *ipso facto* and without special agreement, in relation to any other state accepting the same obligation'.

States which have opted to accept the compulsory jurisdiction of the Court do not today represent the majority of the Members of the UN and the steady increase in their number since the creation of the Court (with the exception of a decrease by one in 1974 and again in 1985 following the withdrawal of their declarations by France and the United States respectively) has reflected the increase in the number of Member States albeit at a far lower rate. As a result, there are today 71 States[18] which have subscribed to the 'optional clause for compulsory jurisdiction' under Article 36, paragraph 2, of the Statute, out of a total of 193 Member States.[19] This figure reflects an international situation that, viewed as a whole, may appear hardly to accord with the expectations and requirements affirmed internationally in the name of the rule of law. In this regard, the General Assembly has called upon States that have not yet done so 'to consider accepting the jurisdiction of the Court in accordance with its Statute'.[20] The Secretary-General of the UN has recently launched 'a campaign to increase the number of Member States that accept as compulsory the jurisdiction of the International Court of Justice'.[21]

However, it should not be forgotten that the 'general' acceptance by a State of the compulsory jurisdiction of the Court, in accordance with Article 36, paragraph 2, of the Statute of the Court, can be accompanied by reservations limiting its scope and this is very often the case in practice. At the same time, acceptance of the Court's jurisdiction for the settlement of a specific case, by means of a special agreement or on the

---

[18] To date Lithuania and Timor-Leste, in 2012, the Republic of Marshall Islands, in 2013, and Italy, in 2014, are the last four States to have made the declaration.

[19] In 1948, of the 58 Member States, 34 (including four out of five permanent members of the Security Council) recognized the compulsory jurisdiction of the Court, some 59 per cent of the United Nations membership as compared to today's rate of 36 per cent (71 States, including only one of the five permanent members of the Security Council, out of 193 Member States).

[20] 2005 World Summit Outcome, A/RES/60/1, 24 October 2005, para 134(f); Declaration on the rule of law at national and international levels, para 31.

[21] 'Delivering justice: a programme of action to strengthen the rule of law at the national and international levels', Report of the Secretary-General, United Nations, A/66/749, para 15(b).

basis of *forum prorogatum* (Art 38, para 5, of the Rules of Court), should not be discouraged. Practice has demonstrated the potential advantages associated with these means of bringing cases before the Court for both States and the Court.

Another factor relating to the Court's jurisdiction should be mentioned here: in accordance with the principle of the free choice by States of the means for the peaceful settlement of their disputes, there is nothing in the Charter preventing them 'from entrusting the solution of their differences to other tribunals by virtue of agreements already in existence or which may be concluded in the future' (Art 95 of the Charter). Notwithstanding its particular place within the UN, the Court does not formally constitute the 'supreme' court of the international legal order, in the sense that it is in particular responsible for ensuring the 'unity' of the jurisprudence of the various international tribunals that have been established. However, in the second part of this chapter, I shall return to this question and to the possible risks for the consistency of international jurisprudence arising from the proliferation of international jurisdiction.

3. Advisory function

The third point to note with respect to the links between the Court and the UN relates to the exercise of the advisory function. This function has been relatively less used in the history of the present Court compared to its jurisdiction in contentious proceedings, unlike in the case of its predecessor, the PCIJ.[22] However, it represents a particularly advantageous – albeit at times neglected – approach in the cause of strengthening compliance with the rule of law in activities of the UN.

The advisory procedure provides an opportunity for the Court to rule on the interpretation to be given to the provisions of the Charter or other legal questions arising within the context of the activities of the organs of the UN and of a number of specialized agencies of the UN system.[23]

---

22 During the 18 years of the Permanent Court's existence, the number of contentious cases and of advisory proceedings was almost identical. Since the establishment of the International Court of Justice the ratio of advisory proceedings (26 since 1946) to judgments (117) is less than one to four.

23 A difference exists depending on the nature of the requesting body. Under the first paragraph of Art 96 of the Charter and of Art 65 of the Statute, the General Assembly and the Security Council may request an opinion from the Court on any 'legal question', whereas, according to para 2 of Art 96, the other organs may refer to the Court only 'legal questions arising within the scope of their activities'.

The advisory function of the Court is rooted in Article 14 of the Covenant of the League of Nations, which was intended to provide the Council and the Assembly with the opportunity of requesting an advisory opinion from the Permanent Court on 'any dispute or question'. Although not using this wording, thereby to some extent restricting the jurisdiction *ratione materiae* of the Court in advisory proceedings (Art 96 of the Charter of the United Nations refers to the more general term of 'legal question'), the drafters of the Charter nevertheless expanded its jurisdiction *ratione personae* with 21 organs and agencies now able to avail themselves of the advisory function.[24]

Although the principles applicable to the exercise of the advisory function have not changed significantly since the practice followed by the Permanent Court, the present Court has very clearly emphasized the particular nature of its power to reply to requests for advisory opinion. Summarizing its earlier jurisprudence on this question, the Court thus noted that:

> the exercise of its advisory jurisdiction represents its participation in the activities of the Organization and, in principle, a request should not be refused (*Interpretation of Peace Treaties with Bulgaria, Hungary and Romania, First Phase, Advisory Opinion, I.C.J. Reports 1950*, pp. 71–72). That indication of a strong inclination to reply is also reflected in the Court's later statement ... that 'compelling reasons' would be required to justify a refusal (1956 Advisory Opinion, *I.C.J. Reports 1956*, p. 86)[25]

and that:

> the purpose of the advisory jurisdiction is to enable organs of the United Nations and other authorized bodies to obtain opinions from the Court which will assist them in the future exercise of their functions.[26]

---

[24] Only four agencies, authorized by the General Assembly, in accordance with Art 96 of the Charter, have to date exercised this facility (UNESCO, IMO, WHO and IFAD).

[25] *Judgment No 2867 of the Administrative Tribunal of the International Labour Organization upon a Complaint Filed against the International Fund for Agricultural Development,* Advisory Opinion, ICJ Reports 2012, 25, para 33. See also *Accordance with international law of the unilateral declaration of independence in respect of Kosovo,* Advisory Opinion, ICJ Reports 2010, 416, para 30 and 417, para 33.

[26] *Accordance with international law of the unilateral declaration of independence in respect of Kosovo,* Advisory Opinion, ICJ Reports 2010 (II), 421, para 44.

Consequently, the advisory opinions of the ICJ do more than simply provide an opportunity to clarify important questions of international law, since, like judgments, they are quite naturally part of the Court's jurisprudence.[27] Despite the fact that they lack binding force, they also contribute to the functioning of the UN and to the exercise of their functions by the requesting bodies. The authority attaching to the Court's pronouncements and the duty on those who go to the Court to take due account of the opinion given by it undoubtedly contribute to ensuring that the advisory function is a particularly valuable instrument in promoting the rule of law at the international level, in particular in order to 'guide all of [the] activities [of the organs of the United Nations] and accord predictability and legitimacy to their actions'.[28]

The general considerations that have just been set out must certainly be viewed in the light of State practice, the extent of recourse to the Court by States (or by organs which may ask for advisory opinions) and, lastly, the effective role played by the Court in its task of settling disputes peacefully by the application of the law.

From this perspective, historical circumstances have had a major impact on fluctuations in the caseload of the Court. With the help of some statistics, I would point out that, across the whole range of its judicial activities, the volume of cases submitted to the Court has increased significantly and steadily since the 1990s especially, reflecting greater confidence on the part of States in the peaceful settlement of their disputes by the Court in particular.

Since it took up its duties in 1946, the Court has given 143 final decisions, namely 117 judgments and 27 advisory opinions. Since 1990, however, it has delivered 66 judgments over a period of 24 years[29] as compared to 50 judgments delivered during the first 44 years of the Court's existence. Since the 2000s, the Court has delivered an average of three judgments per year. And this does not include the many orders made by the Court every year, not only in relation to the conduct of cases (the fixing of time limits), but also in incidental proceedings (applications for permission to intervene, requests for the indication of provisional

---

[27] For certain questions that have recently been considered, see II below.

[28] Declaration of the High-level Meeting of the General Assembly on the Rule of Law at the National and International Levels, adopted 24 September 2012, A/RES/67/1, para 2.

[29] 19 judgments were delivered from 1990 to 2000 and 47 from 2001 to 2015.

measures, counterclaims), which at times require detailed consideration and deliberations on the part of the Court.

Over and beyond the statistical data, the diversity of States appearing before the Court reflects the unparalleled universality and legitimacy of the principal judicial organ of the United Nations. In 2012 alone, for example, the cases decided by the Court involved States from Latin America (Nicaragua and Colombia), Europe (Germany and Italy, Belgium) and Africa (Senegal, Guinea and Democratic Republic of the Congo). And the Court's current docket is particularly diverse, since, with cases involving States from Asia and Oceania (Marshall Islands, India, Pakistan), all the continents are 'represented'.

B. A Judicial Organ: The Requirements of the Rule of Law and the Sound Administration of International Justice before the ICJ

The assertion and promotion of the rule of law at the international level applies, par excellence, to the way the Court conducts its judicial activities. In this regard, while compliance with the requirements of the sound administration of justice before an international court undoubtedly follows common principles which are to a large extent similar to those that have emerged before the domestic courts of democratic States, we should refrain, nevertheless, from too hastily transposing concepts rooted in highly developed court systems in disregard of the characteristics of international society and of the very particular positions of international courts in this regard. As the Permanent Court observed, the rules of procedure before it must be '[those] most suited to procedure before an international tribunal and most in conformity with the fundamental principles of international law'.[30]

Attention should thus be drawn to certain characteristics of the procedure and working methods followed before the ICJ, which reflect both the basic requirements applying to the latter as a judicial body and an international court and the adjustments that are at times required by the development of its role and changes within international society. Here I shall not give a general presentation of how the Court works, but deal only with certain aspects concerning contentious proceedings and then pass on to advisory proceedings.

---

30 *Mavrommatis Palestine Concessions,* Judgment No 2, 1924, PCIJ, Series A, No 2, 16.

1. Contentious proceedings

Respect for the equality of the parties reflects both the task of the judicial settlement of disputes before the Court and the sovereign nature of the States appearing before it. 'The scope of the Court's process [must be] ... such as, in the long run, to neutralize any initial advantage that might be obtained by either side',[31] and the Court must be careful 'to give each of [the parties] the same opportunities and chances to produce their evidence'.[32]

Of course, this has consequences for the organization of cases since ensuring the latter's fairness involves a certain 'cost' and is time consuming. The settlement of certain 'historic' disputes (or non-settlement, where the Court ultimately declared that it lacked jurisdiction to decide on the merits of the dispute before it) has sometimes taken more than a decade, reinforcing the idea of excessively long deadlines, which is hardly in accord with the requirements of the sound administration of international justice. The Court observed during the *Barcelona Traction* case (which lasted 16 years):

> the unusual length of the present proceedings, which has been due to the very long time-limits requested by the Parties for the preparation of their written pleadings and in addition to their repeated requests for an extension of these limits. The Court did not find that it should refuse these requests and thus impose limitations on the Parties in the preparation and presentation of the arguments and evidence which they consider necessary. It nonetheless remains convinced of the fact that it is in the interest of the authority and proper functioning of international justice for cases to be decided without unwarranted delay.[33]

Cases which have given rise to proceedings lasting more than a decade are nonetheless exceptional, although they are necessarily the most spectacular, given the legal and political issues involved.[34]

---

[31] *Barcelona Traction, Light and Power Co, Ltd (New Application: 1962) (Belgium* v *Spain),* Judgment, ICJ Reports 1964, 25.

[32] *Military and Paramilitary Activities in and against Nicaragua (Nicaragua* v *United States),* Merits, Judgment, ICJ Reports 1986, 40, para 59.

[33] ICJ Reports 1970, 30–31, para 27. Instituted initially by Belgium in 1954, before being discontinued and removed from the General List in 1961, this case was the subject of a fresh application in 1962, giving rise to the Judgment on Preliminary Objections in 1964, and a Judgment in 1970 in which the Court rejected the claim on the basis of the preliminary objections which had been joined to the merits.

[34] *Maritime Delimitation and Territorial Questions between Qatar and Bahrain (Qatar* v *Bahrain)* [ten years, 1991–2001]; *Application of the Convention on the Prevention and Punishment of the Crime of Genocide (Bosnia and*

Be that as it may, since the beginning of the 1990s, the Court has found its list becoming increasingly congested. This is due not only to an increase in the number of cases submitted to the Court following renewed interest in the judicial settlement of international disputes; it is also the result of the proliferation of incidental proceedings and the increasingly complex nature of certain cases with an important factual dimension and consequently longer time limits for written pleadings and the filing of voluminous pleadings accompanied by many technical annexes requiring particularly careful consideration (not to mention the additional translation work involved). The average length of time required to deal with a case has thus increased from two and a half years to almost four years. The Court has accordingly taken steps to address this situation, by seeking to improve its procedures at each successive stage of every case. In this connection, it has adopted various measures and 'practice directions', intended for both judges and parties.

The main measures taken with the parties in mind have been aimed at reducing the duration of the written and oral pleadings and, as a corollary, the time between the close of the written proceedings and the opening of the hearings. The Court has thus requested greater cooperation from the parties during the compilation of case files, inviting the latter to reduce the number of pleadings exchanged, to append to their pleadings only strictly selected documents and to provide the Court with any translations of those pleadings available to them – even partial translations – in either of the Court's official languages. The Court has also insisted on the succinctness required of the oral hearings. With the aim of accelerating the handling of preliminary objections to jurisdiction or admissibility made by one party, it has also decided that the time limit for the presentation by the other party of its written observations should generally not exceed four months. At the same time the Court has also amended Articles 79 and 80 of the Rules of Court with the aim of clarifying the implementing conditions and reducing the length of certain incidental proceedings, taking due account of practice.[35] All these efforts have helped to expedite the handling of cases submitted to the Court, in

---

Herzegovina v *Serbia and Montenegro)* [14 years, 1993–2007]; *Land and Maritime Boundary between Cameroon and Nigeria (Cameroon* v *Nigeria: Equatorial Guinea intervening)* [eight years, 1994–2002]; *Application of the Convention on the Prevention and Punishment of the Crime of Genocide (Croatia* v *Serbia)* [15 years, 1999– 2015].

[35] In particular it was decided that the presentation of preliminary objections should be made no later than three months after the filing of the memorial, rather than within the time limit fixed for the filing of the counter-memorial.

particular when it has been fortunate enough to receive support from the States concerned.

The principal measures adopted with the Court in mind have consisted in restricting in principle the drafting of notes by judges to the merits phases of cases (since 1998) and encouraging judges to consider several cases simultaneously.

On this issue, with regard to working methods, the Court, unlike most other international courts, scrupulously observes a bilingual approach to its work. The proclamation in its Statute of French and English as the official languages of the Court (Art 39, para 1) is thus a practical reality and of primary importance in the daily work of the Court which entails additional time and considerable resources. There is thus room for debate as to appropriateness of a bilingual approach, in light of the need to save time and resources in particular, which are legitimate considerations from the perspective of the sound administration of justice. However, it is important always to bear in mind the specific characteristics of international law and of the community of States to which it is applied and to the particular circumstances in which international justice has to be done. Moreover, the Court cannot remain the true 'organ of international law' unless a necessary balance is maintained within it between different legal cultures of which languages are ultimately merely the vehicle. It is from this point of view that, in the work of the Court, a constant interplay between French and English is a significant asset in terms of the proper application of international law and the settlement of international disputes, as well as of the quality of decision.

While safeguarding the principles underlying its jurisdictional mission, as established by its Statute, the Court thus continues on a regular basis to consider possible improvements to its judicial practice.

For example, the Court, taking into account the growth of international organizations, amended its Rules in 2005 in order to widen access to contentious proceedings to such organizations.[36] Thus whenever the construction of a convention to which a public international organization is a party may be in question in a case before the Court, the Court shall

[36] The first para of Art 34 of the Statute forbids international organizations from appearing before the Court as either applicant or respondent; the second and third paras provide for cooperation between those organizations and the Court in contentious proceedings (which was not the case with the PCIJ). Those organizations may thus, on their own initiative or at the request of the parties or the Court, be called upon to provide the Court with all relevant information in a case.

consider whether the Registrar shall so notify the public international organization concerned. This procedure, which is based on the procedure permitting the intervention of States parties to the convention whose construction is at issue in a dispute (Art 63 of the Statute), was introduced into the Rules of Court by an amendment to Article 43 of the Rules which entered into force in 2005.

2. Advisory proceedings

The requirements of the sound administration of justice, and more broadly of the rule of law, also apply to advisory proceedings before the Court. The Court has thus had to deal with the question of the treatment to be accorded to individuals, who in principle do not have access to the Court, in the framework of requests for advisory opinion in respect of the validity of the judgments of international administrative tribunals. This very special remedy was incorporated in the Statute of the ILO Administrative Tribunal (and, until its repeal in 1995, in the Statute of the United Nations Administrative Tribunal), to make it possible, in certain cases in which the validity of a judgment is challenged, for an advisory opinion to be requested from the Court and for the Court's opinion to be binding.

In the most recent advisory opinion, dated 1 February 2012, given under what is known as a 'review' procedure, the Court followed the practice established during earlier similar requests by providing an opportunity to the official directly concerned by the request (ie party to the judgment of ILOAT whose validity was challenged by the International Fund for Agricultural Development) to state her views under the same conditions as the international organization which had originally requested the advisory opinion. The Court nevertheless expressed its concern about the review procedure and, in particular, 'about the inequality of access to the Court arising from the review process under Article XII of the Annex to the Statute of the ILOAT',[37] since it is only the employing agencies which are able to initiate advisory proceedings. At that time the Court made 'one general observation about the development of the concept of equality before courts and tribunals …'[38] considering that '[t]hat principle must now be understood as including access on an equal basis to available appellate or similar remedies unless an exception

---

[37] *Judgment No 2867 of the Administrative Tribunal of the International Labour Organization upon a Complaint Filed against the International Fund for Agricultural Development,* Advisory Opinion, ICJ Reports 2012, 31, para 48.

[38] Ibid., 26, para 38.

can be justified on objective and reasonable grounds'.[39] The Court noted in particular:

> the significant differences between the two General Comments by the Human Rights Committee on Article 14, paragraph 1, of the International Covenant on Civil and Political Rights of 1966. That provision requires that '[a]ll persons shall be equal before the courts and tribunals'. The first Comment, adopted in 1984, just seven years after the Covenant came into force, did no more than repeat the terms of the provision and call on States to report more fully on steps taken to ensure equality before the courts, including equal access to the courts (*Human Rights Committee, General Comment No. 13: Article 14 (Administration of Justice)*, paras 2–3). The later Comment, one adopted in 2007 on the basis of 30 years of experience in the application of the above-mentioned Article 14, gives detailed attention to equality before domestic courts and tribunals. According to the Committee, that right to equality guarantees equal access and equality of arms. While in non-criminal matters the right of equal access does not address the issue of the right of appeal, if procedural rights are accorded they must be provided to all the parties unless distinctions can be justified on objective and reasonable grounds (*Human Rights Committee, General Comment No. 32: Right to equality before courts and tribunals and to a fair trial*, paras 8, 9, 12 and 13). In the case of the ILOAT, the Court is unable to see any such justification for the provision for review of the Tribunal's decisions which favours the employer to the disadvantage of the staff member.[40]

On this question, and aside from the concerns expressed about the fairness of the review procedure, advisory opinions thus apply the rules relating to the administration of justice – which are in principle required for the internal administration of justice by States – to international proceedings involving the Court itself.

II. THE ICJ AS THE 'ORGAN' OF INTERNATIONAL LAW: THE CONTRIBUTION OF THE ICJ'S JURISPRUDENCE TO THE STRENGTHENING OF THE RULE OF LAW AT INTERNATIONAL LEVEL

In its first case decided on the merits (the *Corfu Channel* case), the Court referred to itself as 'the organ' of international law.[41] As such, and given the key institutional and procedural features which have just been

---

[39] Ibid., 29, para 44.
[40] Ibid., 27, para 39.
[41] ICJ Reports 1949, 35. See also PCIJ Series A, No 7, 19 (1926).

recalled, the ICJ's contribution to the promotion and clarification of international law is indeed of paramount importance. The Declaration of the High-level Meeting of the General Assembly on the Rule of Law at the National and International Levels, adopted in September 2012, emphasized 'the positive contribution of the International Court of Justice, the principal judicial organ of the United Nations, including in adjudicating disputes among States, and the value of its work for the promotion of the rule of law' (§ 31).

First, the scope of the Court's contribution is related to its jurisdiction *ratione materiae* and, therefore, to the authority of its jurisprudence in all matters of general international law (A).

Secondly, the Court's role in the promotion of the rule of law, and its contribution thereto, may be viewed in the context of what has been called the 'proliferation' of international judicial bodies in recent decades. Some of the Court's recent cases and decisions may be of interest here, since the ICJ has increasingly been called upon to address issues and questions also dealt with by regional and/or specialized international courts and tribunals (B).

A. The Contribution of the Court's Jurisprudence to the Clarification of Principles of General International Law

As a court of justice, the ICJ cannot legislate. To do so would be contrary to the very essence of the rule of law, according to which adjudicating and law-making functions are to be kept separate in any legal order. The Court's decision in a case has 'no binding force except between the parties and in respect of that particular case' (Art 59 of the Statute). However, the Court, 'whose mission is to decide in accordance with international law such disputes as are submitted to it', does apply the various sources of international law including international conventions, whether general or particular, international custom and the general principles of law recognized by civilized nations (Art 38, para 1, of the Statute). In this way, its jurisprudence indisputably contributes to the establishment of a body of 'precedents' regarding questions of general international law, the authority and significance of which extend far beyond the parties to a particular dispute. The Court's jurisprudence is, therefore, of considerable importance to the promotion of the rule of law at international level, especially in the absence of any 'world legislature' capable of enacting laws equally applicable to all States.

This is generally well known, and therefore only a few words need to be said on the interaction between the Court's jurisprudence and the work of the International Law Commission 'in advancing the rule of law at the international level'[42] through the clarification and progressive development of some basic principles of the international legal order. A few examples may be given from cases involving the law of treaties, the law of international responsibility and the law of State immunity.

As regards the law of treaties, the Court had occasion to rule on the customary nature of the provisions of the Vienna Convention on the Law of Treaties at a time when that instrument, still in the ILC draft, had not yet entered into force. The Court also discussed the conditions for the suspension and termination of a treaty and the effects of reservations and objections by States parties, as well as developing rules and methods for the interpretation of treaties.

Thus in the *Fisheries Jurisdiction* cases the Court stated the following:

> This principle [that a change of circumstances can lead to the termination of a treaty], and the conditions and exceptions to which it is subject, have been embodied in Article 62 of the Vienna Convention on the Law of Treaties, which may in many respects be considered as a codification of existing customary law on the subject of the termination of a treaty relationship on account of change of circumstances.[43]

In the *Gabčíkovo-Nagymaros* case, it examined in detail the conditions for the suspension and termination of a treaty under customary law as codified in the Vienna Convention.[44]

The Court has, moreover, not hesitated to defend a dynamic approach in the interpretation of international instruments. In the case concerning *Reservations to the Convention on the Prevention and Punishment of the Crime of Genocide*, the Court, after referring to traditional conceptions as regards the validity of reservations to multilateral conventions, noted the appearance of new tendencies which represented 'manifestations of a new need for flexibility in the operation of multilateral conventions';[45] the Court thus considered that it was the compatibility of the reservation

---

[42] See the Declaration of the High-level Meeting, para 33: 'We commend the work of the International Law Commission in advancing the rule of law at the international level through the progressive development of international law and its codification.'

[43] *Fisheries Jurisdiction (Federal Republic of Germany* v *Iceland),* Jurisdiction of the Court, Judgment, ICJ Reports 1973, 63, para 36; ibid. *(United Kingdom* v *Iceland*), Jurisdiction of the Court, Judgment, ICJ Reports 1973, 18, para 36.

[44] *Gabčíkovo-Nagymaros Project (Hungary/Slovakia),* Judgment, ICJ Reports 1997, 7.

[45] *Reservations to the Convention on the Prevention and Punishment of the Crime of Genocide,* Advisory Opinion, ICJ Reports 1951, 22.

with the object and purpose of the convention which must furnish the criterion of the attitude of the State making the reservation and of the State objecting thereto.[46] Subsequently, the Court would point out that 'an international instrument has to be interpreted and applied within the framework of the entire legal system prevailing at the time of the interpretation'.[47]

Finally, the Court was able to provide some clarification on the relationship between the law of treaties and State responsibility:

> [T]hose two branches of international law obviously have a scope that is distinct. A determination of whether a convention is or is not in force, and whether it has or has not been properly suspended or denounced, is to be made pursuant to the law of treaties. On the other hand, an evaluation of the extent to which a suspension or denunciation of a convention, seen as incompatible with the law of treaties, involves the responsibility of the State which proceeded to it, is to be made under the law of State responsibility.[48]

Turning to the law of international responsibility, it may be recalled that every legal order presupposes that a subject of that order engages its responsibility when it breaches one of its rules. Within the international community, that principle becomes of particular relevance in the case of States which, in the exercise of their sovereignty, are free to determine their actions. International responsibility then becomes the principal mechanism for regulating relations between States with the aim of reconciling the divergent interests of equal and sovereign entities. However, the law of international responsibility is essentially founded on customary rules; as a result, certain aspects of it are still somewhat controversial and confused. The ILC Articles on State Responsibility for

---

46 As regards the effects of the reservation in relations between States, the Court considered that a State could not be bound by a reservation to which it had not consented. Every State was therefore free to decide for itself whether the State which formulated the reservation was or was not a party to the Convention. While the Court adjudicated only on the specific case referred to it, namely the Genocide Convention, its Advisory Opinion contributed to the further codification of the matter in the Vienna Convention on the Law of Treaties (1969), Art 19 ff.

47 *Legal Consequences for States of the Continued Presence of South Africa in Namibia (South West Africa) notwithstanding Security Council Resolution 276 (1970),* Advisory Opinion, ICJ Reports 1971, 31, para 53.

48 *Gabčíkovo-Nagymaros Project (Hungary/Slovakia)*, above n44 at 38, para 47.

Wrongful Acts,[49] adopted in 2001, can help to clarify these aspects of the law of international responsibility. However, in so far as they develop customary law, that is, go beyond restating the *lex ferenda*, those Articles lack normative character. That is why the judicial activity of the ICJ remains of capital importance in determining what the prevailing law is at any given moment, clarifying its scope and, by the manner in which it applies it, enabling it to develop.

In the case concerning the *Gabčikovo-Nagymaros Project*,[50] the Court addressed for the first time the question whether countermeasures and the state of necessity may constitute circumstances precluding wrongfulness of acts committed by both parties to the dispute. Referring, inter alia, to the ILC Articles, the Court unequivocally stated that a countermeasure 'taken in response to a previous international wrongful act of another State and … directed against that State' could legitimate an act which otherwise would have been unlawful, although, in the particular case, the measures taken by Slovakia failed to respect the proportionality required.[51] The Court also recognized that the existence of a state of necessity may preclude the wrongfulness of an act but did ultimately consider that Hungary could not rely on this principle in order to justify the termination of a treaty.

Article 26 of the ILC's Articles set a general limit to the invocation of circumstances precluding wrongfulness. According to this Article, 'nothing in [the draft articles] precludes the wrongfulness of any act of a State which is not in conformity with an obligation arising under a peremptory norm of general international law'. In other words, a State is not allowed to breach a peremptory norm of international law in taking countermeasures against another State. The most telling example of the principle given by the ILC was that genocide would never allow a counter-genocide. The Court took the same view in the case concerning the *Application of the Convention on Prevention and Punishment of the Crime of Genocide*, by stating that 'in no case could one breach of the Convention serve as an excuse for another'.[52]

The case concerning *Questions relating to the Obligation to Prosecute or Extradite (Belgium* v *Senegal)*, decided by the Court in 2012, reflects

---

49 Draft Articles on the Responsibility of States for Internationally Wrongful Acts, 53 UN GAOR Supp (No 10) at 43, UN Doc A/56/10 (2001). See J Crawford, *The International Law Commission's Articles on State Responsibility* (Cambridge University Press, Cambridge, 2002).

50 *Gabčikovo-Nagymaros Project (Hongary/Slovakia)* above n44.

51 Ibid., 55, para 83.

52 ICJ Reports 1997, 258, para 35.

a recent development in the Court's jurisprudence regarding some of the fundamental aspects of the law of international responsibility. This case, which was brought before the Court by Belgium, concerned 'Senegal's compliance with its obligation to prosecute Mr. H[issène] Habré[, former President of the Republic of Chad, for acts including alleged crimes of torture and crimes against humanity,] or to extradite him to Belgium for the purposes of criminal proceedings'.[53] In its application, Belgium based its claims on the UN Convention against Torture and Other Cruel, Inhuman or Degrading Treatment or Punishment of 10 December 1984 (hereinafter 'the Convention against Torture' or the 'Convention'), as well as on customary international law.

The Court noted the divergence of views between the parties concerning the standing of Belgium, which based its claims not only on its status as a party to the Convention against Torture, but also on the existence of a special interest that would distinguish Belgium from the other parties to the Convention and give it a specific entitlement in the case of Mr Habré, namely the proceedings brought before the Belgian courts by Belgian nationals and the issuance of an arrest warrant directed against Mr Habré.

Relying on the object and purpose of the Convention, which is 'to make more effective the struggle against torture ... throughout the world', the Court found that the States parties to the Convention have a common interest to ensure, in view of their shared values, that acts of torture are prevented and that, if they occur, their authors do not enjoy impunity, regardless of the nationality of the offender or the victims, or of the place where the alleged offences occurred. The Court considered that all the other States parties have a common interest in compliance with these obligations by the State in whose territory the alleged offender

---

[53] After taking power on 7 June 1982 at the head of a rebellion, Mr Hissène Habré was President of the Republic of Chad for eight years, during which time large-scale violations of human rights were allegedly committed, including arrests of actual or presumed political opponents, detentions without trial or under inhumane conditions, mistreatment, torture, extrajudicial executions and enforced disappearances. Overthrown on 1 December 1990, Mr Habré requested political asylum from the Senegalese Government, a request which was granted; he has been living in Dakar ever since. From 25 January 2000 onwards, a number of proceedings relating to crimes alleged to have been committed during Mr Habré's presidency were instituted before both Senegalese and Belgian courts. On 19 September 2005, the Belgian investigating judge issued an international warrant *in absentia* for the arrest of Mr Habré, indicted as the perpetrator or co-perpetrator, inter alia, of serious violations of international humanitarian law, torture, genocide, crimes against humanity and war crimes, on the basis of which Belgium requested the extradition of Mr Habré from Senegal.

is present, that common interest implying that the obligations in question are owed by any State party to all the other States parties to the Convention. It follows that all the States parties 'have a legal interest' in the protection of the rights involved[54] and that these obligations may be defined as 'obligations *erga omnes partes*' in the sense that each State party has an interest in compliance with them in any given case.

The Court concluded that Belgium, as a State party to the Convention against Torture, had standing to invoke the responsibility of Senegal for the alleged breaches of its obligations under the Convention against Torture. This case, while limited to obligations *erga omnes partes*, ie obligations assumed by States under a specific international convention, may be seen as an (implicit) recognition of the rule expressed in Article 48, paragraph 1, *lit* a), of the Articles of the ILC on *Responsibility of States for International Wrongful Acts*.[55] However, as the Court had only jurisdiction, in this case, with regard to the dispute concerning the interpretation and application of the Torture Convention, it did not address the issue further, in the framework of customary international law.[56]

On the merits, the Court found that Senegal, by failing to submit the case of Mr Hissène Habré to its competent authorities for the purpose of prosecution, had breached its obligations under the UN Convention against Torture and that Senegal must, without further delay, submit the case of Mr Hissène Habré to its competent authorities for the purpose of prosecution, if it did not extradite him. Senegal actually complied with the judgment of the Court by instituting within its judicial system a special court, which was inaugurated on 8 February 2013, designed to prosecute Hissène Habré for crimes committed in Chad between 1982 and 1990.

The *law of immunity* is another area in which the Court's jurisprudence has contributed to the strengthening of adherence to the rule of law (at

---

54 *Barcelona Traction, Light and Power Co Ltd*, Judgment, ICJ Reports 1970, 32, para 33.

55 ILC Reports, 2001, 126: 'Any State other than the injured State is entitled to invoke the responsibility of another State … if the obligation breached is owed to a group of States including that State, and is established for the protection of a collective interest of the group.'

56 The Court concluded, from the diplomatic exchanges submitted to it, that at the time of the filing of the application, the dispute between the parties did not relate to breaches of obligations under customary international law and that it thus had no jurisdiction to decide on Belgium's claims related thereto (ICJ Reports 2012, 445, para 55).

both national and international level). The Court has dealt with various aspects of this field, as part of both advisory and contentious proceedings, including the law governing diplomatic and consular relations[57] and the immunities of high officials of the State[58] and of experts of international organizations.[59]

The case concerning *Jurisdictional Immunities of the State (Germany* v *Italy: Greece intervening)*, which was decided by the Court on 3 February 2012, raised many issues relating not only to State immunity as such but also to other general questions of international law.[60]

By its first submission, Germany requested the Court, in substance, to find that Italy had failed to respect the jurisdictional immunity which Germany enjoys under international law by allowing civil claims to be brought against it in the Italian courts seeking reparation for injuries caused by violations of international humanitarian law committed by the German Reich during the Second World War.

In that context, the Court noted that there was a considerable measure of agreement between the parties regarding the fact that immunity is governed by international law and is not a mere matter of comity. It stated that, as between the parties, the entitlement to immunity could be derived only from customary international law. Therefore, the Court had to determine, in accordance with Article 38(1)(b) of its Statute, whether 'international custom, as evidence of a general practice accepted as law' conferring immunity on States exists and, if so, what is the scope and extent of that immunity. The Court noted that, although there has been much debate regarding the origins of State immunity and the identification of the principles underlying that immunity in the past, the

---

57 See: *United States Diplomatic and Consular Staff in Tehran (United States of America* v *Iran)*, Judgment, ICJ Reports 1980, 3; *LaGrand (Germany* v *United States of America)*, Judgment, ICJ Reports 2001, 466; *Avena and Other Mexican Nationals (Mexico* v *United States of America)*, Judgment, ICJ Reports 2004, 12; *Armed Activities on the Territory of the Congo (Democratic Republic of the Congo* v *Uganda)*, Judgment, ICJ Reports 2005, 168.

58 See: *Arrest Warrant of 11 April 2000 (Democratic Republic of the Congo* v *Belgium)*, Judgment, ICJ Reports 2002, 3; *Certain Questions of Mutual Assistance in Criminal Matters (Djibouti* v *France)*, Judgment, ICJ Reports 2008, 177.

59 *Applicability of Article VI, Section 22, of the Convention on the Privileges and Immunities of the United Nations*, Advisory Opinion, ICJ Reports 1989, 177; *Difference Relating to Immunity from Legal Process of a Special Rapporteur of the Commission on Human Rights*, Advisory Opinion, ICJ Reports 1999, 62.

60 *Jurisdictional Immunities of the State (Germany* v *Italy: Greece intervening)*, ICJ Reports 2012, 99.

International Law Commission concluded in 1980 that the rule of State immunity had been 'adopted as a general rule of customary international law solidly rooted in the current practice of States'. In the opinion of the Court, that conclusion was based upon an extensive survey of State practice and is confirmed by the record of national legislation, judicial decisions and the comments of States on what became the United Nations Convention on the Jurisdictional Immunities of States and their Property (2004).

The parties differed as to the scope and extent of the rule of State immunity. Although both agreed that States are generally entitled to immunity in respect of *acta jure imperii*, they disagreed as to whether immunity is applicable to acts committed by the armed forces of a State in the course of conducting an armed conflict. Germany maintained that immunity is applicable and that there is no relevant limitation on the immunity to which a State is entitled in respect of *acta jure imperii*. Italy, for its part, maintained that Germany was not entitled to immunity in respect of the cases before the Italian courts for two reasons: first, that immunity as to *acta jure imperii* does not extend to torts or delicts occasioning death, personal injury or damage to property committed on the territory of the forum State, and, secondly, that, irrespective of where the relevant acts took place, Germany was not entitled to immunity because those acts involved the most serious violations of rules of international law of a peremptory character for which no alternative means of redress was available. The Court addressed each of Italy's arguments in turn.

Regarding the first argument, the Court concluded that customary international law continues to require that a State be accorded immunity in proceedings for torts allegedly committed on the territory of another State by its armed forces and other organs of State in the course of conducting an armed conflict. In order to reach this conclusion, the Court examined carefully the relevant international conventions (namely the European Convention on State Immunity of 1972 and the UN Convention of 2004), State practice in the form of national legislation as well as in the form of the judgments of national courts regarding State immunity in relation to the acts of armed forces. The Court noted that that practice was accompanied by *opinio juris*, as demonstrated by the positions taken by States and the jurisprudence of a number of national courts which have made clear that they considered that customary international law required immunity. It found that the almost complete absence of contrary jurisprudence was also significant, as was the absence of any statements by States in connection with the work of the ILC regarding State immunity and the adoption of the United Nations Convention or, so far as the Court has been able to discover, in any other context asserting that customary international law does not require immunity in such cases.

Regarding the second argument, the Court was called to inquire whether customary international law had developed to the point where a State is not entitled to immunity in the case of serious violations of human rights law or the law of armed conflict. After examining State and international practice, the Court concluded that, under customary international law as it presently stands, a State is not deprived of immunity by reason of the fact that it is accused of serious violations of international human rights law or the international law of armed conflict.[61] Turning to the second strand in Italy's argument, which emphasized the *jus cogens* status of the rules which were violated by Germany during the period 1943–45, the Court came to the opinion there is no conflict between a rule, or rules, of *jus cogens* and the rule of customary law which requires one State to accord immunity to another. Assuming for this purpose that the rules of the law of armed conflict which were violated by Germany are rules of *jus cogens*, the Court took the view that there was no conflict between those rules and the rules on State immunity. The two sets of rules address different matters. The rules of State immunity are procedural in character and are confined to determining whether or not the courts of one State may exercise jurisdiction in respect of another State. They do not bear upon the question whether or not the conduct in respect of which the proceedings are brought was lawful or unlawful. The Court added that the argument about the effect of *jus cogens* displacing the law of State immunity had been rejected by the national courts. It stated that the judgments of the Italian courts which were the subject of the proceedings were the only decisions of national courts to have accepted the reasoning on which Italy's argument was based. It observed, moreover, that none of the national legislation on State immunity has limited immunity in cases where violations of *jus cogens* are alleged.

Thus, the Court's decision placed particular emphasis upon the rationale of the rules on State immunity, and their importance in the international legal order. Indeed, the Court stated that:

> the rule of State immunity occupies an important place in international law and international relations. It derives from the principle of sovereign equality

---

[61] In reaching that conclusion, the Court emphasized that it was addressing only the immunity of the State itself from the jurisdiction of the courts of other States; the question of whether, and if so to what extent, immunity might apply in criminal proceedings against an official of the State was not at issue in the present case.

> of States, which, as Article 2, paragraph 1, of the Charter of the United Nations makes clear, is one of the fundamental principles of the international legal order. This principle has to be viewed together with the principle that each State possesses sovereignty over its own territory and that there flows from that sovereignty the jurisdiction of the State over events and persons within that territory. Exceptions to the immunity of the State represent a departure from the principle of sovereign equality. Immunity may represent a departure from the principle of territorial sovereignty and the jurisdiction which flows from it.[62]

The law on State immunity is undoubtedly of paramount importance to the strengthening of the rule of law both at national and international level. It requires, however, the reconciliation of two principles of equal importance, namely the sovereign equality of States and the effective enforcement of the rules of any given legal order. The case between Germany and Italy illustrates how, in matters such as these, the Court has the difficult task of identifying rules of general customary international law through a careful examination of State practice and *opinio juris*. Indeed, the Court has 'to ensure the unity of international law by taking account of all of its constituent elements'.[63] This task is all the more difficult when the rules – such as those relating to State immunity – are evolving, usually on account of decisions by domestic courts, which may be regarded both as a violation of the established rules and as a precedent for a nascent norm.[64]

The unique way in which proceedings are brought before the ICJ, the Court's universality and its procedures and methods of working appear to be of particular importance in enabling it to contribute to the clarification and development of general international law and, thereby, to the rule of law at international level.

Another aspect of the Court's contribution to the 'rule of law', closely related to the previous one, is the specific role played by the Court in maintaining the coherence and consistency of general international law, in particular with regard to the growing number of international judicial or quasi-judicial bodies.

---

62 *Jurisdictional Immunities of the State (Germany* v *Italy: Greece intervening)*, ICJ Reports 2012, 123–4, para 57.

63 Separate opinion of Judge Bennouna, ICJ Reports 2012, 176–7, para 28 (critical, in this respect, of the reasoning and conclusion of the Court).

64 See the dissenting opinion of Judge Yusuf, ICJ Reports 2012, 304, para 43.

B. The Court's Contribution to the Unity of Interpretation of International Law

A question which has often been discussed, especially in recent years, is whether there is a risk of international law becoming 'fragmented' because of the possible divergent approaches of international courts and tribunals towards the same legal issues and, therefore, a lack of consistency in the application of the law, contrary to the very idea of an international legal order based on the rule of law. While many fears expressed in this respect may have been overamplified and some of them, in retrospect, have proven unfounded, the fact remains, however, that such fears may have prompted international judges to direct their attention to the work of other international courts and tribunals and to embrace the so-called '*dialogue des juges*', thereby diminishing the risks of conflicting jurisprudence.

Be that as it may, and given the 'proliferation' of courts and tribunals whose jurisdiction is restricted to a particular branch of international law or to a specific geographical area, the ICJ's general and universal jurisdiction places it in a unique position, allowing it to play a role in the unifying or streamlining of the interpretation and application of certain rules of international law.

I have chosen to take two examples from the ICJ's recent case law, which relate to the law of the sea and international human rights law.[65]

1. The law of the sea

The law of the sea is a well-known area of law in which fears of 'fragmentation', owing to the multiple courts and tribunals involved in the settlement of disputes relating to the law of the sea, have proved to be exaggerated; it is also an area of law in which the Court's jurisprudence has made a particular contribution to the clarification and development of rules.

---

[65] It is also possible to add here the issue of attributing the conduct of individuals to the State, in the context of the law of State responsibility, in light of the Court's judgment in the *Genocide* case (2007) and the previous 'divergent' approaches of the International Criminal Tribunal for the former Yugoslavia in the *Tadic* case and of the ICJ itself in the *Nicaragua* case. The Court's case law could also be of relative interest with respect to certain general principles of international environmental law; see *Pulp Mills on the River Uruguay (Argentina* v *Uruguay)*, Judgment, ICJ Reports 2010, 14; *Gabčíkovo-Nagymaros Project (Hungary/Slovakia),* Judgment, ICJ Reports 1997, 7; *Legality of the Threat or Use of Nuclear Weapons,* Advisory Opinion, ICJ Reports 1996, 226.

It should be recalled that the ICJ has been involved with the application of the law of the sea from the time of its creation, a total of approximately 30 cases on the Court's list having touched upon such issues.[66] Some of the early cases decided by the Court paved the way for the consolidation of certain rules of customary international law and for their codification in the UN Convention on the Law of the Sea (LOS) adopted in 1982. Conversely, developments at the United Nations Conference on the LOS (which lasted for almost ten years), reflecting the evolution of State practice, have influenced the law applied by the Court, in particular in the field of maritime delimitation.

In this general context, however, two concerns have been expressed regarding, first, the relative unpredictability of the application of the general equitable principles relating to the delimitation of maritime areas such as the continental shelf and the Exclusive Economic Zone (EEZ) and, second, the risk of inconsistency between competing lines of jurisprudence from various international courts and tribunals.[67]

The Court's jurisprudence, which has played a central role in the development of the law governing maritime delimitation, has displaced most of these concerns. The unanimous decision in the *Maritime Delimitation in the Black Sea* case, in 2009, has highlighted the delimitation methodology applied by the Court.[68] In short, drawing on its previous case law, the Court indicated that three defined steps must be contemplated when it is called upon to delimit the continental shelf or EEZ, or when it must determine a single maritime boundary.

As the Court explained in its judgment concerning the *Maritime Delimitation in the Black Sea*, these separate stages, broadly explained in the case concerning the *Continental Shelf (Libyan Arab Jamahiriya/ Malta)*,[69] have in recent decades been specified with precision. First, the

---

66 Address to the United Nations Assembly at the Commemoration of the Thirtieth Anniversary of the Opening for Signature of the 1982 UNCLOS, by HE Judge Christopher Greenwood on behalf of the International Court of Justice, 10 December 2012, p 2. [http://www.icj-cij.org/presscom/files/8/17228.pdf].

67 It may need recalling here that UNCLOS provides for different methods of compulsory dispute settlement (Art 287), States parties to UNCLOS being free to choose between the ICJ, the LOS Tribunal established in Hamburg or arbitral tribunals constituted in accordance with the Convention. Even before the adoption of UNCLOS, law of the sea disputes could give rise to differing interpretations between the ICJ and arbitral tribunals constituted by States on an ad hoc basis.

68 *Maritime Delimitation in the Black Sea (Romania* v *Ukraine),* Judgment, ICJ Reports 2009, 61.

69 ICJ Reports 1985, 46, para 60.

Court will establish a provisional delimitation line, using methods that are geometrically objective and also appropriate for the geography of the area in which the delimitation is to take place. So far as delimitation between adjacent coasts is concerned, an equidistance line will be drawn unless there are compelling reasons that make this unfeasible in the particular case.[70] So far as opposite coasts are concerned, the provisional delimitation line will consist of a median line between the two coasts. No legal consequences flow from the use of the terms 'median line' and 'equidistance line' since the method of delimitation is the same for both.

Equidistance and median lines are to be constructed from the most appropriate points on the coasts of the two States concerned, with particular attention being paid to those protuberant coastal points situated nearest to the area to the delimited. The Court considers elsewhere the extent to which the Court may, when constructing a single purpose delimitation line, deviate from the base points selected by the parties for their territorial seas. When construction of a provisional equidistance line between adjacent States is called for, the Court will have in mind considerations relating to both parties' coastlines when choosing its own base points for this purpose. The line thus adopted is heavily dependent on the physical geography and the most seaward points of the two coasts.

In keeping with its settled jurisprudence on maritime delimitation, the first stage of the Court's approach is to establish the provisional equidistance line. At this initial stage of the construction of the provisional equidistance line, the Court is not yet concerned with any relevant circumstances that may obtain and the line is plotted on strictly geometrical criteria on the basis of objective data.

The course of the final line should result in an equitable solution (Arts 74 and 83 of UNCLOS). Therefore, the Court will at the next, second stage consider whether there are factors calling for the adjustment or shifting of the provisional equidistance line in order to achieve an equitable result.[71] The Court has also made clear that when the line to be drawn covers several zones of coincident jurisdictions, 'the so-called equitable principles/relevant circumstances method may usefully be

---

[70] See *Territorial and Maritime Dispute between Nicaragua and Honduras in the Caribbean Sea (Nicaragua* v *Honduras)*, Judgment, ICJ Report 2007, 745, para 281.

[71] *Land and Maritime Boundary between Cameroon and Nigeria (Cameroon* v *Nigeria: Equatorial Guinea intervening),* Judgment, ICJ Reports 2002, 441, para 288.

applied, as in these maritime zones this method is also suited to achieving an equitable result'.[72]

This is the second part of the delimitation exercise to which the Court will turn, having first established the provisional equidistance line.

Finally, and at a third stage, the Court will verify that the line (a provisional equidistance line which may or may not have been adjusted by taking into account the relevant circumstances) does not, as it stands, lead to an inequitable result by reason of any marked disproportion between the ratio of the respective coastal lengths and the ratio between the relevant maritime area of each State by reference to the delimitation line. A final check for an equitable outcome entails a confirmation that no great disproportionality of maritime areas is evident by comparison to the ratio of coastal lengths.

This is not to suggest that these respective areas should be proportionate to coastal lengths – as the Court has said 'the sharing out of the area is therefore the consequence of the delimitation, not vice versa'.[73]

This methodology was used again recently in the *Territorial and Maritime Dispute (Nicaragua* v *Colombia),* decided on 19 November 2012.[74] Thus, the court has been able to build a predictable approach, which is an important element of legal security for States willing to submit their disputes to the Court, as well as a methodology which may guide other courts and tribunals:

> There is every indication that this three-step methodology now constitutes the usual approach to be espoused in appropriate cases of maritime delimitation. Its validity as a tried and true reflection of the current state of international law has recently been affirmed by ITLOS in its first ever maritime delimitation case. Thus, ITLOS endorsed the Court's three-step methodology in a case where it was called upon to determine a maritime boundary between Bangladesh and Myanmar in the Bay of Bengal.[75,76]

---

72 *Territorial and Maritime Dispute between Nicaragua and Honduras in the Caribbean Sea (Nicaragua* v *Honduras)*, ICJ Reports 2007, 741, para 271.

73 *Maritime Delimitation in the Area between Greenland and Jan Mayen (Denmark* v *Norway),* Judgment, ICJ Reports 1993, 67, para 64.

74 *Territorial and Maritime Dispute (Nicaragua* v *Colombia)*, ICJ Reports 2012, 624.

75 ITLOS, *Delimitation of the Maritime Boundary between Bangladesh and Myanmar in the Bay of Bengal (Bangladesh/Myanmar)*, Judgment of 14 March 2012, 74–6, paras 233–40. The Court's jurisprudence has also been applied by two Annex VII arbitral tribunals in recent cases.

76 Speech by HE Judge Peter Tomka to the Sixth Committee of the General Assembly, 2 November 2012 ('The contributions of the Court to the law

It should also be emphasized that the Court, in turn, draws on the case law of other international tribunals. For example, in its judgment in the case concerning the *Territorial and Maritime Dispute (Nicaragua* v *Colombia)*, the Court made extensive use of and reference to decisions of arbitral tribunals, as well as of the LOS Tribunal, indicating the agreement of the parties 'that the applicable law in [this] case [was] customary international law *reflected in the case law of [the ICJ], the International Tribunal for the Law of the Sea (ITLOS) and international arbitral courts and tribunals*'.[77]

2. International human rights law

While the Court's jurisdiction is limited to inter-State disputes,[78] throughout its history, it has been called upon to deal with issues touching upon international human rights or international humanitarian law. The ICJ's jurisprudence thus contains a range of pronouncements on a variety of aspects of these fields. As the Court has become less reluctant to refer to human rights, it has also become more willing to refer to other international courts and tribunals with exclusive jurisdiction over human rights issues.

In this connection, the recent case concerning *Ahmadou Sadio Diallo (Republic of Guinea* v *Democratic Republic of the Congo)*[79] gave the ICJ the opportunity to address directly a number of issues related to the protection of human rights and, more broadly, to the strengthening of the rule of law.

This case was brought before the Court by the Republic of Guinea against the Democratic Republic of Congo. Guinea claimed that the detention and expulsion of Ahmadou Sadio Diallo, a Guinean national, was in violation of international law. This claim led the Court, first, to consider the proven facts in the case and, second, to examine these facts in the light of the applicable international law.

---

governing maritime delimitation'), p 11. [http://www.icj-cij.org/presscom/files/6/17156.pdf].

77 Ibid., 666, para 114. See also 690–91, paras 178 (entitlement to a territorial sea of 12 nautical miles around an island) and 240 (the 'disproportionality test').

78 And distinct, in this respect, from international criminal courts, whose jurisdiction covers the behaviour of individuals constituting crimes under international law (war crimes, crimes against humanity, genocide).

79 *Ahmadou Sadio Diallo (Republic of Guinea* v *Democratic Republic of the Congo)*, Preliminary Objections, Judgment, ICJ Reports 2010, 639; ibid., Merits, Judgment, ICJ Reports 2010, 639; ibid. *(Compensation owed by the Democratic Republic of the Congo to the Republic of Guinea)*, ICJ Reports 2012, 324.

I will not address the issue of facts raised in this case, except to highlight a particular statement of the Court on the question of the burden of proof, which was made in its judgment on the merits of 30 November 2010.[80] The Court recalled that, as a general rule, it is for the party which alleges a fact in support of its claims to prove the existence of that fact. It pointed out, however, that it would be wrong to regard this rule, based on the maxim *onus probandi incumbit actori*, as an absolute one, to be applied in all circumstances. The determination of the burden of proof is in reality dependent on the subject matter and the nature of each dispute brought before the Court; it varies according to the type of facts which it is necessary to establish for the purposes of the decision of the case.

The Court went on to state that in particular, where, as in these proceedings, it is alleged that a person has not been afforded, by a public authority, certain procedural guarantees to which he was entitled, it cannot as a general rule be demanded of the applicant that it prove the negative fact which it is asserting. A public authority is generally able to demonstrate that it has followed the appropriate procedures and applied the guarantees required by law – if such was the case – by producing documentary evidence of the actions that were carried out. However, it cannot be inferred in every case where the respondent is unable to prove the performance of a procedural obligation that it has disregarded it: that depends to a large extent on the precise nature of the obligation in question; some obligations normally imply that written documents are drawn up while others do not.

Due consideration was therefore given by the Court to the nature of the obligations involved in this case, independently of its formal status as an inter-State dispute. The Court's pronouncement on the general issue of the burden of proof may be seen as reminiscent of the techniques used by specialized/regional judicial bodies when dealing with claims raised directly by individuals against States.

Turning to the law applicable to the dispute, Guinea's claim concerning the arrest, detention and expulsion measures taken against Mr Diallo was based, inter alia, on several provisions of both a regional and an international human rights instrument, to which both States were parties, namely the International Covenant on Civil and Political Rights of 16 December 1966 and the African Charter on Human and Peoples' Rights of 27 June 1981. The Court found, in its judgment, that the circumstances in which Mr Diallo was expelled from Congolese territory,

---

80 ICJ Reports 2010, 660–1, para 55.

as well as the circumstances in which he was arrested and detained, constituted violations of these two instruments entailing the international responsibility of the DRC towards the Republic of Guinea.

The Court made several interesting remarks with respect to the interpretation and application of the rules governing the expulsion by a State of foreigners from its territory.

The Court found that it follows from the two relevant provisions of the Covenant and of the African Charter that the expulsion of an alien lawfully in the territory of a State which is a party to these instruments can only be compatible with the international obligations of that State if it is decided in accordance with 'the law', in other words the domestic law applicable in that respect. Compliance with international law is to some extent dependent here on compliance with internal law. However, it is clear that while 'accordance with law' as thus defined is a necessary condition for compliance with the above-mentioned provisions, it is not a sufficient condition. First, the applicable domestic law must itself be compatible with the other requirements of the Covenant and the African Charter; second, an expulsion must not be arbitrary in nature, since protection against arbitrary treatment lies at the heart of the rights guaranteed by the international norms protecting human rights, in particular those set out in the two treaties applicable in this case.

At this juncture, the Court made reference to 'the jurisprudence of the Human Rights Committee established by the Covenant to ensure compliance with that instrument by the States parties', and stated that:

> [a]lthough it is in no way obliged, in the exercise of its judicial functions, to model its own interpretation of the Covenant on that of the Committee, it believes that it should ascribe great weight to the interpretation adopted by this independent body that was established specifically to supervise the application of that treaty. The point here is to achieve the necessary clarity and the essential consistency of international law, as well as legal security, to which both the individuals with guaranteed rights and the States obliged to comply with treaty obligations are entitled.[81]

[81] *Ahmadou Sadio Diallo (Republic of Guinea* v *Democratic Republic of the Congo),* Merits, Judgment, ICJ Reports 2010, 664, para 66. The Court has already referred to the interpretation given by the Human Rights Committee and other similar bodies in previous case law; see *Legal Consequences of the Construction of a Wall in the Occupied Palestinian Territory,* Advisory Opinion, ICJ Reports 2004, 179, para 109 (application of the Covenant where the State exercises its jurisdiction on foreign territory). See also, more recently, *Judgment No 2867 of the Administrative Tribunal of the International Labour Organization*

Likewise, the Court noted that when it is called upon, as in these proceedings, to apply a regional instrument for the protection of human rights, it must take due account of the interpretation of that instrument adopted by the independent bodies which have been specifically created, if such has been the case, to monitor the sound application of the treaty in question. In the present case, the interpretation given above of Article 12, paragraph 4, of the African Charter was found consonant with the case law of the African Commission on Human and Peoples' Rights established by Article 30 of the said Charter.[82]

On the substance of Guinea's claim, according to which the decision to expel Mr Diallo breached the Covenant and African Charter because it was not taken in accordance with Congolese domestic law, the Court found that the expulsion of Mr Diallo violated the relevant obligations of the DRC.

The Court recalled that it is for each State, in the first instance, to interpret its own domestic law. The Court does not, in principle, have the power to substitute its own interpretation for that of the national authorities, especially when that interpretation is given by the highest national courts.[83] Exceptionally, where a State puts forward a manifestly incorrect interpretation of its domestic law, particularly for the purpose of gaining an advantage in a pending case, it is for the Court to adopt what it finds to be the proper interpretation.

In the particular case of the expulsion of Mr Diallo, the Court found that the expulsion decree was not preceded by consultation of the National Immigration Board, whose opinion was required by the Congolese legislation concerning immigration control before any expulsion measure is taken against an alien holding a residence permit, and that it should have been 'reasoned' pursuant to the Congolese legislation; in other words, it should have indicated the grounds for the decision taken. The Court thus concluded that in two important respects, concerning procedural guarantees conferred on aliens by Congolese law and aimed at protecting the persons in question against the risk of arbitrary treatment, the expulsion of Mr Diallo was not decided 'in accordance with law'.

---

upon a Complaint Filed against the International Fund for Agricultural Development, referred to above (principle of equality of access to the courts).

[82] Ibid., 664, para 67. The Court also referred to the interpretation of the European Court of Human Rights and the Inter-American Court of Human Rights, ibid., 664, para 68.

[83] See *Serbian Loans,* Judgment No 14, 1929, PCIJ, Series A, No 20, 46 and *Brazilian Loans,* Judgment No 15, 1929, PCIJ, Series A, No 21, 124.

Further to the decision of the Court finding that the DRC was under obligation to make appropriate reparation, in the form of compensation, to Guinea for the injurious consequences of the violations of international obligations, the parties failed to find an agreement on the question of compensation. Therefore, the question was settled by the Court, in another judgment, delivered on 19 June 2012.[84] In this decision, the Court fixed the amount of compensation that was owed to the Republic of Guinea by the DRC for the various injuries suffered by Mr Diallo following the breach of his individual rights.[85] The Court's judgment on compensation provides another example of an extensive use of precedents of other courts and tribunals.[86] A Member of the Court further explained, in a declaration appended to the judgment:

> As this [was] the first occasion on which the Court has had to assess damages since the *Corfu Channel* case (*I.C.J. Reports 1949*, p. 4), it [was] entirely appropriate that the Court, recognizing that there is very little in its own jurisprudence on which it can draw … made a thorough examination of the practice of other international courts and tribunals, especially the main human rights jurisdictions, which have extensive experience of assessing damages in cases with facts very similar to those of the present case. International law is not a series of fragmented specialist and self-contained bodies of law, each of which functions in isolation from the others; it is a single, unified system of law and each international court can, and should, draw on the jurisprudence

---

[84] *Ahmadou Sadio Diallo (Republic of Guinea* v *Democratic Republic of the Congo), (Compensation owed by the Democratic Republic of the Congo to the Republic of Guinea)*, ICJ Reports 2012, 324.

[85] The Court indicated that 'the sum awarded to Guinea in the exercise of diplomatic protection of Mr Diallo is intended to provide reparation for the latter's injury', ibid., 344, para 57.

[86] Ibid., 331, para 13:

> The Court has taken into account the practice in other international courts, tribunals and commissions (such as the International Tribunal for the Law of the Sea, the European Court of Human Rights (ECHR), the Inter-American Court of Human Rights (IACHR), the Iran-United States Claims Tribunal, the Eritrea-Ethiopia Claims Commission, and the United Nations Compensation Commission), which have applied general principles governing compensation when fixing its amount, including in respect of injury resulting from unlawful detention and expulsion.

See, in particular, regarding the quantification of compensation for non-material injury, which 'necessarily rests on equitable consideration', the references to the views of the Human Rights Committee and the African Commission on Human Rights, as well as to arbitral tribunals and regional courts, ibid., 334–5, para 24.

of other international courts and tribunals, even though it is not bound necessarily to come to the same conclusions.[87]

Over the years, the Court has managed to adapt to the major developments in international relations. Its composition has diversified to enable it more faithfully to reflect the massive growth in the number of States in the international community. A strictly inter-State organ of justice, the Court was at the service of 51 States at the time of its creation. It is currently a Court with 193 potential litigants. An examination of the Court's General List reveals the true universality of the use of its services for settling international disputes between States from all the regions of the world. The nature of the questions submitted to the Court has also evolved, and so has its mission in view of the recent evolution towards a greater awareness, among the international community, of the international rule of law. Indeed, international law is gradually occupying a larger area in the relations between States as well as in the activities of international organizations.

Looking forwards, a number of ways could be explored in order to further enhance the potential contribution of the International Court of Justice to the 'rule of law' at the international level. To name just a few, one may think, first, of increasing the number of States accepting, in one way or the other (by way of a declaration or a compromissory clause), the compulsory jurisdiction of the Court for settling their disputes. States may also be encouraged to resort with moderation to reservations (ie exclusion of particular categories of disputes) when accepting the compulsory jurisdiction of the Court. The role of the Court, today only accessible to States in contentious proceedings, might also be enhanced by extending its jurisdiction *ratione personae* to public international organizations, which nowadays play an increasing role in international legal relations. Undoubtedly, such an evolution, which would however involve a number of complex legal as well as political questions, could offer the opportunity for the Court to fulfil more effectively its function, not only as the principal judicial organ of the United Nations, but also as the 'highest' Court in the world and the only one to have a universal character and a general jurisdiction.

All-in all, it goes without saying that the role of any Court is dependent upon the society in which it is required to operate. The contribution of the ICJ to the promotion and strengthening of the 'rule of

[87] Declaration of Judge Greenwood, ICJ Reports 2012, 394, para 8.

law' at the international level, should therefore always be evaluated from the standpoint of contemporary international society. In this respect, one may confidently expect that the Court will keep an invaluable place and remain a central element for the advancement of the rule of law at the international level in the future.

4. Constructing the International Criminal Court's rule of law identity

Kenneth Chan and Jan Wouters

I. INTRODUCTION

Although the International Criminal Court (ICC) is a relatively new addition to the landscape of international justice, it has quickly become a tent-pole of the discourse on contemporary transitional justice. This is not terribly surprising, as the institution fills a long-standing accountability gap that has long been recognized to exist in post-conflict situations; one that has not been (and arguably, in the majority of cases, *cannot* be) adequately serviced by domestic courts. Indeed, more often than not, local institutions in the wake of violent conflicts rarely have the capacity or political support necessary to conduct unbiased criminal trials. Although states retain primacy[1] to prosecute all cases where they are 'willing and able' to prosecute individuals for international crimes, a jurisdictional ordering principle known as 'complementarity' within the Rome Statute,[2] the Court nevertheless retains agency to intervene where, in principle, the territorial state is incapable of doing so. This exceptional right granted to the ICC as a third party to perform what is quintessentially the duty of the state to administer its judicial and law enforcement systems uniquely positions the Court at the intersection between domestic and International Criminal Law (ICL) regimes when it comes to the prosecution of atrocity crimes. The ICC, in other words, has an additional responsibility to manage its complex relationship with national courts that hold concurrent authority to prosecute genocides, crimes against humanity and war crimes that take place under their

[1] Indeed, it should be noted that the Statute couches this right as an *obligation* of states – or as it puts it in its preamble, it is the 'duty of every state to exercise its criminal jurisdiction over those responsible for international crimes': Rome Statute, Preamble.

[2] See art 17(1) Rome Statute.

jurisdiction. To date, ICL has not applied a great deal of finesse to this endeavour, adopting what McAuliffe describes as a preference for 'international substitution over domestic empowerment'.[3] This approach emerges, unsurprisingly, because scholarship 'implicitly or explicitly presents the reduction of sovereignty in the name of enforcing international human rights norms as desirable'.[4] But there are obvious reasons why the ICC has begun to deviate from this model where it can. From an institutional perspective, the Court can be easily undone if it spreads its budget too thinly across its vast jurisdictional mandate. Burke-White accordingly notes that despite the Rome Statute's promise to put an end to impunity for international crimes, 'the capacity of the Court and the limited resources made available to it suggest that it will, at best, make a far more limited contribution to ending impunity'.[5] With these limitations clearly in mind, however, the Court's first Prosecutor, the Argentinian lawyer Luis Moreno-Ocampo, made it a priority of his office to focus on expanding the role of states and engaging them in the prosecutorial process in order to lessen the Court's workload where circumstances allowed. He suggested that the kind of comprehensive justice that the Court should pursue would come not from the quantity of tickets in its *own* docket, but through inspiring and supporting domestic courts to conduct their own effective trials. Success, therefore, could only be measured by 'the absence of trials before [thc ICC], as a consequence of the regular functioning of national institutions'.[6] The underlying premise of this message is clear. If transitional governments that take office after conflict hope to claim legitimacy and restore the confidence of their people in the rule of law, they must demonstrate that *local* institutions are capable of bringing justice and accountability to those victimized during its violent past. Indeed, government representatives made this point very clear during the Rome Conference, asserting a 'vital interest' in domestic prosecutions as the main reason they declined to grant the ICC absolute jurisdictional primacy over the state.

---

[3] Padraig McAuliffe, *Transitional Justice and Rule of Law Reconstruction: A Contentious Relationship* (London, Routledge, 2013) 185.

[4] Ibid.

[5] William W W Burke-White, 'Proactive Complementarity: The International Criminal Court and National Courts in the Rome System of Justice' (2008) 49(1) *Harvard International Law Journal* 53 at 54.

[6] Office of the Prosecutor, 'Paper on some policy issues before the Office of the Prosecutor' (September 2003), available at <http://www.icc-cpi.int/nr/rdonlyres/1fa7c4c6-de5f-42b7-8b25-60aa962ed8b6/143594/030905_policy_paper.pdf> (2003 Policy paper).

Accordingly, the Statute favours state prosecution over international interventions, at least in theory. However, the ICC model deliberately courts for itself a broad 'governance' type role in the administration of global war crimes prosecutions. This position is one that ostensibly moves beyond the strictly penal objectives that might be expected of it as a *criminal* court. From this perspective, one can see that it was designed with the intention that domestic trials would take place, meeting the expectations of the international community, and would only assume jurisdiction if this failed to happen. While this is most directly demonstrated through the Rome Statute's incorporation of the principles of complementarity and cooperation, the inclusion of a participatory role for victims in proceedings and the implementation of a restitution and compensation scheme also indicates a more abstract function for the Court in its extensive engagement with national justice systems. Undoubtedly, the intention behind the Court's pursuit of a more 'systemic' role was to establish itself as an authoritative influence over the development of domestic policies relating to the prosecution of atrocities. That is, however, as a precondition to this kind of 'advisory' role, it must first demonstrate that it is itself a sound institutional model for such prosecutions. To date, the Court has struggled to prosecute atrocities with efficacy and efficiently. This has not only disenfranchised victim communities expecting the Court to hold war criminals accountable for their actions, but has undoubtedly weakened their faith in its ability to oversee just and fair trials at home. Thus, it is submitted that a clearer conceptualization of the ICC's role in post-conflict countries undergoing peace-building processes is fundamental to the long-term legitimacy and relevance of the institution. In this regard, this chapter suggests that the Court, at the intersection between global rule of law management and domestic transitional justice processes, must be guided by *the domestic rule of law*. This does not imply that the Court must make a compromise between peace and justice – a false conflation all too often asserted within scholarly literature. Rather, it should demonstrate an awareness of the local impact of its decisions and seek to foster effective domestic institutions and practices through its actions, including how it interprets and applies the Rome Statute. State prosecutions serve the interests, and preserve the value, of both domestic and international legal orders concurrently. Thus, as McAuliffe astutely observes 'the future of international criminal law and the model that clearly emerged from the negotiations on the Rome Statute is … a model of progressive rapprochement and harmonization of national criminal justice systems with international criminal law vis-à-vis the treatment of mass atrocity'.[7] At an elemental level, this means that ICL best serves the domestic and international legal order by supporting national institutions that genuinely wish to conduct trials in observance of the domestic rule of law. In practice, this should not only include, where required, direct provision of capacity, but also requires the Court to model best practice in its own procedural conduct. While the Court has many *sui generis* characteristics, particularly in its incorporation of unique procedural and substantive features not faced by their domestic counterparts – such as its hybrid mix of civil and common law rules of procedure and evidence (reflecting the varied legal systems of its respective states parties) – consistency and coherence with the domestic rule of law should be chief amongst its guiding principles. At the very least, the Court should be cognizant of the domestic impact of its decisions and policies and the perception that local communities are likely to have in response to them.

This chapter will investigate the meaning of the term 'the rule of law' in Part II, before considering the relationship between the ICC and domestic courts in Part III. This section looks at how domestic rule of law support has been conducted by the ICC. Finally, Part IV makes specific recommendations in regards to how the ICC can better apply the international rule of law in support of the domestic rule of law. These proposals are made based on an observation of recent issues that have beleaguered the Court.

II. THE SEMANTICS OF THE RULE OF LAW: A CRIMINAL JUSTICE PERSPECTIVE

The 'rule of law' remains one of the most poorly understood abstractions within the fields of political and legal theory. In common usage, it can be deployed for various purposes, depending on the orator, their intent, and context. Accordingly, because this vague notion is so often empty of specific content, it is particularly attractive to various actors across the political spectrum, where its invocation does not necessarily admit commitment to any particular idea. Indeed, in political discourse, it is often and unjustifiably fetishized through the presumption that obeisance to the rule of law will result in the most just outcome. This kind of *laissez-faire* treatment of its capacities in the public commons famously led philosopher Joseph Raz to criticize the 'promiscuous use made … of

7 McAuliffe, above n3 at 186.

the expression "the rule of law"'.[8] As an ideal type, support for the development and protection of the rule of law is an admirable aspiration, and much needed in regions that lack infrastructural stability due to *inter alia* conflict or corruption, but it is a term too often deployed vacant of meaning or purpose. If it is employed, this should be done with precision, and scrutinized with vigour on application. A lack of consideration, or indeed, an intent to misuse the term to disguise ill intent can fracture unstable post-conflict communities even further.

The rule of law is a term most commonly understood in a domestic context, but over the decades, it has been co-opted into the international justice discourse as well. In this regard, the term develops even greater nuance due to the multilateral character of its objects. Consequently, a lack of clarity in the application of an *international* rule of law – particularly by supervisory bodies such as international human rights and criminal courts and tribunals – poses potential risks to national transitional justice efforts as well. The purpose of this chapter is to advocate a more constructive dialogue between the ICC and domestic courts than has previously taken place. In so doing, it is necessary to briefly unpack some of the occasionally vague *patois* adopted within the scholarship. Indeed, understanding the place of the rule of law in influencing the various goals and functions of international justice is essential to clarifying the rights and responsibilities of the Court. Summarily, the following section explains how the relationship between the domestic and international rule of law is utilized in the context of this chapter, as well as how its normative ideals contribute to the ICC's pursuit of justice. It considers, in short, the concept of justice that the Court embodies, highlighting the tension between the traditional punitive/retributive goals ascribed to regular criminal courts against the broader 'restorative' and transitional justice goals imbued in the Rome Statute, and examines how rule of law protection pursues these ends. Finally, it asserts that support for the domestic rule of law does not warrant a subversion of the Court to political interests – nor does it invoke the so-called debate between 'peace' and 'justice'. As this chapter will further embellish, the Court is responsible for the administration of criminal trials that occur both before it, and at the local level. However, this duty does not extend to politically convenient concessions that afford impunity to any individual. Peace processes that pursue amnesties do not support the rule of law construction, and consequently fall beyond the mandate of the Court.

---

8 Joseph Raz, 'The Rule of Law and its Virtue' in *The Authority of Law: Essays on Law and Morality* (Clarendon Press, 1979) 211.

A. The International Criminal Court and the Interplay between the International and Domestic Rule of Law

This chapter's concern with the rule of law focuses in large part around the reciprocal relationship that the Rome Statute attempts to foster between the international and national rule of law paradigms. The ICC is uniquely placed at the intersection between international and national criminal systems of law. The Statute mandates a more mutually beneficial relationship with national authorities than has been previously encountered within ICL; indeed, it elevates the state above the Court itself in cases of jurisdiction disputes. The Statute further carves out key roles for victims in the participation of trials at the ICC, and grants them rights to reparation, further emphasizing the importance of the Court's role in the post-conflict process of institutional rebuilding. Moreover, under article 21(1)(c) of the Rome Statute, 'general principles of law derived by the Court from national laws of legal systems of the world including, as appropriate, the national laws of states that would normally exercise jurisdiction over the crime … [consistent with the Statute and] international law and internationally recognized norms and standards' are recognized as a valid source of law to draw from when there are deficiencies in the application of the Statute which other relevant authorities fail to address. There are certain implications for the homogenization of legal methods pertaining to the prosecution of Rome Statute crimes that can be drawn from this. Particularly, it is notable that the article is preferential of 'national laws of states that would normally exercise jurisdiction' as a salient interpretive tool. Indeed, the phrase reflects a compromise between two camps of thought that emerged during negotiations at the Rome Conference – the first, seeking to draw from general principles of national law in abstraction, and the second, from those seeking to tie the Court more closely with the trial procedures familiar to national systems that would have otherwise exercised jurisdiction. Despite its tertiary status in the hierarchy of sources, however, it is clear that in its retention, the Statute has recognized that, to the extent possible, it is important that trials conducted before the Court are understood by local populations of the subject state to meet their expectations of the administration of justice.

There is, without question, a significant onus on the ICC as an institution to forge healthy collaborative relationships with national prosecutors and judges and domestic rule of law support. The drafters clearly intended that this exchange would be more robust than that pursued by the ad hoc tribunals. These institutions, in contrast to the ICC, had primacy over states in all matters, and simply required their assistance in arresting and transferring suspects, supplying evidence and witnesses, and so on. The Office of the Prosecutor (OTP) has similarly recognized the need to be proactive in supporting states, both for its benefit and theirs. It observed that 'national investigations and prosecutions, where they can properly be undertaken, will normally be the most effective and efficient means of bringing offences to justice; states themselves will normally have the best access to evidence and witnesses'.[9] Accordingly, the Court has established for itself a pivotal role in shaping the rule of law at both international and national levels respectively. But what does this mean? How does and *should* the rule of law influence the Court in its different roles at the state and supranational level? Equally important, how do these different multilateral obligations relate to each other? In order to answer these questions, which are considered in the subsequent analysis, it is necessary to conceptualize the notion of the international and domestic rule of law, at least as it pertains to the Court. A notional paradigm of an *international* rule of law finds its origins in the vigorous discourse on the *domestic* rule of law. Popularized by international organizations, and certain treaties and multilateral conventions, however, the *international* rule of law is sharply influenced by the global governance movement of the last half century. Due to its cultivation in global institutions like the United Nations, the World Trade Organization, the World Bank, and so on (that is, as opposed to the mechanism of the state), the form of rule of law typically advocated at the international level unsurprisingly incorporates clear human rights and democracy promotion elements. Indeed, these concepts are typically merged when addressed in these forums, as seen in a number of UN General Assembly Resolutions and Security Council thematic debates. For example, the chapeau of the UN General Assembly's resolution on the Rule of Law at the national and international levels, adopted on 14 December 2012, includes the reminder that 'human rights, the rule of law and democracy are interlinked and mutually reinforcing and that they belong to the universal and indivisible core values and principles of the United Nations'.[10]

Of course, such an interpretation is highly controversial. The international rule of law is not a concept that is easily captured in any specific

---

9 2003 Policy paper, above n6 at 2.

10 General Assembly resolution 67/97, *The rule of law at the national and international levels*, A/RES/67/97 (14 December 2012), available at <www.undocs.org/A/RES/67/97>. See already the Outcome Document of the 2005 World Summit, General Assembly resolution 60/1 of 16 September 2005, para. 119.

definition. It is perhaps better considered as a reflection of an ideal of the law itself, a facilitator of the specific goals that the different international and domestic legal regimes in question purport to serve. In transitional justice, the object of the law is to bring to account the wrongs of the past through mechanisms of accountability; in security, international law determines circumstances under which a threat or breach of the peace has occurred, the nature of the harm inflicted, and consequently the nature and level of response that is warranted (which may include a sustained international post-conflict presence on the state, such as with the territorial administrations imposed in Kosovo and East Timor). The role that the rule of law plays in the context of ICL, and particularly in the ICC context, can be difficult to determine due to the complexities of the Court's various goals. Though the Statute does not make express reference to the 'rule of law', it is undoubtedly a key aspect of the Court's work. Subsequently, these should be considered in order to better visualize the purpose of the international rule of law within the framework of the Rome Statute.

B. The Rule of Law and the Pursuit of Justice at the Permanent International Criminal Court

The intimacy of the relationship between 'the rule of law' and the concept of 'justice' belies their respectively complex and highly contestable natures. The latter, in particular, is perennially subjective and frequently disputed. 'Justice' means many things to many people. Within the context of the ICC, the pursuit of justice consequently depends on the characterization of its key goals. This, accordingly, explains what form justice may or should take at the Court (and consequently, what line of inquiry the rule of law must advocate for). Though this explanation is somewhat simplified, it is possible to ascertain the existence of two basic 'types' of justice that emerge in domestic criminal justice systems that are relevant to the current discussion. These are, respectively, the 'retributive' and 'restorative' justice paradigms. The former, Zehr explains, is in essence one where the state is victim, the offence in the violation of the rules it sets, and 'the relationship between victim and offender … irrelevant'.[11] Retribution requires the highest standards of due process and protection of fair trial rights to be preserved, explains Turner, because it is guided by the belief that 'retribution remains

[11] Howard Zehr, *Changing Lenses: A New Focus for Crime and Justice* (Scottdale, PA Herald Press, 1990) 184.

separate from private vengeance and that punishment is determined by law, not by private passions'.[12] This is an ideal starting point for all criminal justice systems. However, there are certain elements in the Rome Statute which indicate this is not the ultimate model applied to the Court itself. Aspects of a restorative concept of justice are present in the Statute's text, which makes victim participation and remuneration an important component of the trial process. If this construction also includes elements of transitional justice, which this chapter submits is the case, then it implies secondary obligations upon the Court to develop policies that assist national courts, and also to ensure that its jurisprudence – wherever possible and consistent with the Statute itself – encourages, facilitates, and enforces best trial practice and respect for due process. Strict retribution of wrongdoers, while essential, would not of itself be sufficient to meet the goals of restoration or transitional justice. The precise contours of the rule of law then would need to take shape around a commonly agreed upon vision of Rome Statute justice, one that clearly draws elements from both paradigms whilst introducing unique elements reflective of the exceptional supranational character of the ICC. It is necessary, therefore, to examine what conception of justice emerges from an examination of the goals of the Court.

Subject to their limited jurisdictions, domestic criminal law systems pursue a more focused set of core objectives than their international counterparts. Without delving too deeply into this analysis, it is broadly noted that first and foremost, national criminal courts seek retribution for crimes committed; they exist to punish those that break the law. Their secondary goals are somewhat tangential to this objective, though they ostensibly include (to varying degrees) deterrence, rehabilitation of offenders, and so on. International criminal courts share the same primary intent, yet their ambitions are far more challenging. International criminal justice is a hybrid of many different elements, and accordingly, serves many different interests. Atrocity crimes cast an extremely long shadow over the societies they impact, and occur in the context of mass criminality under – for example – a specific intent or design, often as part of a broader state or organizational policy. This has no true domestic equivalent. No murder is merely a murder when committed in a genocidal context, no sexual crime occurs in isolation. They occur as part of a destructive strategy intended to harm or decimate a group representing a culture or religion or experience; and accordingly, the main priorities in

---

12 Jenia Turner, 'Defense Perspectives on Law and Politics in International Criminal Trials' (2008) 48 *Virginia Journal of International Law* 529 at 535.

prosecuting these crimes focus on the architects. To unpack the consequences of these acts, ICL purports to be more than the sum of its parts – and its parts are many, drawing from different corners of the legal spectrum. It is neither solely criminal law, nor entirely public international law in its design. In fact, in describing the international law influences on war crimes jurisprudence, former US ambassador at large for war crimes David Scheffer refers to Atrocity Law as an intersection between ICL (which he refers to in its broader, generalized sense – including not only crimes such as genocide, but also transnational crimes such as terrorism, the various types of trafficking and so on), the Laws and Customs of War, International Humanitarian Law and International Human Rights Law.[13] However, there are also distinct elements of domestic criminal law pervasive in the practice of ICL. A global permanent Court, whilst oriented towards its broad supranational objectives, is unlikely to be perceived as legitimate if it does not bear some resemblance to the criminal law systems of the world, and its staff of international lawyers cannot function if they are not able to draw from their experiences in national jurisdictions. Accordingly, general principles and customs of national law have had a far greater influence on the everyday operation of the Court than may be immediately obvious. As ICC Trial Judge René Blattmann observed in a separate opinion in the case of *Thomas Lubanga*:

> Considerable effort was made in the drafting of the Rome Statute and its Rule of Procedure and Evidence ("Rules") to take into account, and reflect, both the Romano-Germanic and the common law legal systems such that a hybrid system was created. This system … is meant to provide procedural certainty to the parties and participants and to limit judicial discretion.[14]

---

[13] He explains that international criminal law inaccurately describes the emerging system of law conducted by international courts:

> Therefore, I know of no way to accurately describe what law is truly on deck in the realm of atrocities and before the war crimes tribunals other than to label it *atrocity law*. The targeted criminal conduct causing the horror may be a mixture of several of the conventional fields of law described. … one body of law – *atrocity law* – marries parts of each of these well established fields of law into its rapidly growing body of jurisprudence

David Scheffer, *All the Missing Souls: A Personal History of the War Crimes Tribunals* (Princeton NJ, Princeton University Press, 2012) 426.

[14] Situation in the Democratic Republic of the Congo in the Case of the Prosecutor v. Thomas Lubanga Dyilo 'Separate Opinion of Judge René Blattmann to the Decision on the defence request to reconsider the "Order on

In the translation of the *customs* of domestic criminal law into the *practice* of ICL, the Rome Statute navigates between and incorporates different legal traditions into its hybrid framework of rules of procedural conduct and substantive norms. This includes not only the civil and common law systems that represent the majority of the world's judicial infrastructures, but also those practices rooted in the customs of *inter alia* religious or tribal legal cultures – particularly Islamic Sharia, which is practiced (for instance) in the Sudan where the ICC is presently investigating. It is important to acknowledge *why* national legal paradigms play a role in shaping the legal system of ICL, and consequently, its objectives. Lawyers and judges from different legal traditions bring to the ICC more than a mere knowledge of the legal empires of states. They are responsible for dictating complex sociological and indigenous perceptions of the world into the source code of atrocity crimes' prosecutions. The community of nations is accountable for moulding together polarized legal cultures, complete with jurisprudential philosophies and sciences, into something greater than the sum of its parts; that is, into a supranational system of international criminal procedure. They are, as Langer argues, more than different techniques for handling legal cases, but also 'legal identities and ways to distribute power and responsibilities between the main actors and institutions [in] the administration of justice'.[15] Therefore, the incorporation of local legal customs within the jurisprudence of the ICC acts as a bridge between local victim communities and the otherwise alien proceedings of the Court, making them comprehensible to local victim communities, and demonstrating the legitimacy of their operations. Thus, given the complexities of atrocity law, the nuances of which continue to appear and be contested every day before the Court, it should be no surprise that the articulation of the Court's procedure remains an ongoing project. Naturally, the rule of law can contribute greatly to this process.

Indeed, the drafters of the Rome Statute have devoted considerable energy into building a new system of law from the bottom up, and what has emerged is a *sui generis* law of atrocities that has hybrid elements from the many distinct sources that it is based upon. As such, there is need to clarify the extent to which the Statute requires the Court to pursue its secondary goals – those that go beyond the standard focus of

---

numbering of evidence" of 12 May 2010' ICC-01/04-01/06 (Trial Chamber I) (30 March 2011), available at <http://www.icc-cpi.int/iccdocs/doc/doc1049659.pdf>, at [7].

[15] Maximo Langer, 'The Rise of Managerial Judging in International Criminal Law' (2005) 53 *Am J Comp L* 835 at 835.

domestic criminal law trials – particularly when these clash with its duty to prosecute and punish. A multitude of sometimes apposite objectives have obfuscated the most direct path towards the conviction and punishment of perpetrators of international crimes at the ad hoc tribunals and has found its way into the ICC's efforts to balance its interests as well. Even the relatively straightforward objective of punishment becomes more challenging in the international criminal justice context, as earlier suggested, because atrocity crimes suspects are typically 'architects and engineers' of these crimes on a grand scale, and are consequently part of or protected by the larger apparatus of national government. Governmental authorities are more often than not complicit with the commissions of such crimes, as these must generally take place within a broader or systemic context. To exact retribution, which is the most important role that these courts observe, they are first faced with the challenge of piercing the veil of sovereign immunity. This problem has become synonymous with the ambitions of the ICC. Indeed, among the various intents that can be determined from examination of the preamble of the Rome Statute, one that is particularly outstanding is the promise to 'put an end to impunity'. Other objectives, however, orient around encouraging or requiring the Court to complement and support efforts to hold national proceedings in compliance with due process. Accordingly, the broad aspirations of international courts are not only warranted but necessary. The Court's substantive and geographic jurisdiction is immense. That it has taken on further aims that speak also to the pursuit of peace and justice, or the development of an accurate historical record of the atrocities committed, is perfectly natural in the circumstances. Additionally, based on his own survey of a cross-section of international lawyers, Klamberg deduces that the Courts have adopted specific policies that relate to 'crime control' (that is, trials conducted with the intent to *deter* or prevent further violations of human rights), ensuring fair trial rights are observed, expeditiousness of trial proceedings (inefficiency of trials which can stretch on for years merely serves to frustrate victim communities seeking justice), the protection of state sovereignty, truth-seeking, and victim participation and protection.[16]

To the extent that these secondary goals reflect the uniquely horrifying nature of atrocity crimes and the additional obligations they place on

---

[16] Mark Klamberg, 'What are the Objectives of International Criminal Procedure? Reflections on the Fragmentation of a Legal Regime' (2010) 79(2) *Nordic Journal of International Law* 279 at 283.

courts to facilitate restorative or transitional justice objectives by conducting trials domestically, how should these be weighed against its most singularly important concern – to ensure accountability through effective prosecutions? Simpson points to this problem of the balancing of interests when he observes that 'international criminal justice seems overwhelmingly committed to promoting the rule of law or the idea of humanity *against* hegemonic ambition or sovereign vanity'.[17] Athough establishing accountability for high-ranking members of states is undeniably essential, the aspiration driving the drafting of the Rome Statute was not merely to create a court to act as a forum for the adjudication of international crimes. Such a limited vision would make the pursuit of comprehensive justice impossible. The ICC is not disposed to prosecute all international crimes that occur upon its watch. It depends on the cooperation of states not only to aide its own investigations, but to contribute to the pursuit of justice through its own initiatives. Consequently, the drafters of the Rome Statute sought to pivot from the Westphalian system's historic state-centrism, which typically favours the interests of states above the rights of the individual, towards the creation of a 'broader political identity'[18] that would grant all human beings equal protection under the law – including the benefit of a functional criminal system when they fall victim to atrocities committed against them, for instance, by their governments. The result of this, as Part IV explores more fully, is that the Statute lays out the basic infrastructure for a mutually supportive system of supranational, national, and regional level war crimes prosecutions. The concept of complementarity, which is addressed in Part III, is the centrepiece of this framework. It grants national authorities, per article 17 of the Statute, a right of first refusal to prosecute where they hold concurrent jurisdiction. This broader strategy, which authors such as Burke-White[19] and Stahn[20] have referred to as a 'Rome System of Justice', is instrumental in understanding how the rule of law is and should be constituted in the context of the ICC. This system, however, also highlights the inherent tension between, on the one

---

[17] Gerry Simpson, 'International Criminal Justice in Historical Context: The post-Second World War Trials and Modern International Criminal Justice' in Gideon Boas, William A Schabas, Michael P Scharf (eds), *International Criminal Justice: Legitimacy and Coherence* (Cheltenham, Edward Elgar Press, 2012) 141.

[18] McAuliffe, above n3.

[19] Burke-White, above n5 at 56.

[20] Carsten Stahn, 'Complementarity: A Tale of Two Notions' (2008) 19 *Criminal Law Forum* 87.

hand, the 'punitive and impunity piercing' goals of the Court, and on the other, those which require greater cooperation with states – and indeed, grants them the prerogative to prosecute ICC crimes. Essentially, the challenge the Court faces in the pursuit of justice is that it considers post-conflict states to be inherently untrustworthy when it comes to prosecuting their own high-ranking officials. There is a risk that this would allow impunity to prevail if the state were to use its position to protect suspects. Yet, the Court cannot exclude the state from conducting trials for many reasons – most obviously, because it has a mandate to support such efforts; because it depends on their assistance to investigate and prosecute many of the incidents and individuals involved with a situation that it itself cannot; and because, if it hopes to assist post-conflict states to restore stability, it must allow them the opportunity to demonstrate their competence. Indeed, trials conducted in local courts (that comply with the rule of law) hold greater weight with local populations than when they are imposed by a third party, where there is often scepticism of the (perceived) hegemony of such actions.

The goals of the restorative and transitional justice paradigms, the authors submit, are ones the Rome Statute has clearly indicated it will be informed by. In doing so, it recognizes that peace can only be restored after violent and repressive rule of a previous regime if societies can undergo transition and establish a new and more legitimate form of government than the one before. Transitional justice is a particularly important part of the post-conflict process because it represents the act of removing the remaining artifacts of the previous regime or acts of violence it committed which fractured the community. According to Đukic, it 'seeks a holistic sense of justice instead of relying solely on a classical, retributive notion of justice'.[21] Therefore, he explains there are four instruments this process employs, of which the administration of trials 'of a civil or criminal nature, conducted before national, foreign, international and/or hybrid courts' is the most important (alongside) truth-seeking commissions, acts of reparation, and reform.[22] In the International Criminal Tribunal for the former Yugoslavia's (ICTY's) *Erdemovic* judgment, the bench commented on this goal, suggesting trials may channel grief by allowing the 'sorely afflicted to mourn those among

21 Drazan Đukic, 'Transitional Justice and the International Criminal Court – in "the Interests of Justice"?' (2007) 89(867) *International Review of the Red Cross* 691.

22 Ibid.

them who had been unjustly killed'.[23] As local populations are most receptive to findings that occur in national courts that they trust to hold fair trials (as well as local truth commissions), these are the most ideal places for facts relevant to the healing process to emerge and have the most profound impact. For example, the Rwandan Gacaca courts, which were developed as a local alternative to the International Criminal Tribunal for Rwanda, hold concurrent jurisdiction with it, and adopt truth-telling elements as local and traditional customs require. This strategy has met with relative success over the years for these very reasons. Restorative justice shares common ties with these objectives, as it too has a clear interest in the healing of wounds, forgiving of harm done, and mending of interpersonal relationships within communities. Referring to the ICTY, Fatic asserts that international courts should take restorative justice goals as seriously as they do the pursuit of punitive measures 'because it is only a comprehensive reconciliation in south-eastern Europe that can facilitate political, economic and social progress and a stabilization of the security situation in the entire region'.[24]

While it is tempting to suggest that this creates a tension between peace and justice, however, one should not make the mistake of conflating the political aspects of the concept of 'peace' with the restorative elements of the concept of 'justice'. The position of the authors is that the kind of rule of law paradigm dictated by the Rome Statute's body of atrocity law demands complicity with *national courts*, to assist them to conduct fair trials locally; it does not require the ICC to subjugate itself to the political whims of governments, which may for example pursue amnesties as part of a peace agreement process. As Prosecutor Bensouda herself puts it, 'the debate about peace versus justice or peace over justice is a patently false choice. Peace and justice are two sides of the same coin. The road to peace should be seen as running via justice, and this peace and justice can be pursued simultaneously.'[25] ICL's contribution to peace is somewhat different to this political conception, and was best explained by the ICTY. In the *Nikolic* Appeals Chamber judgment,

---

[23] *Prosecutor v Erdemovic* (Sentencing Judgment) [29 November 1996] Case No IT-96-22-T ¶ 65.

[24] Aleksandar Fatic, *Reconciliation via the War Crimes Tribunal* (Ashgate Publishing Ltd, 2000) 1.

[25] Fatou Bensouda, 'International justice and diplomacy', *The New York Times*, (18 March 2013), available at <http://www.nytimes.com/2013/03/20/opinion/global/the-role-of-the-icc-in-international-justice-and-diplomacy.html?_r=0>.

the tribunal drew a specific link between the achievement of justice in legal proceedings and the provision of stability, explaining that:

> [by] holding individuals responsible for the crimes committed, it [is] hoped that a particular ethnic or religious group (or even political organization) would not be held responsible for such crimes by members of other ethnic or religious groups, and that the guilt of the few would not be shifted to the innocent.[26]

The same observation holds true of cases and situations that appear before the ICC, perhaps more so given the flexibility afforded the Prosecutor to target specific crimes within the Court's jurisdiction – allowing her to focus on those where such societal divisions can be tempered by judicial proceedings.

What conclusions then can be drawn about the meaning of the rule of law to the ICC? First, there is a clearly complementary relationship between the rule of law's ideals and the Court's pursuit of justice – the observance of the former strongly assures the success of the latter. It demands, at the very least, certainty and consistency in the application of the law. This is easier said than done when faced with the multiple objectives of ICL. Indeed, the international rule of law, at least where the Rome Statute is concerned, refers to the idea of its singular supranational law of atrocities being applied to all individuals equally without the potential bias that comes from the state acting as an intermediary; while at the same time, it is required to defer to sovereignty under the principle of complementarity, and support national efforts because of the vital role it plays in restorative and transitional justice paradigms. Because different goals and many visions of justice limit the ability of the Court to apply a strict code of conduct in every possible case where it may be in question, it is perhaps better to approach the rule of law by supporting a particular set of principles that should be applied where there is a need to resolve uncertainties. In the context of armed conflict, Bassiouni views post-conflict justice as consisting of the need to pursue retribution for acts committed, and restoration of those things – both physical and metaphysical – destroyed during the fighting.[27] However, this can be clarified further: in the *sui generis* context of crimes committed by individuals in violation of international law, 'justice' should be concerned with restoration and reparations for past acts *to the extent that it is*

---

[26] *Prosecutor v Momir Nikolic* (Sentencing Judgment) [2 December 2003] Case No IT-02-60/1-S at ¶ 60.

[27] M Cherif Bassiouni (ed.), *Post-Conflict Justice* (New York, Transnational Publishers Inc, 2002) xv.

necessary to pave the way for peace and reconciliation in the future, so long as this does not undermine efforts to pursue accountability through the conduct of fair trials (whether domestically or internationally). Given this formulation, for example, ambiguities of procedural conduct should be determined by assessing what is most consistent with due process, particularly as understood in the state where the crimes were committed. The rule of law, accordingly, should be developed as a non-instrumental framework that works towards that end.

The subsequent sections of this chapter will build upon this proposal, first in Part III by examining the nature of the relationship between international criminal courts/tribunals and domestic criminal courts over the last two decades. This, it submits, precedes and provides context for the Rome Statute's infrastructural design. Part IV ties together this analysis by expanding upon what such a 'rule of law' construction might look like, using a number of examples that have emerged during the ICC's first decade of work.

III. A HISTORY OF INTERNATIONAL CRIMINAL LAW AND TRANSITIONAL JUSTICE IN POST-CONFLICT STATES

The fight to give life to a permanent judicial body for international crimes was waged for many years before the creation of the ICC in The Hague in 2002. Since the end of the Second World War, now 70 years ago, the global community has attempted on numerous occasions to pursue accountability for the commission of atrocities through the establishment of international criminal courts and tribunals. The intention behind supplanting domestic courts with external judicial bodies is perhaps obvious. There was, and remains, a ubiquitous belief within the international community that post-conflict communities, those that have suffered the serious atrocities which warrant global attention, are not able to hold perpetrators accountable without, at a minimum, third-party oversight. Indeed, it is almost universally assumed by Western liberal democracies that the prospects of conducting legitimate trial diminish even further if the primary suspects of the prosecuted crimes hold positions of authority within the state's executive branch. Yet, efforts to establish an exclusive and permanent judicial body to prosecute war crimes have yielded mixed results. For many decades, tribunals with limited substantive, temporal and/or geographic jurisdictions were created as a compromise. The Nuremberg, Tokyo, and ad hoc tribunals for the former Yugoslavia and Rwanda, as well as the hybrid tribunals, represent the high water mark of these negotiations. However, as already stated, such Courts were only conferred limited and temporary jurisdiction. Thus, they were capable of prosecuting only the barest margin of atrocities representing the extraordinary breadth and depth of criminality experienced across the world over the decades. Indeed, their existence merely highlighted the need for the creation of an institution or institutions whose grasp could extend beyond the impunity gap that exists at the highest echelons of the State, preserved by the notion of Westphalian sovereignty. Increasingly, calls to establish a permanent war crimes institution became stronger and more determined. Yet, despite considerable support amongst legal scholars and international civil society, time and again, such efforts were defeated by a resilient community of diplomats and state officials fiercely guarding against potential intrusions of their sovereignty. Thus, there was much to celebrate with the establishment of the ICC. Indeed, its formation has been quite rightly lauded widely as one of the most significant triumphs of justice in decades, and a major blow against impunity. Even in its infancy, scholars, politicians and international civil society alike were immediately unreserved in their praise of the Court. As Weller argued, before the institution had even opened its first case, the mere existence of a permanent court for atrocity crimes represented 'the culmination of international law-making [in] the twentieth century'.[28] McAuliffe makes a similarly lavish observance, noting the emergence of a 'triumphalist discourse of international criminal law … wherein ICC accession is seen as the moral imperative of the times, as a manifestation of the international community's self-constitutionalization incorporating individuals as "world citizens", as the triumph of law over barbarism'.[29] While such enthusiasm was somewhat premature given that the Court was barely beyond its infancy, it does not diminish the miracle of its establishment in the least. Indeed, as those close to the negotiations in Rome would assuredly attest, at no point during the process of the Statute's negotiation – not even during the final moments of the conference – was it clear that the parties would agree upon a text that would bring the institution into being. The Court's supporters properly recognized that with its birth, there would now exist an institution that had the potential to be a true arbiter of a global rule of law, one that would pierce impunity at the highest levels and afford

---

[28] Marc Weller, 'Undoing the Global Constitution: UN Security Council Action on the International Criminal Court' (2002) 78(4) *International Affairs* 693 at 693.

[29] McAuliffe, above n3 at 182.

justice to the most vulnerable victims of the most heinous international crimes. Indeed, the prosecution of *any* potential war crime is prima facie to be lauded as a triumph of the global rule of law, which stands against the culture of impunity that has developed under the Westphalian state system. This cannot be made any more explicit than in the observation by the International Centre for Transitional Justice that 'investigations and trials of powerful leaders (whether political or military) help strengthen the rule of law and send a strong signal that such crimes will not be tolerated in a rights-respecting society'.[30] As Chesterman succinctly puts it, analytically juxtaposing the notion of high-level war crimes prosecutions against the stability of the international order, the fact that 'leaders who violate the law may themselves be prosecuted is an important part of the core definition [of the rule of law]'.[31]

Due to the massive scale of human rights violations that took place during and after the end of the cold war era, the discourse on international criminal law, which had become relatively dormant after the Nuremberg trials, found itself again a matter of considerable global interest during the 1990s. Looking to deter future atrocities, and seeking to end those that were ongoing, scholars and politicians sought to facilitate the creation of new institutions to prosecute individuals who would commit international crimes. Of these, the ad hoc International Criminal Tribunals for the former Yugoslavia and Rwanda (the ICTY and ICTR respectively); as well as the hybrid or mixed tribunals, which include inter alia the Special Court for Sierra Leone (SCSL), the Extraordinary Chambers in the Courts of Cambodia (ECCC), the Special Tribunal for Lebanon (STL), and the Special Panels for Serious Crimes in Timor Leste (SPSC), played the most critical roles in defining the relationship between international criminal law institutions and state judiciaries. Indeed, one can see their different approaches towards concurrent domestic prosecutions as a kind of precursor to the complementarity regime that the ICC would later adopt. Thus, a brief consideration of their approach to domestic prosecutions provides an important context to the understanding of the ICC's attitude towards domestic trials today. For the purpose of this consideration, it is necessary to distinguish between the policies and strategies represented by the philosophies of the hybrid and ad hoc tribunals, which are prima facie quite distinct.

---

30 International Centre for Transitional Justice, 'Criminal Justice', available at file://localhost/<http/::www.ictj.org:id:node:23>.

31 Simon Chesterman, 'An International Rule of Law?' (2008) 56 *American Journal of Comparative Law* 331 at 343.

The ad hoc tribunals were the international community's first major foray into supranational criminal justice after Nuremberg. As institutions, they crystallized in the 1990s as a response to the escalation of certain post-cold war conflicts. Perhaps due to the urgency behind their creation – notably, both were the product of Security Council Chapter VII authorizations, whose mandate strictly covers 'threats to international peace and security'[32] – international criminal justice efforts became wholly vested in their success. This had the troubling effect of marginalizing the role of the state as the primary forum for prosecution, a result that had been in the works for years, as academia became increasingly preoccupied with the ineffectualness of post-conflict societies in engaging their national judiciaries. Indeed, the intellectualization of international criminal law has in some regards developed at odds with the discourse on transitional justice which shapes the post-conflict state-building process and emphasizes local forms of accountability through domestic prosecutions. The moral imperative driving international prosecutions has long held itself, particularly in scholarship, as superior to those that might take place in 'flawed' and 'politicized' national forums. This contention, not unusual within the discourse on international criminal law, establishes an indisputable tension between global rule of law aspirations and the inherent desire of the state to preserve sovereignty (which is sometimes a precondition to restoring the domestic rule of law). The occasional tendency of ICL scholars to trivialize the state's duty to prosecute (in essence the principle of *aut dedere aut judicare*) when there is significant political interest in an international trial, occurs in part outside of transitional justice debates because of the perceived secondary nature of 'judicial sovereignty' in the rebuilding of post-conflict societies.[33]

This attitude is admittedly understandable. It is instinctually difficult not to relegate domestic criminal systems to secondary status given the highly unstable conditions of national judiciaries after wars. The example of the ad hoc tribunal's surrender regime demonstrates this tension at its height. The tribunals were granted primacy of jurisdiction by the Security Council over the territorial state, requiring all accused sought by the

---

32 Within the chapeau of United Nations Security Council Resolution 955, the ICTY's foundational document, it is explicitly stated that 'all States shall cooperate fully' with the Tribunal. This is similarly replicated in the authorizing resolution of the ICTR.

33 McAuliffe puts this elegantly, warning that, atlhough 'judicial sovereignty has been pilloried as a political fetish, it is in fact a central aspect of sovereignty itself': McAuliffe, above n3 at 184.

tribunals to be surrendered to them rather than undergo domestic trials. While concurrent jurisdiction would take place, all high-level accused desired by the international prosecutor would go to the tribunals. According to the ICTY's appeals chamber in *Tadic*, 'when an international tribunal such as the present one is created, it must be endowed with primacy over national courts. Otherwise, human nature being what it is, there would be a perennial danger of international crimes being … "designed to shield the accused", or cases not being diligently prosecuted'.[34] Similarly, the ICTY president, Antonio Cassese, once rationalized the dilemma facing the ad hoc tribunals in these stark terms: 'So long as states retain some essential aspects of sovereignty and fail to set up an effective mechanism to enforce arrest warrants and to execute judgments, international criminal tribunals may have little more than normative impact.'[35] Collectively, he suggests, experience indicates that states will by default resist holding war criminals accountable for atrocity crimes as part of their process of *jus post bellum*. Indeed, instances of true high-level prosecutions and lustration of government officials have been so limited that the international community has rarely been able to overcome its overarching scepticism of the intentions of incoming governments. Neither tribunal had a specific mandate in regards to supporting and rebuilding judicial institutions in the Balkans and Rwanda, and as such, ignored this dimension of the pursuit of justice until the need to develop a completion strategy arose years later.[36]

As other authors have surmised, to exclude the state entirely from the possibility of conducting domestic trials can be problematic. For example, the absence of support from local communities can serve to de-legitimize international efforts to conduct investigations and hold effective trials. This is particularly an issue for intervening third parties in situations where political divisions continue to wreak havoc. The manipulation of the circumstances surrounding the ICTY's prosecution of Slobodan Miloševic are demonstrative. The former communist dictator's trial began in 2002, and ended prematurely in 2005 with his untimely death. Ever the consummate politician, Miloševic sought to conduct his own defence, using the position as a pulpit to discredit the tribunal and espouse his own narrative of the events of the Kosovo war, largely in

---

[34] *Prosecutor v Tadic* (Appeals Decision on the Defence Motion for Interlocutory Appeal on Jurisdiction), IT-9401 App Ch. (2 October 1995), at [58].

[35] Antonio Cassese, 'On the Current Trends Towards Criminal Prosecution and Punishment of Breaches of International Humanitarian Law' (1998) 9 *European Journal of International Law* 2 at 17.

[36] McAuliffe, above n3 at 190.

order to rally support for his previously discredited political agenda. Thus, not a week after his trial had started, his approval ratings had doubled from single digits to more than 20 per cent, while consequently '[a]pproval of the [ICTY, who was prosecuting him] conversely [continued] to drop … [such that] even the NATO [North Atlantic Treaty Organization] alliance that bombed Belgrade, polls say, [were being] held in higher public esteem'.[37] In fact, the swell of support for the accused's brand of ultra-nationalism proved so powerful that in 2007 Miloševic's Serbian Radical Party attempted to replicate the effect by coercing Serbian state television into broadcasting proceedings against one of the defendant's former henchmen, Miloševic's previously hand-selected heir-apparent, Vojislav Šešeljšelj.[38] In Serbia, where the impact of the ICTY's trial should have mattered most, the perception of imperialism instead catalysed the nationalist sentiment that had originally inspired the atrocities it was investigating.

Naturally, the tribunal model's successes and failures informed (or rather, served as caution in) the design of the ICC framework. Many of the ICTY's and ICTR's features, including their limited ability to contribute to local capacity-building efforts, made it unsuitable for future replication. Thus, the development of a mixed/hybrid criminal tribunal model emerged as a result of a desire to establish a compromise between the different objectives and customs found within domestic criminal systems and ICL. Neither entirely domestic nor completely internationalized, mixed tribunals operate under an amalgam of procedural and substantive rules, norms, and practices unique to each court, and borrow their components freely from both the legal system of the territorial state and from established norms of international justice.[39] Such arrangements serve a specific purpose, relevant to the needs of the post-conflict society. They demonstrate international solidarity with the transitional government, which can be essential in their

---

37 Andrew Purvis, 'Star power in Serbia', *Time Magazine* (22 September 2002), available at <http://content.time.com/time/magazine/article/0,9171, 353524,00.html>.

38 Vesna Zimonjic, 'Trial opens of Serb "who gave Ethnic Cleansing to World"' *The Independent* (London, United Kingdom, 8 November 2007) 32.

39 'A tribunal may be classified as hybrid or internationalized based on a number of criteria: legal basis, function/mandate, location within or without the domestic court system, subject-matter-jurisdiction, oversight, and composition/ personnel. … The aim of these tribunals is to "marry the best of two worlds – the expertise of the international community with the legitimacy of local actors.": Lindsey Raub, 'Positioning Hybrid Tribunals in International Criminal Justice' (2008–2009) 41 *New York University Journal of International Law & Policy* 1013 at 1023.

efforts to reclaim the support of the civilian population, while supporting local ownership efforts by ensuring trials take place on home soil. Further, supervision by international judges and lawyers affords legitimacy and objectivity, where necessary, to trials taking place in highly volatile post-conflict contexts. Domestic prosecutions in post-conflict societies are typically *politically* driven, often part of a transitional process that involves distinguishing a new regime from a previous one through rejection and punishment of those who facilitated the violent and illiberal order it emerged from. Similarly, such trials may be oriented at non-state groups that have had de facto governmental control over a region. Despite an intent to condemn the previous leadership's corruption of the nomocracy, however, these same political motivations make such trials untenable from a rule of law perspective. Put differently, the rule of law cannot support trials where there is significant potential for political bias. The hybrid model moderates such trials through the supervision of impartial third parties, establishing legitimacy through the enforcement of fair trial standards. For some, therefore, a quintessential characteristic of this model is the involvement of the United Nations in their creation and administration, even though the organization's part in the formation of the ad hoc tribunals is relatively similar.[40]

However, the contribution of the hybrid model to national capacity building assistance has been disappointing in practice. The expectation of hybrid tribunals was that they would rely on international supervision only in the early stages of transition, and would be phased out over time as domestic prosecutors developed competence in war crimes prosecution. In practice, instability merely pushed states to increase their dependence on international actors, who would increasingly revert responsibility back to the Court for the sake of convenience or comfort. McAuliffe provides a powerful condemnation of the tribunal's efforts:

> … In the years between 2000 and 2003 when hybrid tribunals were in their infancy … UN officials were simultaneously vetoing negotiations with Cambodia because local participation was too great, UNMIK was progressively weakening Kosovar participation in the most important trials, and the Sierra Leonean Government was voluntarily relinquishing ever-greater control over the bench and prosecution to internationals.[41]

---

[40] See, for example, Luigi Condorelli and Theo Boutruche, 'Internationalized Criminal Courts and Tribunals: Are They Necessary?' in Cesare Romano et al. (eds), *Internationalized Criminal Courts and Tribunals* (Oxford, Oxford University Press, 2004) 429.

[41] McAuliffe, above n3 at 194.

As he explains, over time, national judges in hybrid tribunals sought and accepted increasingly smaller roles, whilst the court's internationalized staff would conversely take on greater responsibilities. Yet, the goals of domestic and international actors in such courts are indisputably different. The latter are – and rightfully, in the theoretical context of the hybrid tribunal and its distinct composition of actors – focused on the operational functions of the Court rather than the capacity-building side, which should properly be spearheaded by national judges and legal officers. For example, prosecutors typically seek to pursue criminal law's primary punitive goal, on the one hand, while local stakeholders – including victims groups – demand greater time to develop a full picture of the event (and not strictly what is relevant to the prosecution). During early development stages, such tensions can be properly managed when equal representation from both groups engages on the perceived priorities of the institution, but this balance of participation should eventually lead to the international actors ceding control to the state. However, if the domestic goals of the court are not allowed to flourish at the preliminary stage, they are unlikely to succeed when the international community eventually withdraws. This was the concern expressed in a report by the UN High Commissioner for Human Rights, who observed that without a 'specific mandate on legacy or capacity-building[,] … prosecutors and judges simply focused on the task at hand of trying cases'.[42] The transitional aspects of hybrid courts, arguably their most important and distinguishing feature, are consequently lost as the tribunals pursue the effective disposition of cases instead.

The point of the preceding analysis is not to disparage the gains made by the advancement of the ICL agenda over the last few decades, rightly celebrated as it is. Rather, it seeks to capture the nuances of the tension between domestic and international rule of law in international law, and highlight the problem with ICL's tendency to paint the state as an obstacle to justice; consequently failing to integrate the latter within its broader strategy to pursue accountability. Consequently, the practice followed by the international community and leading up to the creation of the ICC has been primarily to ignore the need to fortify the rule of law in domestic forums, troublingly championing diminished responsibility of supranational institutions to guide and support local reconstruction and development efforts of local courts. With the installation of a permanent

---

[42] Office of the United Nations High Commissioner for Human Rights, 'Rule of law tools for post-conflict states: maximizing the legacy of hybrid courts', United Nations (2008), available at <http://www.ohchr.org/Documents/Publications/HybridCourts.pdf>, at 7.

Court, such lessons become even more important. As the Court must divide its time across a number of different situations it is investigating, it lacks the capacity to prosecute as comprehensively as its predecessors could with their restricted jurisdictions. Thus, its capacity issues suggest that the Court should secure competent national judicial systems if it hopes to have more than a merely superficial effect. Although the ICC is its own institution, in the development of its strategy of engagement with domestic prosecutions, which is predominantly defined in its complementarity and cooperation regime, the influence of the international community's experiences with the *ad hoc* and *hybrid* tribunals is evident. Indeed, one might see these paradigms of international judicial intervention as early 'test cases' of complementarity.

The concept of complementarity was introduced in the Rome Statute to clarify the relationship between the ICC and national authorities in regard to jurisdiction to prosecute. As UN Secretary General Kofi Annan explains, the crucial purpose behind complementarity's delicate balance of interests is to 'ensure that mass murderers and other arch-criminals cannot shelter behind a State run by themselves or their cronies, or take advantage of a general breakdown of law and order'.[43] Its mechanics is prefaced in the preamble of the Rome Statute, which proclaims that the 'International Criminal Court established under this Statute shall be complementary to national criminal jurisdictions'.[44] As such, it serves as a hierarchical ordering principle, and determines whether the Court's jurisdiction is triggered when there exists a clash with a concurrent domestic claim. The principle requires the ICC to *complement* rather than *supersede* national courts in investigating and prosecuting the Statute's core crimes. Accordingly, the principle is determinative of the Court's prerogative in a given situation, and thus acts as the lynch pin of the ICC's admissibility regime. Its machinery is laid out under article 17. Article 17(1)(a) of the Rome Statute explains that a case sought by the ICC is inadmissible if a state has jurisdiction over it 'unless the State is unwilling or unable genuinely to carry out the investigation or prosecution'.[45] In other words, it places the jurisdiction of the state to prosecute

---

[43] Kofi Annan, 'Secretary-General urges "Like-minded" states to ratify Statute of International Criminal Court', United Nations (1 September 1998) Press Release SG/SM/6686, available at <http://www.un.org/News/Press/docs/1998/19980901.sgsm6686.html>

[44] Rome Statute, Preamble. The Statute immediately confirms this relationship in art 1, which reiterates that the Court 'shall be complementary to national criminal jurisdictions'.

[45] Article 17(1)(a), Rome Statute.

international crimes ahead of the Court's own jurisdiction. This assessment is conducted by the Prosecutor at a preliminary situational investigation phase, and again when a specific accused is sought. From a rule of law perspective, the compromise reached by the Statute's negotiators strikes a good balance between the potentially valid claims of both parties – at least in theory. Notionally, states hold first right of refusal to bring those responsible for planning and committing atrocities to trial, which is a vindication of sovereignty; and it is only in the absence of action for reasons outlined in article 17 – that is inability due to 'total or substantial collapse or unavailability of its national judicial system'[46] on the one hand, or unwillingness on the other, as determined by the genuineness of attempts to conduct timely proceedings in an independent and impartial manner not designed to shield a suspect from criminal responsibility.[47]

Undoubtedly, such circumstances were shaped by the law's experiences in the Balkans and Rwanda. To put the relationship between the Court and the tribunals in perspective, early drafts of the Statute ultimately adopted in Rome began in the mid-1990s. The International Law Commission (ILC) submitted a final draft of the Statute to the UN General Assembly in 1994. This draft received revisions between 1994 and 1998, first from the General Assembly's Ad Hoc Committee on the Establishment of an International Criminal Court, and later its Preparatory Committee. In July 1998, the final consolidated text was adopted at the Rome Conference. During the negotiations, the primary form that international criminal justice took was that administered by the ad hoc tribunals. Although, as the name suggests, ad hoc tribunals represented 'temporary' emergency responses to two specific shocking international crimes, their model of primacy has indelibly shaped the 'complementarity' model applied by the Statute. Rwanda and the former Yugoslavia, in other words, represented the existence of two crucial forms of hostile circumstances that would militate against granting the state primary authority. Yugoslavian courts, for example, were still besieged by rampant ethnic hatred at the bureaucratic level, and the judicial system had subsequently demonstrated an unwillingness to conduct trials free of vindictive political bias. Similarly, the Rwandan court system had been so thoroughly decimated as a result of the Rwandan genocide that it was

46 Article 17(3), Rome Statute.
47 Article 17(2)(a), (b) and (c), Rome Statute.

physically unable to conduct trials. Accordingly, these cases demonstrated situations where international primacy represented the only possible solution. Complementarity specifically preserves these circumstances as the only genuine circumstances under which the ICC can, under the Statute, usurp the judicial sovereignty of the national state (although the OTP later implemented a third policy-driven category of 'state inactivity', recognizing the possibility that the state may still subvert justice if it is willing and able, but simply sedentary in pursuit of war criminals). The strict onus established under the principle is a clear concession to state sovereignty. It warrants ICC interference only in the strictest of circumstances. At the same time, it should not be mistaken as an absolute vindication of sovereignty, as the Statute still permits the Court to pierce national supremacy when the circumstances warrant. Rather, it reflects the importance of the interests of both the international community to ensure that impunity does not exist for international crimes due to the failures of the state to act in good faith, and the sovereign state's prerogative to assume responsibility for war crimes prosecutions as a means of restoring legitimacy and competency to the infrastructure of the post-conflict state on its own terms. McAuliffe describes this compromise as an 'integrated check on state sovereignty, [with] its precise statutory form [representative of] a check on this check'.[48] That is, in effect, it imposes *realpolitik* punishment on states that use sovereignty as a veil to rebuff their duty to implement fundamental international law norms.

Since the Nuremberg trials, when the Allies wrested control for the prosecutions of Nazi war crimes from German hands, the international community has steadily returned to a more balanced consideration of the tension between global and domestic interests in the war crimes discourse. In this context, the Rome Statute is the culmination of such efforts. The concessions to sovereignty found within are unsurprisingly the result of the influence of states during the development of the drafts of the Statute. Indeed, it reflects numerous interests of various stakeholders, the ICC being the first truly collaborative effort in ICL to develop a permanent court, a fact demonstrated by its foundation in a multilateral treaty as opposed to the Security Council resolutions or compromise between a host state and the UN as an organization that characterized its predecessors. The efforts of the drafters to create a better working relationship with the state and support the domestic rule of law is evident not only in the Statute's complementarity scheme, but

---

[48] McAuliffe, above n3 at 20.

also in the advancement of its victims participation and reparations schemes alongside its new Victims and Witnesses Unit, a relatively significant deviation from the strictly legalistic position adopted by the ad hoc tribunals, which saw victims as relevant to the trial process only insofar as they were witnesses to the crimes being investigated. The international community's reaction to the ICC's limited intrusive powers has, not so shockingly, received mixed reactions – particularly in academic and civil society circles. Perhaps after bearing witness to too many bad faith efforts to bring accountability at the state level, there is a fundamental dissonance in the views held by those who represent international criminal justice versus transitional justice interests. Typically, the former view the compromises made to ICC primacy under the principle of complementarity as an obstacle to justice, while the latter are more receptive to the possibility of political institutions having a genuine commitment to justice and the rule of law. Perhaps the most infamous description of this competition comes from Cryer's colourful commentary about sovereignty:

> When sovereignty appears in international criminal law scholarship, it commonly comes clothed in hat and cape. A whiff of sulphur permeates the air. Generally, international criminal law scholars see sovereignty as the enemy. It is seen as the sibling of realpolitik, thwarting international criminal justice at every turn.[49]

As an observation of the discipline's attitude towards the Westphalian state model, it strays not terribly far from the truth. Certainly, there has been sufficient cause for ongoing scepticism of the state as the primary administrator of international justice.

One example that critics provide of the problem with complementarity's subordination of the ICC to state sovereignty relates to the implementation of Colombia's so-called 'Justice and Peace Laws'. This case study has been previously considered by the authors.[50] Here, therefore, observations of this situation will be kept brief. The situation in Colombia, whose government has been involved in an asymmetric intractable armed conflict against (among others) the Revolutionary

---

49 Robert Cryer, 'International Criminal Law vs State Sovereignty: Another Round?' (2005) 16(5) *European Journal of International Law* 979 at 980.

50 See Jan Wouters and Kenneth Chan, 'Policies, Not Politics: The Pursuit of Justice in Prosecutorial Strategy at the International Criminal Court', in S Muller and S Zouridis (eds), *Law and Justice: A Strategy Perspective* (Torkel Opsahl Academic EPublisher (TOAEP), 2013) 143.

Armed Forces of Colombia (also known as *Fuerzas Armadas Revolucionarias Colombianas* or FARC) and the National Liberation Army for several decades, has been under an ICC preliminary examination since 2006. The issues faced by the Office of the Prosecutor (OTP) in conducting its examination, which is a precursor to its determination to open an investigation, are highly contentious. The now eight-year-long examination is a peculiarity of international justice, some viewing this as a representation of the industry's inability to administer justice in a timely manner. The primary contention made by the Prosecutor in his 2011 report on preliminary examinations is that an assessment of complementarity prevents the OTP from opening an investigation,[51] specifically because it was continuing to monitor the ongoing efforts of the Colombian authorities to carry out criminal proceedings under its Justice and Peace Law 975 of 2005. The determination of genuineness of domestic proceedings required more information, although the tenor of the report implied a belief that the proceedings were being conducted in good faith. Human rights NGOs, however, strongly reject the legitimacy of these 'trials', which they argue are used as a shield to deflect culpability away from important state officials, who if prosecuted, are primarily charged with minor administrative crimes instead.[52] Rather, the law, which grants an extraordinary amount of power to government officials rather than judicial officers, demonstrating a callous disregard for the *trias politica,* allows the state significant control over who to prosecute, and who to provide amnesty to. Under such conditions, concern for the ability of the state to compromise the effectiveness of the ICC through manipulation of complementarity remains justified.

As with the hybrid tribunals, whose development during the early 2000s follows a similar trajectory, the ICC's international staff has the primary responsibility to implement policies and infrastructure that defines its institutional relationship with domestic courts. However, the ICC can be distinguished from these predecessors due to a much clearer institutional remit to assist and support national institutions – terms clearly dictated by states prior to and during the negotiations at the Rome Conference. Complementarity, as discussed, is the foundation of this strategy, and it has very much shaped the work of the Court, and

[51] Office of the Prosecutor, 'Report on Preliminary Examination Activities' (13 December 2011) at 15–16.

[52] See Avocats Sans Frontières, 'The principle of complementarity in the Rome Statute and the Colombian situation: a case that demands more than a "positive" approach' (May 2012), available at <http://www.iccnow.org/documents/asf_rapport-anglais-complementarity_and_colombia.pdf>.

particularly the OTP. Recognizing the need to coopt national criminal prosecutions into its external relations strategy in order to extend its reach, the Prosecutor used the concept of complementarity to develop a blueprint for encouraging and facilitating states to fulfil their duty to prosecute.[53] The concept of 'positive complementarity' would, according to the office, allow the Court to '[encourage] genuine national proceedings where possible; [rely] on national and international networks; and [participate] in a system of international cooperation'.[54] Through such engagements, the Court may act directly to supply resources, supervision and advice to domestic courts that would be otherwise *unable* to prosecute. As Ocampo explains, the policy has already paid dividends in situations presently under investigation. For example, he notes that in the Democratic Republic of Congo (DRC), his office seeks to:

> [coordinate an] approach whereby it will transfer background information, contextual analysis or evidence on alleged perpetrators of crimes in the Kivus to relevant national judicial authorities in order to support complementary national efforts … [that have] a credible local system of protection for judges or witnesses and … integrity of domestic proceedings.[55]

In many ways, the policy of positive complementarity reflects the same principles followed by the hybrid tribunal model, which was developed during the same period.

While such evidence points to an increasingly progressive recognition of the importance of domestic trials by the Court, certainly driven by the recognition that caseload undoubtedly exceeds capacity, in practice, there are reasonable concerns that this philosophy has been employed only selectively, and ignored when circumstances do not suit the interests of the Court. That is, although the ICC was established to act as a court of

---

[53] See 'Paper on some policy issues before the Office of the Prosecutor', above n6 at 5.

[54] The Office of the Prosecutor, 'Report on Prosecutorial Strategy' (14 September 2006), available at <http://www.icc-cpi.int/NR/rdonlyres/D673DD8C-D427-4547-BC69-2D363E07274B/143708/ProsecutorialStrategy20060914_English.pdf> (further 2006 Prosecutorial Strategy)

[55] Luis Moreno-Ocampo, 'A Positive Approach to Complementarity: The Impact of the Office of the Prosecutor' in Carsten Stahn and Mohammed el Zeidy (eds), *The International Criminal Court and Complementarity: From Theory to Practice* (Cambridge, Cambridge University Press, 2011) 27.

'last resort'[56] in order to allow post-conflict communities the opportunity to rebuild and restore upon their own terms, there is some evidence that this is only applied when it does not inconvenience the Court's own design for its investigative and prosecutorial docket. This is undoubtedly troubling, as the development of the domestic rule of law is an especially volatile process, and risks destabilization if it is subject to arbitrary political whim. Take, for example, Schabas's description of the arrest warrant for Congolese warlord Thomas Dyilo Lubanga, which paints a picture of a Court somewhat unconcerned with the capability of the national court to prosecute insofar as it does not bar jurisdiction subject to complementarity. In 2006, the Prosecutor issued an arrest warrant for the accused, who was at that present moment already in the custody of the DRC, awaiting trial for crimes of genocide. However, the ICC, which had not yet opened a trial in the four years since it was created, was eager to demonstrate its relevance. Thus, it sought to divest the Congo of its prisoner – but not because they were incapable of conducting the trial themselves, it would seem. As Schabas opined, '... arguably, the justice system of the DRC was doing a *better* job than the Court itself, because it [charged Lubanga with] crimes of greater gravity [than those the Prosecutor ultimately laid charges for at the ICC]'.[57] In his view, the decision of the ICC to take the defendant's trial away from his home country was a political compromise which suited all parties, as the defendant would face lesser charges with lesser consequences, the state would be relieved of the financial burden of the trial, and the Court would have its first accused to demonstrate it had been active. The only 'losers' in these circumstances, he argued, were the victims of Lubanga's crime who had pursued prosecution for the more serious charges, and for the trial to take place locally where they could observe and monitor proceedings. That the Court so casually dismissed the very real prospect that a domestic trial could have and would have taken place prior to its intervention is troubling, if not surprising. Even though it had obtained the consent of the Congolese government to assume custody of Lubanga, allowing it to end its own preparations for the trial, the law should not be so at ease with the political convenience of the resolution – especially given its detrimental impact on victim communities. After all, the DRC

---

56 A term used deliberately by the Court itself: 'ICC at a glance' *The International Criminal Court,* available at <http://www.icc-cpi.int/en_menus/icc/about the court/icc at a glance/Pages/icc at a glance.aspx>.

57 William A. Schabas, 'Prosecutorial Discretion v. Judicial Activism at the International Criminal Court' (2008) 6(4) *Journal of International Criminal Justice* 731 at 743.

had demonstrated it was both willing and able to prosecute, albeit reluctant to do so. (Of course, 'reluctance' does not represent an aspect of the admissibility test.) Indeed, in a test of complementarity, a plain reading of the text in the circumstances would suggest the case would be inadmissible. The ICC, adopting an interpretation of the text of article 17 that would allow it to take proceedings if domestic courts were 'inactive', developed what some have suggested is a third prong of the complementarity test. Indeed, inactivity as a grounds for admissibility has received considerable support in a number of Chambers in the Court.[58] This is itself somewhat dubious, as article 17 already require an assessment of whether a case is being investigated and prosecuted by the state *prior* to a determination of complementarity. As such, the Court's jurisdiction should have been discharged prior to the point where it would need to apply the complementarity test. Thus, it is surprising that the case was deemed admissible due to 'inactivity' in the circumstances.

There have similarly been inconsistencies in the application of the so-called 'same conduct' test in regard to article 17. That is, in the application of complementarity under article 17(1)(a) and 17(1)(b), when required to assess whether 'the case' is being or has been investigated and prosecuted, the Court has sometimes endorsed a test to determine if the domestic prosecution is for the 'same case' that it would bring against the accused for 'substantially the same conduct'. Initially adopted by the Pre-trial Chamber in the *Lubanga Arrest Warrant Decision*,[59] and confirmed half a decade later by the Appeals Chamber as the 'correct test'

---

[58] For example, in the Trial Chamber's decision on the admissibility of the case against Germain Katanga et al., they explain that 'in the case of inaction, the question of unwillingness or inability does not arise; inaction on the part of a State having jurisdiction (that is, the fact that a State is not investigating or prosecuting, or has not done so) renders a case admissible before the Court, subject to article 17(1)(d) of the Statute': *Prosecutor v Germain Katanga and Mathieu Ngudjolo Chui, Judgment on the Appeal of Mr Germain Katanga against the Oral Decision of Trial Chamber II of 12 June 2009 on the Admissibility of the Case,* ICC-01/04-01/07 OA 8 (25 September 2009), available at file://localhost/<http/::www.icc-cpi.int:iccdocs:doc:doc746819.pdf>, at [78].

[59] Pre-Trial Chamber I explains that 'it is a *conditio sine qua non* for a case arising from the investigation of a situation to be inadmissible that national proceedings encompass both the person and the conduct which is the subject of the case before the Court': *Situation in the Democratic Republic of Congo, Decision on the Prosecutor's Application for Warrants of Arrest, Article 58*, Pre-Trial Chamber I, 10 February 2006, ICC-01/04-520-Anx2, at [31].

during the *Ruto Admissibility Appeal*,[60] the exacting standards of this threshold test has been the cause of considerable vexation for national courts seeking to rebuff the Court's attempts to take over their cases. Under the test, if national courts do not tailor their prosecutions to ensure that they prosecute the *same person for the same conduct* alleged by the Prosecutor, the case would be prima facie admissible and the Court could then assert jurisdiction (assuming the secondary conditions of the complementarity test were also met). There are, as Heller suggests, numerous criticisms of this approach which would '[require] governments to be mind-readers: [because] if they do not accurately anticipate the precise conduct that will draw the ICC's attention … they will be deemed "inactive" with regard to the international proceedings and the Court will admit the case'.[61] At the crux of this problem is the issue of the homogenization of ICL under a single jurisprudential mandate. In its attempt to ensure that all actions that constitute the commission of a specific crime as defined by the Statute are prosecuted as such, whether or not the trial takes place before the ICC, the Statute has established a threshold that attempts to ensure that the 'appropriate' crime is prosecuted if it occurs at the domestic level. The intent behind the policy is admirable. It seeks to ensure that the proceedings reflect the actual crimes committed as determined by the facts of the case. In effect, it could be seen to impute an assessment of the 'gravity' of the national proceedings into the assessment of complementarity. That is, it rejects attempts to prosecute serious crimes as lesser charges, perhaps due to an accused's political position or connections. However, the test problematically ignores the practical limitations of state judicial systems, who may yet lack the expertise to prosecute for specialized crimes, and/or have instead conducted good faith prosecutions for such actions under their ordinary penal codes as ordinary crimes. In some circumstances, this is the very antithesis of constructive support of the domestic rule of law, as it can actively undermine genuine local efforts simply to secure jurisdiction for a case that the Court desires for itself. The 'disturbing' result of this strategy is that it can, in practice 'effectively [transform]

---

60 *The Prosecutor v William Samoei Ruto, Henry Kiprono Kosgey and Joshua Arap Sang, Judgment on the Appeal of the Republic of Kenya Against the Decision of Pre-Trial Chamber II of 30 May 2011 Entitled 'Decision on the Application by the Government of Kenya Challenging the Admissibility of the Case Pursuant to Article 19(2)(b) of the Statute*', Appeals Chamber, 20 May 2011, ICC-01/09-01/11-307.

61 Kevin J. Heller, 'A Sentence-Based Theory of Complementarity' (2012) 53(1) *Harvard International Law Journal* 85 at 125.

complementarity into primacy … [as] the ICC will always have final say over whether a case remains at the national level; a Prosecutor that wants to ensure that a particular defendant is prosecuted by the ICC can simply nullify an existing national investigation or prosecution by selecting different conduct to investigate'.[62] There are, assuredly, good reasons to revisit the test, as states will undoubtedly contest its application in the future.

Indeed, Pre-trial Chamber I was recently required to revisit the same conduct test when Libya contested the admissibility of the case relating to Abdullah al-Senussi, the chief of intelligence under Qaddafi's former regime. Libya, having jurisdiction over the accused, asserted that the Court should be precluded from exercising jurisdiction because of the active investigations being conducted by its national judicial system for the crimes against humanity potentially committed. Complementarity, in other words, would demand Libya's primacy be respected in the circumstances. Although the Prosecutor was in agreement with Libya's assessment, both the Defence for the accused and the Office of Public Council for Victims (OPCV) contested this appraisal, arguing that the evidence produced to corroborate the claim lacked both sufficient specificity and probative value. Accordingly, they asserted that it would not be possible to make an adequate assessment of the scope and depth of the investigations taking placed based on the evidence. In its determination of whether the evidence gave sufficient indication of the parameters of the factual matrix being investigated by Libya, the Court notably loosened its previously strict attitude towards the assessment of complementarity, which required the precise minutiae of the national proceedings to be indicated. It found, accordingly, that the evidence adduced need not be clearly demonstrative of the full extent of its activities, but was satisfied that it was indicative of 'concrete and progressive steps … being undertaken by the domestic authorities in the proceedings against Mr Al-Senussi', as well as the 'scope and subject-matter of such proceedings'.[63] That the Pre-trial Chamber considered evidence of 'identifiable, concrete and progressive investigative steps in relation to … criminal responsibility'[64] as being sufficient to satisfy the same conduct test is an important concession to the Court's duty to respect the primacy of the state when the latter acts in good faith.

---

62 Ibid.

63 *Situation in Libya, Decision on the admissibility of the case against Abdullah Al-Senussi*, Pre-Trial Chamber I, 11 October 2013, ICC-01/11-01/11, at [158].

64 Ibid. [162].

The inconsistency with which the ICC has addressed the rights it affords to national courts has undoubtedly soured its relationship with them, the most obvious example of this being its frigid *détente* with the African Union, which recently called upon its members to withdraw from the Statute. The organization's frustration arises not only from its express concern that Africa is being (unjustly) targeted by the Prosecutor, but more acutely, because the judicial systems of states' targeted by investigations find themselves increasingly frozen out of the decision-making process. Indeed, it would not be unfair to say that the Court's jurisprudence – which is determined entirely by the ICC's international judges and prosecutors – is indicative of a narrower view of state sovereignty than is evidenced by the Statute. While there is evidence that the Court has become more aware of its potential overreach and is increasingly demonstrating greater respect for the domestic rule of law, the uncertainty that emerges from its unevenness of application is itself injurious to local peace-building efforts. In order to neutralize the antagonism that is growing between the Court and subject states, establishing a strong precedent of cooperation with and support for the domestic rule of law is essential. Not only should the Court directly support domestic prosecutorial efforts, but it should do so *indirectly* as well, through the development of clear procedural jurisprudence that is cohesive with the principles of domestic criminal justice. That is, despite the Court's *sui generis* characteristics, its goals can only be served by interpreting and applying the law in a manner that local judicial systems can comprehend and utilize as a model of best practice. Indeed, as the following section will elaborate, because the ICC stands at the intersection between domestic and international rule of law, it is in an ideal position to advocate for stronger harmonization of legal practice at both the local and supranational level, but to do so, it must demonstrate reciprocity.

IV. THE ICC AND SUPPORT FOR THE DOMESTIC RULE OF LAW: RECENT DEVELOPMENTS AND RECOMMENDATIONS FOR BEST PRACTICE

As the ICC enters its second decade of work, it can no longer rely on the initial good will it was afforded upon creation. Today, it must stand on its own merits, effectively pursue its vision of justice, and uphold the rule of law wherever it holds influence. This is no small task, and those that have looked to the Court to act decisively against genocidaires and violent despots have seen little evidence of this occurring. In the past decade, questionable policy and unnecessary bloat have hampered the Court as it manages its ever-increasing caseload, and this must be excised. Increasingly, post-conflict communities seeking a measure of justice from the institution have found it the embodiment of bureaucracy. While the Court has promised them much in the way of support for their transitional justice efforts, it has largely failed to deliver. Disenfranchised communities recovering from conflict perceive the institution as having fallen short of its towering aspirations. Although not always deserved, the ICC has received some scathing criticisms from those frustrated by its limitations. These were particularly prominent during the prosecution of Thomas Dyilo Lubanga, a mid-level war criminal from the DRC, the first case to be successfully prosecuted by the Court. There can be no dispute that the prosecution of the accused was a 'victory', as non-governmental organizations like Human Rights Watch have described it; nor that it is not the major 'first step in bringing justice to the tens of thousands of children forced to fight in conflicts'.[65] Yet, as other critics have succinctly countered – observing that shy of its first decade the Court had only successfully completed one trial – frequent and spurious delays highlight 'the weaknesses of the ICC model, as well as the prosecutor's own failings'.[66] Even at the ad hoc tribunals, whose rules and regulations were far less meticulous than the Courts, trials did not drag on and delay to the extent that they do at the ICC. Thus, as others have done following the Lubanga verdict,[67] the Court must ask itself whether the relatively modest gains achieved by pursuing a narrow line of investigation and an indictment focussed exclusively on war crimes relating to the enlistment and conscription of child soldiers (which also meant the exclusion of charges for gender-based and sexual crimes, which proved a major point of contention among victims and human rights organizations alike)[68] are enough to justify the distinct perception that it has been ineffective in

---

[65] Human Rights Watch, 'ICC: landmark verdict a warning to rights abusers' (14 March 2012), available at <http://www.hrw.org/news/2012/03/14/icc-landmark-verdict-warning-rights-abusers>.

[66] Joshua Rozenberg, 'Delay in Lubanga judgment demonstrates ICC weaknesses' (14 March 2012), *The Guardian,* available at <http://www.theguardian.com/law/2012/mar/14/delay-lubanga-weaknesses-icc-model>.

[67] See for example, Alpha Sesay, 'Long proceedings in trial of Thomas Lubanga finally reach end' *International Justice Monitor* (26 August 2011), available at <http://www.ijmonitor.org/2011/08/long-proceedings-in-trial-of-thomas-lubanga-finally-reach-end/>.

[68] See, for example, Passy Mubalama and Experance Nzigire, 'ICC still facing rape case challenges', *Institute for War and Peace Reporting* (8 August

engaging with contemporary atrocities. It is not hard, after all, to see how victims could be frustrated with Lubanga's relatively conservative 14-year prison sentence[69] following a convoluted six-year-long trial (spanning from the transfer of the accused to the publication of the final judgment), which in at least two instances threatened to implode when the trial court considered a dismissal of the case due to intractable evidentiary disputes between the Court and the OTP, which effectively undermined the accused's right to due process, and as a result of the dubious use of unvetted and untrained local intermediaries to conduct investigations, compromising the integrity of the evidence adduced. As the adage goes, justice delayed is justice denied – and indeed, so is justice ignored. Even if one considers the numerous delays, clumsy management of procedural disputes, and occasional failure of due diligence (such as with the prosecutorial manipulation of local assets, as discussed below) which have undermined the institution throughout its first decade of work[70] to be part of a vital learning curve, it is unclear whether the Court has taken relevant lessons on board – or indeed, if there is even agreement on what these may be. More recent cases before the Court, such as the high-profile prosecutions launched against Saif Al-Islam Gaddafi, son of former Libyan Dictator Muammar Gaddafi, and Abdullah Al-Senussi, the former regime's intelligence officer, are languishing as the Court disputes the application of its jurisdiction over the state. Indeed, Heller recently described the unwarranted delays of the Appeals Chamber in its determination of appeals of admissibility as a case of 'the ICC [fiddling] while Libya burns'.[71]

2011), available at <http://iwpr.net/report-news/icc-still-facing-rape-case-challenges>.

[69] Unsurprisingly, local non-governmental organizations have received the sentence with some ire, with one referring to it as 'joke'. Instead, they suggest that 'for his victims – and their families – who agreed to testify in court, Lubanga's return to DRC will spark fear of reprisals. It would be good for him to be tried for other crimes he committed in Ituri, in addition to the recruitment and use of minors as combat troops in his militia': Emmanuel Chaco, 'DRC warlord sentence a joke, says NGOs' (12 July 2012) Inter Press Service News Agency, available at <http://www.ipsnews.net/2012/07/drc-warlord-sentence-a-joke-say-ngos/>.

[70] See, for a closer analysis of the myriad of problems that plagued the trial: Patrick Wegner, 'What went wrong during the Lubanga trial', Justice in Conflict (14 March 2012), available at <http://justiceinconflict.org/2012/03/14/what-went-wrong-during-the-lubanga-trial/>.

[71] Kevin Jon Heller, 'The ICC fiddles while Libya burns' *Opinio Juris* (24 March 2014), available at <http://opiniojuris.org/2014/03/24/30477/>.

How should the Court refocus its efforts in the next decade of its existence? Now under its second prosecutor, the ICC has indicated renewed vigour in its pursuit of justice. If it is to win back the support of its sceptics, it is clear that the Court must confidently demonstrate an ability to provide justice effectively to and within post-conflict communities. It must shed the 'trial by error' mentality that has so decisively characterized the institution's first years, and real gains must be made on its promise of global justice and ending impunity. The recommendations made in this chapter are not comprehensive, but a few modest thoughts are offered.

A. Supporting the Domestic Rule of Law Through Technical Assistance

First, international lawyers must attempt to move beyond their inherent suspicions of the efficacy of domestic proceedings. An international rule of law demands that the ICC ensure that the law is applied unequivocally to all who commit atrocities, irrespective of their political affiliations. Yet, it does not assert whether this should take place in domestic or international forums, and as the Rome Statute under complementarity has itself indicated a deference to national courts in specific circumstances, *their specific interests as post-conflict states* must be used to guide this relationship – at least, to the extent that it does not undermine the primary goal of due process prosecutions of war criminals. At face value, the nature of the relationship between the ICC and post-conflict states – not only those over whom it has jurisdiction, per se, but all those actively seeking transitional justice – is primarily articulated through the concepts of complementarity and cooperation, located respectively in article 17 and part IX of the Statute. These concepts describe, at least superficially, the nature of the expected interaction between the institution and the state, demanding a high degree of synergy to secure the most comprehensive level of prosecutions possible. Yet, with a robust appreciation of the post-conflict context of the Court's work, a closer sub-textual reading of the Statute intimates the existence of a far more complex relationship between these bodies – one that remains largely under-theorized and poorly augmented in the Court's jurisprudence. However, as Chesterman suggests, 'rule of law assistance is supported because … in addition to promoting human rights and providing a stable foundation for economic development, it has also been used to establish non-violent mechanisms for resolving political disputes'.[72] These are, undeniably, attractive goals for the Court, and ones it should pursue robustly.

Of course, it is understandable why there has been such a major discipline-wide suspicion of domestic criminal law trials. First and most significantly, there is a strong belief that fair, unbiased trials that observe due process cannot take place where the crimes were committed – for reasons ranging from the ongoing ethnic divisions to the failure of post-conflict communities to effectively purge community leaders who have had a hand in fanning the flames of instability.[73] The chaotic, and highly criticized 'show' trial and eventual execution of former Iraqi President Saddam Hussein in 2005–06, coordinated by the Iraqi Special Tribunal under the country's domestic laws, is the most infamous modern example of such concerns. Indeed, Human Rights Watch goes so far as to declare the 'flawed trial' 'a significant step away from the rule of law in Iraq';[74] while Amnesty International determined that 'due to political interference … and other serious failings',[75] the independence of the tribunal had been seriously undermined. In view of these concerns, which are prescient after any major forceful change of regime, complementarity directly addresses situations where such forms of 'unwillingness' to provide due process trials are evidenced, and exempts them from the protections of state sovereignty.

---

72 Chesterman, above n31 at 341.

73 Hussain puts it thus:

> The goal of supporting the reconstruction of a domestic legal culture – although now becoming accepted as a necessary starting point – has been the most neglected of principles behind justifying the establishment of tribunals. Notably, the lack of such a focus is not simply a result of scarce resources. The human rights community has concerns about whether it is even normatively desirable to elevate the goal of capacity-building to the level of the other goals of accountability mechanisms. This position assumes that certain important principles intrinsic to fully achieving accountability will be sacrificed if collaboration increases with domestic institutions and people.

Varda Hussain, 'Sustaining Judicial Rescues: The Role of Outreach and Capacity-Building Efforts in War Crimes Tribunals' (2004–5) 45 *Virginia Journal of International Law* 547 at 551.

74 Human Rights Watch, 'Iraq: Saddam Hussein put to death' (30 December 2006), available at <http://www.hrw.org/en/news/2006/12/29/iraq-saddam-hussein-put-death>.

75 Amnesty International, 'Iraq: Amnesty International condemns Iraqi Appeal Court verdict against Saddam Hussein and co-accused' (28 December 2006), available at <https://www.amnesty.org/en/library/asset/MDE14/044/2006/en/a85375ab-d34c-11dd-a329-2f46302a8cc6/mde140442006en.html>.

Secondly, and perhaps more pragmatically, there are reasonable concerns that domestic courts are ill-equipped to prosecute 'unimaginable atrocities that deeply shock the conscience of humanity'.[76] There is no question that the commission of crimes on a grand scale, or as part of some broader genocidal strategy, revolts the human spirit – but this has clear practical implications as well. Genocides, crimes against humanity, and war crimes are irregular acts of barbarity that fall beyond the normal scope of what a functional judiciary in stable, functional states were designed to anticipate or independently manage. National criminal courts are not purposed to prosecute international crimes emerging from the exceptional circumstances of protracted armed conflict, or to do battle with such deeply entrenched levels of state corruption and nihilistic violence at the executive level. Rather, they are designed to address the commission of 'ordinary' breaches of law such as theft, sexual violence, or murder – where these occur in 'regular' circumstances, outside the broader orchestrations of atrocity crimes. Put differently, the vast complexities and massive scale typical of international crimes tend to require specialized infrastructure and personnel, which the ICC was uniquely created to provide. As Judge Hans Peter-Kaul persuasively argued in 2010, in a dissenting opinion about the Court's decision to authorize the investigation into Kenya's 2007 post-election violence:

> There are, in law and in the existing systems of criminal justice in this world, essentially two different categories of crimes … . There are, on the one side, international crimes of concern to the international community as a whole, in particular genocide, crimes against humanity, and war crimes pursuant to articles 6, 7 and 8 of the Statute. There are, on the other side, common crimes, albeit of a serious nature, prosecuted by national criminal justice systems … . [Thus, a] demarcation line must be drawn between international crimes and human rights infractions; between those crimes subject of international jurisdiction and those punishable under domestic penal legislation.[77]

Substantively, international crimes under the Rome Statute are uniquely distinguished from 'ordinary' crimes because – as has been previously alluded to – they require proof of the presence of a special *chapeau* element. All four crimes under the substantive jurisdiction of the ICC require this. A crime against humanity has only occurred, for example, if

---

76 Rome Statute, preamble.

77 Dissenting Opinion of Judge Hans-Peter Kaul on the '*Decision Pursuant to Article 15 of the Rome Statute on the Authorization of an investigation into the Situation in the Republic of Kenya*' 31 March 2010, ICC 01/09-19-Corr, at [8] ("Dissenting Opinion of Judge Hans Peter-Kaul").

the act takes place as part of a widespread or systematic attack against a civilian population. For genocide, there exists the need to prove specific intent, also known as the *dolus specialis*. That is, in genocide, the existence of both a general intent (the *mens rea* of an act) to commit the specific act (the *actus reus*) constituting the crime must be present, as well as a *dolus specialis* ulterior intent to bring about the 'destruction' of a protected group. The assessment of this additional subjective requirement is as much academic as it is political or legal in nature, and considerable work has gone into articulating its precise character, not only in the case law of the ad hoc tribunals which preceded the work of the Court,[78] but in special commissions of inquiry,[79] civil society contributions, and in scholarly literature. This pedigree is not raised merely for posterity, but to demonstrate the highly complex and nuanced task of managing war crimes cases – a task that regular national courts would be unlikely to have the competence or the experience to handle.

However, neither reason provides an entirely compelling case for the prioritization of international over domestic trials. Rather, they establish a strong onus on international institutions to strengthen national prosecutions and reinforce the domestic rule of law through training, capacity support, and so on – all elements evident in the prosecutorial strategy of positive complementarity. They further indicate a need for vigilance against political bias and dysfunction, which the Rome Statute adequately regulates in its admissibility regime. The ICC must, therefore, work with these courts to ensure the different goals it prioritizes are adequately balanced, and to ensure the principles that stand as a *conditio sine qua non* to the rule of law are not compromised. The ICC has expressly rejected any preconception that it may play a 'political' role, painting itself exclusively as an arbiter of justice. This must be translated into its domestic rule of law programme. Local trials, particularly successor trials, are frequently at risk of being subsumed by their political nature. As Teitel notes:

---

[78] The 'special intent' concept which was adopted by the Rome Statute finds its origins from the ICTR decision *Prosecutor v Jean-Paul Akayesu*, Trial Judgement, Case No ICTR-96-4-T, 2 September 1998.

[79] See, for further assessment of the elements of genocide: International Commission of Inquiry on Darfur, Report of the International Commission of Inquiry on Darfur to the UN Secretary-General, pursuant to SC Res 1564, 18 September 2004, Annex to letter dated 31 January 2005 from the UN Secretary-General addressed to the President of the Security Council, S/2005/60, 1 February 2005.

> While trials in these political contexts are intended to serve political purposes – relating to the extraordinary message of transitional justice to lay the foundation of the political transition, to disavow predecessor political norms, and to construct a new legal order – these very features are in tension with conventional understandings of the rule of law. The core dilemma relates to the central feature of transition: the political context of the normative shift. This core dilemma raised by the political shift from illiberal to liberal rule is inextricably enmeshed in the problem of retroactivity in the relevant norms during the change of regime and the exercise of the successor regime's new normative rules as applied to the past regime's behavior.[80]

Ultimately, efficacious criminal proceedings are quintessential to a functioning state, and conducting such trials in local courts has an extremely profound effect in assisting communities, still strongly divided by their ethnic and religious divisions, resolve their differences and prevent the resurgence of conflict. Even if it is not possible to host trials on local soil, there remains a need to provide training and support for local judicial institutions if they are to be expected not only to host lower level trials not sought by international courts, but to take over, continue and complete outstanding prosecutions once the international court has closed down. Accordingly, Alvarez summarizes the international communities' experiences with domestic judicial engagement under the ad hoc tribunals by asserting, and not unjustly so, that:

> international proceedings should be truly complementary to national processes that are pursued in good faith. Indeed, such national proceedings may need to be accorded jurisdictional primacy, except with respect to particular cases presenting due process concerns. Generally, the jurisdictional limits, procedures, and sentences of international processes should avoid conflicts with and enhance the effectiveness of concurrent national efforts.[81]

B. A Rome System of Justice: Implications for Jurisprudence

It is submitted that the ICC's obligation to cooperate with states and uphold the domestic rule of law applies not only to technical assistance, but should also extend to its own jurisprudential development. Accordingly, the second recommendation offered is that the Court must set a clear example in its own rulings and determinations, which should as clearly as possible be demonstrative of best practice to national courts.

---

[80] Ruti G Teitel, *Transitional Justice* (New York, Oxford University Press, 2000), at 30.

[81] Jose E Alvarez, 'Crimes of States/Crimes of Hate: Lessons from Rwanda' (1999) 24 *Yale Journal of International Law* 365 at 463.

This refers to what some authors have referred to as the systemic dimension of the Rome Statute. Robinson asserts that the Court should be expected to 'contribute to a climate of accountability not only through the demonstrative effect of its own prosecutions but, more importantly, through the "multiplier effect" of its complementary jurisdiction, as it encourages states to more diligently apprehend and prosecute international criminal'.[82] In 2006, the Prosecutor explained his office's view that the concept of complementarity was not merely a simple tool to determine primacy of judicial fora, but formed the basis of an 'interdependent, mutually reinforcing international system of justice',[83] which extended from the ICC. It was, accordingly, responsible for facilitating the homogenization of goals, and ensuring cooperation and assistance were provided where necessary. Burke-White similarly shares the view of the Statute 'not just as the foundational instrument of the ICC, but also as the basis of the Rome System of Justice ... [the purpose of which] is to "put an end to impunity"'.[84] In establishing the ICC as the spine of a broader central nervous system of international criminal justice, the Court assumes a responsibility to, in essence, set a good example for domestic courts. What this means, ostensibly, is that it should – wherever there is uncertainty in application or interpretation of the law and sources of international law do not immediately clarify it – apply the Rome Statute in a manner that demonstrates to national courts how they should address similar procedural problems. In so doing, the Court must interpret the law in a way that resists bowing to political pressure, for instance, so as to demonstrate to domestic courts the importance of maintaining the *trias politica*. A number of recent developments in the work of the Court highlight the need to develop a principled guideline for the development of procedural jurisprudence, one which this chapter has suggested should be influenced by an interest in supporting the domestic rule of law. Consider the following examples.

1. The legal characterization of facts and regulation 55: A challenge to due process?

One of the most contested procedural issues that has emerged in recent ICC jurisprudence relates to a largely unassuming regulation adopted by the bench in 2004 to assist it in the application of article 74(2) of the

---

[82] Darryl Robinson, 'Serving the Interests of Justice: Amnesties, Truth Commissions and the International Criminal Court' (2003) 14(3) *European Journal of International Law* 481 at 482.

[83] 2006 Prosecutorial Strategy, above n54.

[84] Burke-White, above n5 at 79.

Statute. Yet, regulation 55 has had a significant impact on due process, and continues to pose a serious risk to the rights of the accused at trial. Under the regulation, the Court is permitted to amend charges against an accused *during a trial* in order to convict a defendant of crimes *different* from those laid out in the initial charges. It also allows for the Trial Chamber to alter the mode of liability applied to the accused. Accordingly, regulation 55 has the potential to create significant due process problems, and consequently, its implementation has been troubling.

To understand the challenges posed by regulation 55, it is necessary to provide context about the article to which it relates. Article 74(2) was drafted in anticipation of the possibility that the evidence that would emerge during the trial process would portray the contested facts of a case in a different light than that initially conceived by the Prosecutor.

Article 74(2) specifies that:

> The Trial Chamber's decision shall be based on its evaluation of the evidence and the entire proceedings. The decision shall not exceed the facts and circumstances described in the charges and any amendments to the charges. The Court may base its decision only on evidence submitted and discussed before it at the trial.

Accordingly, the article allows for the Trial Chamber to ensure the crime charged matches the evidence accordingly, even if it is not the one originally asserted. The motivations behind the adoption of the regulation is perhaps understandable given the nature of the different international crimes. In ICL, individual acts of violence take on the legal character of a specific international crime dependent on the existence of a broader context – a murder becomes a genocide because of genocidal intent, or a crime against humanity if such an intent is absent but instead occurs as part of a broader organizational policy. It can be, as the article anticipates, unclear what the appropriate legal character to apply to the facts is, and this may only reveal itself in the course of proceedings. Accordingly, the introduction of this rule was intended to streamline the prosecutorial process and, in part, make it more efficient by mitigating the need for the Prosecutor to prepare alternate or cumulative charges at the outset.

As a buffer against the potential subversion of the accused's fair trial rights, which would obviously be violated to some degree by *any* sudden change in the nature of the charges levelled against him (as this would clearly prevent the accused from being properly informed of the charges against him in due time to mount an adequate defence) the article strictly prohibits the Prosecutor from using the article to introduce new facts and essentially lay fresh charges. Regulation 55 was adopted by the judges of the ICC to elaborate on the machinery of article 74(2). The regulation states that:

> In its decision under article 74, the Chamber may change the legal characterisation of facts to accord with the crimes under articles 6, 7 or 8, or to accord with the form of participation of the accused under articles 25 and 28, without exceeding the facts and circumstances described in the charges and any amendments to the charges.

Perhaps unsurprisingly, the regulation has either been invoked by the Prosecutor or flagged by the Trial Chamber as being subject to potential legal recharacterization in numerous cases, including *Lubanga*, *Bemba Gombo*, *Katanga*, *Ruto and Arap Sang*, *Kenyatta*, and most recently in the confirmation of charges in *Gbagbo* and *Ntaganda*. The most significant of these invocations relates to the case of Germain Katanga. In 2012, the Trial Chamber – in its case against the Congolese national charged with the commission of war crimes and crimes against humanity relating to an attack on the village of Bogoro in the Ituri province of the DRC – sought to apply the regulation in order to recharacterize the mode of liability that the accused would be charged with. Notably, this decision took place *after* the Court had heard both the evidence against the defendant as well as his own testimony. They sought to install a different mode of liability, namely 'common purpose liability', which had a lower threshold of proof than the initial charge of indirect co-perpetration. The purpose of this appears evident – having heard the evidence, the Court was uncertain it would be able to secure a conviction on the higher charge, and thus sought a form of responsibility with a lower evidentiary threshold where there was a greater chance of success. Judge van den Wyngaert rightly expressed outrage at this decision in a strong dissent, asserting that it would 'fundamentally [encroach] upon the accused's right to a fair trial'. She went on further to claim that this would put 'both the fairness and the expeditiousness of the trial in grave jeopardy'. To add insult to injury, the majority also determined that it could use the previous testimony provided by the accused when litigating the previous indictment to prove the *new* charges – in effect, using evidence provided by the accused when testifying to the previous charges with the higher burden of proof *against him* once the evidentiary standard had been lowered. The right against self-incrimination was clearly abrogated in this case, and sends a disturbing message to domestic courts that they may employ whatever tactics deemed necessary to secure convictions, even if they fundamentally compromise due process.

There is no doubt that the implications of this application have been vigorously debated behind closed doors, and the result has been a more cautious application in future decisions. Indeed, in the recent confirmation of charges in *Gbagbo*, the Court's willingness to comply with the OTP's request at this early stage to cumulatively charge the accused with several different possible modes of liability – a situation which regulation 55 was designed in part to negate the need for – is indicative of its concern with future application. Accordingly, the Court made its mindset clear in a key passage of its decision:

> Taking stock of past experience of the Court, the Chamber is also of the view that confirming all applicable alternative legal characterisations on the basis of the same facts is a desirable approach as it may reduce future delays at trial, and provides early notice to the defence of the different legal characterisations that may be considered by the trial judges. This more flexible approach is, of course, without prejudice to the possibility that trial judges, following the applicable procedure, consider other alternatives as well.[85]

Caution is certainly warranted due to the regulation's essentially foreign nature. It does not exist nor have an equivalent counterpart in any domestic criminal justice system, for the very reason of its threat to due process and the legitimacy of the trial process. It is somewhat difficult to justify the need for the regulation at the ICC. Even with its *sui generis* character, there is no real justification for mitigating these rights. Indeed, if one takes the view that the Court should be mindful of the example it sets for domestic systems, then the regulation should not have been adopted in the first place, and should be struck down. Certainly, it is hard to align the expectations of the rule of law with the practice of regulation 55.

2. Requirement for the accused to be present at trial

The Court has struggled to maintain its hard line in the fight against impunity, particularly where the prosecution of sitting heads of states are concerned. Spurred on by considerable pressure from the African Union (AU) to defer the trial of Kenya's sitting Deputy President William Samoei arap Ruto, concessions were made that have consequently had a negative impact on the the high standards expected of an international criminal trial. For example, the Assembly of States Parties (ASP) recently adopted a new rule (Rule 134*quater*) which would ostensibly permit 'an

---

[85] *The Prosecutor v Laurent Gbagbo* (Pre-Trial Chamber I), 12 June 2014, ICC-02/11-01/11, at [228].

accused subject … who is mandated to fulfill extraordinary public duties at the highest national level … to be excused and to be represented by counsel only'.[86] The introduction of this rule has been met with strong criticism, and indeed appears contrary to one of the most basic requirements of due process necessary for the observance of the rule of law within trial proceedings.The adoption of the rule is something of a curiosity, given that it followed only a few months after the Appeals Chamber had roundly rejected Ruto's earlier request to be excused from being present at trial. As the Court's consideration of Ruto's request for excusal a few months earlier indicated, 'article 63(1) of the Statute establishes that the accused shall be present during the trial, reflecting the central role of the accused person in proceedings and the wider significance of the presence of the accused for the administration of justice'.[87] The Chamber affirmed the centrality of this due process protection, reminding the defendant that his presence was essential to the rule of law because he was not just a 'passive observer of the trial, but the subject of the criminal proceedings'.[88] Thus, he was required to be in attendance, to follow the production of evidence, the testimony of witnesses, and so on. Based upon the adoption of the new rule shortly after, Ruto again sought excusal given his 'extraordinary public duties'. This time, the Trial Chamber obliged, allowing the trial to be conducted essentially *in absentia*.

This situation presents an interesting dilemma to the rule of law, as it highlights the tension between the principle of legality and the political elements which drive the Rome System of Justice – essentially, that the states that compose the ASP and have certain law-making powers will have inevitably different *political* interests than the staff of international lawyers and judges at the Courts will have. The conduct of a trial *in absentia* is an unacceptable practice which threatens due process – even if it occurs at the request of the accused, because *inter alia* he can later leverage his absence to suggest impropriety by the court; or deny its jurisdiction from outside its custody once a verdict has been rendered. In

---

86 Assembly of States Parties, 'Amendments to the Rules of Procedure and Evidence', Resolution ICC-ASP/12/Res.7, adopted at the 12th plenary meeting on 27 November 2013, Rule 134*quater* (1).

87 See *The Prosecutor v William Samoei Ruto and Joshua Arap Sang,* Judgment on the appeal of the Prosecutor against the decision of Trial Chamber V(a) of 18 June 2013 entitled 'Decision on Mr. Ruto's Request for Excusal from Continuous Presence at Trial', No. ICC-01/09-01/11 OA 5 (25 October 2013), available at <http://www.icc-cpi.int/iccdocs/doc/doc1669852.pdf>, at 18–19.

88 Ibid.

no circumstances could a trial without an accused present meet basic standards of domestic due process. Accordingly, the rule of law would demand rejection of Rule 134*quater*, and wherever possible, the Court should seek to mitigate the detrimental consequences of this rule in its application.

3. A code of conduct for the ICC's engagement with intermediaries

The use of intermediaries is essential to the Court's work, and both the OTP and the Victims Participation and Reparations Section (VPRS) have regular interactions with them. Intermediaries are typically local individuals or groups that have intimate knowledge of the local customs of a community, and are contracted by the Court to assist it in gathering information, conducting interviews, seeking viable witnesses, and so on. Their presence on the ground is often necessary because of the limitations of the Court's own staff of investigators, whether due to language, difficulties with addressing local customs, or due to hostile attitudes towards the Court by locals which may pose a real threat to security. Despite the significance of their role and their vast influence over the collection of evidence, the Court did not have any standing regulations or oversight practices in place to monitor how they were being used. In *Lubanga*, the consequences of these actions manifested in the disastrous revelation that the evidence procured and testimony provided by witnesses solicited by intermediaries on the Prosecutor's behalf had been fundamentally corrupted due to their misconduct. Allegations of influencing and bribing witnesses resulted in the Court heavily criticizing the prosecution for having 'delegated its investigative responsibilities to intermediaries. A series of witnesses have been called during this trial whose evidence, as a result of the essentially unsupervised actions of three of the principal intermediaries, cannot safely be relied on'.[89] A clear breach of professional ethics expected of the international bar, the topic has become something of a wedge issue for the defence, which have strongly advanced their case that this is a violation of fair trial rights. In the interim, precautionary measures have been adopted in cases which have used intermediaries, particularly in relation to disclosure of information. Nonetheless, the Court must pursue these claims with vigour, and ensure a proper response is provided – a failure to mitigate

---

89 *The Prosecutor v Thomas Lubanga Dyilo,* Summary of the 'Judgment pursuant to Article 74 of the Statute', No. ICC-01/04-01/06 (14 March 2012), available at <www.icc-cpi.int/iccdocs/doc/doc1379843.pdf> at 17–18.

these consequences will undoubtedly sow national dissent amongst the accused's supporters.

It was not until early 2014, however, that a formal set of (non-binding and non-enforceable) guidelines were adopted for the management of intermediaries – not only those approved by the Court, but also procedures for dealing with information provided by those acting on an ad hoc or informal basis. This episode has been particularly unsettling from the perspective of the international rule of law, and the previously cavalier attitude towards collection of evidence sends a strong message to local courts modelling their post-conflict docket after the ICC. Accordingly, therefore, it is heartening to see positive momentum in the immediate presence, and strong condemnation of past actions is highly necessary to mitigate the harm caused.

V. CONCLUSION

According to Chesterman, 'assertions that the rule of law is a meaningful concept at the international level depend on a coherent meaning at the national level'.[90] For ICL, this could not be more accurate. Atrocity crimes are extraordinary in nature. They are a violation of mankind's dignity. Yet, if one hopes for comprehensive prosecutions that pursue more than just the most exceptional cases, this will fall to the state to do – and it must do it well, if it hopes to avoid becoming fuel to incite further divisions in fragile communities looking for any excuse to go to war again. It must be above impropriety, and because of circumstances, it is possible that this can only occur with external supervision. Thus, the International Criminal Court plays a vital role in the future of states looking to restore stability through the process of post-conflict justice, and the Court must oblige by providing guidance. But this relationship flows in both directions, and it must be similarly willing to be informed by the expectations of domestic due process. As the Court moves towards its second decade, it must begin to engage with the communities it serves in order to advance the kind of sustainable, collaborative agenda necessary to strengthen its position as a global actor.

---

[90] Chesterman, above n31 at 360.

5. The Appellate Body of the World Trade Organization

Peter Van den Bossche

Since its establishment in 1995, the dispute settlement system of the World Trade Organization has been the most frequently used international mechanism for the resolution of state-to-state disputes. Within this system for the resolution of trade disputes, the WTO Appellate Body serves as a permanent court of last resort, which has established itself over the past 18 years in what is now, in all but name, the 'World Trade Court'.[1] This chapter focuses first on facts and figures regarding WTO dispute settlement in general and the WTO Appellate Body in particular. It discusses the number and nature of the disputes brought to, and resolved by, the WTO since 1995, the identity of the complainants and respondents in these disputes, and the incidence of, and (most importantly) compliance with, rulings of WTO-inconsistency. Subsequently, this chapter focuses on the genesis and key features of WTO dispute settlement in general, and the Appellate Body in particular. It discusses the jurisdiction of and access to the WTO dispute settlement system, its objectives, its institutions and their mandate, the remedies for breach of WTO law and the process of WTO dispute settlement. By way of conclusion, this chapter looks at the main problem of the WTO dispute settlement system and the Appellate Body. While anything but perfect, the WTO dispute settlement system is a remarkable system. It is in many respects, including the fact that it provides for appellate review, unique among state-to-state dispute settlement systems and may serve as a

[1] It was Claus-Dieter Ehlermann, a former Director-General of the Legal Service and of DG Competition of the European Commission and Member of the Appellate Body from 1995 to 2001, who referred in a 2002 article to the Appellate Body as the 'World Trade Court'. See C-D Ehlermann, 'Six Years on the Bench of the "World Trade Court": Some Personal Experiences as Member of the Appellate Body of the WTO' (2002) *Journal of World Trade* 605–39.

source of inspiration for other systems set up to ensure the rule of law in international relations.

I. FACTS AND FIGURES ON WTO DISPUTE SETTLEMENT

A brief look at the facts and figures on WTO dispute settlement reveals that the WTO dispute settlement system has been much used by many WTO Members, developed countries and developing countries alike. As discussed below, disputes on issues of great political sensitivity and/or huge economic significance have been brought to the WTO for resolution and were in all but a few instances resolved within a relatively short time frame.

A. Number of WTO Disputes and Dispute Settlement Reports

Between 1 January 1995 and 31 December 2013, a total of 474 disputes have been brought to the WTO for resolution.[2] The number of disputes brought to the WTO has fluctuated from year to year with an all time high of 50 disputes in 1997 and an all-time low of eight disputes in 2011. The latter did not, however, herald the end of the WTO dispute settlement system. In both 2012 (with 27 disputes) and in 2013 (with 20 disputes) more disputes were brought to the WTO than in any other year since 2001. One might expect there to be a correlation between, on the one hand, the state of the global economy or intensive diplomatic efforts to bring trade negotiations to a successful end, and, on the other hand, an increase or decrease, respectively, in the number of WTO disputes. However, the fluctuation in the number of disputes brought to the WTO often defies such logic and remains without obvious explanation.

With regard to the 474 disputes brought to the WTO between 1995 and 2013, the WTO dispute settlement system 'generated' 188 reports, ie WTO speak for 'judgments', of first instance ad hoc dispute settlement panels, and 110 appellate reports of the standing Appellate Body.[3] When

---

[2] This number refers to the number of requests for consultations by WTO Members notified to the WTO Dispute Settlement Body during this period. For statistical data on WTO dispute settlement, see www.wto.org or www.worldtradelaw.net.

[3] Note that when in a dispute multiple reports are issued in a single document, these reports are counted as one. Eg in *US – Steel Safeguards (2003)*, the panel rendered a separate report for each of the eight complainants in that

compared to the number of disputes brought to, and resolved by, other international mechanisms for the settlement of state-to-state disputes, such as the International Court of Justice (ICJ) or the International Tribunal for the Law of the Sea (ITLOS), it is clear that the WTO dispute settlement system is by far the most prolific of all international state-to-state dispute settlement mechanisms. In the period from 1995 to 2013, the ICJ rendered 57 judgments and six advisory opinions.[4] The ITLOS has since 1996, the year in which it was inaugurated, rendered 11 judgments and one advisory opinion.[5] As noted above, the Appellate Body rendered since 1995 110 reports, ie judgments. This is almost twice as many as the ICJ and ten times as many as the ITLOS.

B. Nature of the Disputes Brought to the WTO

Some of the disputes brought to the WTO have been disputes on technical trade issues of little interest to (and importance for) anyone except the traders and/or producers directly concerned. This is the case, for example, for disputes to relating the customs duties imposed on specific products, such as *EC – Computer Equipment (1997)* (complaint by the United States) or *EC – Chicken Cuts (2005)* (complaints by Brazil and Thailand), or disputes relating to the calculation of a dumping margin, such as *EC – Bed Linen* (complaint by India) and *US – Zeroing (EC)* (complaint by the European Union).[6] Many other WTO disputes, however, have triggered much public debate and have attracted considerable media attention. This has been the case, for example, for disputes on national legislation for the protection of the environment, public health or public moral, such as *US – Shrimp (1998)*, a dispute on the US import ban on shrimp harvested with nets that kill sea turtles (complaints by India, Malaysia, Pakistan and Thailand); *Brazil – Retreaded Tyres (2007)*, a dispute on a Brazilian ban for environmental reasons on the importation of retreaded tyres (complaint by the European Union); *EC – Approval and Marketing of Biotech Products (2006)*, a dispute on measures

---

dispute, but it did so in *one single document* with a common set of findings. These eight reports are counted as one report.

[4] See http://www.icj-cij.org.

[5] In addition, the ITLOS rendered in six disputes an Order prescribing preliminary measures pending a decision by an Article VII arbitral tribunal. See https://www.itlos.org.

[6] Note, however, that the Appellate Body's case law on 'zeroing', ie the method for the calculation of a dumping margin at issue in these disputes, is very controversial in at least one WTO Member.

affecting the approval and marketing of genetically modified products in the European Union (complaint by the US, Canada and Argentina); *US – Clove Cigarettes (2012),* a dispute concerning a US measure to reduce youth smoking, which prohibited flavoured cigarettes but excluded menthol cigarettes from this prohibition (complaint by Indonesia); *US – Tuna II (Mexico) (2012)*, a dispute concerning US regulation on the use of the dolphin-safe label on tuna cans (complaint by Mexico); and *EC – Seal Products (2014)* a dispute concerning an EU ban on seal products adopted to address EU public moral concerns regarding seal welfare (complaint by Canada and Norway). Also *EC – Bananas III (1997)* on the EU's preferential import regime for bananas (complaints by Ecuador, Guatemala, Honduras, Mexico and the US); *EC and certain Member States – Large Civil Aircraft (2011)* (complaint by the US) and *US – Large Civil Aircraft (2012)* (complaint by the EU) on billions of EUR or USD of subsidies to Airbus and Boeing respectively; and *China – Raw Materials (2012)* on restrictions imposed by China on the exportation of certain raw materials (complaints by the European Union, Mexico and the US), were or are the subject of heated public debate and frequently made headline news.

C. Users of the WTO Dispute Settlement System

The WTO dispute settlement system has been used by developed country and developing country Members of the WTO alike, see Table 5.1 below. In half of the years since 2000, developing country Members brought *more* disputes to the WTO for resolution than developed country Members.[7] The most active user of the system has been the US, closely followed by the EU.[8] The WTO dispute settlement system has, however, also been used 'against' the US more often than against any other Member, the EU being a distant second in this respect. The most active users of the system among developing country Members have been Brazil, Mexico, India, Argentina, Thailand, and in recent years, also China (which joined the WTO only in 2001). The most frequent respondents among developing country Members have been China, India, Argentina, Brazil and Mexico.

---

[7] In 2000, 2001, 2003, 2005, 2008, 2010 and 2012 developing country Members initiated more cases than developed country Members. In 1995, 2006, 2009 and 2011, developing country and developed country Members initiated the same number of cases.

[8] Note that until 2009 the European Union (EU) was officially referred to as the European Communities (EC) in the WTO.

Table 5.1 Disputes brought to the Appellate Body of the World Trade Organization

Complainants		Respondents	
United States	106	United States	122
EU	90	EU	77
Canada	33	China	31
Brazil	26	India	22
Mexico	23	Argentina	22
India	21	Canada	17
Argentina	20	Japan	15
Japan	19	Brazil	15
Korea	16	Korea	14
Thailand	13	Mexico	14
China	12	Australia	14

In 2013, the WTO dispute settlement system was used by the US (3), the EU (3), Argentina (2), Indonesia (2), Japan (1), China (1), Cuba (1), Denmark (1), Guatemala (1), Korea (1), New Zealand (1), Panama (1) and Russia (1) *against* the EU (4), US (3), Indonesia (3), Russia (2), Australia (1), Brazil (1), China (1), Colombia (1), India (1), Pakistan (1), Peru (1) and Ukraine (1).[9] To date, 101 of the 160 WTO Members (ie almost two out of three WTO Members) have been involved in WTO dispute settlement. Particularly noteworthy is the use of the WTO dispute settlement system by small developing country Members against the largest among the developed country Members.[10] In the WTO system, might does not necessarily prevail over right.

D. Findings of WTO-inconsistency and Compliance with Adverse Rulings

In 89 per cent of all cases adjudicated, panels and/or the Appellate Body found an inconsistency with at least one WTO provision. This does not

9 See http://www.worldtradelaw.net/dsc/database/searchcomplaints.asp.

10 Eg *US – Gambling (2005)*, a dispute between Antigua and Barbuda (a Caribbean island state with less than 90.000 inhabitants) and the US.

reflect any bias in favour of complainants but rather the careful consideration by complainants of the likelihood of success before initiating WTO dispute settlement proceedings.

As for all international dispute settlement systems, the ultimate test for the WTO dispute settlement system is whether respondents comply with adverse rulings and withdraw (or modify) the measures that were found to be WTO-inconsistent. To date, the compliance record of the WTO dispute settlement system is impressive. In more than four out of five disputes in which the respondent is called upon to withdraw (or modify) a WTO-inconsistent measure, the respondent has done so. While much attention in the media and in academic writing goes to those disputes in which resolution was delayed (e.g. *EC – Bananas III (1997)*; *EC – Hormones (1999)*; *US – FSC (2000)*; *US – Section 211 Appropriations Act (2002)*; and *US – Gambling (2005)*) it should also be noted that many of these disputes were eventually resolved.

II. GENESIS OF THE WTO DISPUTE SETTLEMENT SYSTEM

When it started operating on 1 January 1995, the WTO dispute settlement system was not an entirely novel system. On the contrary, this system was based on, and took on board, almost 50 years of experience in the resolution of trade disputes in the context of the General Agreement on Tariffs and Trade of 1947 (the GATT 1947).

A. Dispute Settlement under the GATT 1947

The GATT 1947 contained only two brief provisions on dispute settlement (Articles XXII and XXIII), which neither explicitly referred to 'dispute settlement' nor provided for detailed procedures to handle disputes. However, the GATT Contracting Parties 'transformed', in a highly pragmatic manner over a period of five decades, what was initially a rudimentary, power-based system for settling disputes through diplomatic negotiations into a fairly elaborate, rules-based system for settling disputes through adjudication. While for decades it was quite successful in resolving disputes to the satisfaction of the GATT Contracting Parties, GATT dispute settlement had some shortcomings which became ever more acute in the course of the 1980s. In fact, the gradual change from settling disputes through diplomatic negotiations to settling disputes through adjudication resulted in a situation in which these shortcomings all but paralysed the GATT dispute settlement system. The most important inadequacy related to the fact that the conclusions of the panels of experts adjudicating disputes only became legally binding when adopted *by consensus* by the GATT Council (the 'adoption-by-consensus requirement'). The responding party could thus prevent any unfavourable conclusion from becoming legally binding upon it. Of the panel reports circulated during the last ten years of the GATT dispute settlement system, almost 40 per cent remained unadopted by the GATT Council. Of the ten last GATT dispute settlement reports only three were adopted. Because of the failure of the GATT dispute settlement system, some GATT Contracting Parties, and in particular the US, resorted more and more to unilateral action against alleged violations of GATT rules by other Contracting Parties.

B. Negotiations on the WTO Dispute Settlement System

The growing concern of many GATT Contracting Parties regarding the ever more aggressive unilateralism in addressing trade disputes was the driving force behind the attempt to fix the shortcomings of GATT dispute settlement in the context of the GATT Uruguay Round (1986–94). These negotiations on dispute settlement eventually resulted in the *Understanding on Rules and Procedures for the Settlement of Disputes*, commonly referred to as the *Dispute Settlement Understanding* or DSU, which sets out the current WTO dispute settlement system.[11] The DSU is generally considered to be one of the most significant achievements of the Uruguay Round. The DSU remedied the most serious shortcoming of GATT dispute settlement, namely the 'adoption-by-*consensus* requirement' for panel reports, by replacing this requirement with an 'adoption-by-*reverse-consensus* requirement'. As further explained below, adoption by reverse consensus means that a decision is adopted unless there is a consensus not to adopt the decision. As a result, the responding party could no longer prevent any unfavourable panel conclusions from becoming legally binding upon it and thus paralyse dispute settlement. In addition to remedying this shortcoming of GATT dispute settlement, the DSU also provided for strict timeframes for dispute settlement proceedings, for the surveillance and enforcement of compliance with dispute settlement recommendations and rulings, and for appellate review by a standing Appellate Body. As noted by Claus-Dieter Ehlermann, the

---

[11] The DSU is attached to the *Agreement on the Establishment of the World Trade Organization* (the '*WTO Agreement*') as Annex 2 thereof, and can be found at http://www.wto.org/english/docs_e/legal_e/legal_e.htm.

successful negotiation of the DSU was 'an extraordinary achievement that comes close to a miracle'.[12] The establishment of the WTO dispute settlement system in 1995 was an important step in the process of 'judicialization' of, and ensuring the rule of law in, the settlement of international trade disputes.

The distinguishing features of the WTO dispute settlement system will be discussed in more detail below but it should already be noted that the provision of appellate review by a standing Appellate Body was initially an 'afterthought' rather than the reflection of a grand design to create a strong, new international court. After agreeing that panel reports would be adopted (and become legally binding) by reverse consensus, the negotiators were apprehensive that it would no longer be possible to stop 'bad' panel reports from becoming legally binding. The introduction of appellate review was primarily intended by the DSU negotiators to ensure that the (quasi-) automatic adoption of panel reports would not have the undesirable side effect of leaving WTO Members without protection from the occasional 'bad' panel report. It was not the negotiators' intention to establish the Appellate Body as the centrepiece of the WTO dispute settlement system, although that is undoubtedly what it has become. After its establishment in 1995, the WTO dispute settlement system, and the role of the Appellate Body within that system, developed further in a pragmatic and incremental manner and in response to the evolving needs of the multilateral trading system.

III. JURISDICTION OF AND ACCESS TO THE WTO DISPUTE SETTLEMENT SYSTEM

Both the jurisdiction of, and the access to, the WTO dispute settlement system distinguish the WTO dispute settlement system from other international dispute settlement mechanisms.

A. Jurisdiction of the WTO Dispute Settlement System

The jurisdiction of the WTO dispute settlement system is compulsory. A responding Member has, as a matter of law, no choice but to accept the jurisdiction of the WTO dispute settlement system when a complaint is brought against it.[13] The jurisdiction is also exclusive. A complaining Member is obliged to bring WTO disputes to the WTO dispute settlement

[12] C-D Ehlermann, above n1 at 639.

[13] Article 6.1 of the DSU.

system rather than another system of dispute settlement.[14] Both compulsory jurisdiction and exclusive jurisdiction are uncommon features in international dispute settlement. Furthermore, the jurisdiction of the WTO dispute settlement system is very broad in scope. It covers disputes arising under all but two of the WTO agreements.[15] These 'covered agreements' include inter alia the GATT 1994 and 11 other multilateral agreements on trade in goods, the General Agreement on Trade in Services (the GATS), the Agreement on Trade Related Aspects of Intellectual Property Rights (the TRIPS Agreement) and the Agreement on Government Procurement.[16] In terms of the kind of measure that can be challenged in WTO dispute settlement, any act or omission attributable to a WTO Member can in principle be subject to WTO dispute settlement.

B. Access to the WTO Dispute Settlement System

Access to the WTO dispute settlement system is limited to WTO Members. A WTO Member can have recourse to the system when it claims that a benefit accruing to it under one of the 'covered agreements' is being nullified or impaired.[17] A complainant will almost always argue that the respondent violated a provision of WTO law and thus file a *violation complaint*. If the violation is shown, there is a presumption of nullification or impairment of a benefit.[18] Alternatively, and this is quite unique in international or national adjudication, a complainant can file a *non-violation complaint*.[19] In that case the complainant does not argue

---

[14] Article 23.1 of the DSU. Note, however, that in addition to adjudication by panels and the Appellate Body, Article 25 of the DSU allows WTO Members to have recourse to 'expeditious arbitration within the WTO'. To date, Members had recourse to arbitration under Article 25 of the DSU once. See Award of the Arbitrators, *United States – Section 110(5) of the US Copyright Act – Recourse to Arbitration under Article 25 of the DSU*, WT/DS160/ ARB25/1, 9 November 2001, DSR 2001:II, 667.

[15] The 'WTO agreements' include the *WTO Agreement* and the 18 agreements annexed to the *WTO Agreement*.

[16] The two WTO Agreements which are not 'covered agreements' are the *Trade Policy Review Mechanism* and the *Agreement on Trade in Civil Aircraft*.

[17] See eg Article XXIII:1 of the GATT 1994.

[18] See eg Article XXIII:1(a) of the GATT 1994 and Article 3.8 of the DSU.

[19] See eg Article XXIII:1(b) and Article 26.1 of the DSU. Pursuant to eg Article XXIII:1(c) and Article 26.2 of the DSU, WTO Members can also file a *situation complaint*. Note, however, that no WTO Member has ever done so and

that the respondent violated any specific provision of WTO law but contends that the respondent has nevertheless nullified or impaired a benefit of the complainant under one of the covered agreements. Non-violation complaints are rare and have never been successful in WTO dispute settlement to date. Generally speaking, WTO Members have broad discretion in deciding whether to bring a case against another Member, but they are expected to exercise their judgment 'as to whether [such] action … would be fruitful'.[20]

International organizations, non-governmental organizations, industry associations, companies or individuals have no direct access to the WTO dispute settlement system. However, it should be noted that most disputes are brought to the WTO for resolution at the instigation of companies and/or industry associations. The latter often are the 'driving force' behind the initiation of dispute settlement proceedings by WTO Members. Moreover, companies or industry associations will not only lobby governments to bring disputes to the WTO, they (and their law firms) will often also play an important, 'behind-the-scenes' role in planning the legal strategy and drafting the submissions. It could be argued that companies and industry associations have 'indirect' access to the WTO dispute settlement system and make abundant use thereof.

IV. OBJECTIVES OF WTO DISPUTE SETTLEMENT

The principal objective of any dispute settlement system is obviously the resolution of the disputes brought to it. This is also the case for the WTO dispute settlement system. Article 3.3 of the DSU states that the 'prompt settlement' of disputes is 'essential to the effective functioning of the WTO and the maintenance of a proper balance between the rights and obligations of Members'. However, the DSU identifies also other, albeit closely related, objectives of WTO dispute settlement.

A. Clarification of Provisions of WTO Agreements

Pursuant to Article 3.2, second sentence, of the DSU, WTO dispute settlement serves not only 'to preserve the rights and obligations of Members under the covered agreements', but also 'to clarify the existing

that there is considerable uncertainty as to the circumstances under which such a complaint can be filed.

[20] See Article 3.7 of the DSU.

provisions of those agreements'. Like many other international agreements, the WTO agreements are a masterpiece of 'constructive ambiguity' with many provisions that Members understand differently. As a result there is much need for clarification, a task explicitly assigned to the WTO dispute settlement system, ie WTO panels and, ultimately, the Appellate Body. The scope and nature of this clarification mandate is, however, circumscribed by Article 3.2, third sentence, and 19.2 of the DSU, which explicitly state that the WTO dispute settlement system, and in particular panels and the Appellate Body, 'cannot add to or diminish the rights and obligations provided in the covered agreements'. The DSU does not condone judicial activism. For panels and the Appellate Body to stay within their mandate to clarify existing provisions, it is therefore important that they interpret and apply the provisions concerned correctly, ie in accordance with customary rules of interpretation of international law, as codified in Articles 31 and 32 of the *Vienna Convention on the Law of Treaties (VCLT).* Georges Abi-Saab, Member of the Appellate Body from 2000 to 2008, described the Appellate Body's 'judicial policy of interpretation' as 'strict constructionism'.[21] As the Appellate Body ruled in *Japan – Alcoholic Beverages (1996)*, Article 31 of the VCLT provides that the *words* of the treaty form the foundation for the interpretative process.[22] The results of an interpretative approach that gives primary importance to the wording actually used are more easily accepted by the parties to the treaty than the often 'surprising' results of interpretative approaches that, for example, give more importance to the object and purpose of the treaty. If WTO Members now hold the Appellate Body in high esteem, this is to a large extent due to the Appellate Body's choice for, and consistent application of, a 'text first' approach to interpretation.[23] Note, however, that the Appellate Body also stated in *Japan – Alcoholic Beverages (1996)* that 'WTO rules are not so rigid or so inflexible as not to leave room for reasoned judgments in confronting the endless and ever-changing ebb and flow of real facts in real cases in the real world' and that WTO rules should be interpreted

---

21 D Terris, C Romano and L Swigart, *The International Judge: An Introduction to the Men and Women Who Decide the World's Cases* (Brandeis University Press, 2007) 139.

22 See Appellate Body Report, *Japan – Alcoholic Beverages (1996)* 11.

23 See P Van den Bossche, 'The Making of the "World Trade Court": The Origins and Development of the Appellate Body of the World Trade Organization' in R Yerxa and B Wilson, *Key Issues in WTO Dispute Settlement: The First Ten Years* (Cambridge University Press, 2005) 72.

with that in mind.[24] In recent years, the Appellate Body's multiple clarifications of WTO provisions and contributions to the development of WTO law have been criticized by some for being too timid and text-bound and by others as inadmissible instances of judicial activism.

B. Providing Security and Predictability to the Multilateral Trade System

With regard to the objectives of WTO dispute settlement, Article 3.2, first sentence, of the DSU further states: 'The dispute settlement system of the WTO is a central element in providing security and predictability to the multilateral trading system.' In the context of the divisive debate on the role of precedent in WTO dispute settlement, the Appellate Body stated in *US – Stainless Steel (Mexico) (2008)* that: '[e]nsuring "security and predictability" in the dispute settlement system, as contemplated in Article 3.2 of the DSU, implies that, absent cogent reasons, an adjudicatory body will resolve the same legal question in the same way in a subsequent case'.[25]

C. Resolve Disputes through Consultations

Finally, with regard to the objectives of WTO dispute settlement, it should be noted that the DSU, as stated in Article 3.7 thereof, prefers Members to resolve a dispute through consultations, ie negotiations, rather than through adjudication. In other words, the DSU prefers parties *not* to go to court but to settle their dispute amicably out of court. This is inter alia reflected in the requirement – further discussed below – that every WTO dispute settlement process starts with consultations between the parties to the dispute with the aim of reaching a mutually acceptable solution. In one out of five disputes brought to the WTO for resolution, the parties are able to resolve the dispute without recourse to adjudication. Parties are encouraged to continue seeking an amicable solution to the dispute even after it has been referred to adjudication.[26]

---

24 See Appellate Body Report, *Japan – Alcoholic Beverages (1996)* 31.

25 Appellate Body Report, *US – Stainless Steel (Mexico) (2008)* at para 160.

26 See Article 11 of the DSU. Occasionally such efforts have been successful. See eg *EC – Butter*, a 1999 dispute in which New Zealand and the EU reached a mutually agreed solution shortly before the panel was to make its report public.

D. Withdrawal of the WTO-inconsistent Measure

When a dispute on the WTO-consistency of a measure is referred to adjudication and it is found that the measure at issue is WTO-inconsistent, the 'first objective' of WTO dispute settlement is, pursuant to Article 3.7 of the DSU, to secure the withdrawal (or modification) of the WTO-inconsistent measure. The DSU provides for one, and only one, *final* remedy for breach of WTO law, namely, the withdrawal (or modification) of the WTO-inconsistent measure. It is important to note that it is not an objective of WTO dispute settlement to award the complainant compensation for the damage suffered as a result of the WTO-inconsistent measure. Under customary international law, as codified in the International Law Commission's *Articles on Responsibility of States for Internationally Wrongful Acts*, a State responsible for an internationally wrongful act is under an obligation to compensate for the damage caused by this act. Under WTO law, however, such an obligation does not exist. By providing a detailed set of rules regarding the legal consequences of a breach of WTO law, the DSU has *contracted out* of customary international law on State responsibility. The rule on compensation for damage caused therefore does not apply.

In addition to its one and only *final* remedy for breach of WTO law, namely the withdrawal (or modification) of the WTO-inconsistent measure, the DSU provides, as is discussed in more detail below, for two *temporary* remedies, namely, suspension of concessions or other obligations (ie 'retaliation') and *compensation*.[27] To avoid confusion, it is important to note that this *compensation* only concerns the damage caused *after* the reasonable period of time for the withdrawal (or modification) of a WTO-inconsistent measure has expired.[28] This *compensation* does not concern the damage that *was* caused (often over a period of many years) by the WTO-inconsistent measure to the complainant's trade and/or its economy at large. That damage is never compensated under WTO law. Generally speaking, remedies for breach of WTO law are prospective and not retroactive. While this may be considered a shortcoming, compensation for damage caused is not an objective of WTO dispute settlement.

---

27 The purpose of these temporary remedies is to 'encourage' a Member to withdraw (or modify) a measure that was found to be WTO-inconsistent. See also below, p. 200.

28 On the reasonable period of time to withdraw (or modify) a WTO – inconsistent measure, see below, p. 199.

V. INSTITUTIONS OF WTO DISPUTE SETTLEMENT

Among the institutions involved in WTO dispute settlement one must distinguish between a political institution, the Dispute Settlement Body or DSB, *and* two independent, adjudicative institutions, the ad hoc dispute settlement panels and the standing Appellate Body.

A. Dispute Settlement Body

The DSB, which is composed of all 160 WTO Members, 'administers' the dispute settlement system.[29] It has the authority to establish the ad hoc dispute settlement panels, adopt panel and Appellate Body reports, and authorize retaliation in case of non-compliance. As already mentioned above with regard to the adoption of panel reports, it takes decisions on these critical matters by *reverse consensus*. This means that the DSB shall be deemed to have taken a decision on these matters unless there is a consensus among WTO Members *not* to take that decision. Since there is normally at least one Member with a strong interest in the establishment of a panel (namely the Member requesting the establishment), the adoption of the panel and/or Appellate Body reports (namely the 'winning' Member) or the authorization to suspend concessions (namely the Member requesting authorization), it is highly unlikely that there will be a consensus in the DSB *not* to adopt these decisions. As a result, the DSB decisions on these matters are (quasi-) automatic.[30] The (quasi-) automatic character of these decisions does not deprive them of meaning. The fact that these decisions must be taken by the DSB and the debate that may precede these decisions ensures a high degree of interest as well as knowledge among diplomats and trade officials of what happens in WTO dispute settlement. The DSB's involvement in dispute settlement provides Members with a welcome opportunity to express – when they consider this necessary – concern about or disagreement with any matter relating to WTO dispute settlement.

B. Panels

The adjudication of disputes brought to the WTO is done, at the first instance level, by dispute settlement panels and, at the appellate level, by the Appellate Body. Panels are ad hoc bodies established for the purpose

---

[29] See Article 2 of the DSU.

[30] Note that the DSB takes other decisions, such as the appointment of Appellate Body Members, by positive consensus.

of adjudicating a particular dispute and are dissolved once they have accomplished this task. Panels are established by the DSB at the request of the complainant and, as noted above, the DSB takes decisions on panel establishment by reverse consensus.[31] After the establishment of a panel, the parties to the dispute decide on the composition of the panel by mutual accord. However, if they fail to do so within 20 days, either party can ask the Director-General of the WTO to appoint the panellists. In fact, in most cases it has been the WTO Director General who decided on the composition of the panel.[32] As a rule, panels are composed of three well-qualified governmental and/or non-governmental individuals, who are not nationals of the parties or third parties to the dispute. Since 1995, 240 trade experts from more than 50 different countries have served or are serving as panellists.[33] Some of them have served on multiple panels.[34] Pursuant to the *Rules of Conduct* for WTO dispute settlement, panellists must be independent and impartial, avoid direct and indirect conflicts of interest and respect the confidentiality of proceedings.[35] The WTO Secretariat counts about 50 dispute settlement lawyers to assist panels on the legal and procedural aspects of disputes.[36] The overall cost of panel proceedings to the WTO budget amounted in 2012 to CHF 5.4 m.[37]

With regard to the mandate of panels, ie the scope and nature of the task(s) entrusted to panels, several aspects deserve particular attention. *First,* almost all panels have standard terms of reference which refer back to the complainant's request to establish a panel. Hence, a claim and/or

---

[31] See Article 6.2 of the DSU.

[32] To date three out of five panels were composed by the WTO Director General.

[33] To date, nationals from New Zealand served on 48 panels and nationals from Australia and Switzerland on 43 and 42 panels respectively.

[34] Michael Cartland (from Hong Kong) served on 11 panels, and Christian Härberli (from Switzerland) and Crawford Falconer (from New Zealand) on ten and nine panels respectively.

[35] To date, no panellist has ever been found to have committed a material violation of *the Rules of Conduct* which would result in his or her disqualification as a panellist.

[36] Note, however, that these dispute settlement lawyers of the Legal Affairs Division or Rules Division of the WTO Secretariat also fulfill other tasks in addition to assisting panels.

[37] Ie EUR 4.4 m or USD 6.1 m. In 2012 the WTO spent in total CHF 19 m (or 9 per cent of its overall budget) on dispute settlement. Other dispute settlement expenses related to the DSB, the Appellate Body and general support to dispute settlement.

measure falls within the panel's terms of reference, ie within its jurisdiction, only if that claim or measure is identified in the panel request. A panel cannot consider claims and/or measures, which are not identified in the panel request. *Second*, the standard of review of panels, as set forth in Article 11 of the DSU, is to 'make an objective assessment of the matter before it, including an objective assessment of the facts of the case and the applicability of and conformity with the relevant covered agreements'. Pursuant to Article 11 of the DSU, a panel, as the trier of facts: (1) must base its findings on a sufficient evidentiary basis on the record; (2) may not apply a double standard of proof; (3) must treat evidence in an 'even-handed' manner; (4) must consider evidence before it in its totality (which includes consideration of submitted evidence in relation to other evidence); and (5) should not disregard evidence that is relevant to the case of one of the parties. *Third,* panels may exercise judicial economy. They need only address (but at the same time *are required* to address) those claims which must be addressed in order to resolve the matter at issue in the dispute. Where a panel concludes that a Member's measure is inconsistent with WTO law, it shall recommend that the Member concerned bring that measure into conformity with WTO law. Panels take decisions by consensus, or, if consensus cannot be achieved, by majority vote (two to one). Panellists can express a separate opinion in the panel report, be it dissenting or concurring. However, if they do, they must do so anonymously. To date, in less than 10 per cent of the panel reports one of the panellists set out a separate opinion.

VI. APPELLATE BODY

The WTO dispute settlement system distinguishes itself from other state-to-state dispute settlement systems in a number of ways. Arguably the most notable difference is the provision of appellate review by a standing Appellate Body. The Appellate Body is a permanent, international tribunal of seven judges, who are appointed by the DSB for a term of four years (renewable once). When compared with other international courts, such as the ICJ (15 judges appointed for nine-year terms renewable) or the ITLOS (21 judges appointed for nine-year terms renewable), both the modest size of the Appellate Body and the relatively short term in office of Appellate Body Members stand out. As stated in Article 17.3 of the DSU, the Appellate Body shall comprise 'persons of recognized authority, with demonstrated expertise in law, international trade and the subject matter of the covered agreements'. Moreover,

Article 17.3 requires Appellate Body membership to be broadly representative of membership in the WTO. Since 1995, 24 persons from 16 different countries and with very diverse professional backgrounds have served or are serving on the Appellate Body. At present the Appellate Body is composed of nationals from Belgium, China, India, Korea, Mexico and the US with a professional background in academia, government, international organizations and/or private practice. Since December 2013, the Appellate Body has had six rather than seven Members as disagreement between WTO Members has prevented the DSB from appointing a seventh Member. This deadlock reflects the contentious nature of the appointment process and the importance WTO Members give to Appellate Body appointments. Serving Appellate Body Members must be unaffiliated with any government and the *Rules of Conduct* further require that they be independent and impartial, avoid direct and indirect conflicts of interest and respect the confidentiality of proceedings. Any Member having a direct or indirect conflict of interest or being involved in a situation that is likely to affect, or give rise to justifiable doubts as to, that Member's independence or impartiality, is recused from the case with regard to which the conflict or situation occurs. These rules are applied strictly. The Appellate Body is assisted in the exercise of its functions by its Secretariat, which is separate from the WTO Secretariat and currently comprises 15 lawyers.[38] By way of comparison, note that that ICJ has a staff of 26 lawyers to assist it.[39] The overall cost of the Appellate Body to the WTO budget amounted in 2012 to CHF 7.9 m.[40] The ICJ budget for 2012 was more than 250 per cent bigger while, as discussed above, the ICJ's output (in terms of number of judgments) was only 50 per cent of the output of the Appellate Body.[41]

The Appellate Body hears and decides appeals in divisions, ie ad hoc chambers, of three of its Members. The Members constituting a division

---

[38] This number includes the Director of the Appellate Body Secretariat, five senior lawyers, and nine junior lawyers.

[39] This number includes the Registrar, the Deputy Registrar, two special assistants to the President of the ICJ and the Registrar, eight lawyers at the ICJ Department of Legal Matters, and the 14 associate legal officers seconded to the judges. See Report of the International Court of Justice, 1 August 2012 – 31 July 2013, UN General Assembly, Official Records, 68th Session, Supplement No 4, 14 and 18.

[40] Ie EUR 6.5 m and USD 9 m.

[41] The ICJ's budget for the biennium 2012–13 amounted to USD 48 m (ie CHF 42 m and EUR 34 m). See Report of the International Court of Justice, 1 August 2012 – 31 July 2013, UN General Assembly, Official Records, 68th Session, Supplement No 4, 53–4.

are selected on the basis of rotation, while taking into account the principles of random selection, unpredictability and opportunity for all Members to serve regardless of their national origin.[42] A division decides by consensus and, if consensus cannot be reached, by majority vote (two to one). Appellate Body Members sitting on the division hearing an appeal can express a separate opinion (be it dissenting or concurring) in the Appellate Body report. However, if they do, they must do so anonymously. To date, only four Appellate Body reports have included separate opinions.

Only parties to the dispute can appeal against a panel report. Third parties, let alone other WTO Members, cannot appeal against a panel report. Pursuant to Article 17.6 of the DSU, an appeal is limited to issues of law covered in the panel report and legal interpretations developed by the panel. Issues of fact cannot be appealed. However, the treatment of the facts or evidence by a panel may raise the question of whether the panel has made an objective assessment of the facts as required under Article 11 of the DSU. This is a legal issue and can therefore be examined by the Appellate Body. Consequently, the Appellate Body is tasked in many appeals to assess not only the panel's legal interpretations and the panel's application of the law to the facts, but will also have to assess whether the panel's fact finding met the requirements of Article 11 of the DSU, discussed above. Generally speaking, the size and complexity of appeals has increased significantly in recent years and this is reflected in the average length of Appellate Body reports.

To date, 67 per cent of all panel reports have been appealed. This high appeal rate should not be seen as an indication of poor quality of the panel reports appealed but rather of the fact that a party unsuccessful in the panel proceedings has often little to lose by appealing against the unfavourable panel report. Pursuant to Article 17.13 of the DSU, the Appellate Body may uphold, modify or reverse the legal findings and conclusions of the panel that were appealed. Relatively few panel findings are reversed, more are upheld and most are modified. In the latter case, the Appellate Body agrees with the panel as to the WTO consistency or inconsistency but on the basis of a different argumentation. On occasion, the Appellate Body has also – in the absence of the authority to remand a case to the panel – felt compelled to 'complete the legal analysis' on issues within the panel's terms of reference but not addressed by the panel (because eg it exercised judicial economy). The

---

42 See Rule 6(2) of the *Working Procedures for Appellate Review*.

Appellate Body then acted as a first instance court and did so in order to provide a prompt resolution to the dispute.

VII. PROCESS OF WTO DISPUTE SETTLEMENT

The WTO dispute settlement process may – and often does – entail four major steps: (1) consultations; (2) panel proceedings; (3) Appellate Body proceedings; and (4) implementation and enforcement. As discussed below, the WTO dispute settlement has procedural features which distinguish it from other international adjudication (eg (very) short timeframes; involvement of political organs; interim review; appellate review; exchange of views; surveillance of compliance; and enforcement of compliance). However, as also discussed below, some other procedural features, which initially set apart the WTO dispute settlement, have in the past 18 years undergone changes which now make WTO dispute settlement more akin to other international adjudication (eg public observation; and role of private legal counsel). As with other international adjudication, WTO dispute settlement pays much attention to the protection of due process. The Appellate Body has described the protection of due process to be an 'essential feature of a rules-based system of adjudication, such as that established under the DSU'.[43] Consequently, in WTO dispute settlement all parties must always be afforded an adequate opportunity to pursue their claims, make their defences, and establish the facts in the context of proceedings conducted in a balanced and orderly manner, according to established rules.[44] The Appellate Body has also given importance to the requirement, set out in Article 3.10 of the DSU, that WTO Members must 'engage in [WTO dispute settlement] procedures in good faith in an effort to resolve the dispute'. In *US – FSC (2000)*, the Appellate Body found that the US had failed to 'engage in good faith' by failing to bring procedural deficiencies 'seasonably and promptly' to the attention of the complainant and the panel so that corrections, if needed, could have been made.[45]

---

[43] See Appellate Body Report, *US/Canada – Continued Suspension (2008)* at para 433.

[44] See Appellate Body Report, *Thailand – Cigarettes (Philippines) (2011)* at para 147.

[45] See Appellate Body Report, *US – FSC (2000)* at paras 165–6.

A. Consultations

The WTO dispute settlement process always begins with consultations (or, at least, an attempt to engage in consultations) between the parties to the dispute. The consultations, ie negotiations, are of course in the first place aimed at allowing the parties to resolve through diplomatic means their dispute out of court, ie amicably. As noted above, in 20 per cent of the disputes brought to the WTO, consultations lead to this preferred outcome. However, even if consultations are not successful, they play an important role as they allow the disputing parties to obtain a better understanding of the factual situation and the legal claims at issue in the dispute. This frequently leads to a narrowing down of the dispute referred to the panel. Parties have broad discretion regarding the manner in which they conduct the consultations. Members other than the parties to the dispute may be allowed to join the consultations when they have a substantial trade interest in the matter at issue in the dispute. Consultations take place behind closed doors and without the presence of WTO Secretariat officials. Consultations are confidential and without prejudice to the rights of parties in any further proceedings.[46] If consultations do not resolve the dispute within 60 days after the request for consultations, the complainant may request the DSB to establish a panel. In many disputes, however, complainants try to reach an amicable solution for a period much longer than 60 days and thus delay the initiation of panel proceedings.

B. Panel Proceedings

The basic rules governing panel proceedings are set out in Article 12 of the DSU. Article 12.1 of the DSU directs a panel to follow the *Working Procedures* contained in Appendix 3 to the DSU, but at the same time authorizes a panel, after consultations with the parties, to do otherwise. A panel will – whenever possible within one week of its composition – fix the timetable for its work and decide on detailed ad hoc working procedures that deviate from and/or complement the *Working Procedures* of Appendix 3. Each party to a dispute normally submits two written submissions to the panel: a 'first written submission' and a 'rebuttal submission'. During the proceedings, the panel will meet with the parties twice, first after the filing of the 'first written submissions' and then after the filing of the 'rebuttal submissions'. Until 2006, panel meetings were

---

[46] See Article 4.6 of the DSU.

held behind closed doors. The 2004 Sutherland Report on *The Future of the WTO* commented in this respect that: 'the degree of confidentiality of the current dispute settlement proceedings can be seen as damaging to the WTO as an institution'.[47] In recent years, however, panel meetings with the parties are open to public observation if the parties so request and the panel so rules.

Pursuant to Article 13 of the DSU, panels have the authority to seek information and technical advice from any source in order to help them to understand and evaluate the evidence submitted and the arguments made by the parties. Especially in disputes concerning sanitary and phytosanitary measures (eg disputes concerning growth hormones or genetically modified organisms), panels have made much use of scientific experts. The parties are under an obligation to provide the panel with the information or the documents that the panel requests at any time during the proceedings. A panel may draw negative inferences from instances of non-cooperation. In most panel proceedings, WTO Members other than the parties will participate as third parties. The rights of third parties in the panel proceedings are limited but have been, in some cases (in which vital economic interests of third parties were at stake), extended to include inter alia the right to participate in *all* meetings of the panel with the parties rather than in one dedicated session of the first of such meetings.

Under the GATT dispute settlement system and in the first years of the WTO dispute settlement system, parties to disputes were not allowed to be represented in dispute settlement proceedings by private legal counsel and could therefore only rely on government lawyers to argue their case. However, in *EC – Bananas III (1997),* Saint Lucia, a third party in this case with vital economic interests at stake, challenged this ban on private lawyers. While the US objected to the presence of a private lawyer acting on behalf of Saint Lucia, the Appellate Body ruled that a party or third party is free to decide to include private legal counsel in its delegation to present its arguments in WTO dispute settlement proceedings. The Appellate Body noted in its ruling: 'that representation by counsel of a government's own choice may well be a matter of particular significance – especially for developing country Members – to enable them to participate fully in dispute settlement proceedings'.[48] Today, most parties in panel and Appellate Body proceedings will be represented by, or at the

---

[47] Report by the Consultative Board to the Director-General Supachai Panitchpakdi, *The Future of the WTO: Addressing Institutional Challenges in the New Millennium* (the 'Sutherland Report') (WTO, 2004) at para 261.

[48] Appellate Body Report, *EC – Bananas III (1997)* at para 12.

very least have as part of their delegation, private legal counsel. This development has undoubtedly further strengthened the rule-based character of WTO dispute settlement. Another related development has been the establishment in, and successful operations since, 2001 of the Advisory Centre on WTO Law (ACWL). The ACWL is an intergovernmental organization, fully independent of the WTO, which functions essentially as a law firm specializing in WTO law, providing legal services at low or no cost to developing country Members of the WTO. In 2013, the ACWL assisted developing country Members in eight separate disputes.[49] 'Legal aid' as provided by the ACWL is quite unique in international adjudication.

Panels submit their draft reports to the parties for 'interim review', seeking the parties' comments on the draft report. This is a procedural feature very uncommon in national or international adjudication. Note that this interim review very seldom results in substantial changes in the panel report. After this interim review, the panel finalizes the report, issues it to the parties and eventually – when the report is available in the three official languages (English, French and Spanish) – makes the report public by circulating it to all WTO Members. Within 60 days of its circulation, a panel report is either adopted by the DSB by reverse consensus or appealed to the Appellate Body.

According to Article 12.9 of the DSU, panel proceedings (from the establishment of the panel to the circulation of the panel report) *should* not take more than nine months. In fact, panel proceedings to date have taken on average 15 months,[50] but this is, when taking into account the size and complexity of the disputes and compared with the average time taken by other international dispute settlement systems, still remarkably short.

C. Appellate Body Proceedings

In contrast to panels, the Appellate Body has detailed standard working procedures set out in the *Working Procedures for Appellate Review*.[51] Appellate Body proceedings are initiated by a notice of appeal. A party to the dispute other than the original appellant may also appeal alleged legal errors in the panel report by filing a notice of other appeal. The *Working*

---

49 ACWL, *Report on Operations 2013*, 16.

50 This count includes exceptionally complex cases, such as Airbus and Boeing subsidy cases in which the panel proceedings took more than five years.

51 *Working Procedures for Appellate Review*, WT/AB/WP/6, dated 16 August 2010, replacing earlier versions of the *Working Procedures*.

Procedures for Appellate Review set out a strict and very demanding timetable for appeals. The appellant's and other appellant's submissions are filed at the same time as the notice of appeal or the notice of other appeal. The appellee's submission(s) and the third participants' submissions are due within respectively 18 and 21 days after the date of the notice of appeal. An oral hearing generally takes place between day 30 and day 45 of the appellate process. Only in exceptional circumstances, where strict adherence would result in manifest unfairness, will the Appellate Body division hearing the appeal modify a time period set out in the *Working Procedures for Appellate Review.*[52] Note that third participants in Appellate Body proceedings have much broader rights to participate in these proceedings than third parties have in panel proceedings.

Where a procedural question arises that is not covered by the DSU or the *Working Procedures,* a division may, in the interest of fairness and orderly procedure in the conduct of an appeal, adopt an appropriate additional procedure for the purposes of that appeal only. In the exercise of this authority, Appellate Body divisions have adopted procedures to handle *amicus curiae* briefs submitted to the division, to provide for additional protection to business confidential information and to allow for public observation of the oral hearing. With regard to *amicus curiae* briefs, note that a total of about 60 *amicus curiae* briefs have been submitted to the Appellate Body in various proceedings. While strongly criticized by most WTO Members, the Appellate Body has repeatedly confirmed its case law on its authority (and that of panels) to accept and consider *amicus curiae* briefs when that would be useful. However, in no proceeding thus far has the Appellate Body considered it useful to consider *amicus curiae* briefs submitted to it. With regard to the public observation of the oral hearing, note that at the request of the parties, the Appellate Body may authorize public observation by means of real time or delayed closed circuit television broadcast to a separate viewing room at the WTO Headquarters. Many developing country Members strongly object to this practice of public observation. To safeguard their rights of confidentiality, the transmission is turned off when they make statements at an oral hearing in which they participate as a third participant.

After the oral hearing and before finalizing its report, the Appellate Body division responsible for deciding an appeal will always exchange views on the issues raised by the appeal with the Members of the Appellate Body not serving on the division. This procedural feature,

[52] Rule 16.2 of the *Working Procedures for Appellate Review.*

commonly referred to as the 'exchange of views', is quite uncommon in international or national adjudication but has allowed the Appellate Body to ensure consistency and coherence in its case law and to draw on the individual and collective expertise of *all* seven Members.

When the Appellate Body's report in an appeal is available in the three official languages, it is circulated to all WTO Members and made public. Article 17.5 of the DSU requires that Appellate Body proceedings not exceed 90 days. When compared with the time taken by other international courts to adjudicate cases of similar length and complexity, this timeframe for Appellate Body proceedings seems unrealistic. Yet, in most cases, the Appellate Body has been able to complete its review within that very short timeframe. In only two cases has the Appellate Body taken much longer than 90 days. In *US – Large Civil Aircraft (2nd complaint) (2012)* and *EC and certain member States – Large Civil Aircraft (2011)*, the Appellate Body proceedings lasted for 346 days and 301 days respectively. Note, however, that the panel proceedings in these cases lasted 1,868 days and 1,806 days, respectively, and the Appellate Body reports in these cases were 599 pages and 645 pages long.

Within 30 days of its circulation, the Appellate Body report, together with the panel report, as upheld, modified or reversed by the Appellate Body, is adopted by the DSB by reverse consensus. As discussed above, it is this (quasi-) automatic adoption by the DSB that makes the recommendations and rulings of the Appellate Body (and the panels) legally binding on the parties to the dispute.

D. Implementation and Enforcement

As stated in Article 21.3 of the DSU, the recommendations and rulings adopted by the DSB must be implemented immediately or, if that is impracticable, within a 'reasonable period of time'. Usually the parties are able to agree on the duration of the 'reasonable period of time' for implementation, but if they cannot, the duration of that period can – at the request of either party – be determined through binding arbitration.[53] The 'reasonable period of time' determined through binding arbitration has ranged from six months to 15 months and one week.

During the 'reasonable period of time' for implementation, the DSB keeps the implementation of adopted recommendations and rulings under surveillance.[54] At any time following adoption of the recommendations

53 See Article 21.3(c) of the DSU.
54 See Article 21.6 of the DSU.

and rulings, *any* WTO Member may raise the issue of implementation at the DSB. Shortly after the establishment of the reasonable period of time, the issue of implementation is automatically placed on the agenda of *each* regular DSB meeting and the Member concerned must provide the DSB with a monthly status report on its progress in the implementation of the recommendations and rulings. The issue of implementation remains on the DSB's agenda until the issue is resolved. This degree of surveillance by a political body of the implementation of court judgments is lacking in other international dispute settlement systems.

If by the end of the 'reasonable period time' for implementation, there is disagreement as to whether implementing measures were taken or whether the implementing measures are WTO-consistent, the original complainant can have recourse to the so-called 'compliance proceedings' set out in Article 21.5 of the DSU. These Article 21.5 compliance proceedings differ little from the proceedings in the original dispute, discussed above. If still available, the panel in the original dispute will act as the Article 21.5 panel and the Article 21.5 panel report can be appealed to the Appellate Body. To date, there have been 24 disputes in which there was recourse to Article 21.5 proceedings to determine whether the respondent in the original dispute implemented the relevant recommendations and rulings and did so in a WTO-consistent manner.[55]

If a respondent fails to implement correctly the recommendations and rulings within the 'reasonable period of time', Article 22.1 of the DSU provides that compensation (of future damages) and the suspension of concessions or other obligations (ie retaliation) are 'temporary measures' available to 'enforce' compliance by 'encouraging' the respondent to implement the relevant recommendations and rulings. Note that Article 22.1 of the DSU explicitly states that neither compensation nor retaliation 'is preferred to full implementation'. Parties are required to negotiate first on mutually acceptable compensation for future damages. However, it is very exceptional for parties to agree on what constitutes appropriate compensation for future damages. If agreement on compensation cannot be reached within 20 days of the expiry of the 'reasonable period of time' for implementation, Article 22.2 of the DSU provides that the original complainant(s) may request the DSB authorization to take retaliation measures against the respondent that failed to implement in time. As discussed above, the DSB decisions on the authorization of

---

[55] Note that in a number of these disputes, the complainant(s) resorted to Article 21.5 proceedings more than once. In *EC – Bananas III* there were in total five separate Article 21.5 proceedings.

retaliation are taken by reverse consensus. The authorization is therefore (quasi-)automatic.[56] While requests for authorization to retaliate often attract much attention, it should be noted that to date the DSB has authorized the taking of retaliation measures in only nine cases and that in only four of these cases the complainants actually applied retaliation measures.[57] In *US – FSC (2000)* the EU was authorized to retaliate against the US for an amount of US$ 4 billion per year. The retaliation measures in this case took the form of an increase of EU customs duties on selected US products. It is clear that retaliation measures put economic and political pressure on the respondent to bring their WTO-inconsistent measure(s) into compliance. It is often pointed out, however, that for complainants that are small developing countries, applying retaliation measures to respondents that are large developed countries is not a genuine option, as they would cause severe harm to their own economy without inflicting much pain on the economy of the respondent. Imperfect as this enforcement mechanism may be, it should be noted that other state-to-state dispute settlement systems, such as the ICJ, have no specific enforcement mechanism at all.

VIII. THE MAIN PROBLEM WITH THE WTO DISPUTE SETTLEMENT SYSTEM

As discussed above, the WTO dispute settlement system is the most prolific of all state-to-state dispute settlement mechanisms. Since its establishment in 1995, it has been widely used by developed as well as developing countries. Almost two out of three WTO Members have been involved in WTO dispute settlement. Disputes on issues of great political sensitivity and/or economic significance have been brought to the WTO for resolution and were in all but a few instances quickly resolved. The degree of compliance with rulings of WTO-inconsistency has been remarkably high. As discussed above, WTO dispute settlement has a number of features that distinguish it from other international adjudication and that help to explain its success.

While successful, it is broadly recognized that the current WTO dispute settlement system has a number of deficiencies. In the context of

---

[56] If the respondent objects to the level of retaliation for which authorization is requested, the matter may be referred to arbitration (under Article 22.6 of the DSU) before the DSB takes a decision.

[57] See *EC – Bananas III (1997)*, *EC – Hormones (1998)*, *US – FSC (2000)*, and *US – Offset Act (Byrd Amendment) (2003)*.

the Doha Round negotiations, WTO Members have been engaged since 2001 in discussions on amendments to the DSU to remedy some of the current deficiencies. These discussions on mostly technical amendments (eg on the joining of consultations; the facilitation of panel composition; third-party rights; remand; and sequencing) have not been successful to date.[58] However, the main problem of the WTO dispute settlement system and the Appellate Body is not any of the technical deficiencies of the system. Its main problem is, paradoxically, its success. This success has created a dangerous institutional imbalance in the WTO between its 'judicial' branch and its political 'rule-making' branch. It is uncontested that the WTO has not been successful in negotiating much-needed new and/or improved rules for international trade. In the face of the ineffectiveness of the political branch of the WTO, WTO Members may be ever more tempted to use the dispute settlement system to bring about new or improved rules, rather than seeking political agreement on such rules. However, as discussed above, the DSU does not condone judicial activism. Unwarranted judicial activism would seriously undermine the authority that the dispute settlement system and the Appellate Body currently enjoy and would drastically weaken their contribution to the rule of law in international trade.

---

[58] For the last publicly available progress report on these negotiations, see Special Session of the Dispute Settlement Body, *Report by the Chairman, Ambassador Ronald Saborío Soto, to the Trade Negotiations Committee*, TN/DS/25, 21 April 2011.

6. The contribution of the International Tribunal for the Law of the Sea to the rule of law

Philippe Gautier*

I. INTRODUCTION: THE MECHANISM FOR THE SETTLEMENT OF DISPUTES UNDER PART XV OF THE UNITED NATIONS CONVENTION FOR THE LAW OF THE SEA

A distinct feature of public international law, in comparison with municipal law, is the lack of a compulsory judicial system. Recourse to international judges or arbitrators depends on the consent of the parties to the dispute. In the absence of consent, international courts or tribunals do not have jurisdiction to deal with alleged violations of international obligations. Certainly, States may accept, prior to the existence of a dispute, the jurisdiction of an international court or tribunal. Several mechanisms do exist to that effect, through general, regional, or bilateral treaties, or optional declarations under Article 36 of the Statute of the International Court of Justice (the ICJ), and with respect to a narrow, specialized or broad scope of disputes. It must be acknowledged, however, that, in practice, these mechanisms are inserted in a only limited number of treaties.[1] In this context, a major achievement of the United Nations Convention for the Law of the Sea (the Convention) is to

* The opinions contained in this article are expressed by the author in his personal capacity and do not reflect the views of the Tribunal.

[1] See eg, Revised General Act for the Pacific Settlement of International Disputes, 28 April 1949; American Treaty on Pacific Settlement (Pact of Bogotá), 30 April 1948; European Convention for the Peaceful Settlement of Disputes, 29 April 1957; or the mechanisms established under the European Convention on Human Rights and the Dispute Settlement Understanding of the WTO.

include in its Part XV a mechanism for largely compulsory settlement of disputes arising out of the interpretation or application of its provisions. Actually, since 1982, no other major multilateral treaty has been adopted which would provide for such a robust and comprehensive judicial mechanism.[2] It is therefore against this background that the system for the settlement of disputes in law of the sea matters, as contained in Part XV of the Convention, should be analysed.

Part XV of the Convention contains three sections. Section 1 repeats the general obligation to settle disputes by peaceful means and reserves the right of the parties to a dispute to have recourse to the diplomatic means referred to in Article 33 of the UN Charter. Where no settlement has been reached through Section 1, Section 2 (Compulsory procedures entailing binding decisions) comes into play. On that basis, any dispute concerning the interpretation or application of the Convention may be submitted, at the request of any party to the dispute, to the court or tribunal having jurisdiction under the Convention.

Section 2 of Part XV combines two principles: the obligation to submit disputes arising out of the Convention to a compulsory procedure entailing binding decisions and the freedom of States to select their preferred means. In this connection, the following procedures are available to States Parties pursuant to Article 287: the International Tribunal for the Law of the Sea (the Statute of which is contained in Annex VI to the Convention), the International Court of Justice, arbitration under Annex VII to the Convention and special arbitration under Annex VIII to the Convention.[3] Pursuant to Article 287 of the Convention, States Parties may select the forum to which they wish to submit their disputes by virtue of declarations submitted to the Secretary-General of the United Nations, the depositary of the Convention. In the absence of declarations made by the parties to a dispute or if the declarations do not select the same forum, the dispute will be submitted to arbitration under Annex VII, except if otherwise agreed by the parties. Declarations under Article 287 may be made at any time. Withdrawal or modification of declarations does not affect pending proceedings and a declaration 'shall remain in

[2] With the exception of the Dispute Settlement Understanding of the WTO, to the extent that it might be characterized as a 'judicial' mechanism.

[3] Article 1 of Annex VIII provides that special arbitration is available to States Parties to the Convention for disputes relating to '(1) fisheries, (2) protection and preservation of the marine environment, (3) marine scientific research, or (4) navigation, including pollution from vessels and by dumping'.

force until three months after notice of revocation has been deposited with the Secretary-General of the United Nations'.[4]

Declarations under Article 287 of the Convention do not represent the only way by which States Parties to the Convention may confer jurisdiction on the different fora referred to in Part XV. Cases involving law of the sea matters may also be instituted on the basis of a special agreement or provisions to that effect contained in other general, regional or bilateral agreements. In addition, as will be examined later, under the Convention the Tribunal has compulsory jurisdiction to deal with specific categories of disputes.

The compulsory mechanism under Part XV is subject to certain limitations and exceptions which are contained in Section 3. By virtue of Article 297, disputes relating to the sovereign rights (or their exercise) of the coastal State with respect to the living resources in its exclusive economic zone (Article 297, paragraph 3), and disputes relating to the exercise by the coastal State of its rights regarding marine scientific research in its exclusive economic zone (Article 297, paragraph 2) are excluded from the compulsory judicial mechanism provided for in Part XV, Section 2, of the Convention. Article 298 of the Convention provides for optional exceptions to the application of Part XV of the Convention whereby States may declare that they exclude from the mechanism disputes relating to the delimitation of maritime areas, military activities[5] or disputes in respect of which the Security Council of the United Nations is exercising the functions assigned to it by the Charter. These exceptions are activated by way of declarations deposited by States Parties with the Secretary-General of the United Nations. Disputes which are subject to the limitations covered by Article 297 or by declarations made under Article 298 may still be submitted to the Tribunal if the parties to the dispute so agree (Article 299, paragraph 1).

---

4 Article 287, para 6, of the Convention.

5 Paragraph 1(b) of Article 298 covers disputes concerning military activities and disputes 'concerning law enforcement activities in regard to the exercise of sovereign rights or jurisdiction excluded from the jurisdiction of a court or tribunal under article 297, paragraph 2 or 3'.

II. THE INTERNATIONAL TRIBUNAL FOR THE LAW OF THE SEA (ITLOS): AN OVERVIEW

The International Tribunal for the Law of the Sea (the Tribunal) was created by the 1982 United Nations Convention on the Law of the Sea.[6] Pursuant to Article 1 of the Statute of the Tribunal (the Statute), its seat is in the Free and Hanseatic City of Hamburg in the Federal Republic of Germany.

The Tribunal is composed of 21 members elected[7] by the States Parties to the Convention 'from among persons enjoying the highest reputation for fairness and integrity and of recognized competence in the field of the law of the sea' (Statute, Article 2). They serve for a term of nine years and may be re-elected. Elections take place on a triennial basis. The composition of the Tribunal has to ensure the representation of the principal legal systems of the world and equitable geographical distribution.

The Tribunal received its first case on 13 November 1997 (*The "SAIGA" Case*). So far, 22 cases have been submitted to the Tribunal. In its decisions, the Tribunal has dealt with legal issues regarding inter alia the protection of the marine environment and the importance of procedural rights relating thereto, the right of hot pursuit and the use of force at sea, liability, delimitation of maritime areas and prompt release of vessels and crews.

A. Jurisdiction of the Tribunal in Contentious Cases

1. Disputes arising out of the interpretation and application of the Convention

(i) Jurisdiction ratione materiae The core competence of the Tribunal is to deal with disputes arising out of the Convention. In other words, whenever a dispute relates to a provision of the Convention or whenever it is alleged that a State has not complied with a provision of the Convention, the Tribunal has jurisdiction to deal with such a case, subject to the limitations contained in Articles 297 and 298.

---

[6] The Convention entered into force on 16 November 1994. As of 1 June 2014, 165 States and one international organization (European Union) are parties to it.

[7] The first election took place on 1 August 1996.

(ii) Jurisdiction ratione personae With respect to disputes relating to the Convention, the Tribunal is open to States Parties to the Convention. The expression 'States Parties'[8] refers to the 165 States which have ratified or acceded to the Convention as well as the European Union.

It is also possible for non-States Parties, such as the International Seabed Authority, a State enterprise or a natural or juridical person,[9] to appear before a chamber of the Tribunal composed of 11 Judges – the Seabed Disputes Chamber – with respect to disputes relating to the exploration and exploitation of the Area ie, 'the seabed and ocean floor and subsoil thereof, beyond the limits of national jurisdiction'.[10]

According to Article 20, paragraph 2, of the Statute, 'the Tribunal shall be open to entities other than States Parties in any case submitted pursuant to any other agreement conferring jurisdiction on the Tribunal which is accepted by all the parties to that case'. The fact that this provision, only applicable to the Tribunal, refers to an 'agreement' – and not to an 'international agreement' as in the case of Article 288, paragraph 2, which applies to any 'court or tribunal referred to in Article 287' – has sometimes been interpreted as encompassing agreements which could be concluded with private entities, eg, an agreement between a flag State and an insurance company or a classification society. The Tribunal has not yet had the opportunity to pronounce itself on this question.

It should be added that, whenever an entity which is not party to the Convention (eg, a State or an international organization not party to the Convention) is party to a case before the Tribunal, such entity will have to contribute to the expenses of the Tribunal. In this respect, Article 19, paragraph 2, of the Statute of the Tribunal provides that, in such a situation, the Tribunal 'shall fix the amount which that party is to contribute towards the expenses of the Tribunal'.

(iii) Compulsory jurisdiction of the Tribunal The Tribunal is competent to deal with certain cases through unilateral applications independently of any declaration or expression of consent by the respondent State. This so-called 'compulsory jurisdiction' of the Tribunal applies to the following categories of disputes:

---

8 See Article 1, para 2(1) and (2), of the Convention.

9 Article 20, para 2 of the Statue; Articles 187 and 188 of the Convention.

10 Article 1, para 1(1) of the Convention.

- Disputes relating to Part XI of the Convention (exploration and exploitation of deep seabed resources (see Convention, Article 187 and 188)). With the exception of disputes concerning the interpretation or application of a contract,[11] the Seabed Disputes Chamber of the Tribunal has exclusive jurisdiction over these disputes.
- Disputes submitted pursuant to Article 292 of the Convention (prompt release of vessels and crews). Under certain provisions of the Convention, a State which has detained a vessel on specific charges (eg, fishery offences) is required to release the vessel and/or its crew upon the posting of a reasonable bond.[12] Where the flag State of the detained vessel alleges that the detaining State has failed to comply with these provisions, the dispute relating to the release of the vessel and its crew may be submitted to the Tribunal if, after ten days from the date of detention, no agreement has been reached between the two parties to the dispute. The case may be brought by the flag State or on its behalf.
- Disputes submitted under Article 290, paragraph 5, of the Convention (prescription of provisional measures pending the constitution of an arbitral tribunal). When arbitral proceedings are instituted (eg, in the event that the parties have not made a declaration under Article 287 of the Convention), the constitution of the arbitral tribunal may take some months. During this period of time, any party to the dispute is entitled to request the Tribunal to prescribe provisional measures 'to preserve the respective rights of the parties or to prevent serious harm to the marine environment'.[13] The Tribunal may prescribe provisional measures 'if it considers that prima facie the tribunal which is to be constituted would have jurisdiction and that the urgency of the situation so requires'.[14]

---

[11] See, however, Article 188, para 2, of the Convention which provides that disputes between parties to a contract ('being States Parties, the Authority or the Enterprise, state enterprises and natural or juridical persons') concerning the interpretation or application of a contract or a plan of work 'shall be submitted, at the request of any party to the dispute, to binding commercial arbitration, unless the parties otherwise agree'. In this case, the 'commercial arbitral tribunal to which the dispute is submitted shall have no jurisdiction to decide any question of interpretation of this Convention. When the dispute also involves a question of the interpretation of Part XI and the Annexes relating thereto, with respect to activities in the Area, that question shall be referred to the Seabed Disputes Chamber for a ruling.'

[12] See, for instance, Article 73 of the Convention.

[13] Article 290, para 1, of the Convention.

[14] Article 290, para 5, of the Convention.

2. Disputes arising out of agreements other than the Convention

The jurisdiction of the Tribunal is not limited to disputes arising out of the Convention. In accordance with Article 21 of the Statute, the jurisdiction of the Tribunal comprises all matters provided for in any other agreement which confers jurisdiction on the Tribunal. A number of agreements have been concluded which contain provisions stipulating that disputes arising out of the interpretation or application of these agreements could be submitted to the Tribunal.[15]

B. Advisory Proceedings

The Convention provides that the International Seabed Authority may address requests for advisory opinions to the Seabed Disputes Chamber. Further to a request submitted by the Council of the International Seabed Authority, a first advisory opinion was delivered by the Chamber on 1 February 2011 on questions relating to the responsibility of States sponsoring activities in the Area.[16]

Requests for advisory opinions may also be submitted to the Tribunal pursuant to Article 138 of the Rules of the Tribunal which states that the Tribunal 'may give an advisory opinion on a legal question if an international agreement related to the purposes of the Convention specifically provides for the submission to the Tribunal of a request for such an opinion'.

---

15 See eg, the 1996 Protocol to the Convention on the Prevention of Marine Pollution by Dumping of Wastes and Other Matter, 1972; the 1995 Agreement for the Implementation of the Provisions of the United Nations Convention on the Law of the Sea of 10 December 1982 relating to the Conservation and Management of Straddling Fish Stocks and Highly Migratory Fish Stocks; the Agreement to Promote Compliance with International Conservation and Management Measures by Fishing Vessels on the High Seas; the UNESCO Convention on the Protection of the Underwater Cultural Heritage; the Convention on the Conservation and Management of Highly Migratory Fish Stocks in the Western and Central Pacific Ocean; the Convention on the Conservation and Management of Fishery Resources in the South-East Atlantic Ocean.

16 See the advisory opinion delivered on 1 February 2011: *Responsibilities and obligations of States with respect to activities in the Area*, Advisory Opinion, 1 February 2011, ITLOS Reports 2011, 10.

III. THE JURISPRUDENCE OF THE TRIBUNAL AND ITS CONTRIBUTION TO THE RULE OF LAW

A. The Role of Part XV of the Convention

Before addressing specific aspects which illustrate the contribution of the Tribunal to the rule of law, it is appropriate to highlight the role of Part XV of the Convention in the promotion of justice. As already mentioned, treaties containing a compulsory mechanism for the settlement of disputes are not numerous in international law and the very fact that such a mechanism is set up in Part XV is already remarkable. In addition, Part XV not only exists on paper; it also functions in a successful way. As an illustration, we may compare the number of cases relating the law of the sea which were brought to an international court during a similar period of time (18 years) before (1977–94) and after (1995–2012) the entry into force of the Convention on 16 November 1994. This shows a sharp increase (from 12[17] to 37[18]) in the number of cases brought to a judicial

[17] 1994: *Land and Maritime Boundary between Cameroon and Nigeria (Cameroon* v *Nigeria: Equatorial Guinea intervening*), Judgment, ICJ Reports 2002, 303; 1991: *Maritime Delimitation and Territorial Questions between Qatar and Bahrain,* Merits, Judgment, ICJ Reports 2001, 40; *Passage through the Great Belt (Finland* v *Denmark),* Order of 10 September 1992, ICJ Reports 1992, 348; 1989: *Case concerning the Delimitation of Maritime Areas between Canada and France,* Decision of 10 June 1992, ILM, Vol. 31 (1992), 1145; 1988: *Maritime Delimitation in the Area between Greenland and Jan Mayen,* Judgment, ICJ Reports 1993, 38; 1986: *Land, Island and Maritime Frontier Dispute (El Salvador/Honduras: Nicaragua intervening),* Judgment, ICJ Reports 1992, 351; 1985: *Case concerning the delimitation of the maritime boundary between Guinea-Bissau and Senegal,* Arbitral Award of 31 July 1989, 1990, ILR 83, 1; *Dispute concerning Filleting within the Gulf of St. Lawrence between Canada and France,* Decision of 17 July 1986, ILR 82 (1990), 591.

[18] ITLOS: Prompt release: *M/V "SAIGA" (Saint Vincent and the Grenadines* v *Guinea), Prompt Release,* Judgment, ITLOS Reports 1997, 16; *"Camouco" (Panama* v *France),* Order of 17 January 2000, ITLOS Reports 2000, 4; *"Monte Confurco" (Seychelles* v *France),* Prompt Release, Judgment, ITLOS Reports 2000, 86; *"Grand Prince" (Belize* v *France),* Prompt Release, Judgment, ITLOS Reports 2001, 17; *"Chaisiri Reefer 2" (Panama* v *Yemen),* Order of 13 July 2001, ITLOS Reports 2001, 82; *"Volga" (Russian Federation* v *Australia),* Prompt Release, Judgment, ITLOS Reports 2002, 10; *"Juno Trader" (Saint Vincent and the Grenadines* v *Guinea-Bissau),* Prompt Release, Judgment, ITLOS Reports 2004, 17; *"Hoshinmaru" (Japan* v *Russian Federation),* Prompt Release, Judgment, ITLOS Reports 2005–2007, 18; *"Tomimaru" (Japan* v *Russian Federation),* Prompt Release, Judgment, ITLOS Reports 2005–2007, 74;

body after the Convention came into force. It may be added that a majority of these cases were submitted to a judicial process on the basis of the compulsory mechanism provided for in the Convention.

At the time of the entry into force of the Convention, concerns were expressed vis-à-vis the risk of conflicting decisions which could be pronounced by the different courts and tribunals provided for by Part XV. In light of the judicial practice generated by Part XV of the Convention, it may be stated that this risk did not materialize. On the contrary, it

---

Provisional measures: *Southern Bluefin Tuna (New Zealand* v *Japan; Australia* v *Japan),* Provisional Measures, Order of 27 August 1999, ITLOS Reports 1999, 280; *MOX Plant (Ireland* v *United Kingdom*), Provisional Measures, Order of 3 December 2001, ITLOS Reports 2001, 95; *Land Reclamation in and around the Straits of Johor (Malaysia* v *Singapore),* Provisional Measures, Order of 8 October 2003, ITLOS Reports 2003, 10; "ARA Libertad" (*Argentina* v *Ghana),* Provisional Measures, Order of 15 December 2012, ITLOS Reports 2012, 332; Merits: *M/V "SAIGA" (No. 2) (Saint Vincent and the Grenadines* v *Guinea),* Judgment, ITLOS Reports 1999, 10; *Conservation and Sustainable Exploitation of Swordfish Stocks (Chile/European Union),* Order of 16 December 2009, ITLOS Reports 2008–2010, 13; *Delimitation of the maritime boundary in the Bay of Bengal (Bangladesh/Myanmar),* Judgment, ITLOS Reports 2012, 4; *M/V "Louisa" (Saint Vincent and the Grenadines* v *Kingdom of Spain),* Judgment, ITLOS Reports 2013, to be published; *M/V "Virginia G" (Panama/Guinea-Bissau),* Judgment, ITLOS Reports 2014, to be published; **ICJ:** 1995: *Fisheries Jurisdiction (Spain* v *Canada),* Order of 2 May 1995, ICJ Reports 1995, 87; 1999: *Territorial and Maritime Dispute between Nicaragua and Honduras in the Caribbean Sea (Nicaragua* v *Honduras),* Judgment, ICJ Reports 2007, 659; 2001: *Territorial and Maritime Dispute (Nicaragua* v *Colombia),* Judgment, ICJ Reports 2012, 624; 2003: *Sovereignty over Pedra Branca/Pulau Batu Puteh, Middle Rocks and South Ledge (Malaysia/Singapore),* Judgment, ICJ Reports 2008, 12; 2004: *Maritime Delimitation in the Black Sea (Romania* v *Ukraine),* Judgment, ICJ Reports 2009, 61; 2008: *Maritime Dispute (Peru* v *Chile*), Judgment of 27 January 2014; 2010: *Whaling in the Antarctic (Australia* v *Japan: New Zealand intervening),* Judgment of 31 March 2014; **Arbitration:** 1996: Award of the Arbitral Tribunal in the Second Stage – Maritime Delimitation (Eritrea/Yemen), 17 December 1999; 2004: Award of the Arbitral Tribunal (Barbados v Trinidad and Tobago), 11 April 2006; 2009: Bay of Bengal Maritime Boundary Arbitration between Bangladesh and India; 1999: *Southern Bluefin Tuna (New Zealand – Japan, Australia – Japan),* Decision of 4 August 2000, RIAA, Vol XXIII, 1; 2001: *Ireland* v *United Kingdom* ("*MOX Plant Case*") (2008); Final Award, *Ireland* v *United Kingdom* ("OSPAR" Arbitration) (2 July 2003); 2003: Award on Agreed Terms (*Land Reclamation by Singapore in and around the Straits of Johor* (*Malaysia* v *Singapore*), (1 September 2005); 2009: *Arbitration Between the Republic of Croatia and the Republic of Slovenia*; 2010: *The Republic of Mauritius* v *The United Kingdom of Great Britain and Northern Ireland*; 2012: The *ARA Libertad Arbitration* (*Argentina* v *Ghana*) (2013).

seems that the arbitral and judicial bodies which have been dealing with issues concerning the law of the sea were particularly keen in taking into account the existing international jurisprudence. As an illustration of this development, reference may be made to the recent statements delivered by Judge Yanai, President of the Tribunal, and Judge Greenwood, of the ICJ, on the occasion of the celebration of the 30th anniversary of the opening for signature of the Convention in New York on 10 December 2012. With respect to the freedom of choice given to States Parties under Article 287 of the Convention, President Yanai stated:

> This option given to States to choose one or more international courts or tribunals has sometimes given rise to fears of a fragmentation of international law and of conflicting judgments being delivered by different international courts and tribunals. This concern has proved to be unfounded. The Tribunal has regularly referred to judgments of the International Court of Justice and its predecessor, the Permanent Court of International Justice, and to decisions by other courts and tribunals, both on substantive issues and on procedural points.[19]

This assessment was largely shared by Judge Greenwood who, in his intervention, noted that:

> when the Convention was adopted, a number of commentators expressed concern that the choice of different methods of dispute settlement in Article 287 … might lead to a fragmentation of this area of international law and even to competing lines of jurisprudence from different courts and tribunals. In fact, there has been a remarkable harmony between the pronouncements of the [ICJ], the [ITLOS] and the Annex VII arbitration tribunals.[20]

Incidentally, it may be added that the options offered by Article 287 – a provision sometimes seen as promoting a form of 'forum shopping' – remain largely theoretical. Out of 166 States Parties – as of 1 June 2014 – 49 States made a declaration under Article 287 of the Convention. This

---

[19] Statement of the President of the Tribunal on the occasion of the commemoration of the thirtieth anniversary of the opening for signature of the 1982 United Nations Convention on the Law of the Sea, New York, 10 December 2012, text available on the website of the Tribunal at: http://www.itlos.org/fileadmin/itlos/documents/statements_of_president/yanai/GA_Statement_30th_anniversary_101212.E_FINALE.pdf.

[20] Judge C Greenwood, Address to the United Nations General Assembly at the commemoration of the Thirtieth Anniversary of the opening for signature of the 1982 United Nations Convention on the Law of the Sea, text available on the website of the ICJ at: http://www.icj-cij.org/presscom/files/9/17229.pdf.

means that in the majority of disputes between the 166 States Parties, when no declaration was made by a party to the dispute or when the declarations do not select the same forum, there will simply be no choice: arbitration will be the only compulsory mechanism available under the Convention.

B. 'Justice Delayed, Justice Denied'

Access to international justice is not sufficient to ensure an efficient application of the rule of law. It is also necessary that a decision be rendered within a reasonable period of time. In this respect, the Tribunal has demonstrated its ability to deal swiftly with cases submitted to it. The importance that the Tribunal attaches to this point is reflected in provisions of its Rules requiring that proceedings be 'conducted without unnecessary delay or expense'[21] and that time-limits prescribed for the completion of procedural steps (for example, the date for the filing of written pleadings) should be 'as short as the character of the case permits'.[22] The attention paid by the Tribunal to the need to deal promptly with cases is particularly noticeable in its Rules and its practice regarding urgent proceedings (ie, request for prompt release of vessels and crews under Article 292 of the Convention and request for the prescription of provisional measures pending the constitution of an arbitral tribunal under Article 290, paragraph 5, of the Convention). Indeed, the period of time required to deal with these urgent proceedings amounts to approximately one month, from the day of the filing of the application until the delivery of the judgment or the order.

C. Flag State and the Functional Protection of the Vessels Flying its Flag

In its jurisprudence, the Tribunal had the opportunity to revisit the application of rules relating to the admissibility of international claims brought by States in connection with damage caused to private persons. In the *M/V "SAIGA" (No. 2) Case*, the Tribunal was faced with a situation where different persons – crew members, the shipowner and the owner of the cargo – suffered damage due to the arrest and detention of the *Saiga*, a ship flying the flag of Saint Vincent and the Grenadines, by the authorities of Guinea. During the proceedings, the respondent, Guinea, raised objections to the admissibility of the claims, arguing that

21 Article 49 of the Rules.
22 Article 46 of the Rules.

the rule of exhaustion of local remedies had not been complied with. In its view, the persons whose rights were prejudiced as a result of alleged violations of international law by Guinea should have first exhausted legal remedies before Guinean Courts. In addition, it referred to the principle of diplomatic protection according to which a State can only claim reparation for its nationals. The application of the nationality of claims' rule would then have prevented the Tribunal from dealing with the issue of damages caused to the persons on board of the vessel, who were nationals of Ukraine and Senegal, as well as the shipowner of the vessel (Tabona Shipping Company Ltd. of Nicosia, Cyprus[23]) and the owner of the cargo (Addax BV of Geneva, Switzerland[24]).

Pursuant to Article 295 of the Convention, local remedies have to be exhausted 'where this is required by international law'. In other words, the rule is not applicable in all circumstances. In 1999, when the Tribunal dealt with the case, the ILC had adopted on first reading its Draft Articles on State Responsibility (the 'Draft'). Article 22 of the Draft specified that the rule that local remedies must be exhausted is applicable in cases where the alleged violation relates to 'an international obligation concerning the treatment to be accorded to aliens'. The rule is therefore not applicable to cases involving a direct violation of the rights of a State. On the basis of this approach, the Tribunal considered that the rule was not applicable to the case before it, since the claims brought by Saint Vincent and the Grenadines were made in relation to rights belonging to that State under the Convention. As an example, reference may be made to Article 90 of the Convention which expressly refers to the freedom of navigation as a right directly conferred upon the flag State.[25] That said, whenever the flag State brings an international action for violation of its own rights, it will then claim reparation for the whole damage resulting from the said violation and this may include the prejudice caused to private persons placed under its protection.[26]

On the issue relating to the nationality of the claims, the Tribunal took a position centred on the need to ensure an efficient protection of the ship and those involved in its operation:

---

23 *M/V "SAIGA" (No. 2) (Saint Vincent and the Grenadines* v *Guinea)*, Judgment, ITLOS Reports 1999, 10 at 27.

24 Ibid., at 28.

25 'Every State, whether coastal or land-locked, has the right to sail ships flying its flag on the high seas.'

26 See *M/V "SAIGA" (No. 2)*, above n23 at 46.

> the Convention considers a ship as a unit, as regards the obligations of the flag State with respect to the ship and the right of a flag State to seek reparation for loss or damage caused to the ship by acts of other States … Thus the ship, every thing on it, and every person involved or interested in its operations are treated as an entity linked to the flag State. The nationalities of these persons are not relevant.[27]

As a consequence, the flag State is entitled to claim reparation for the whole damage caused to the ship, regardless of the nationalities of the persons concerned.

The approach adopted by the Tribunal on these two issues (exhaustion of local remedies and nationality of claims) seems to be based on some form of functional protection offered by the flag State to the vessels flying its flag. Such functional protection is not identical to diplomatic protection since it is not based on the nationality of the persons involved. The flag State of the vessel then plays a pivotal role, which is reinforced by the principle of the unity of the ship. Incidentally, it may be observed that the notion of functional protection is not entirely new in international law; it had already been developed by the ICJ in the Reparation case where the Court referred to the United Nations' right of functional protection vis-à-vis its agents.[28]

Another issue which arose in the *M/V "SAIGA" (No. 2) Case* relates to the compensation that Guinea had to pay to Saint Vincent and the Grenadines in respect of damages caused to private persons. In the context of diplomatic protection, the amount of compensation is paid to the national State of the victims and it is for that State to decide on how, and to what extent, this amount will be allocated among the persons who suffered damage. Nothing prevents, however, an international court from being more precise and from taking a decision as to the amount to which each person would be entitled as compensation for damage caused by violation of international law. That is what the Tribunal did in its judgment of 1999. Paragraph 175 of the judgment gives a precise list of the allocation of damages, including compensation for medical expenses and pain for the persons who were injured during the arrest of the vessel, as well as compensation for the detention of the captain and the members of the crew. The amount of damage for detention is further detailed in an annex to the judgment, which lists each person with the amount of compensation allocated to him.

---

27 Ibid., 48.

28 *Reparation for Injuries Suffered in the Service of the United Nations*, Advisory Opinion, ICJ Reports 1949, 174 at 185.

D. Protection of Procedural Rights in Environmental Cases[29]

Over the past few years the number of international cases involving environmental legal issues has increased. This trend is also visible in the practice of the Tribunal relating to the prescription of provisional measures pending the constitution of an arbitral tribunal. The objective of this urgent procedure is to offer legal remedies to the parties to a dispute in a situation where arbitral proceedings have been instituted but the arbitral tribunal has not yet been constituted. Indeed, the constitution of the arbitral tribunal may take several months and, during this period of time, there is a need for legal protection. Then, under Article 290, paragraph 5, of the Convention, the Tribunal has compulsory competence to prescribe provisional measures 'to preserve the respective rights of the parties to the dispute or to prevent serious harm to the marine environment'. This is, however, subject to the condition that 'the urgency of the situation so requires', the urgency here being assessed in light of the relatively short period of time which will be needed to constitute the arbitral tribunal and enable it to deal with a request for interim measures of protection. Provisional measures under Article 290, paragraph 5, of the Convention are proceedings which may be particularly useful in the context of environmental cases where there is a need to act promptly to avoid further deterioration of the marine environment. This may explain that the four cases which were submitted to the Tribunal under this provision were all related to environmental matters.[30] In this context, an interesting aspect of the jurisprudence of the Tribunal concerns the protection of the procedural rights of the parties to the dispute. In environmental cases, the importance of procedural obligations (eg, the obligation to notify, to consult, to exchange information, to conduct an environmental impact assessment ...) should not be underestimated in comparison with substantive obligations (eg, the obligation to comply with specific standards for the emission of pollutants ...). Very often a dispute will arise due to the breach of a procedural obligation requiring eg, prior consultation or exchange of information. In its orders, the

---

[29] See eg, P Gautier 'Urgent proceedings before the International Tribunal for the Law of the Sea' (2009) 8(1) *Issues in Legal Scholarship*.

[30] *Southern Bluefin Tuna (New Zealand* v *Japan; Australia* v *Japan),* Provisional Measures, Order of 27 August 1999, ITLOS Reports 1999, 280; *MOX Plant (Ireland* v *United Kingdom),* Provisional Measures, Order of 3 December 2001, ITLOS Reports 2001, 95; *Land Reclamation in and around the Straits of Johor (Malaysia* v *Singapore),* Provisional Measures, Order of 8 October 2003, ITLOS Reports 2003, 10.

Tribunal took the view that provisional measures could be an appropriate tool to ensure the efficient protection of procedural rights. For example, in the *MOX Plant Case*,[31] it ordered the parties to cooperate with a view to exchanging information on the consequences of the operation of the plant and monitoring the risks resulting from it. Likewise, in the *Land Reclamation* case,[32] the Tribunal went further and not only requested the parties to cooperate and exchange information but also ordered them to establish a group of independent experts with a precise mandate.[33]

E. Delimitation of the Continental Shelf beyond 200 Nautical Miles

In a recent judgment, the Tribunal dealt with a new issue in respect of which the existing jurisprudence is rather inconclusive.[34] The question,

---

[31] *MOX Plant*, above n30 at 95.

[32] *Land Reclamation in and around the Straits of Johor*, above n30 at 10.

[33] See operative provision 1(a) in the Order of 8 October 2003:

> Malaysia and Singapore shall cooperate and shall, for this purpose, enter into consultations forthwith in order to: (a) establish promptly a group of independent experts with the mandate (i) to conduct a study, on terms of reference to be agreed by Malaysia and Singapore, to determine, within a period not exceeding one year from the date of this Order, the effects of Singapore's land reclamation and to propose, as appropriate, measures to deal with any adverse effects of such land reclamation; (ii) to prepare, as soon as possible, an interim report on the subject of infilling works in Area D at Pulau Tekong … .

[34] In the *Arbitration between Barbados and the Republic of Trinidad and Tobago,* the arbitral tribunal considered that it had jurisdiction to delimit the maritime boundary of the continental shelf beyond 200 nm (Decision of 11 April 2006, RIAA, Vol XXVII, 147 at 209, para 217). In *Territorial and Maritime Dispute between Nicaragua and Honduras in the Caribbean Sea (Nicaragua* v *Honduras),* the ICJ stated that 'any claim of continental shelf rights beyond 200 miles must be in accordance with Article 76 of UNCLOS and reviewed by the Commission on the Limits of the Continental Shelf established thereunder' (Judgment, ICJ Reports 2007, 759, para 319). After the judgment of the Tribunal, the ICJ dealt with a request addressing the continental shelf beyond 200 nautical miles in the *Territorial and Maritime Disputes (Nicaragua* v *Columbia).* In its Judgment of 19 November 2012, the Court noted that:

> Nicaragua submitted to the Commission only 'Preliminary Information' which, by its own admission, falls short of meeting the requirements for information on the limits of the continental shelf beyond 200 nautical miles which 'shall be submitted by the coastal State to the Commission' in accordance with paragraph 8 of Article 76 of UNCLOS. (para 127)

and took the view that:

which arose in the dispute concerning *Delimitation of the maritime boundary between Bangladesh and Myanmar in the Bay of Bengal*,[35] related to the delimitation of the outer continental shelf ie, the continental shelf beyond 200 nautical miles (from the baselines from which the breadth of the territorial sea is measured). More precisely, the Tribunal had to decide whether it should exercise its jurisdiction in order to delimit the outer continental shelf between Bangladesh and Myanmar in the absence of recommendations of the Commission on the Limits of the Continental Shelf (CLCS). Pursuant to Article 76, paragraph 8, of the Convention, States have to establish the limits of their continental shelf beyond 200 nautical miles on the basis of the recommendations of the CLCS. However, in the circumstances of this case, due to the existing dispute between the two States, the Commission was prevented from considering their entitlements to an outer continental shelf. Faced with this situation, the Tribunal observed that it had a role to play since the Convention expressly provides for recourse to judicial means for the delimitation of the continental shelf in the absence of an agreement between the States concerned. It also noted that some States had in practice concluded agreements on the delimitation of their outer continental shelf even prior to any recommendations made by the CLCS on the delineation of their outer continental shelf. Therefore it would be difficult to consider that the Tribunal would be prevented from settling, through a judgment, a matter on which States could agree through a treaty. The Tribunal then came to the conclusion that 'it would be contrary to the object and purpose of the Convention not to resolve the existing impasse. Inaction in the present case, by the Commission and the Tribunal … would leave the Parties in a position where they may be unable to benefit fully from their rights over the continental shelf.'[36] As a consequence of its decision, the Tribunal had to verify that the entitlements of both States were not hypothetical. On the basis of a legal interpretation of Article 76 of the Convention, and in particular as regards the terms 'natural prolongation' and 'outer edge of the continental margin', it concluded

since Nicaragua, in the present proceedings, has not established that it has a continental margin that extends far enough to overlap with Colombia's 200-nautical-mile entitlement to the continental shelf, measured from Colombia's mainland coast, the Court is not in a position to delimit the continental shelf boundary between Nicaragua and Colombia, as requested by Nicaragua, even using the general formulation proposed by it. (para 129)

[35] *Delimitation of the maritime boundary between Bangladesh and Myanmar in the Bay of Bengal (Bangladesh/Myanmar),* Judgment, ITLOS Reports 2012, 4.

[36] Judgment of 14 March 2012, para 392.

that the two States were entitled to a shelf beyond 200 miles. At the same time, the Tribunal made it clear that this approach was made possible due to 'uncontested scientific evidence regarding the unique nature of the Bay of Bengal and information submitted during the proceedings'[37] showing that 'there is a continuous and substantial layer of sedimentary rocks extending from Myanmar's coast to the area beyond 200 nm'.[38] In other words, the Tribunal would not necessarily adopt the same approach in other circumstances. It even made it clear that it 'would have been hesitant to proceed with the delimitation of the area beyond 200 nm had it concluded that there was significant uncertainty as to the existence of a continental margin in the area in question'.[39]

F. Advisory Opinions Before the Tribunal[40]

Contrary to the advisory jurisdiction of the Seabed Disputes Chamber which is contemplated in Article 191 of the Convention, the possibility of submitting a request for a legal opinion to the Tribunal is not expressly addressed in any provision of the Convention. The advisory jurisdiction of the Tribunal is nevertheless based on an interpretation of a particular provision thereof ie, Article 21 of the statute of the Tribunal. Article 21 first refers to the contentious jurisdiction of the Tribunal, with respect to 'all disputes and all applications submitted to it in accordance with this Convention', but this provision immediately goes on and adds 'and all matters specifically provided for in any other agreement which confers jurisdiction on the Tribunal'.[41] Obviously, the expression 'all matters' is broader than the term 'dispute'[42] and may be understood as comprising requests for a legal opinion, on the condition that such possibility is provided for in an international agreement related to the purposes of the

---

37 Ibid., para 446.

38 Ibid., para 446.

39 Ibid., para 443.

40 See eg, P Gautier, 'Advisory Proceedings before the International Tribunal for the Law of the Sea' in Haisheng Zhang, Jiabiao Li, Zhiguo Gao and Haiwen Zhang (eds), *Technical and Legal Aspects of the Continental Shelf and the Area* (Beijing, Science Press, 2012,) 129–43.

41 Article 21, entitled 'Jurisdiction', reads as follows: 'The jurisdiction of the Tribunal comprises all disputes and all applications submitted to it in accordance with this Convention and all matters specifically provided for in any other agreement which confers jurisdiction on the Tribunal.'

42 See also Article 288, para 3, of the Convention where the expression 'any matter', in the case of the Seabed Disputes Chambers clearly refers to contentious and advisory jurisdictions of the Chamber.

Convention. Advisory proceedings before the Tribunal are regulated by Article 138 of the Rules and this provision was recently activated: on 28 March 2013, the Tribunal received its first request for an advisory opinion based on Article 138 of its Rules.

It could be argued that the role of an international court is to adjudicate disputes and not to render non-binding legal opinions. However, it should be recognized that the difference between contentious and advisory proceedings is not always crystal clear: in the *North Sea Continental Shelf Cases*, the ICJ was requested to determine the principles and rules of international law applicable to the delimitation of the continental shelf in the North Sea,[43] and it may be stated that a similar result could have been achieved through a legal opinion. Likewise, States have developed, through agreements, the practice of requesting the ICJ to give advisory opinions in order to settle disputes between States and international organizations and those opinions are accepted by the parties to the dispute as legally binding. It may be acknowledged that such a 'binding advisory opinion' – a form of oxymoron – looks very close to a judgment.

On this matter, it should be recalled that States, pursuant to Part XV of the Convention and the UN Charter, have the duty to settle peacefully their disputes. In this context, it is difficult to understand the reasons which would prevent States from jointly requesting an advisory opinion on a legal question which, if properly addressed, could help them in settling a pending issue between them. What really matters is to assess whether advisory proceedings serve the needs of the international community and constitute a useful tool in the administration of international justice.

That said, this should not imply in any way that advisory proceedings could be a suitable substitute for contentious proceedings. Indeed, while it is well recognized in the practice of the ICJ that advisory proceedings

---

[43] Article 1 of the special agreement was drafted as follows:

(1) The International Court of Justice is requested to decide the following question: What principles and rules of international law are applicable to the delimitation as between the Parties of the areas of the continental shelf in the North Sea which appertain to each of them beyond the partial boundary determined by the above-mentioned Convention of 1 December 1964?

(2) The Governments of the Federal Republic of Germany and of the Kingdom of the Netherlands shall delimit the continental shelf of the North Sea as between their countries by agreement in pursuance of the decision requested from the International Court of Justice

North Sea Continental Shelf, Judgment, ICJ Reports 1969, 6–7.

may relate to legal aspects of an existing dispute[44] – judges ad hoc may even be nominated in advisory proceedings – it is equally important to keep in mind the basic principle applicable to all international cases requiring that no dispute should be settled by a judicial body without thc consent of the States concerned.[45] In dealing with advisory proceedings, the Tribunal will certainly have to give to States Parties to the Convention some guidance on the scope of its advisory jurisdiction and on the kind of legal questions which may be submitted to it on the basis of Article 138 of the Rules.

IV. CONCLUSION

Through this overview of some issues addressed in the jurisprudence of the Tribunal, the objective was to illustrate the role of the Tribunal in contributing to the development of the rule of law. In the selection of the questions highlighted above, the focus was placed on issues relating to the access to the Tribunal, its functioning (compulsory mechanism, time frame for handling cases) and the admissibility of claims (functional protection of the flag State). These issues are closely related to the need to administer justice promptly and efficiently and to ensure reparation of damages caused not only to States but also to private persons who are under their protection. A similar approach may be found in the other decisions commented on above, which contribute to a sound administration of justice through the adoption of concrete measures with a view to protecting procedural rights in environmental matters and through the settlement of a complex maritime dispute involving a new issue relating to the delimitation of the outer continental shelf. Likewise, in drafting

---

[44] For example, in the *Interpretation of Article 3, Paragraph 2, of the Treaty of Lausanne* (Advisory Opinion, 1925, PCIJ, Series B, No. 12), several States accused Bulgaria, Hungary and Romania of violating the provisions for the protection of human rights and fundamental freedoms contained in the Peace Treaties concluded by these countries. The Permanent Court of International Justice entertained the request despite the objection raised by the three States concerned that the issue related to a legal question pending between States and thus could not be subject of judicial proceedings without their consent.

[45] 'It is well established in international law that no State can, without its consent, be compelled to submit its disputes with other States either to mediation or to arbitration, or to any other kind of pacific settlement.' *Status of Eastern Carelia,* Advisory Opinion, 1923, PCIJ, Series B, No. 5, 27–8.

Article 138 of its Rules, the Tribunal developed a tool which might assist States in the fulfilment of one of their basic obligations under international law ie, to settle their disputes peacefully.

PART III

Regional courts

7. The contribution of the European Court of Human Rights to the rule of law

Paul Lemmens

I. A BRIEF PRESENTATION OF THE EUROPEAN COURT OF HUMAN RIGHTS

Before examining the contribution of the European Court of Human Rights to the rule of law, it seems useful to recall briefly its organisation, its competence and its role as a reviewing organ.

A. The European Court as a 'Court'

The European Court should in the first place be seen as a 'court', ie a judicial body. It is composed of 47 judges, one per State Party to the European Convention on Human Rights. When a vacancy occurs, the relevant State Party submits a list of three names to the Council of Europe, and the Parliamentary Assembly elects the judge out of that list. Judges serve on a full-time basis, which makes the Court a 'permanent' court, in session during the whole year. The Court is furthermore assisted by a registry, which is its 'engine': the registry plays a key role in identifying the manifestly inadmissible complaints and in dealing with these complaints, and its lawyers (around 300) prepare the drafts of decisions and judgments in the more complex cases.

The Court sits in various formations. A single judge, assisted by a non-judicial rapporteur (a senior lawyer of the registry), can declare a complaint inadmissible, 'where such a decision can be taken without further examination', in proceedings that are extremely summary (Article 27 of the Convention). A committee of three judges can unanimously declare an application inadmissible, admissible and ill founded, or even admissible and well founded, if the decision can be based on so called 'well established case law' (Article 28 of the Convention). If the case is not decided by a single judge or by a committee, it is for a chamber of seven judges to examine the admissibility and the merits of the application (Article 29 of the Convention). This is the 'ordinary' form of proceedings, although not in terms of numbers. A chamber may relinquish jurisdiction to the Grand Chamber (Article 30 of the Convention). After a case has been decided by a chamber it can, exceptionally, be accepted by a filtering panel for rehearing by the Grand Chamber (Article 43 of the Convention). The Grand Chamber thus deals with cases raising serious questions affecting the interpretation or application of the Convention.

The judgments of the Court are, like decisions of a domestic court, binding on the parties to the proceedings (Article 46(1) of the Convention). Their execution is supervised by the Committee of Ministers of the Council of Europe, a political body composed of the permanent representatives of the Member States with the Council (Article 46(2)).

B. A Court 'of Human Rights'

The Court has been set up to deal with complaints about violations of human rights. Its jurisdiction is limited to violations allegedly committed by an organ of one of the States Parties to the Convention. Unlike an international criminal court, it cannot examine the individual responsibility of private persons, not even of State agents.

While the Court can receive – and has received – applications from one State against another State (Article 33 of the Convention), in practice it deals almost exclusively with applications brought by a person, a non-governmental organisation or a group of individuals against a State (Article 34 of the Convention): it is thus called upon to deliver 'individual justice'.

The statistics show that from this point of view the Court is responding to a clear and overwhelming demand. At the beginning of 2013, 128,100 applications were pending before the Court. In 2013 and 2014, 65,800 viz 56,250 new applications were filed, which were allocated to one of the judicial formations of the Court (which means that the Court would have to take a decision on these applications). In 2013 and 2014, 93,401 viz 86,063 applications were decided, either by decision declaring the application inadmissible or striking it out of its list (89,740 viz 83,675) or by judgment on the merits (3,661 viz 2,388). At the end of 2014, there were 69,900 applications pending.[1] It should be noted, incidentally, that

---

1 See European Court of Human Rights, *Analysis of statistics 2014*, 6, available at http://www.echr.coe.int/Documents/Stats_analysis_2014_ENG.pdf.

the (further) decrease of the backlog in these two years (from 128,100 to 69,900) is to a large extent the result of the further use of the single judge procedure.

The fact that the Court is a human rights court is reflected in the way it interprets the Convention. The Convention is indeed 'intended to guarantee not rights that are theoretical or illusory but rights that are practical and effective'.[2] This feature, which follows in particular from the fact that the Convention is a human rights treaty protecting individuals on an objective basis, calls for an interpretation and application of the Convention provisions 'in a manner that renders its guarantees practical and effective'.[3] This regularly results in an evolutive interpretation, whereby the Convention is explicitly seen as 'a living instrument, to be interpreted in present-day conditions'.[4] The fact that the Convention is a human rights treaty and the Court a human rights court, does not mean that all or even many cases end with a favourable outcome for the applicant. To the contrary, in 2014 about 97 per cent of all decisions taken were decisions declaring the application inadmissible or striking it out (83,675 decisions of a total of 86,063 decisions and judgments). This low success rate is to a large extent due to the strict admissibility conditions (see Articles 34 and 35 of the Convention).

Moreover, it is a significant feature of the law on human rights, including the European Convention on Human Rights, that human rights are in general not absolute rights. There is room for explicitly or sometimes even implicitly accepted limitations. In assessing whether human rights have been respected, the European Court often has to examine whether the domestic authorities struck a fair balance between the human rights of the applicant, on the one hand, and rights of others or the general interest, on the other hand (see below). Given the potential weight of the opposing rights and interests, it should not come as a surprise that violations of human rights are in fact not easily found.

On 30 June 2015, 63,800 applications were pending (see European Court of Human Rights, *Statistics 1/1 – 30/6/2015*).

[2] ECtHR, 13 May 1980, Artico v Italy, *Publ Court*, Series A, vol 37, § 33.

[3] ECtHR [GC], 12 September 2012, Nada v Switzerland, *ECHR*, 2012-V § 182; ECtHR [GC], 26 November 2013, X v Latvia, no 27853/09, § 94.

[4] ECtHR, 25 April 1978, Tyrer v United Kingdom, *Publ. Court*, Series A, vol 26, § 31. For recent confirmations, see ECtHR [GC], 19 February 2013, X and Others v Austria, no 19010/07, § 139; ECtHR [GC], 7 November 2013, Vallianatos and Others v Greece, nos 29381/09 and 32684/09, § 84.

C. A 'European' Court

The European Court is a supranational court, set up by an international treaty. While the original text of the European Convention was signed in 1950 by 12 Member States of the Council of Europe, now 47 Member States are party to the Convention. This also means that the Court is somewhat dependent on the support of these 47 States. Such support is not self-evident, given the fact that it is precisely these same States that can be held responsible by the Court for violations of human rights.

As an international court, the European Court has jurisdiction only over States. It examines whether the States have violated human rights. Obviously, the acts or omissions of any organ of a State (such as the legislature, the government, regional or local authorities or the judiciary) can give rise to the State's responsibility.

The Court has no jurisdiction with respect to acts or omissions attributable to private individuals or entities. However, it is not impossible to accuse a State of not having offered sufficient protection against such acts or omissions. In that case, the complaint is presented as one relating to the State's failure to fulfil a positive obligation,[5] namely the obligation to protect individuals, 'even in the sphere of the relations of individuals between themselves'.[6]

Nor does the Court have jurisdiction with respect to acts or omissions attributable to international organisations. Difficult questions may arise, however, when a complaint is directed against a State for action taken in its capacity of Member State of an international organisation,[7] or for action taken in the implementation of a decision taken by an international organisation.[8]

---

[5] See ECtHR, 13 June 1979, Marckx v Belgium, *Publ Court*, Series A, vol 31, § 31.

[6] ECtHR, 26 March 1985, X and Y v Netherlands, *Publ Court*, Series A, vol 91, § 23.

[7] If the action is entirely attributable to the international organisation in question, it falls outside the jurisdiction of the European Court. See eg, with respect to acts attributable to the United Nations Mission in Kosovo, ECtHR [GC], dec 2 May 2007, Behrami and Behrami v France and Saramati v France, Germany and Norway, nos 71412/01 and 78166/01.

[8] See eg, with respect to the implementation of an EU regulation, ECtHR [GC], 30 June 2005, Bosphorus Airways v Ireland, *ECHR*, 2005-VI, and with respect to the implementation of a decision taken by the UN Security Council, ECtHR [GC], 12 September 2012, Nada, above n3.

As a court for Europe, the Court's task is to give authoritative interpretations of the European Convention. The Court refers as follows to this aspect of its role:

> [...] (I)ts judgments serve not only to decide those cases brought before it but, more generally, to elucidate, safeguard and develop the rules instituted by the Convention, thereby contributing to the observance by the States of the engagements undertaken by them as Contracting Parties [...]. Although the primary purpose of the Convention system is to provide individual relief, its mission is also to determine issues on public-policy grounds in the common interest, thereby raising the general standards of protection of human rights and extending human rights jurisprudence throughout the community of the Convention States.[9]

As the Court indicates in the text quoted, it thus combines two roles that in domestic law are often fulfilled by judicial organs of different natures: on the one hand, it provides individual relief in individual cases (like a civil, criminal or administrative court) (see above), on the other hand, it sets general human rights standards for the whole of Europe (like a constitutional court would do, on the basis of the national constitution). This combination of roles creates a certain tension, as both roles in fact require specific and sometimes conflicting ways of dealing with cases.

Notwithstanding its quasi-constitutional role, the European Court plays (only) a subsidiary role in the protection of human rights. Already in one of its first cases, the Court acknowledged that 'it cannot assume the role of the competent national authorities, for it would thereby lose sight of the subsidiary nature of the international machinery of collective enforcement established by the Convention'.[10] A few years later, it clarified that:

> the machinery of protection established by the Convention is subsidiary to the national systems safeguarding human rights [...]. The Convention leaves to each Contracting State, in the first place, the task of securing the rights and liberties it enshrines. The [former Commission and the Court] make their own contribution to this task but they become involved only through contentious proceedings and once all domestic remedies have been exhausted [...].[11]

---

[9] ECtHR, 24 July 2003, Karner v Austria, *ECHR*, 2003-IX, § 26; ECtHR, 7 January 2010, Rantsev v Cyprus and Russia, *ECHR*, 2010-I, § 197; ECtHR [GC], 22 March 2012, Konstantin Markin v Russia, *ECHR*, 2012-III, § 89.

[10] ECtHR, 23 July 1968, Belgian linguistic case, *Publ Court*, Series A, vol. 6, § 10.

[11] ECtHR, 7 December 1976, Handyside v United Kingdom, *Publ Court*, Series A, vol 24, § 48.

Later, referring to Article 1 of the Convention,[12] it emphasised that the responsibility of the States Parties is the 'primary' one: '[T]he primary responsibility for implementing and enforcing the guaranteed rights and freedoms is laid on the national authorities.'[13] Human rights are thus a 'shared responsibility' of the national States and the European Court, with the primary responsibility resting upon the States and the secondary responsibility vested upon the European Court. This idea will in the future be confirmed in the preamble of the Convention, as an expression of the understanding of the States Parties, when Protocol No 15 to the Convention has entered into force.[14]

The subsidiary character of the Convention mechanism is apparent, from a procedural point of view, in Articles 13 and 35(1) of the Convention. According to the former provision, anyone who alleges a violation of his or her human rights has a right to an effective remedy in the domestic system in respect of the alleged breach. According to the latter provision, an applicant before the Court must have exhausted available domestic remedies, thus affording the State Party the opportunity of preventing or putting right – usually through the courts – the violations alleged against it before those allegations are submitted to the European Court.[15]

The subsidiary character of the Convention mechanism is also reflected in the way the Court exercises its power of review over decisions taken by domestic authorities. Ever since 1976, the Court holds that, where the Convention subjects the lawfulness of a measure limiting human rights to the requirement of 'necessity in a democratic society', it 'leaves to the Contracting States a margin of appreciation. This margin is given both to the domestic legislator [...] and to the bodies, judicial amongst others,

---

[12] According to Article 1 of the Convention, the High Contracting Parties 'shall secure to everyone within their jurisdiction the rights and freedoms defined in Section I of this Convention'.

[13] ECtHR [GC], 26 October 2000, Kudła v Poland, *ECHR,* 2000-XI, § 152.

[14]

> Affirming that the High Contracting Parties, in accordance with the principle of subsidiarity, have the primary responsibility to secure the rights and freedoms defined in this Convention and the Protocols thereto, and that in doing so they enjoy a margin of appreciation, subject to the supervisory jurisdiction of the European Court of Human Rights established by this Convention

(new recital of the preamble, as inserted by Article 1 of Protocol No 15, adopted in Strasbourg on 24 June 2013).

[15] See, eg, ECtHR [GC], 21 January 1999, Fressoz and Roire v France, *ECHR*, 1999-I, § 37.

that are called upon to interpret and apply the laws in force'.[16] While the margin of appreciation was initially granted with respect to the assessment of whether a limitation of human rights was necessary, the Court later extended the notion to the assessment of the obligation of domestic authorities to adopt positive measures designed to protect human rights.[17] The theory of the margin of appreciation means in essence that, whenever policy choices have to be made, implying a balancing of competing interests, the Convention secures to the competent domestic authorities an area in which they legitimately can choose among available options.[18]

That area is not unlimited: 'The domestic margin of appreciation [...] goes hand in hand with a European supervision.'[19] However, here again the subsidiarity principle comes into play: 'The Court's task in exercising its supervision is not to take the place of the national authorities but rather to review, in the light of the case as a whole, the decisions that they have taken pursuant to their margin of appreciation.'[20] In other words, '[t]he Court's supervisory function being of a subsidiary nature, it is limited to reviewing whether or not the particular solution adopted can be regarded as striking a fair balance'.[21]

II. THE RULE OF LAW IN THE EUROPEAN COURT'S CASE LAW

A. The Rule of Law in the European Convention

Before turning to the specific contribution by the European Court to the development of the rule of law in Europe, it is useful to pay some attention to the text of the European Convention.

In the preamble of the Convention, the drafters stated that they were 'resolved, as the governments of European countries which are like-minded and have a common heritage of political traditions, ideals, freedom and the rule of law, to take the first steps for the collective enforcement of certain of the rights stated in the Universal Declaration [of Human Rights]'. The rule of law was thus seen as one of the elements

16 ECtHR, 7 December 1976, Handyside, above n11, § 48.
17 ECtHR, 26 March 1985, X and Y v Netherlands, above n6, § 24.
18 ECtHR [GC], 8 July 2003, Hatton v United Kingdom, *ECHR*, 2003-VIII, § 123.
19 ECtHR, 7 December 1976, Handyside, above n11, § 49.
20 ECtHR [GC], 15 March 2012, Aksu v Turkey, *ECHR*, 2012-I, § 65.
21 ECtHR [GC], 8 July 2003, Hatton, above n18, § 123.

of the 'common heritage' of the democratic States that formed the Council of Europe. The European Court has developed this idea further, and considers that 'the rule of law, one of the fundamental principles of a democratic society, is inherent in all the Articles of the Convention'.[22]

An expression of the principle of the rule of law can indeed be found in a number of provisions of the Convention which refer to the 'law' (eg Article 5(1) – 'in accordance with a procedure prescribed by law', 'lawful' – and Article 8(2) – 'in accordance with the law'). Such references are essentially to domestic law, and the relevant provisions lay down the requirement for an individual measure to have some basis in domestic law and to conform to domestic law.[23]

One can conclude from the foregoing that the rule of law is an underlying principle of the Convention and that the provisions of the Convention reflect that principle, to a greater or lesser extent.

B. Some Elements of the Rule of Law, According to the European Court's Case Law

There are numerous judgments of the European Court in which the rule of law is used as a tool to interpret a provision of the Convention. Naturally, the Court approaches the rule of law on a case-by-case basis. While it has not tried to give a definition of the term,[24] it is possible to distil from its case law a number of elements of the rule of law. Taken together, these elements give an indication of what the Court understands by the term.

In his book on the rule of law, Bingham writes that he chose to write on the subject 'because the expression was constantly on people's lips, [he] was not quite sure what it meant, and [he] was not sure either that all

22 ECtHR, 25 June 1996, Amuur v France, *Rep*, 1996-III, § 50; ECtHR [GC], 25 March 1999, Iatridis v Greece, *ECHR*, 1999-II, § 58.

23 ECtHR [GC], 12 June 2014, Fernández Martínez v Spain, no 56030/07, § 117 (with respect to Art 8(2)); ECtHR [GC], 3 July 2014, Georgia v Russia (I), no 13255/07, § 182 (with respect to Art 5(1)).

24 Some other terms, although widely used in the Court's case law, are equally not defined by the Court. The Court consistently states, for example, with respect to the term 'private life', that this 'is a broad term not susceptible to exhaustive definition' (see, as a recent authority, ECtHR [GC], 16 June 2015, Sargsyan v. Azerbaijan, no 40167/06, § 255; see also, as an older authority, ECtHR, 16 December 1992, Niemietz v Germany, *Publ Court*, Series A, vol 251-B, § 29). The same seems to apply to the term 'rule of law'.

those who used the expression knew what they meant either, or meant the same thing'.[25] He then suggests that:

> the core of the [...] principle [of the rule of law] is [...] that all persons and authorities within the state, whether public or private, should be bound by and entitled to the benefit of laws publicly made, taking effect (generally) in the future and publicly administered in the courts.[26]

This is also the definition that has been endorsed by the Venice Commission in a report on the rule of law.[27] It seems fair to assume that the Court's implicit understanding of the rule of law corresponds to Bingham's.

A number of elements of the rule of law, according to the Court's case law, will be discussed below.[28] An attempt has been made to group these elements in three categories, building somewhat on the traditional '*trias politica*': the rule of law and laws and regulations, the rule of law and the implementation or application of the law by administrative bodies, and the rule of law and the judiciary.

1. The rule of law and laws and regulations

In a number of cases the Court has stressed that an effective protection of human rights may require the setting up of a normative framework in order to deal with a problematic issue. In other words, the legislature or the regulator is sometimes required to act.

For example, the positive obligation to take all appropriate steps to safeguard life for the purposes of Article 2 of the Convention, or to protect an individual against ill-treatment prohibited by Article 3, entails a primary duty on the State to put in place a legislative and administrative framework designed to provide effective deterrence against threats to the

---

[25] Tom Bingham, *The Rule of* Law (Penguin 2010) vii.

[26] Ibid., at 8.

[27] European Commission for Democracy Through Law (Venice Commission), 25–6 March 2011, *Report on the Rule of Law*, CDL-AD (2011) 003rev, § 36.

[28] For recent and more detailed studies of the relevance of the rule of law in the Court's case law, see Xavier Souvignet, *La prééminence du droit dans le droit de la Convention européenne des droits de l'homme* (Bruylant 2012); Geranne Lautenbach, *The Concept of the Rule of Law and the European Court of Human Rights* (OUP 2013).

right to life[29] or against ill-treatment.[30] There may be an obligation to adopt a normative framework in purely private matters as well. The Court has held, for instance, that in determining in its domestic legal system the regime applicable to certain family ties such as those between an unmarried mother and her child, the State must act in a manner calculated to allow those concerned to lead a normal family life. Respect for family life, guaranteed by Article 8 of the Convention, implied in the Court's view the existence in domestic law of legal safeguards that rendered possible as from the moment of birth the child's integration in his family.[31] In a case involving the protection of an individual against interferences in his right to the peaceful enjoyment of his possessions by a private entity, the Court placed the obligation explicitly within the context of the rule of law. It considered that it was part of the States' duties under Article 1 of Protocol No 1:

> at least to set up a minimum legislative framework including a proper forum allowing persons who find themselves in a position such as the applicant's to assert their rights effectively and have them enforced. Indeed, by failing to do so a State would seriously fall short of its obligation to protect the rule of law and prevent arbitrariness.[32]

In order for an interference with human rights to be compatible with the Convention, it has to be 'provided by law' or 'in accordance with the law'. The European Court reads into this condition a quality requirement for the law in which an interference must find a basis. The law in question should, among other things, be accessible to the person concerned, who must moreover be able to foresee its consequences for him or her. The latter requirement implies, inter alia, 'that domestic law must be sufficiently foreseeable in its terms to give individuals an adequate indication as to the circumstances in which and the conditions on which the authorities are entitled to resort to measures affecting their rights under the Convention'.[33] There is also a requirement with respect to the

---

29 ECtHR [GC], 30 November 2004, Öneryildiz v Turkey, *ECHR*, 2004-XII, § 89; ECtHR [GC], 20 December 2004, Makaratzis v Greece, *ECHR*, 2004-XI, § 57.

30 ECtHR [GC], 28 January 2014, O'Keeffe v Ireland, no 35810/09, §§ 146 and 152.

31 ECtHR, 13 June 1979, Marckx, above n5, § 31.

32 ECtHR [GC], 3 April 2012, Kotov v Russia, no 54522/00, § 117.

33 ECtHR, 24 April 2008, CG and Others v Bulgaria, no 1365/07, § 39; ECtHR [GC], 12 June 2014, Fernández Martínez, above 23, § 117.

conferral of discretionary powers to administrative authorities: 'In matters affecting fundamental rights it would be contrary to the rule of law, one of the basic principles of a democratic society enshrined in the Convention, for a legal discretion granted to the executive to be expressed in terms of an unfettered power.'[34]

The foreseeability requirement is in fact a specific application of the more general principle of legal certainty.

Another application of the principle of legal certainty is the prohibition of retrospective application of the law. While this prohibition is expressly provided, even in absolute terms, with respect to criminal law at the disadvantage of the accused (Article 7 of the Convention), it also plays a role with respect to civil law, in particular where the retrospective application of the new law has the effect of extinguishing existing claims.[35]

2. The rule of law and the implementation or application of the law by administrative bodies

From the point of view of human rights, a fundamental aspect of the rule of law is that State authorities are, like individuals, bound by the law. This aspect is expressed in the Convention by the above-mentioned requirement that interferences with human rights must be 'provided by law' or 'in accordance with the law'. Even where such a requirement is not explicitly provided for, as for example in the general rule of Article 1, first paragraph, first sentence, of Protocol No 1, the Court holds that 'the first and most important requirement' of that Article 1 is that any interference by a public authority with the peaceful enjoyment of possessions should be 'lawful'. The Court bases this interpretation not only on the context of the said provision, but also on the rule of law, 'which is inherent in all the Articles of the Convention'.[36]

---

34 See, eg, ECtHR, 2 August 1984, Malone v United Kingdom, *Publ Court*, Series A, vol 82, § 68; ECtHR [GC], 17 February 2004, Maestri v Italy, *ECHR*, 2004-I, § 30; ECtHR [GC], 14 September 2010, Sanoma Uitgevers bv v Netherlands, no 38224/03, § 82.

35 The retrospective application of the law can thus result in an interference with a creditor's right to the peaceful enjoyment of possessions (Article 1 of Protocol No 1). There is no absolute prohibition of the retrospective application of civil law, but any interference with the right to property will have to be compatible with the proportionality principle. See, eg, ECtHR, 20 November 1995, Pressos Compania Naviera v Belgium, *Publ Court*, Series A, vol 332, §§ 38–44.

36 ECtHR [GC], 25 March 1999, Iatridis, above n22, § 58.

Individual measures taken by administrative authorities thus have to be based on pre-existing general rules (of domestic law), adopted by the competent rule maker. As such, the requirement contributes to avoiding arbitrary action by administrative authorities. Of course, it is not sufficient that such rules exist: the requirement also implies that measures taken in the implementation of the law should comply with the applicable (domestic) rules, and in particular respect the conditions set by the law for its implementation.

The rule of law does not only set limits on the exercise of State power by administrative authorities, it also may oblige them to take action.

For instance, where the law grants citizens certain rights, which however need further implementation before they can become enforceable, the rule of law requires the State to ensure the legal and practical conditions necessary for the effective enjoyment of these rights.[37] In a case involving the non-execution of laws which recognised the right to compensation of a large group of owners, including the applicant, for the loss of their property, the European Court held that:

> it was incumbent on the [...] authorities to remove the existing incompatibility between the letter of the law and the State-operated practice which hindered the effective exercise of the applicant's right of property. [The rule of law underlying the Convention and the principle of lawfulness in Article 1 of Protocol No 1] also required the [...] State to fulfil in good time, in an appropriate and consistent manner, the legislative promises it had made in respect of the settlement of the [...] claims [of the owners].[38]

The Court found that by not taking the necessary measures of implementation, and by in fact applying practices that made the applicant's statutory right unenforceable and unusable in practice, the authorities had rendered that right illusory and destroyed its very essence.[39]

Similarly, the State has a duty to enforce the laws that are intended to protect citizens against human rights violations committed by other individuals or private entities.

The fulfilment of this duty supposes in the first place action of a preventive nature. For example, the obligation to protect the right to life against the risks created by dangerous industrial activities, requires the State not only to establish a proper legislative and regulatory framework (see above), but also to execute the applicable norms through a system of

---

37 ECtHR [GC], 22 June 2004, Broniowski v Poland, *ECHR*, 2004-V, § 184.
38 Ibid.
39 Ibid., at 185.

licensing and supervision of the activities so as to ensure the effective protection of citizens.[40] In this connection the Court has also held that in certain circumstances the authorities may have a duty to provide information enabling individuals to assess risks to their health and lives created by dangerous activities.[41] Another example is that of the protection of children against sexual abuse. Having regard to the nature of such abuse, particularly in situations where the abuser is in a position of authority over the child, the Court held that 'the existence of useful detection and reporting mechanisms are fundamental to the effective implementation of the relevant criminal laws'.[42]

Where violations of human rights have taken place, remedial action is called for. Generally speaking, in cases of serious violations of human rights, including cases of infliction of bodily harm, the competent police and judicial authorities are under a duty to promptly establish the facts, hold accountable those at fault and provide appropriate redress to the victims.[43] This requirement may, and under certain circumstances must, include recourse to the criminal law. In such cases, the investigation must be capable of leading to the identification and punishment of those responsible.[44] It should be noted, however, that if the infringement of the right to life or to physical integrity is not caused intentionally, the positive obligation to set up an effective judicial investigation does not necessarily require the provision of a criminal law remedy. For instance, in the sphere of medical negligence:

> the obligation may [...] also be satisfied if the legal system affords victims a remedy in the civil courts, either alone or in conjunction with a remedy in the criminal courts, enabling any liability of the doctors concerned to be established and any appropriate civil redress, such as an order for damages

---

40 ECtHR [GC], 30 November 2004, Öneryildiz, above at n29, § 90.

41 See eg ECtHR, 24 July 2014, Brincat and Others v Malta, nos 60908/11 and other, § 102.

42 ECtHR, 2 December 2008, Juppala v Finland, no 18620/03, § 42; ECtHR [GC], 28 January 2014, O'Keeffe, above n30, § 148.

43 ECtHR [GC], 17 July 2014, Centre for Legal Resources on behalf of Valentin Câmpeanu v Romania, no 47848/08, § 132.

44 See, eg, ECtHR [GC], 6 July 2005, Nachova v Bulgaria, *ECHR*, 2005-VII, § 110; ECtHR [GC], 17 September 2014, Mocanu and Others v Romania, nos 10865/09 and other, § 318; ECtHR [GC], 14 April 2015, Mustafa Tunç and Fecire Tunç v. Turkey, no 24014/05, § 172.

> and for the publication of the decision, to be obtained. Disciplinary measures may also be envisaged[45]

All this brings us to the role of the judiciary.

3. The rule of law and the judiciary

In a State based on the rule of law, citizens should not be dependent on the authorities to obtain redress for violations of their rights, whether fundamental rights or other rights. They should be able themselves to take the initiative to obtain respect for the law when they believe that their rights have been violated.

Indeed, as the European Court has noted, 'in civil matters one can scarcely conceive of the rule of law without there being a possibility of having access to the courts'.[46] Having regard to the rule of law, the Court interpreted Article 6(1) of the Convention, which guarantees the right to a fair trial, in such a way that it:

> secures to everyone the right to have any claim relating to his civil rights and obligations brought before a court or tribunal. In this way the Article embodies the 'right to a court', of which the right of access, that is the right to institute proceedings before courts in civil matters, constitutes one aspect […].[47]

The right to a court implies an obligation for the State to provide for 'judicial procedures that [offer] the necessary procedural guarantees and therefore (enable) the domestic courts and tribunals to adjudicate effectively and fairly any disputes between private persons'.[48]

The right to a court acquires particular significance when a citizen considers on arguable grounds that there has been an interference with the exercise of his or her civil rights because of an administrative measure taken by the competent body in the exercise of public authority. In such a case, the citizen is entitled to have the dispute relating to the lawfulness of the administrative measure determined by a court.[49] Where no civil rights are at stake, but there is an interference with fundamental

---

[45] ECtHR [GC], 17 January 2002, Calvelli and Ciglio v Italy, *ECHR*, 2002-I, § 51.

[46] ECtHR, 21 February 1975, Golder v United Kingdom, *Publ Court*, Series A, vol 18, § 34.

[47] Ibid., at 36.

[48] ECtHR [GC], 3 April 2012, Kotov, above n32, § 114.

[49] ECtHR, 23 September 1982, Sporrong and Lönnroth v Sweden, *Publ Court*, Series A, vol 52, §§ 80–81.

rights, the rule of law implies that the interference by the administrative authorities with the individual's rights 'should be subject to effective supervision, which should normally be carried out by the judiciary, at least in the last resort, since judicial control affords the best guarantees of independence, impartiality and a proper procedure'.[50] In both situations, the right to a court takes the form of a right to judicial review of administrative action. Courts should be able to review, at the end of adversarial proceedings, the reasons of an administrative decision, their factual basis and their compatibility with the law.[51]

Article 6(1) of the Convention provides furthermore for a number of structural and procedural guarantees to be offered by courts. Some of these guarantees have been explicitly linked to the rule of law. Hereunder, a few examples, taken from the case law of the Grand Chamber, will be mentioned.

The Court has held, for instance, that the principle of the rule of law and the notion of fair trial in principle preclude any interference by the legislature with the administration of justice designed to influence the judicial determination of a given dispute.[52]

Turning to the decisions of a criminal court, the European Court has held that for the requirements of a fair trial to be satisfied, the accused, and indeed the public, must be able to understand the verdict that has been given; this is a vital safeguard against arbitrariness. As the Court has often noted, the rule of law and the avoidance of arbitrary power are principles underlying the Convention.[53]

On another occasion, relying on the principle of legal certainty, which is one of the fundamental aspects of the rule of law and which guarantees, inter alia, a certain stability in legal situations, the Court has held that persistence of conflicting court decisions 'can create a state of legal uncertainty likely to reduce public confidence in the judicial

---

[50] See, with respect to the right guaranteed by Article 8 of the Convention, ECtHR, 6 September 1978, Klass v Germany, *Publ Court*, Series A, vol 28, § 55; ECtHR [GC], 4 May 2000, Rotaru v Romania, *ECHR*, 2000-V, § 59.

[51] Consult ECtHR [GC], 21 October 2013, Janowiec and Others v Poland, nos 55508/07 and 29520/09, § 213.

[52] ECtHR [GC], 28 October 1999, Zielinski and Pradal and Gonzalez and Others v France, *ECHR*, 1999-VII, § 57; ECtHR [GC], 8 April 2004, Assanidze v Georgia, *ECHR*, 2004-II, § 129.

[53] ECtHR [GC], 16 December 2010, Taxquet v Belgium, *ECHR*, 2010-VI, § 90.

system, whereas such confidence is clearly one of the essential components of a State based on the rule of law'.[54] Courts, in particular supreme courts, should try to be consistent in their case law.

The requirement of a decision within a reasonable time is also linked to the rule of law. Where this requirement is frequently violated, there is according to the Court an 'important danger' for the rule of law as such a situation might jeopardise the effectiveness and credibility of the system of administration of justice.[55]

Finally, the rule of law is also concerned with the execution of decisions. The principle of legal certainty, which has already been identified above as a fundamental aspect of the rule of law, 'requires, inter alia, that where the courts have finally determined an issue, their ruling should not be called into question'.[56] As a consequence, legal systems which allowed the procurator-general – who had not been a party to proceedings – to apply for a final judgment to be quashed, without being subject to any time limit, infringed the principle of legal certainty and were thus incompatible with the rule of law.[57] For the same reason, it cannot be accepted that the execution of a judicial decision is unduly delayed.[58]

III. CONCLUDING REMARKS

What can one conclude from this overview of some cases in which the rule of law is explicitly mentioned?

First, the European Court does not see the rule of law as an autonomous source of the law it has to apply. Rather, it invokes the rule of law as an interpretational tool, in order to give a meaning to a Convention article. In other words, the rule of law is always used in

---

54 ECtHR [GC], 20 October 2011, Nejdet Şahin and Perihan Şahin v Turkey, no 13279/05, § 57.

55 ECtHR [GC], 28 July 1999, Bottazzi v Italy, *ECHR*, 1999-V, § 22, referring to Resolution DH (97) 336 of the Committee of Ministers of the Council of Europe of 11 July 1997 (Length of civil proceedings in Italy: supplementary measures of a general character). See also ECtHR [GC], 26 October 2000, Kudła, above n13, § 148.

56 ECtHR [GC], 28 October 1999, Brumărescu v Romania, *ECHR*, 1999-VII, § 61.

57 Ibid., at 62.

58 ECtHR [GC], 28 July 1999, Immobiliare Saffi v Italy, *ECHR*, 1999-V, § 66.

combination with an article of the Convention, which the Court considers to constitute a specific application of the principle.

Second, very often it is apparent that one of the main aims of the rule of law is to protect the individual against arbitrary action. As such, it is, as the Court states, a principle underlying all articles of the Convention.

Third, there are other principles that are closely related to the principle of the rule of law. In the case law of the European Court, this is in particular the case with the principle of legal certainty.

Fourth, the rule of law not only sets limits to State action, but also obliges the competent authorities to take measures. It thus colours both the negative and the positive obligations of the State under human rights law.

Finally, it is to be noted that the rule of law applies to any sort of State action or inaction, whether by the legislature, the executive or the judiciary. This is one of the reasons why it can be considered to be a 'general' principle of law.

8. The Court of Justice as the guarantor of the rule of law within the European Union

Koen Lenaerts*

In accordance with Article 19 of the Treaty on European Union (TEU), the European Court of Justice (the ECJ) 'shall ensure that in the interpretation and application of the Treaties the law is observed'. It follows that all EU acts must be interpreted so as to guarantee that 'the European Union is based on the rule of law'.[1]

However, as Koopmans notes,[2] the original version of the EEC Treaty told 'us nothing about its substantive principles'. It thus provided little guidance as to the content of the 'law' to be observed. Nonetheless, in the aftermath of World War II, legitimacy could not be based upon a formalistic conception of the rule of law. In order to reassure the Member States, the EU (or Community as it then was) legal order needed to embrace a particular conception of public morality reflecting both the universal values shared by mankind and, more specifically, the basic values of European liberal democracies. With a view to accomplishing this mission, the ECJ had to create new norms that would supplement and complete the legal order established by the Treaty, aligning it with both public international law and the fundamental constitutional tenets common to its Member States.

* All opinions expressed herein are strictly personal to the author.

1 See the judgment in *E and F*, C-550/09, EU:C:2010:382, para 44. See also the judgments in *Unión de Pequeños Agricultores v Council*, C-50/00 P, EU:C:2002:462, paras 38 and 40; and *Kadi and Al Barakaat International Foundation v Council and Commission ('Kadi I')*, C-402/05 P and C-415/05 P, EU:C:2008:461, para 281.

2 T Koopmans, 'The Birth of European Law at the Crossroads of Legal Traditions' (1991) 39 *American Journal of Comparative Law* 495.

Ever since the landmark decision in *van Gend en Loos*,[3] the ECJ has consistently held that the Union is a distinct and autonomous legal order. Yet autonomy could hardly be achieved by a legal system that was not both self-sufficient and coherent. In order for the EU legal order to find its own independent space between national and international law, constitutional and legislative gaps cannot be allowed to persist. Although they may be inspired by the constitutional traditions common to the Member States or by international treaties, norms intended to give a substantive meaning to the 'rule of law' must derive from within the Union's legal order itself.

It follows that when providing the rule of law with a substantive content, the ECJ must strike a balance between, on the one hand, the autonomy of the EU legal order and, on the other hand, rules already enshrined in public international law and national constitutions. Thus, the EU constitutional autonomy should not be confused with complete detachment. In light of *van Gend en Loos* and the cases that followed, it is clear that the ECJ seeks to define the EU constitutional space without denying that EU law influences and is influenced by the legal orders that surround it.[4]

The purpose of my chapter is thus to explore the way in which the rule of law within the EU legal order interacts with public international law and the constitutional law of the Member States. To that end, it is divided into two parts. Part I explores the incorporation of public international law into the EU legal order. In that regard, it is argued that public international law becomes the 'law of the land', provided that two cumulative conditions are fulfilled, namely that the norm of public international law at issue is binding upon the EU and, most importantly, that it is compatible with the rule of law within the EU. This point will be illustrated by looking at the seminal judgment of the ECJ in *Kadi I* and its progeny. Part II is devoted to examining the interaction between EU law and national constitutions in the area of fundamental rights. In this regard, it is submitted that the rule of law within the EU does not oppose value diversity, but rather that it favours constitutional pluralism. A cumulative application of national constitutions and EU law is not to be ruled out. However, like the constitutional autonomy of the EU,

---

[3] Judgment in *NV Algemene Transport- en Expeditie Onderneming van Gend & Loos v Netherlands Inland Revenue Administration* ('*van Gend en Loos*'), 26/62, EU:C:1963:1, p. 1.

[4] See A Tizzano, J Kokott and S Prechal (eds), *50th Anniversary of the judgment in van Gend en Loos*, Conference proceedings, Luxembourg, 13 May 2013 (Luxembourg, Office des publications de l'Union européenne, 2013).

constitutional pluralism is not an absolute value, but a relative one. This means that different standards of fundamental rights protections may coexist, in so far as 'the primacy, unity and effectiveness of EU law are not thereby compromised'.[5] Finally, a brief conclusion supports the contention that the rule of law within the EU operates as a 'transnational rule of law', since it is influenced by and in turn influences, the legal orders that surround it.

I. THE RULE OF LAW WITHIN THE EU AND PUBLIC INTERNATIONAL LAW

A. General Observations

The incorporation of an international agreement into the EU legal order takes place where the EU is a contracting party to such an agreement. As Article 216(2) TFEU states, international '[a]greements concluded by the Union are binding upon the institutions of the Union and on its Member States'. In addition, the incorporation of an international agreement into EU law may also take place in accordance with the 'theory of succession',[6] ie where the EU has 'assumed, and thus had transferred to it, all the powers previously exercised by the Member States that fall within the [international agreement] in question'.[7] Stated differently, the incorporation of an international agreement into EU law may occur by means of 'field pre-emption': if the EU has occupied a policy field to which an international agreement concluded by the Member States applies, then national authorities no longer enjoy the powers to honour the obligations entered into under such an agreement. In order to respect Member States' commitment to remain bound by such an agreement, it is thus for the EU to assume those obligations. In *International Fruit Company and Others*, the seminal case where the theory of succession was first applied, the ECJ found that the then Community had 'progressively assumed powers previously exercised by the Member States, with the consequence that it became bound by the obligations flowing from [the 1947 GATT]'.[8]

---

[5] See the judgments in *Melloni*, C-399/11, EU:C:2013:107, para 60 and *Åkerberg Fransson*, C-617/10, EU:C:2013:105, para 29.

[6] Judgment in *International Fruit Company and Others*, 21 to 24/72, EU:C:1972:115.

[7] Judgment in *Bogiatzi*, C-301/08, EU:C:2009:649, para 33.

[8] Judgment in *Intertanko*, C-308/06, EU:C:2008:312, para 48.

Principles of customary international law may also be incorporated into the EU legal order. In this connection, the ECJ has ruled that 'the powers of the [EU] must be exercised in observance of international law, including provisions of international agreements in so far as they codify customary rules of general international law'.[9] Accordingly, provisions contained in international agreements not binding upon the EU which codify principles of customary international law may nevertheless be incorporated into the EU legal order as such principles. This is so for the 1969 Vienna Convention on the law of Treaties and for Article 1 of the Chicago Convention.[10]

The incorporation of public international law into EU law follows, to some extent, a 'monist approach'.[11] Once it has been established that the EU is bound by an international agreement, the latter becomes an integral part of EU law. In other words, for an international agreement to be 'the law of the land', there is no need for EU institutions to pass secondary EU law 'translating' such an agreement into EU law. As will be discussed below, subject to compliance with the constitutional tenets of the EU legal order,[12] the incorporation of international obligations binding upon the EU into the latter's constitutional fabric is automatic.[13]

B. Limits to the Incorporation of International Law

The ECJ has consistently held that 'by virtue of Article 216(2) TFEU, where international agreements are concluded by the [EU] they are

---

9 See, to this effect, the judgments in *Poulsen and Diva Navigation*, C-286/90, EU:C:1992:453, paras 9 and 10; *Mondiet*, C-405/92, EU:C:1993:906, paras 13–15; and *Racke*, C-162/96, EU:C:1998:293, para 45.

10 In this regard, the ECJ has held that 'even though the [1969] Vienna Convention does not bind either the [EU] or all its Member States, a series of provisions in that convention reflect the rules of customary international law which, as such, are binding upon the [EU] institutions and form part of the EU legal order'. See the judgment in *Brita*, C-386/08, EU:C:2010:91, para 42. See also the judgments in *Racke*, paras 24, 45 and 46; *El-Yassini*, C-416/96, EU:C:1999:107, para 47, and *Jany and Others*, C-268/99, EU:C:2001:616, para 35.

11 K Lenaerts, 'Droit international et monisme de l'ordre juridique de l'Union' (2010) *Revue de la Faculté de droit de l'Université de Liège* 505.

12 *Kadi I*, above n1 and Opinion 1/09, EU:C:2011:123.

13 The same applies in relation to a principle of customary international law. See eg T Konstadinides, 'When in Europe: Customary International Law and EU Competence in the Sphere of External Action' (2011) 13 *German Law Journal* 1177.

binding upon its institutions and, consequently, they prevail over acts of the European Union'.[14] This means that international agreements concluded by the EU enjoy *supra-legislative* status.[15]

However, the incorporation of international law into the EU legal order must be respectful of the constitutional integrity of the EU legal order. This means that an international agreement binding upon the EU must not call into question the constitutional structure put in place by the authors of the Treaties. Notably, as the ECJ made clear in its Opinion 1/09, 'an international agreement may affect [the ECJ's] own powers provided that the indispensable conditions for safeguarding the essential character of those powers are satisfied and, consequently, there is no adverse effect on the autonomy of the [EU] legal order'.[16] This means that all international agreements to which the EU becomes a party must ensure compliance with 'the system set up by Article 267 TFEU [which] establishes between the [ECJ] and the national courts direct cooperation as part of which the latter are closely involved in the correct application and uniform interpretation of [EU] law and also in the protection of individual rights conferred by that legal order'.[17] Indeed, 'the tasks attributed to the national courts and to the [ECJ] respectively are indispensable to the preservation of the very nature of the law established by the Treaties'.[18]

Substantively, all international obligations must comply with the constitutional tenets upon which the EU is founded. In particular, the incorporation of international law must ensure compliance with fundamental rights. As is well known, this point is illustrated by the ruling of the ECJ in *Kadi I*.[19] In that case, the ECJ held that 'the obligations

---

[14] *Kadi I*, above n1, para 50. See also the judgments in *Commission v Germany*, C-61/94, EU:C:1996:313, para 52; *Algemene Scheeps Agentuur Dordrecht*, C-311/04, EU:C:2006:23, para 25; *Intertanko*, above n8, para 42, and *Kadi I*, above n1, para 307.

[15] In the US, this is not the case. In the event of a conflict between an international agreement to which the US is a party and a federal statute passed after the conclusion of such an agreement, the latter prevails over the former. This is known as the 'last-in-time' principle. This is so even for UN Security Council Resolutions. A Bianchi, 'International Law and US Courts: The Myth of Lohengrin Revisited' (2004) 15 *European Journal of International Law* 751.

[16] Opinion 1/09, above n12, para 76 (see also, in the same way, Opinion 1/00, EU:C:2002:231, paras 21, 23 and 26).

[17] Ibid., para 84.

[18] Ibid., para 85.

[19] *Kadi I*, above n1.

imposed by an international agreement cannot have the effect of prejudicing the constitutional principles of the [Treaties]'. For the case at hand, this meant that Regulation No 881/2002 implementing a UN Security Council Resolution was not exempt from judicial review, as this would run counter to 'the [constitutional] principle that all [EU] acts must respect fundamental rights, that respect constituting a condition of their lawfulness which it is for the [ECJ] to review in the framework of the complete system of legal remedies established by the Treat[ies]'.[20] Accordingly, an international agreement which is in breach of those constitutional principles cannot form part of the EU legal order.

Moreover, it is true that by virtue of Article 351 TFEU, EU institutions must not impede the performance of the obligations of Member States which stem from an agreement prior to 1 January 1958 or the date of their accession to the EU. This means that, under certain circumstances,[21] Article 351 TFEU allows primacy of those agreements over secondary EU law. However, as the ECJ stressed in *Kadi I*, 'that primacy … would not … extend to primary [EU] law, in particular to the general principles of which fundamental rights form part'.[22]

Accordingly, the ECJ annulled Regulation No 881/2002 in so far as it concerned the appellants, since '[their] rights of the defence, in particular the right to be heard, and the right to effective judicial review of those rights, were patently not respected'.[23] This was so because they had not been informed of the grounds for their inclusion in the list containing the names of the persons whose assets had to be frozen.[24] Regarding the

---

[20] Ibid., para 285.

[21] N Lavranos, 'Revisiting Article 307 EC: The Untouchable Core of Fundamental European Constitutional Law Values and Principles' in P Carrozza, F Fontanelli and G Martinico (eds), *Shaping the Rule of Law Through Dialogue* (Groningen, European Law Publishing, 2009) 119.

[22] *Kadi I*, above n1, para 308.

[23] Ibid., para 334.

[24] Ibid. In this regard, the ECJ found that the Council had failed to comply with its obligation to communicate to the appellants the grounds on which their names were included in the list laying down a body of restrictive measures, 'so far as possible, either when that inclusion is decided on or, at the very least, as swiftly as possible after that decision in order to enable [them] to exercise, within the periods prescribed, their right to bring an action'. Ibid., para 336. It is true that:

> overriding considerations to do with safety or the conduct of the international relations of the [EU] and of its Member States may militate against the communication of certain matters to the persons concerned and, therefore, against their being heard on those matters. However, that does not mean, with

right to property, the ECJ recognised that threats to international peace and security posed by acts of terrorism may justify the freezing of assets of the persons identified by the UN Security Council as being associated with Al-Qaeda.[25] However, since Regulation No 881/2002 did not enable Mr Kadi to put his case before the competent authorities, the freezing of his assets constituted an unjustified restriction of his right to property.[26]

Kadi I was commented on by academia at length.[27] Scholars have traditionally examined that judgment from three different, albeit closely related, perspectives, namely from a constitutional perspective, from an international perspective and from a fundamental rights perspective.

On the constitutional level, the *Kadi* judgment stresses the fact that EU law is an autonomous legal order and that the EU Courts play a fundamental role in protecting that autonomy. Those Courts are first and foremost committed to upholding the 'EU rule of law' which reflects fundamental rights recognised as general principles of EU law (which are now enshrined in the Charter of Fundamental Rights of the European Union, the Charter).[28] Thus, when EU fundamental rights are at stake, the incorporation of international law into EU law is not automatic. In order for international law to become 'the law of the land', it must pass muster under the Charter.

Internationally, it is true that the *Kadi I* judgment demonstrates that international obligations entered into by the EU are not absolute, as they may not prevail over the basic constitutional tenets of the EU legal order. However, this does not mean that EU law has completely broken away from its international law origins. On the contrary, it shows that the EU

> regard to the principle of effective judicial protection, that restrictive measures such as those imposed by the contested regulation escape all review by the [EU] judicature once it has been claimed that the act laying them down concerns national security and terrorism

Ibid., paras 342–3.

Moreover, the ECJ ruled that 'the contested regulation, in so far as it concerns the appellants, was adopted without any guarantee being given as to the communication of the inculpatory evidence against them or as to their being heard in that connection, so that it must be found that that regulation was adopted according to a procedure in which the appellants' rights of defence were not observed, which has had the further consequence that the principle of effective judicial protection has been infringed'. Ibid., para 352.

25 Ibid., para 363.

26 Ibid., paras 369–70.

27 For a survey of the literature, see S Poli and M Tzanou, 'The *Kadi* Rulings: A Survey of the Literature' (2009) 28 *Yearbook of European Law* 533.

28 [2012] OJ C 326/02.

Courts do take into account the EU's international obligations when exercising their powers of judicial review. When striking the balance between the EU principle of effective judicial protection and the EU's international commitments, those judgments reveal that the EU Courts have paid due attention to the general interest of protecting international peace and security.

From a fundamental rights perspective, the *Kadi I* judgment shows that the EU Courts are seriously committed to the protection of fundamental rights. In so doing, the EU Courts have shown that they are the guarantors of individual rights and that the EU's international obligations may not deprive fundamental rights of their substance. The EU Courts have honoured their role as protectors of those who do not enjoy sufficiently strong political representation to have their voices heard, ie the persons blacklisted.

Soon after the ECJ delivered its judgment in *Kadi I*, the Commission sent to Mr Kadi a 'narrative summary' elaborated by the Sanctions Committee of the UN Security Council, which stated the main reasons why his name was included in the list. In light of that summary, the Commission decided to keep his name on the list, giving him the opportunity to comment on those reasons and to provide it with any information that he might consider relevant. Mr Kadi sent his comments to the Commission, requesting disclosure of the evidence supporting the assertions and allegations made in the narrative summary. In its reply, the Commission stated that the *Kadi I* judgment did not require it to disclose further information and decided to include Mr Kadi's name on the list by adopting Regulation No 1190/2008 amending Regulation No 881/2002. Mr Kadi successfully challenged that regulation before the European General Court (the EGC).[29]

In *Kadi II*, the Commission, the Council and the UK each brought an appeal against the ruling of the EGC.[30] They argued, in essence, that the EGC had erred in law by applying a level of judicial scrutiny which was, in their view, excessive. However, the ECJ dismissed the appeals. Confirming its previous findings in *Kadi I*, it ruled that the EU Courts 'must ensure the review, in principle the full review, of the lawfulness of all Union acts in the light of the fundamental rights forming an integral part of the European Union legal order, including review of such

[29] Judgment in *Kadi*, T-85/09, EU:T:2010:418.

[30] Judgment in *Commission, Council and UK v Kadi* ('*Kadi II*'), C-584/10 P, C-593/10 P and C-595/10 P, EU:C:2013:518.

measures as are designed to give effect to resolutions adopted by the Security Council under Chapter VII of the Charter of the United Nations'.[31]

Notably, this means that the EU Courts must examine whether rules as to procedure and rules as to competence, including whether or not the legal basis is adequate, are observed. They must also determine whether the competent EU authority has:

> (i) disclose[d] to the person concerned the summary of reasons provided by the Sanctions Committee which is the basis for listing or maintaining the listing of that person's name in Annex I to Regulation No 881/2002[32]; (ii) enable[d] him effectively to make known his observations on that subject[33] and (iii) examine[d], carefully and impartially, whether the reasons alleged [were] well founded, in the light of the observations presented by that person and any exculpatory evidence that [might] be produced by him.[34]

In that regard:

> it is for that authority to assess … whether it [was] necessary to seek the assistance of the Sanctions Committee and, through that committee, the Member of the UN which proposed the listing of the individual concerned on that committee's Consolidated List, in order to obtain … the disclosure of information or evidence, confidential or not, to enable it to discharge its duty of careful and impartial examination.[35]

Additionally, the EU Courts must verify whether the competent EU authority has complied with the requirements flowing from Article 296 TFEU, and whether the contested decision is taken on a sufficiently solid factual basis (ie 'whether [the] reasons [set out in the summary] or, at the very least, one of those reasons, deemed sufficient in itself to support that decision, is substantiated').[36] Consequently, 'it is for [the EU Courts] in order to carry out that examination, to request the competent [EU]

---

[31] Ibid., para 97.

[32] See, in this regard, the judgment in *France v People's Mojahedin Organization of Iran*, C-27/09 P, EU:C:2011:853, para 62.

[33] See, by analogy, the judgments in *Technische Universität München*, C-269/90, EU:C:1991:438, para 14; *Spain v Lenzing*, C-525/04 P, EU:C:2007:698, para 58 and *M*, C-277/11, EU:C:2012:744, para 88.

[34] *Kadi II*, above n30, para 135.

[35] Ibid., para 115.

[36] Ibid., para 119.

authority, when necessary, to produce information or evidence, confidential or not, relevant to such an examination'.[37]

If the competent EU authority is unable to obtain the relevant information or evidence from the UN:

> it is then the duty of [the EU Courts] to base their decision solely on the material which has been disclosed to them, namely, in this case, the indications contained in the narrative summary of reasons provided by the Sanctions Committee, the observations and exculpatory evidence that may have been produced by the person concerned and the response of the competent [EU] authority to those observations.[38]

It follows that 'the fact that the party concerned and the [EU] Courts … do not have access to information or evidence which the competent [EU] authority does not have in its possession [does not constitute], as such, an infringement of the rights of the defence or the right to effective judicial protection'.[39]

If, on the other hand, the competent EU authority manages to obtain the relevant information or evidence from the UN, the EU Courts must have access to all the relevant information and evidence which has been obtained by that authority. This means that vis-à-vis those Courts, 'the secrecy or confidentiality of that information or evidence is no valid objection'.[40] In that regard, it is for the EU Courts, 'when carrying out an examination of all the matters of fact or law produced by the competent EU authority, to determine whether the reasons relied on by that authority as grounds to preclude … disclosure [to the person concerned] are well founded'.[41]

If those reasons do not preclude disclosure, the EU Courts:

> shall give the competent [EU] authority the opportunity to make such disclosure to the person concerned. If that authority does not permit the disclosure of that information or evidence, in whole or in part, the EU Courts shall then undertake an examination of the lawfulness of the contested measure solely on the basis of the material which has been disclosed.[42]

Conversely, if the EU Courts find that the competent EU authority was right to oppose disclosure:

---

37 Ibid., para 120.
38 Ibid., para 123.
39 Ibid., para 139.
40 Ibid., para 125.
41 Ibid., para 126.
42 Ibid., para 127.

> it is necessary to strike an appropriate balance between the requirements attached to the right to effective judicial protection, in particular respect for the principle of an adversarial process, and those flowing from the security of the European Union or its Member States or the conduct of their international relations.[43]

It follows from *Kadi II* that considerations relating to international peace and security may not, as such, render decisions imposing restrictive measures upon named persons and entities immune from judicial review. Those considerations are not 'political questions' outside the scope of such review. On the contrary, in compliance with Article 19 TEU, the EU Courts, as guarantor of the rule of law within the EU, must exercise their review powers in full.

II. THE RULE OF LAW WITHIN THE EU AND NATIONAL CONSTITUTIONS: THE PROTECTION OF FUNDAMENTAL RIGHTS

A. General Observations

In Europe, fundamental rights are protected by a plurality of legal sources, namely national constitutions, the Charter and international treaties, notably the European Convention on the Protection of Human Rights and Fundamental Freedoms (the ECHR), as well as by various judicial bodies, namely national courts, both ordinary and constitutional, the ECJ and the European Court of Human Rights (the ECtHR).

It follows that fundamental rights are protected at national, supranational and international levels. As a result of that multilevel system of fundamental rights protection, there is a risk that conflicts of jurisdiction and conflicts of interpretation may arise between courts operating at different levels. When a national measure implements EU law, it falls within the scope of the Charter.[44] This means that it must be compatible with the standard of fundamental rights protection set out in the Charter. Logically, the question arises whether a national court may, when

---

43 Ibid para 128.

44 Article 51 of the Charter provides that '[t]he provisions of this Charter are addressed … to the Member States only when they are implementing Union law'. In this regard, see K Lenaerts, 'The Court of Justice of the European Union and the Protection of Fundamental Rights' (2011) 31 *Polish Yearbook of International Law* 79 and 'Exploring the Limits of the EU Charter of Fundamental Rights' (2012) 8 *European Constitutional Law Review* 375.

examining the validity of that measure, also apply a constitutional provision which provides for a higher standard of protection than that guaranteed by EU law.

In that regard, Article 52(4) of the Charter states that '[i]n so far as [the latter] recognises fundamental rights as they result from the constitutional traditions common to the Member States, those rights shall be interpreted in harmony with those traditions'. By referring to the constitutional traditions common to the Member States, the Charter does not seek to define the fundamental rights recognised thereby in accordance with the 'smallest common denominator' of the Member States' constitutions, but to interpret the fundamental rights enshrined therein in a way that offers a high level of protection; that is adapted to the nature of EU law; and that is in harmony with the national constitutional traditions.

Moreover, Article 53 of the Charter provides that '[n]othing in this Charter shall be interpreted as restricting or adversely affecting human rights and fundamental freedoms as recognised, in their respective fields of application, … by the Member States' constitutions'. The question is then whether Article 53 of the Charter must be interpreted as a codification of the '*Solange*' approach,[45] according to which the primacy of EU law is made conditional upon that law offering a level of fundamental right protection, at least, equivalent to that guaranteed by the legal orders of the Member States.[46]

One should not read Article 53 of the Charter as a rule of conflict,[47] but as a rule which seeks to strengthen the primacy of EU law by demanding from the ECJ that it states the reasons why it decided to

---

[45] See the judgments of the German *Bundesverfassungsgericht* of 29 May 1974, known as *Solange I* (2 BvL 52/71) and of 22 October 1986, known as *Solange II* (2 BvR 197/83); the judgment of the Italian *Corte Costituzionale* of 21 April 1989 (No 232, Fragd, in Foro it, 1990, I, 1855); the declaration of the Spanish *Tribunal Constitucional* of 13 December 2004 (DTC 1/2004). See also ECtHR, *Bosphorus Hava Yolları Turizm v Ireland ve Ticaret Anonim Şirketi*, judgment of 30 June 2005, ECHR 2005-VI.

[46] J Bering Liisberg, 'Does the EU Charter of Fundamental Rights Threaten the Supremacy of Community Law?' (2001) 38 *Common Market Law Review* 1171.

[47] C Ladenburger, European Institutional Report, in J Laffranque (ed.) *The Protection of Fundamental Rights Post – Lisbon, FIDE XXV Congress*, Vol 1 (Tartu, Tartu University Press, 2012), at 175 (who argues that 'Article 53 refers to Member States' constitutions (as well as to Union law, international law and international agreements) only *within their respective fields of application*. Those words were chosen by the first Convention precisely to leave primacy of Union law unaffected').

follow (or depart from) the level of fundamental right protection provided for by the Member States' constitutions. Article 53 of the Charter thus mandates the ECJ to engage in a dialogue with the national constitutional courts or, as the case may be, with the national supreme courts. Methodologically, this means, for example, that the ECJ must continue to rely on the constitutional traditions common to the Member States when determining the content, limitations and scope of fundamental rights.[48] In accordance with such a reading, Article 53 of the Charter would be an expression of constitutional pluralism.

In light of a pluralist reading of Article 53 of the Charter, the latter provision would not endorse the primacy of an EU law measure which does not pay due homage to the constitutional traditions common to the Member States. As Article 4(2) TEU stresses,[49] the EU legal order is committed to respecting the identities of the Member States, of which

---

[48] S Iglesias Sánchez, 'The Court and the Charter: The Impact of the Entry into Force of the Lisbon Treaty on the ECJ's Approach to Fundamental Rights' (2012) 49 *Common Market Law Review* 1565 at 1605.

[49] See generally, L Besselink, 'National and Constitutional Identity Before and After Lisbon' (2010) 6 *Utrecht Law Review* 36 (who argues that Article 4(2) TEU is an 'exception to the primacy of EU law [that] seem[s] to be restricted to issues of constitutional *identity*, which would suggest that constitutional provisions which are not fundamental and hence do not contribute to the very identity of the constitution do not share in that privileged position vis-à-vis EU law'); A von Bogdandy and S Schill, 'Overcoming Absolute Primacy: Respect for National Identity under the Lisbon Treaty' (2011) 48 *Common Market Law Review* 1417 at 1419 (who posit that 'Article 4(2) TEU … provides a perspective for overcoming the idea of absolute primacy of EU law and the underlying assumption of a hierarchical model for understanding the relationship between EU law and domestic constitutional law, because this provision endorses a pluralistic vision of the relationship between EU law and domestic constitutional law'). However, see B Guastaferro, 'Beyond the *Exceptionalism* of Constitutional Conflicts: The Ordinary Functions of the Identity Clause' (2012) 31 *Yearbook of European Law* 263 (who reads Article 4(2) TEU as a provision that does not limit the primacy of EU law, but seeks to contain the EU 'competence creep'. She also argues that the expression 'national identities' laid down in Article 4(2) TEU should not be read as a synonym of 'constitutional identity' as defined by national law. In her view, such expression should be 'coupled' with existing concepts of EU law, such as public policy. Finally, the author supports the contention that normative conflicts between national constitutional law and EU law are rather exceptional. Accordingly, the application of Article 4(2) TEU should not be limited to exceptional cases, but should regulate the 'ordinary functioning of EU law' by helping improving competence monitoring).

constitutional arrangements are part and parcel.[50] Nor would that provision of the Charter deprive EU law of its primacy because of a national constitution which, although offering a higher level of protection than that guaranteed under EU law, does not take into account the essential elements of that law. Accordingly, Article 53 of the Charter is not to be interpreted in accordance with the '*Solange*' approach, but in light of the rulings of the ECJ in *Omega*[51] and *Sayn-Wittgenstein*.[52] In those cases, the ECJ ruled that:

> it is not indispensable for the restrictive measure issued by the authorities of a Member State to correspond to a conception shared by all Member States as regards the precise way in which the fundamental right or legitimate interest in question is to be protected and that, on the contrary, the need for, and proportionality of, the provisions adopted are not excluded merely because one Member State has chosen a system of protection different from that adopted by another State.[53]

This means that, in so far as the essential interests of the EU are not adversely affected by national measures implementing EU law, the ECJ defers to the Member States the question of determining the level of protection of fundamental rights they consider consistent with their national constitution. Provided that Member States enjoy a margin of discretion in implementing EU law, the Charter does not oppose a 'cumulative application' of fundamental rights.[54]

B. The Judgment of the ECJ in *Melloni*

1. Factual and legal background

Melloni offered a good opportunity for the ECJ to interpret Article 53 of the Charter and in so doing to engage, for the first time, in a constructive dialogue with the Spanish Constitutional Court.[55] In that case, the ECJ

---

[50] Judgment in *Sayn-Wittgenstein*, C-208/09, EU:C:2010:806, para 92. See also the judgments in *Runevič-Vardyn and Wardyn*, C-391/09, EU:C:2011:291, para 86, and *Commission v Luxembourg*, C-51/08, EU:C:2011:336, para 124.

[51] Judgment in *Omega*, C-36/02, EU:C:2004:614.

[52] *Sayn-Wittgenstein*, above n50.

[53] Ibid., para 91 (referring to *Omega*, above n51, paras 37 and 38).

[54] C Ladenburger, above n47, at 173–5.

[55] *Melloni*, above n5. See, in this regard, A Torres Pérez, 'Constitutional Dialogue on the European Arrest Warrant: the Spanish Constitutional Court Knocking on Luxembourg's Door' (2012) 8 *European Constitutional Law*

was called upon to strike the right balance between the principle of mutual recognition in the Area of Freedom, Security and Justice and compliance with fundamental rights.[56] The facts of the case are as follows. In 1996, the Spanish judicial authorities authorised the extradition of Mr Melloni to Italy so that he could be tried in Italy in relation to criminal charges brought against him on account of bankruptcy fraud. After being released on bail, he fled and could not be surrendered to the Italian authorities. In 2000, Mr Melloni, who did not appear in person at the trial, was convicted and sentenced to ten years' imprisonment by the Tribunale di Ferrara. In 2003, the latter's ruling was confirmed on appeal by the Bologna Appeals Court and in 2004, by the Supreme Court of Cassation. Mr Melloni was defended by two lawyers, chosen by him, who represented him at the trial and in the subsequent appeal and cassation proceedings. In 2004, a European arrest warrant for the execution of the sentence imposed by the Tribunale di Ferrara was issued against Mr Melloni. The Spanish executing judicial authority authorised his surrender. However, Mr Melloni filed a '*recurso de amparo*' before the Spanish Constitutional Court,[57] alleging that his right to a fair trial, as provided for by Article 24 of the Spanish Constitution, had been violated, since his surrender was not conditional upon his being entitled to a retrial in Italy.

In accordance with Article 24 of the Spanish Constitution, which protects the right to a fair trial and the rights of the defence, Spanish judicial authorities may only consent to extradite a person who has been

---

Review 105. More generally, see J Malenovský, 'Le renvoi préjudiciel perçu par trois Cours "souveraines"'(2013) *Journal de droit européen* 214.

[56] See also the judgment in *Radu*, C-396/11, EU:C:2013:39.

[57] See Article 53(2) of the Spanish Constitution which provides that '[a]ny citizen may assert his or her claim to the protect the liberties and rights recognised in Article 14 and in Section 1 of Chapter Two [of the Spanish Constitution], by means of a preferential and summary procedure in the ordinary courts and, when appropriate, by submitting an individual appeal for protection ("*recurso de amparo*") to the Constitutional Court.' As explained by the Spanish Constitutional Court:

> [t]he protection of fundamental rights and freedoms of the individual is first of all entrusted to [ordinary courts as provided for by the relevant rules of procedure]. However, the [Spanish] Constitution has established a specific and ultimate [remedy] to protect these rights [, namely the '*recurso de amparo*' which is] a constitutional appeal for [the] protection of fundamental rights [that may be brought before] the [Spanish] Constitutional Court.

This information is available in English at: http://www.tribunalconstitucional.es/en/Pages/Home.aspx.

convicted *in absentia* if that person is given the opportunity to apply for a retrial in the requesting State. For the Spanish Constitutional Court, that interpretation of Article 24 of the Spanish Constitution also applies in the context of a European arrest warrant. However, Article 4a(1) of Framework Decision 2002/584,[58] as amended by Framework Decision 2009/299,[59] which seeks to foster the application of the principle of mutual recognition to decisions rendered in the absence of the person concerned at the trial, limits the grounds on which the executing judicial authority may refuse to execute such decisions. For example, Article 4a(1)(b) states that refusal of execution of a decision rendered *in absentia* may not take place where the person concerned, who is aware of the scheduled trial, has appointed legal counsel, and he or she was in fact defended by that person at the trial.

Taking the view that its interpretation of Article 24 of the Spanish Constitution might be at odds with Article 4a(1) of Framework Decision 2002/548, the Spanish Constitutional Court referred three questions to the ECJ. First, it asked whether Article 4a(1) of Framework Decision 2002/584 must be interpreted as precluding national authorities, in the circumstances specified in that provision, from making the execution of a European arrest warrant conditional upon the possibility of a retrial in the issuing Member State, in order to guarantee the rights of the defence of the person whose transfer is requested under the warrant.[60] If so, it also asked the ECJ to determine whether Article 4a(1) of Framework Decision 2002/584 is valid in light of Articles 47 and 48(2) of the Charter. Finally, if such examination does not disclose any factor of such a kind as to affect the validity of Article 4a(1) of Framework Decision 2002/584, the

---

[58] Council Framework Decision 2002/584/JHA of 13 June 2002 on the European arrest warrant and the surrender procedures between Member States, [2002] OJ L 190/1.

[59] Council Framework Decision 2009/299/JHA of 26 February 2009 amending Framework Decisions 2002/584/JHA, 2005/214/JHA, 2006/783/JHA, 2008/909/JHA and 2008/947/JHA, thereby enhancing the procedural rights of persons and fostering the application of the principle of mutual recognition to decisions rendered in the absence of the person concerned at the trial, [2009] OJ L 81/24.

[60] In this regard, the factual scenario in *Melloni* differs from that in *Radu*, above n56, para 38, which concerned the execution of a European arrest warrant issued for the purposes of prosecution. In this regard, the ECJ found that 'the fact that the European arrest warrant has been issued for the purposes of conducting a criminal prosecution, without the requested person having been heard by the issuing judicial authorities, does not feature among the grounds for non-execution of such a warrant as provided for by the provisions of Framework Decision 2002/584'.

referring court asked whether Article 53 of the Charter may be relied upon with a view to applying the level of fundamental rights protection guaranteed by Article 24 of the Spanish Constitution.

2. The ECJ's response

At the outset, some Member States raised an objection of inadmissibility on the ground that Article 4a(1) of Framework Decision 2002/584 was not applicable *ratione temporis* to the case at hand. In their view, the date on which the Spanish executing judicial authority decided to surrender Mr Melloni, ie 12 September 2008, preceded the deadline for transposing Framework Decision 2009/299, ie 28 March 2011. Thus, they argued that the situation of Mr Melloni was not governed by Article 4a(1), but by Article 5(1) of Framework Decision 2002/584 which allowed Member States to make the execution of a European arrest warrant issued for the purposes of executing a sentence rendered *in absentia* conditional upon a guarantee of a retrial in the issuing Member State. However, the ECJ rejected that objection. It noted that in light of the wording of Article 8(2) of Framework Decision 2009/299, the latter applied, as from 28 March 2011, 'to the recognition and enforcement of decisions rendered in the absence of the person concerned at the trial', 'without any distinction whatsoever being drawn between decisions rendered prior or subsequently to that date'.[61] Such a literal reading of Article 8(2) was confirmed by the case law according to which 'procedural rules are generally held to apply to all proceedings pending at the time when they enter into force, whereas substantive rules are usually interpreted as not applying to situations existing before their entry into force'.[62]

As to the first question, the ECJ noted that by adopting Framework Decision 2009/299, the EU legislator sought to harmonise the grounds for non-recognition of decisions rendered following a trial at which the person concerned did not appear in person, whilst fully respecting that person's rights of the defence.[63] Stated differently, it sought to improve the principle of mutual recognition by narrowing down the margin of discretion enjoyed by the executing Member State when deciding whether to surrender – and if so, under what conditions – a person convicted *in absentia*. To that end, the EU legislator decided to repeal Article 5(1) of Framework Decision 2002/584 and replaced it by a new Article 4a(1) which 'precludes, in the four situations set out therein, the

---

[61] *Melloni*, above n5, para 31.
[62] Ibid., para 32.
[63] Ibid., para 43.

executing judicial authority from making the surrender of a person convicted *in absentia* conditional upon the conviction being open to review in his presence'.[64] As noted by AG Bot, Article 4a(1) of Framework Decision 2002/584 contains an 'exhaustive list … of the circumstances in which it must be considered that the procedural rights of a person who has not appeared in person at his trial have not been infringed and that the European arrest warrant must therefore be executed'. This means that a person who was, for example, 'aware of the scheduled trial, had given a mandate to a legal counsellor, who was either appointed by the person concerned or by the State, to defend him or her at the trial, and was indeed defended by that counsellor at the trial', must be regarded as having waived his or her right to appear at the trial, so that he or she may not invoke a right to a retrial.[65]

Regarding the second question, the ECJ went on to examine the compatibility of Article 4a(1) of Framework Decision 2002/584 with the principle of effective judicial protection and the rights of the defence enshrined in Articles 47 and 48(2) of the Charter.[66] In this regard, it recalled that, 'although the right of the accused to appear in person at his trial is an essential component of the right to a fair trial, that right is not absolute'.[67] This means that '[t]he accused may waive that right of his own free will, either expressly or tacitly, provided that the waiver is established in an unequivocal manner, is attended by minimum safe-guards commensurate to its importance and does not run counter to any important public interest'.[68] For example, if the accused was aware of the place and time of the trial or gave instructions to a legal counsellor to defend him at the trial, he may be convicted *in absentia* without his rights of the defence being violated. In addition, the ECJ observed that such a reading of the right of the accused to appear in person was fully

---

64 Ibid., para 40.

65 Opinion of AG Bot in *Melloni*, C-399/11, EU:C:2012:600, paras 64–5.

66 It is worth noting that those fundamental rights do not impose the same requirements on the executing judicial authority when dealing with a European Arrest Warrant issued for the purposes of conducting a criminal prosecution. See *Radu*, above n56, para 39, where the ECJ held that 'the observance of Articles 47 and 48 of the Charter does not require that a judicial authority of a Member State should be able to refuse to execute a European arrest warrant issued for the purposes of conducting a criminal prosecution on the ground that the requested person was not heard by the issuing judicial authorities before that arrest warrant was issued'.

67 *Melloni*, above n5, para 49.

68 Ibid.

consistent with the case law of the ECtHR.[69] Accordingly, given that '[a]rticle 4a(1)(a) and (b) of Framework Decision 2002/584 lays down the circumstances in which the person concerned must be deemed to have waived, voluntarily and unambiguously, his right to be present at his trial',[70] the ECJ found that that provision was compatible with Articles 47 and 48(2) of the Charter.

As to the third question, the ECJ held that Article 53 of the Charter may not be interpreted as 'allow[ing] a Member State to disapply EU legal rules which are fully in compliance with the Charter where they infringe the fundamental rights guaranteed by that State's constitution'.[71] Provided that the EU measure at issue – for the case at hand, Article 4a(1) of Framework Decision 2002/548 – complies with primary EU law, notably the Charter, national courts are bound to set aside conflicting national measures, including those of constitutional ranking.[72] However, that does not mean that Article 53 opposes a cumulative application of fundamental rights. 'Member States are free', the ECJ wrote, 'to apply national standards of protection of fundamental rights, provided that the level of protection provided for by the Charter, as interpreted by the [ECJ], and the primacy, unity and effectiveness of EU law are not thereby compromised.'[73]

Logically, the question is then under what circumstances 'the primacy, unity and effectiveness of EU law' are compromised. For the ECJ, the answer to that question is conditional upon the existence or absence of a

---

69 See ECtHR, *Medenica v Switzerland*, no 20491/92, § 56 to 59, ECHR 2001-VI; *Sejdovic v Italy* [GC], no 56581/00, § 84, 86 and 98, ECHR 2006-II; and *Haralampiev v Bulgaria*, no 29648/03, § 32 and 33, 24 April 2012.

70 *Melloni*, above n5, para 52.

71 Ibid., para 58.

72 Ibid., para 59. Moreover, AG Bot pointed out that Article 53 of the Charter does not, however, preclude a Member State from challenging an act of secondary EU legislation which adversely affects its national identity, as defined by Article 4(2) TEU. In his view, the validity of Article 4a(1) of Framework Decision 2002/584 could thus be examined in light of that Treaty provision. However, he noted that there was no need to do so in the present case, as the Spanish government had submitted that the application of the right to a fair trial and the rights of the defence to judgments rendered *in absentia* did not form part of the national identity of the Kingdom of Spain. See the Opinion of AG Bot in *Melloni*, above n65, para 139. However, the judgment of the ECJ in *Melloni* does not mention Article 4(2) TEU, deferring to future developments the question whether Article 4(2) TEU may operate as an independent ground of review of secondary EU law.

73 *Melloni*, above n5, paras 60 and 61.

uniform standard of fundamental rights protection which has been defined by the EU legislator. Where the EU measure at issue reflects a consensus regarding the level of fundamental rights protection enjoyed by the persons to whom such a measure applies, then the application of higher national standards of protection is ruled out. This is so because, when adopting such a measure, the EU legislator struck a balance between the general interest the EU pursues and the protection of fundamental rights. Applying higher standards of protection would thus disturb such a balance, thus compromising the 'primacy, unity and effectiveness of EU law'. Needless to say, this does not mean that the protection of fundamental rights is entirely left to the EU political process. As *Melloni* shows, the balance resulting from political deliberations at EU level must always pass muster under the Charter. Conversely, where the measures adopted by the EU legislator do not define a uniform standard of fundamental rights protection, then Member States are free to impose higher standards of protection, provided that such standards do not adversely affect the objectives pursued by the EU legislator.[74] The discretion enjoyed by the Member States as to the standards of fundamental rights protection they apply is therefore not absolute, but is circumscribed by the Charter and the EU principle of effectiveness ('*effet utile*').

This reading of Article 53 of the Charter is highlighted by contrasting *Melloni* with *Åkerberg Fransson*.[75] In *Melloni*, the ECJ held that Article 4a(1) of Framework Decision 2002/584 does not allow Member States to refuse to execute a European arrest warrant when the person concerned is in one of the situations provided for therein. By adopting Article 4a(1), the EU legislator indeed struck a balance between the principle of mutual trust and the protection of the procedural fundamental rights enjoyed by persons convicted *in absentia*. Since that balance complied with the

---

[74] See, in this regard, V Skouris, 'Développements récents de la protection des droits fondamentaux dans l'Union européenne: les arrêts *Melloni* et *Åkerberg Fransson*' (2013) *Il diritto dell'Unione Europea* 229 at 241. See also N de Boer, Case Note on *Melloni*, (2013) 50 *Common Market Law Review* 1083 at 1096; D Ritleng, 'De l'articulation des systèmes de protection des droits fondamentaux dans l'Union: les enseignements des arrêts *Åkerberg Fransson* et *Melloni*' (2013) *Revue trimestrielle de droit européen* 267 at 283; and D Sarmiento, 'Who's Afraid of the Charter? The Court of Justice, National Courts and the New Framework of Fundamental Rights Protection in Europe' (2013) 50 *Common Market Law Review* 1267.

[75] *Åkerberg Fransson*, above n5.

Charter, Member States were precluded from imposing higher standards of fundamental rights protection.

By contrast, in *Åkerberg Fransson*, after holding that the national legislation at issue constituted implementation of EU law for the purposes of Article 51(1) of the Charter,[76] the ECJ was called upon to determine whether the *ne bis in idem* principle enshrined in Article 50 of the Charter had to be interpreted as precluding criminal proceedings for tax evasion from being brought against a defendant where a tax penalty had already been imposed upon him for the same acts of providing false information. At the outset, the ECJ noted that in order for the *ne bis in idem* principle to apply to a situation such as that of Mr Åkerberg Fransson, the tax penalty has to be final and criminal in nature. The ECJ also observed that, as a means of ensuring the effective collection of VAT revenue which guarantees the financial interests of the EU, the *ne bis in idem* principle does not preclude Member States from adopting penalties in the form of administrative penalties, criminal penalties or a combination of the two. If a Member State opts for a combination of penalties, it must make sure that tax penalties – which are final and adopted prior to criminal penalties – are not criminal in nature. Next, the ECJ went on to define what is to be understood by 'criminal in nature'. In this regard, it observed that 'three criteria are relevant for the purpose of assessing whether tax penalties are criminal in nature', namely (1) the legal classification of the offence under national law, (2) the very nature of the offence, and (3) the nature and degree of severity of the penalty that the person concerned is liable to incur.[77] In doing so, the ECJ referred to its previous ruling in *Bonda*[78] which, in turn, referred to the case law of the ECtHR.[79] Accordingly, the EU legislator had not struck a balance between the protection of the EU financial interests and the *ne bis in idem* principle. Provided that tax penalties complied with the Charter (ie they were not criminal in nature) and provided that the '*effet utile*' of EU law was guaranteed (ie penalties had to be effective, proportionate and dissuasive for ensuring the collection of VAT), Member States were free

76 See, in this regard, K Lenaerts and JA Gutierrez-Fons, 'The Place of the Charter in the EU Constitutional Edifice' in S Peers, T Hervey, J Kenner and A Ward (eds), *The EU Charter of Fundamental Rights: A Commentary* (Oxford, Hart Publishing, 2014) 1559–93.

77 *Åkerberg Fransson*, above n5, para 35.

78 Judgment in *Bonda*, C-489/10, EU:C:2012:319, para 37.

79 See ECtHR, *Sergey Zolotukhin v Russia*, judgment of 10 February 2009, [GC], no 14939/03, ECHR 2009, §§ 52 and 53.

to apply higher standards of fundamental rights protection when assessing the lawfulness of combining tax and criminal penalties for the same wrongful conduct.

III. CONCLUSION

The autonomy of the EU legal order is not absolute, but relative. The ECJ does not seek to break away from the international legal order, but neither does it allow the latter law to call into question the autonomy of EU legal order. Provided that international law complies with the basic constitutional tenets of EU law, international obligations binding on the EU may prevail over secondary EU law. In so far as other international legal orders – such as that of the UN – require EU implementing measures but fail to offer a level of fundamental rights protection equivalent to that of the EU, the ECJ may not reduce the intensity of its judicial review by deference to the international law origin of the relevant obligations. That rationale underpins the rulings of the ECJ in *Kadi I* and *II* and makes it possible to reconcile the EU's openness to international law with its own constitutional autonomy. As the ECJ made clear in *van Gend en Loos*, the EU legal order must find its own constitutional space within which to operate. However, the autonomy of the EU legal order does not imply 'isolationism'. EU law must continue to influence and be influenced by the legal orders that surround it.

In the same way, the autonomy of the EU legal order does not rule out the possibility for Member States to apply the standard of fundamental rights protection defined by their respective constitutions. It follows from *Melloni* that the ECJ has embraced a pluralist model of fundamental rights protection.[80] When Member States are implementing EU law, they are free to apply their own standards of fundamental rights protection, 'provided that the level of protection provided for by the Charter, as interpreted by the [ECJ], and the primacy, unity and effectiveness of EU law are not thereby compromised.'[81] *Melloni* thus welcomes a cumulative application of fundamental rights, whilst rejecting an EU system of protection grounded in 'dual-federalism', whereby national and supranational systems of fundamental rights protection are insulated from one another. As interpreted by the ECJ, Article 53 of the Charter serves to articulate the different systems of fundamental rights protection that form part of the EU 'common constitutional space', thus preventing conflicts

---

80 D Sarmiento, above n74, at 1302.

81 *Melloni*, above n5, para 60.

between them whilst favouring value diversity. In addition, *Melloni* pays due attention to the principle of separation of powers, given that it is not the ECJ but the EU legislator who, subject to compliance with the Charter, determines whether it is possible for Member States to opt for higher standards of fundamental rights protection. Thus, the question whether a uniform standard of fundamental rights protection is adopted at EU level is left to the political process, which enjoys the necessary democratic legitimacy and institutional capacity to strike a balance between the collective good and individual liberty. As *Melloni* demonstrates, the role of the ECJ is then limited to that traditionally reserved to national constitutional courts, ie policing the compliance with the Charter of that uniform standard of protection.

The rule of law within the EU must be interpreted in light of an external and internal balance. Externally, while the EU must remain open to international law, compliance with Article 19 TEU requires that the ECJ guarantees the constitutional autonomy of the EU legal order. Internally, while it is for the EU political process to decide whether national diversity must be set aside in favour of European unity, compliance with Article 19 TEU also requires that the ECJ examines whether such policy choices comply with the Charter. The rule of law within the EU is thus composed of a nucleus of core values which must be protected at all times. Beyond that nucleus, the rule of law within the EU is defined by its openness to international law and by a pluralist model of fundamental rights protection.

By demonstrating that it is possible to interlock different legal orders, I believe that the rule of law within the EU indicates the path to be followed for the establishment of a global community of law where all participants can, nonetheless, preserve their own constitutional autonomy.

PART IV

Tribunals pertaining to particular situations

9. International criminal justice and the rule of law: The experience of the International Criminal Tribunal for the Former Yugoslavia (ICTY)*

Serge Brammertz

I. INTRODUCTION

The brevity of the phrase 'the rule of law' belies its extraordinary scope and significance – it is a term which sets out not only a fundamental tenet of the criminal justice process but also many of the core principles of a fair society.[1] It is thus unsurprising that the rule of law is assuming ever greater significance for the international community.[2]

Looking back over the last decades, rule of law perspectives have become more and more closely integrated in the mainstream of UN business. Both the UN General Assembly and the Security Council

* This chapter is based on a speech made at the University of Leuven in April 2013. I am grateful to Matthew Cross for his support in preparing this chapter.

1 See eg Lord Bingham, 'The rule of law,' (2007) 66(1) *Cambridge Law Journal* 67–85 (identifying eight 'sub-rules': the law must be accessible, intelligible, clear and predictable; legal rights and liabilities must be resolved according to the law and not by discretion; the law must apply equally to all; the law must afford adequate protection to fundamental human rights; the law must provide means of resolving *bona fide* disputes; public officials must exercise powers conferred upon them reasonably, in good faith, and subject to the law; adjudicative procedures must be fair; nation states must comply with international law). See also Kramer, MH, 'On the moral status of the rule of law,' (2004) 63(1) *Cambridge Law Journal* 64 at 64 (citing Fuller, L, *The Morality of Law* (Yale University Press, revised ed, 1969)).

2 See 'Delivering justice: programme of action to strengthen the rule of law at the national and international levels,' Report of the UN Secretary-General, 16 March 2012, UN Doc A/66/749, *especially* paras 1–9.

regularly consider the rule of law as an agenda item,[3] and these debates have gained greater prominence in recent years. Most notably, the UN General Assembly held its first ever high-level meeting on the rule of law in 2012.[4] Likewise, the UN has created a specialized Rule of Law Coordination and Resource Group,[5] supported by the Rule of Law Unit,[6] to supplement and draw together the work of more than 30 UN and other

---

[3] At the UN General Assembly, see eg 'The rule of law at the national and international levels,' GA Res 61/39 (18 December 2006), UN Doc A/RES/61/39; 'The rule of law at the national and international levels,' GA Res 62/70 (8 January 2008), UN Doc A/RES/62/70; 'The rule of law at the national and international levels,' GA Res. 63/128 (15 January 2009), UN Doc A/RES/63/128; 'The rule of law at the national and international levels,' GA Res 64/116 (15 January 2010), UN Doc A/RES/64/116; 'The rule of law at the national and international levels,' GA Res 65/32 (10 January 2011), UN Doc A/RES/65/32; 'The rule of law at the national and international levels,' GA Res 66/102 (13 January 2012), UN Doc A/RES/66/102; 'The rule of law at the national and international levels,' GA Res 67/97 (14 January 2013), UN Doc A/RES/67/97; 'Strengthening the rule of law and the reform of criminal justice institutions, particularly in the areas related to the United Nations system-wide approach to fighting transnational organized crime and drug trafficking,' GA Res 67/186 (12 March 2013), UN Doc A/RES/67/186. At the UN Security Council, see eg statement by the President of the Security Council, UN Doc S/PRST/2012/1 (19 January 2012), p1 ('The Security Council recognizes the need for universal adherence to and implementation of the rule of law and emphasizes the vital importance it attaches to promoting justice and the rule of law as an indispensable element for peaceful coexistence and the prevention of armed conflict. The Security Council reaffirms its commitment to international law and the Charter of the United Nations, and to an international order based on the rule of law and international law, which are essential for cooperation among States in addressing common challenges, thus contributing to the maintenance of international peace and security.'). *See also* UN Doc S/PRST/2003/15 (24 September 2003); UN Doc S/PRST/2006/28 (22 June 2006); UN Doc S/PRST/2010/11 (29 June 2010).

[4] See 'The rule of law at the national and international levels,' GA Res 66/102 (13 January 2012), UN Doc A/RES/66/102; 'Declaration of the High-level Meeting of the General Assembly on the Rule of Law at the National and International Levels,' GA Res 67/1 (30 November 2012), UN Doc A/RES/67/1. *See also* 'High-level Meeting on the Rule of Law, 24 September 2012', available at http://www.unrol.org/article.aspx?article_id=168 (accessed 5 December 2013).

[5] See 'Rule of Law Coordination and Resource Group,' available at http://www.unrol.org/article.aspx?article_id=6 (accessed 5 December 2013).

[6] See 'Rule of Law Unit,' available at http://unrol.org/article.aspx?article_id=7 (accessed 5 December 2013).

agencies whose mandates include rule of law issues.[7] And, of course, we have seen the rising tide of international criminal justice – not just the ad hoc tribunals of the 1990s[8] but also the permanent International Criminal Court[9] and UN partnerships such as the Special Court for Sierra Leone

---

[7] Eg United Nations Department of Economic and Social Affairs (DESA), United Nations Department of Political Affairs (DPA), United Nations Department of Peacekeeping Operations (DPKO), Office for Coordination of Humanitarian Affairs (OCHA), Office of the High Commissioner for Human Rights (OHCHR), Office of Legal Affairs (OLA), Office of the Special Representative for Children and Armed Conflict (OSRSG/CAAC), Office of the Special Representative of the Secretary-General on Sexual Violence in Conflict, United Nations Peacebuilding Support Office (PBSO), United Nations Democracy Fund (UNDEF), United Nations Development Programme (UNDP), United Nations Human Settlements Programme (UN-HABITAT), United Nations High Commissioner for Refugees (UNHCR), United Nations Children's Fund (UNICEF), United Nations Office on Drugs and Crime (UNODC), United Nations Office for Project Services (UNOPS), United Nations Entity for Gender Equality and the Empowerment of Women (UN WOMEN), Counter-Terrorism Committee Executive Directorate (CTED), Food and Agriculture Organization (FAO), International Labour Organization (ILO), Office for Disarmament Affairs (ODA), Office of the Special Adviser for Gender Issues (OSAGI), United Nations Commission on International Trade Law (UNCITRAL), United Nations Conference on Trade and Development (UNCTAD), United Nations Environment Programme (UNEP), United Nations Educational, Scientific and Cultural Organization (UNESCO), United Nations Interregional Crime and Justice Research Unit (UNICRI), United Nations International Research and Training Institute for the Advancement of Women (UN-INSTRAW), United Nations Population Fund (UNFPA), UN Regional Commissions (Economic and Social Commission for Western Asia (ESCWA), Economic Commission for Africa (ECA), Economic Commission for Europe (ECE), Economic Commission for Latin America and the Caribbean (ECLAC), Economic and Social Commission for Asia and the Pacific (ESCAP)), World Bank Group (comprising *inter alia* the International Bank for Reconstruction and Development (IBRD) and International Development Association (IDA)).

[8] See International Criminal Tribunal for the Former Yugoslavia (ICTY), available at http://www.icty.org/ (accessed 5 December 2013); International Criminal Tribunal for Rwanda (ICTR), available at http://www.unictr.org/ (accessed 5 December 2013). See also Mechanism for International Criminal Tribunals (MICT), available at http://www.unmict.org/ (accessed 5 December 2013).

[9] See International Criminal Court (ICC), available at http://www.icc-cpi.int/en_menus/icc/Pages/default.aspx (accessed 5 December 2013).

and the Special Tribunal for Lebanon.[10] These courts and tribunals not only clarify and publicize international criminal law but also reassert the vital truth that every person, at every level of seniority and influence, is subject to that law. They model the highest standards of substantive and procedural fairness.

The experience of the ICTY offers a particular insight into the relationship between the rule of law and international criminal justice. At the time of writing, we are in the final phase of our work, with our last four trials well under way[11] and seven ongoing cases now on appeal.[12] Two of these last trials, the *Karadžić* and *Mladić* trials, are some of our most important. With Slobodan Milošević and others, Karadžić and Mladić are alleged to be the architects of the ethnic cleansing in Bosnia and Herzegovina. The indictments against Karadžić and Mladić include charges relating to ethnic cleansing in the Bosnian municipalities, the siege of Sarajevo, and the genocide at Srebrenica.[13] Both sought to evade justice for many years. But both face it now. 2013 saw another milestone, when the ICTY branch of the Mechanism for International Criminal Tribunals began operating.[14] This mechanism will look after the ICTY's

---

[10] See Special Court for Sierra Leone (SCSL), available at http://www.sc-sl.org/ (accessed 5 December 2013); Special Tribunal for Lebanon (STL), available at http://www.stl-tsl.org/en/ (accessed 5 December 2013).

[11] *Prosecutor v Radovan Karadžić*, Case No IT-95-5/18-T (mid-way through the defence case at trial); *Prosecutor v Ratko Mladić*, Case No IT-09-92-T (end of the prosecution case at trial); *Prosecutor v Goran Hadžić*, Case No IT-04-75-T (end of the prosecution case at trial); *Prosecutor v Vojislav Šešelj*, Case No IT-03-67-T (adjourned for judicial deliberations).

[12] *Prosecutor v Nikola Šainović et al.*, Case No IT-05-87-A (appeal judgment anticipated for early 2014); *Prosecutor v Vlastimir Đorđević*, Case No IT-05-87/1-A (appeal judgment anticipated for early 2014); *Prosecutor v Vujadin Popović et al*, Case No IT-05-88-A (judicial deliberations pending); *Prosecutor v Zdravko Tolimir*, Case No IT-05-88/2-A (awaiting appeal hearing); *Prosecutor v Mićo Stanišić and Stojan Župljanin*, Case No IT-08-91-A (awaiting appeal hearing); *Prosecutor v Jovica Stanišić and Franko Simatović*, Case No IT-03-69-A (awaiting appeal hearing); *Prosecutor v Jadranko Prlić et al.*, Case No IT-04-74-A (appeals in preparation).

[13] *Prosecutor v Radovan Karadžić*, Case No IT-95-5/18-PT, Prosecution's Marked-Up Indictment, 19 October 2009; *Prosecutor v Ratko Mladić*, Case No IT-09-92-PT, Prosecution Submission of the Fourth Amended Indictment and Schedules of Incidents, 16 December 2011.

[14] 'Mechanism for International Criminal Tribunals (MICT) begins work in The Hague,' available at http://www.unmict.org/news/2013/130701_PR10.html (accessed 5 December 2013).

affairs once the current trials and appeals are finished (scheduled for mid-2017) and our mandate comes to an end.[15]

The story of the ICTY is one of challenges as well as achievements. Both are important. From our experience, other courts, such as the ICC and STL, may be able to borrow ideas of what to do – and, sometimes, perhaps even what *not* to do. For we all confront the same basic problems: access to evidence, access to suspects, the challenges of conducting long and complex trials. And we are all agents of the international community, required to work within the political realities of international decision making. The ICC does, of course, face the unique challenge of working simultaneously and often at relatively short notice in many different situations. But it is no longer a new institution. It is now judged not just on its ability to assert jurisdiction over situations but on the basis of what it achieves: investigations, arrests, fair trials, judgments.

However, there is a paradox underlying these reflections about the contributions of international criminal justice to the rule of law. On the one hand, we have the view of the ICTY, a tribunal whose completion is drawing near and which can look back on two decades of accomplishments – as well as lessons learned. But, on the other, crimes every bit as serious as those in the former Yugoslavia appear to be taking place in the conflict in Syria. It is currently estimated that hundreds of thousands of people have been killed, 2.4 million people made refugees, and 6.5 million people displaced from their homes.[16] The international community is paralysed while the law in Syria has been silenced. There can be no greater demonstration of the importance of using the experience of our successes to address our failures, in order to further the realization of the rule of law.

---

15 See SC Res 1966 (22 December 2010), UN Doc S/RES/1966, *especially* paras 1, 3–4, 17, Annex 1 (MICT Statute), Annex 2 (Transitional Arrangements).

16 See eg Report of the Independent International Commission of Inquiry on the Syrian Arab Republic, UN Human Rights Council, 16 August 2013, UN Doc A/HRC/24/46, para 35 (estimating 1.85 million refugees); Press Statement of the Independent International Commission of Inquiry on the Syrian Arab Republic, 11 September 2013, available at http://www.ohchr.org/EN/NewsEvents/Pages/DisplayNews.aspx?NewsID=13708&LangID=E (accessed 5 December 2013) (estimating 'tens of thousands' killed and 6 million displaced from their homes).

II. CONTEXT: THE ICTY WAS CREATED AS A TOOL TO REASSERT THE RULE OF LAW

The starting point for any consideration of the ICTY's contribution to the rule of law must be its mandate.

The ICTY was established by the UN Security Council on 25 May 1993.[17] At this time, although serious crimes had already been committed in Croatia and across the Bosnian municipalities over the previous 12–18 months, the war was still in its early stages. It showed no sign of stopping. Yet the Security Council was convinced, as Resolution 827 states, that the existence of a body like the ICTY 'would contribute to the restoration and maintenance of peace'.[18] It believed that the existence of a body like the ICTY would not only be able to provide redress for violations of the law but that it would also be able to 'halt' ongoing crimes.[19] For a criminal court, this was a very ambitious mandate indeed.

Underlying the ICTY's mandate was an expansive – and radical – conception of the way in which a court can promote all aspects of the rule of law. Not only was the ICTY charged (like any court) with the duty of modelling and maintaining the rule of law through its own judicial proceedings, but, uniquely, it was also mandated to assist in *reasserting* the rule of law in a dynamic political situation where it had been lost. More than just a forum for hearing trials, the ICTY was also obliged to work cooperatively with the countries and people of the former Yugoslavia as they sought to strengthen the rule of law for themselves.[20] For this reason, although it is common to compare the

---

17 SC Res 827 (25 May 1993), UN Doc S/RES/827.

18 SC Res 827 (25 May 1993), UN Doc S/RES/827, Preamble ('Convinced that [...] the establishment [...] of an international tribunal [...] would contribute to the restoration and maintenance of peace').

19 SC Res 827 (25 May 1993), UN Doc S/RES/827, Preamble ('Believing that the establishment of an international tribunal [...] will contribute to ensuring that such violations are halted').

20 See eg SC Res 1503 (28 August 2003), UN Doc S/RES/1503, para 1 (calling 'on the international community to assist national jurisdictions, as part of the completion strategy, in improving their capacity to prosecute cases transferred from the ICTY and the ICTR and encourages the ICTY and ICTR Presidents, Prosecutors and Registrars to develop and improve their outreach programmes'); SC Res 1534 (26 March 2004), UN Doc S/RES/1534, para 9 (recalling 'that the strengthening of competent national judicial systems is crucially important to the rule of law in general and to the implementation of the ICTY and ICTR Completion Strategies in particular').

'primacy' jurisdiction of the ICTY with the 'complementarity' jurisdiction of the ICC,[21] the truth is a little more complicated. In reality, we at the ICTY are in the business of complementarity too. Like the so-called 'positive complementarity' idea at the ICC,[22] our mission includes assisting in the development of the rule of law in the former Yugoslavia, as a way to restore and maintain peace, and not just to hold individuals accountable.

In order for the ICTY to achieve its mandate, it was essential that it was – and was seen to be – a legitimate body. And in the context of the ICTY, legitimacy had two factors: the legality of its creation and its exercise of jurisdiction; and the fairness of its proceedings. These are the very principles we see underlying instruments such as Article 6 of the European Convention on Human Rights, which guarantees the right to a trial before a tribunal 'established by law'.[23] And again they are facets of the rule of law: to exercise jurisdiction, a tribunal must be part of the community which it judges. It is itself a subject of the law, and it must be bound by that law.

It is a sign of the ICTY's and the international community's commitment to the rule of law that scope exists for the legitimacy of the ICTY to be reasonably challenged. Indeed, the ICTY Appeals Chamber examined the legality of the ICTY's creation by the UN Security Council in one of its very earliest decisions, in the *Tadić* case.[24] It upheld the principle of 'competence-competence', that a tribunal must be empowered to consider

---

21 Compare ICTY Statute, as amended, September 2009, Art 9(2), with ICC Statute, as amended, 2011, Art 17.

22 See eg Burke-White, WW, 'Implementing a policy of positive complementarity in the Rome system of justice,' (2008) 19 *Criminal Law Forum* 59–85, at 61 ('From this systemic perspective, the ICC and its OTP may be seen as having a broader role in ending impunity by encouraging national governments to undertake their own investigations and prosecution of international crimes [...] [P]ositive complementarity[] refers to the potential for the ICC to contribute to the effective functioning of national judiciaries'). See further ICC, Office of the Prosecutor, Prosecutorial Strategy 2009-2012, 1 February 2010, available at http://www.icc-cpi.int/en_menus/icc/structure%20of%20the%20court/office%20of%20the%20prosecutor/policies%20and%20strategies/Pages/report%20on%20prosecutorial%20strategy.aspx (accessed 6 December 2013), paras 15–17.

23 European Convention on Human Rights, Art 6(1). *See also* American Convention on Human Rights, Art 8(1); International Covenant on Civil and Political Rights, Art 14(1).

24 *Prosecutor v Duško Tadić*, Case No IT-94-1, Decision on the Defence Motion for Interlocutory Appeal on Jurisdiction, 2 October 1995.

the legality of its own creation in order to ensure that it acts fairly.[25] And it is a testament to the abiding importance of this rule of law principle that the Appeals Chamber for the Special Tribunal for Lebanon engaged in the same exercise (and on a very similar issue) more than 15 years later.[26]

Challenges to the legitimacy of the ICTY are not just a legal matter. Part of the challenge of our work is communicating our mission and our values with the people of the former Yugoslavia.[27] This remains, 20 years on, a work in progress. In 2013, the UN General Assembly hosted a controversial debate on the 'Role of International Criminal Justice in Reconciliation', in which the ICTY was prominently discussed. In that debate, the President of Serbia, Tomislav Nikolić, criticized the ICTY as biased against Serbs and stated his belief that it will never reach 'the real truth'.[28] I disagree with both of President Nikolić's assertions, and do not think they are well informed. However, whatever opinion one may hold, the debate showed that 'acceptance' of the ICTY and its rulings is still an issue in some communities, even 20 years on. It is vital that the UN is and continues to be a forum where the realities of international justice can be measured against our hopes for it – even if this debate missed the opportunity to contribute much of substance to the real issues with which it might have engaged.

---

[25] Ibid., paras 18–22.

[26] *Prosecutor v Salim Ayyash et al.*, Case No STL-11-01/PT/AC/AR90.1, Decision on the Defence Appeals against the Trial Chamber's 'Decision on the Defence Challenges to the Jurisdiction and Legality of the Tribunal', 24 October 2012. *See also Prosecutor v Salim Ayyash et al.*, Case No STL-11-01/PT/TC, Decision on the Defence Challenges to the Jurisdiction and Legality of the Tribunal, 27 July 2012.

[27] See SC Res 1503 (28 August 2003), UN Doc S/RES/1503, para 1.

[28] See eg Balkan Insight, Ristić, M, BIRN, 'Serbia Slams Hague Tribunal at UN Debate,' 11 April 2013, available at http://www.balkaninsight.com/en/article/un-debate-turns-as-criticism-of-the-icty (accessed 5 December 2013). See also Permanent Mission of the Republic of Serbia to the United Nations, Recent Statements, April 2013, Statement by HE Mr Tomislav Nikolić, President of the Republic of Serbia, UN General Assembly, Thematic Debate: Role of International Criminal Justice in Reconciliation, 10 April 2013, available at http://www.un.int/serbia/rstatements.html (accessed 5 December 2013).

III. CASE SELECTION

Before considering the legal developments contained in the ICTY's extensive body of jurisprudence, it is appropriate to first focus on the cases themselves and, in particular, the process by which cases are selected for investigation and prosecution. Given the guarantee of equal protection implicit in the rule of law, international tribunals like the ICTY must have a reasoned basis upon which they select their cases.[29]

A. The ICTY has Issued Many Indictments but it Cannot Prosecute Every Perpetrator

The ICTY has issued 161 indictments.[30] This is more than any other international tribunal – and, potentially, more than any other international tribunal is ever likely to issue. Yet even so, it leaves a considerable number of cases to be prosecuted by other authorities. In Bosnia and Herzegovina alone, some 800 war crimes cases against more than 2,500 alleged perpetrators remain to be prosecuted. Given the scale of the crimes in the former Yugoslavia, no institution could hope to alone address them all. And other international courts and tribunals seized of international crimes are likely to face the same challenge. Yet if we consider that the rule of law requires us to end impunity, and to ensure that all society has equal access to justice, how do we reconcile the practical need for an institution like the ICTY to make choices and to be selective?

The answer is that international criminal justice must be seen as *part* of the accountability process but not the *entirety* of it. It is equally important that national capacity is developed and that there is a process by which the international institution can work with and assist national institutions. This is not just a matter of pragmatism; as I have said, this kind of 'positive complementarity' is a vital aspect of our work in rebuilding the rule of law where it has been lost or diminished. Indeed, this need for international and national partnership is one of the aspects of the recent General Assembly debate with which I agree.[31] Yet it must

---

[29] Cf Cryer, R, *Prosecuting International Crimes: Selectivity and the International Criminal Law Regime* (Cambridge University Press, 2005) at 194–9.

[30] See ICTY, Infographic: ICTY Facts & Figures, available at http://www.icty.org/sid/11186 (accessed 5 December 2013).

[31] See eg UN Secretary-General Ban Ki-Moon, Latest Statements, Secretary-General's Remarks to General Assembly thematic debate on the Role

not be assumed that national processes are a cheap or easy alternative to international processes – not only are national processes a *complement* to international justice rather than a replacement, they often require considerable financial support and expertise transfer from other members of the international community.

B. Targeting of Indictments

If we accept that an international tribunal must be selective in the number of cases that it investigates or prosecutes, then the question remains as to *how* selective? And by *what criteria* does it select?

There appears to be some consensus today that international prosecutions should focus on the highest level perpetrators, those who are considered to be 'most responsible'.[32] This notion clearly informs the practice of institutions such as the ICC, which operates a very selective policy about the indictments it issues, and tends to target its investigations at the leadership level from an early stage.[33] However, although this

---

of International Criminal Justice in Reconciliation, 10 April 2013, available at http://www.un.org/sg/statements/index.asp?nid=6726 (accessed 5 December 2013) ('both the ICTY and the ICTR have transferred cases to national jurisdictions. Such transfers help to ensure justice. They also facilitate the building of strong and independent domestic legal systems in which the rule of law flourishes'); EU Statement – United Nations General Assembly: Thematic Debate on the Role of International Criminal Justice in Reconciliation, 10 April 2013, available at http://www.eu-un.europa.eu/articles/en/article_13382_en.htm (accessed 5 December 2013) ('national judicial institutions are not always able to address some or all international crimes that were committed [...] The Rome Statute embodies a system where national and international court work together in an interdependent manner').

[32] See eg Law on Amendments [...] [to] the Law on the Establishment of the Extraordinary Chambers in the Courts of Cambodia for the Prosecution of Crimes Committed During the Period of Democratic Kampuchea, 2004, Art 2; SCSL Statute, 2002, Art 1. But see STL Statute, 2007, Art 1. Compare ICTY Statute, Art.1 ('The International Tribunal shall have the power to prosecute persons responsible for serious violations of international humanitarian law'), with SC Res 1534 (26 March 2004), UN Doc S/RES/1534, para 5 (calling on the ICTY and ICTR, in reviewing and confirming new indictments, 'to ensure that any such indictments concentrate on those most senior leaders suspected of being most responsible').

[33] Compare ICC Statute, as amended, 2011, Art 1 (the ICC 'shall have the power to exercise its jurisdiction over persons for the most serious crimes of international concern'), with ICC, Office of the Prosecutor, Paper on Some Policy Issues before the Office of the Prosecutor, September 2003, available at

approach is economical, there are a number of practical considerations which might suggest that a slightly broader approach is likely to be more effective. This has been the experience of the ICTY.

International criminal tribunals may often be concerned with situations in which the relevant states or regions are difficult to access. This may be due to ongoing conflict, or uncooperative local authorities. In these circumstances, not only may investigative activities be more difficult, but so also will be the process of taking an indictee into custody. This applies particularly if the indictee is a high-level individual.

---

http://www.icc-cpi.int/nr/rdonlyres/1fa7c4c6-de5f-42b7-8b25-60aa962ed8b6/143594/030905_policy_paper.pdf (accessed 6 December 2013), p 3 (the OTP:

> will initiate prosecutions of the leaders who bear most responsibility for the crimes. [...] In some cases the focus of an investigation by the Office of the Prosecutor may go wider than high-ranking officers if, for example, investigation of certain types of crimes or those officers lower down the chain of command is necessary for the whole case);

ICC, Office of the Prosecutor, Report on Prosecutorial Strategy, 14 September 2006, available at http://www.icc-cpi.int/en_menus/icc/structure%20of%20the%20court/office%20of%20the%20prosecutor/policies%20and%20strategies/Pages/report%20on%20prosecutorial%20strategy.aspx (accessed 6 December 2013), para 2(b) ('The second principle guiding the Prosecutorial Strategy is that of focused investigations and prosecutions. Based on the Statute, the Office adopted a policy of focusing its effort on the most serious crimes and on those who bear the greatest responsibility for these crimes'). But see *Situation in the Democratic Republic of the Congo*, Case No ICC-01/04-169, Judgement on the Prosecutor's Appeal against the Decision of Pre-Trial Chamber I entitled 'Decision on the Prosecutor's Application for Warrants of Arrest, Article 58,' 13 July 2006, paras 73–79, especially 74 ('The imposition of rigid standards primarily based on top seniority may result in neither retribution nor prevention being achieved'), 77 ('individuals who are not at the very top of an organization may still carry considerable influence and commit, or generate the widespread commission of, very serious crimes [...] [P]redetermination of inadmissibility on the above grounds could easily lead to the automatic exclusion of perpetrators of most serious crimes in the future'), 79

> (the Preamble to the Rome Statute mentions 'most serious crimes' but not 'most serious perpetrators'. [...] The reference in paragraph five of the Preamble to 'perpetrators' is not prefixed by the delineation 'most serious' or 'most responsible'. Such language does not appear elsewhere in the Statute in relation to the category of perpetrators. Had the drafters of the Statute intended to limit its application to only the most serious leaders suspected of being most responsible they could have done so expressly.)

At the ICTY, we found that a combination of 'top down'[34] and 'bottom up'[35] approaches delivered the best results. This enabled us to begin our work – at a time when we confronted the most significant barriers to access and cooperation – by prosecuting lower-level individuals over whom it was easier to obtain custody, and who might potentially plead guilty and even be 'flipped' to assist in our investigations. Over time, as our knowledge base grew and circumstances became more favourable for securing evidence and indictees, we were able to implement a prosecution strategy which was more representative of the scope and scale of the crimes as a whole, and which targeted leadership perpetrators. Smaller cases, or those involving lower-level perpetrators, could be transferred back to the region.[36]

A closely-related question concerns what crimes we indict a person *for*. Early on, our approach was to make each indictment as comprehensive as possible. In principle, this gives the fullest representation of the nature and scale of the crimes for which we believe a person is responsible. Yet such large indictments can also create a risk that no findings on responsibility will be made for any crimes. For example, Slobodan Milošević died midway through his trial for extensive crimes committed in Bosnia and Herzegovina, Croatia and Kosovo over an

[34] For example, the Prosecution has indicted both political and military leadership figures. These have included the most senior military officers in the armies of Serbia, Republika Srpska, Bosnia and Herzegovina, and Herceg-Bosna, as well as senior military officers in the army of Croatia: *Prosecutor v Dragoljub Ojdanić*, Case No IT-05-87; *Prosecutor v Momčilo Perišić*, Case No IT-04-81; *Prosecutor v Ratko Madić*, Case No IT-09-92; *Prosecutor v Rasim Delić*, Case No IT-04-83; *Prosecuor v Milivoj Petković*, Case No IT-04-74; *Prosecutor v Ante Gotovina and Mladen Markač*, Case No IT-06-90. The Prosecution has also indicted a wide variety of political leaders: eg *Prosecutor v Slobodan Milošević*, Case No IT-02-54; *Prosecutor v Radovan Karadžić*, Case No IT-95-5/18; *Prosecutor v Momčilo Krajišnik*, Case No IT-00-39; *Prosecutor v Milan Martić*, Case No IT-95-11; *Prosecutor v Milan Babić*, Case No IT-03-72; *Prosecutor v Biljana Plavšić*, Case No IT-00-39&40/1; *Prosecutor v Jadranko Prlić*, Case No IT-04-74; *Prosecutor v Slobodan Praljak*, Case No IT-04-74; *Prosecutor v Vojislav Šešelj*, Case No IT-03-67; *Prosecutor v Milan Milutinović*, Case No IT-05-87; *Prosecutor v Nikola Šainović*, Case No IT-05-87.

[35] For example, the Prosecution has indicted notorious physical perpetrators such as Milan Lukić, Goran Jelišić and Dragan Nikolić for crimes in Višegrad, Brčko, and Sušica Camp respectively: *Prosecutor v Milan Lukić and Sredoje Lukić*, Case No IT-98-32/1; *Prosecutor v Goran Jelišić*, Case No IT-95-10; *Prosecutor v Dragan Nikolić*, Case No IT-94-2.

[36] See below n100.

eight-year period.[37] We have to balance the representational value of an indictment, therefore, against considerations of practicality. We saw this recently when Ratko Mladić was arrested, in advanced age and experiencing some health difficulties. First, we requested that his case be split into two separate indictments, so the process of delivering a verdict on one could be started before the evidence was heard on the other. After deliberation, the Chamber refused this request.[38] So, instead, we decided to trim the existing indictment to make it more manageable – while ensuring that it remained representative by taking into account factors such as gender, geography and temporal scope.[39]

C. Investigations and Conflict Prevention

One other point is apposite to the issue of case selection. As previously discussed, the UN Security Council tasked the ICTY not just with investigating and providing redress for crimes, but also with *halting* them.

History, of course, tells us that some of the most high-profile crimes in the former Yugoslavia were committed well after the establishment of the ICTY: the genocidal killing of 8,000 Bosnian Muslim men and boys was committed at Srebrenica in 1995; the enforced displacement of up to 700,000 Kosovo Albanians was committed in 1999. At first glance, one might think that the ICTY clearly did not deter or halt these crimes. But, equally, we cannot know what potential crimes might have been deterred or mitigated by ICTY activities. At the very least, the evidence tells us that actors in the former Yugoslavia were mindful of future investigation – after the crimes in both Srebrenica and Kosovo, we saw sophisticated

---

[37] See *Prosecutor v Slobodan Milošević*, Case No IT-02-54-T, Order Terminating the Proceedings, 14 March 2006 (terminating proceedings after 467 trial days). See further *Prosecutor v Slobodan Milošević*, Case No IT-02-54-T, Second Amended Indictment (Croatia), 28 July 2004; *Prosecutor v Slobodan Milošević*, Case No IT-02-54-T, Amended Indictment (Bosnia and Herzegovina), 22 November 2002; *Prosecutor v Slobodan Milošević et al.*, Case No IT-99-37-PT, Second Amended Indictment (Kosovo), 16 October 2001.

[38] *Prosecutor v Ratko Mladić*, Case No IT-09-92-PT, Decision on Consolidated Prosecution Motion to Sever the Indictment, to Conduct Separate Trials, and to Amend the Indictment, 13 October 2011.

[39] See eg *Prosecutor v Ratko Mladić*, Case No IT-09-92-PT, Prosecution Submission of the Fourth Amended Indictment and Schedules of Incidents, 16 December 2011, para 4.

attempts to conceal the evidence.[40] Likewise, during the conflict, officials of the Tribunal took steps to warn the parties to comply with the law – and to assure them of future accountability – by means including the circulation of draft indictments, private communications, and public hearings.[41] These measures may all have had an effect.

IV. JURISPRUDENCE

The ICTY is distinctive for the quality, breadth and erudition of the vast majority of its case law. This tradition contributes to the rule of law by the progressive elucidation of the law's meaning, contributing not only to the cases which fall within the ICTY's mandate but to international criminal law as a whole. Two key themes in the ICTY's jurisprudence are especially prominent: an emphasis on the legal mechanisms by which individual responsibility can be imposed for what are often enormous and complex crimes and a clarification of the concrete elements of offences under customary international law.

A. An Emphasis on Individualizing Responsibility for Crimes

Perhaps the most notable theme we have seen in the ICTY caselaw is the judicial emphasis on explaining how, even in the most complicated situations, an individual is (or is not) responsible for crimes which are committed. We call these doctrines 'modes of liability'. Concern with

---

[40] See eg *Prosecutor v Vidoje Blagojević and Dragan Jokić (Blagojević and Jokić)*, Case No IT-02-60-T, Judgement, 17 January 2005, paras 380–390, *especially* para 382 (describing efforts to conceal crimes, opining 'that the opening of the mass graves and the reburial of the victims in other locations was an attempt to conceal the evidence of the mass killings'); *Prosecutor v Milan Milutinović et al.*, Case No IT-05-87-T, Judgement, 26 February 2009, vol 2, paras 1263–1357, especially paras 1356–57 (describing efforts to conceal crimes, determining the existence of a "clandestine operation" and "institutional cover-up" to "conceal over 700 bodies scattered throughout Kosovo from both citizens of the FRY and Serbia, and from the international community, including this Tribunal and NATO ground forces'). See also *Prosecutor v Vlastimir Đorđević (Đorđević)*, Case No IT-05-87/1-T, Judgement, 23 February 2011, paras 1290–1366, 1967–1982; *Prosecutor v Vujadin Popović et al. (Popović et al.)*, Case No IT-05-88-T, Judgement, 10 June 2010, paras 600–606.

[41] Eg ICTY, Rules of Procedure and Evidence, Rule 61 ('Procedure in Case of Failure to Execute a Warrant'). Rule 61 hearings were held for accused including Radovan Karadžić, Ratko Mladić, Ivica Rajić, Mile Mrkšić, Miroslav Radić, Veselin Šljivančanin, and Dragan Nikolić.

this issue again lies at the heart of the rule of law, in the 'principle of culpability':[42] the innocent should go free; only the guilty should be punished. And we have to be able to explain in a reasoned way the difference between the two.

Although the basic principle sounds obvious, sorting out who is legally responsible for a crime is often not an easy job. It is now commonly understood, I think, that the man who pulls the trigger is sometimes only a small part of a much bigger picture. Identifying the links between a 'crime' and its masterminds can be very difficult, since these links are often subtle. They may draw upon a person's legitimate functions or the activities of public institutions. Sometimes, they may even rely upon or be concealed by other organized criminal activity. Hundreds or even thousands of people might be involved, many of them mere tools or functionaries, working in different places and at different times. Just discovering these links is a huge investigative challenge. Yet we also require the law to explain these links in a rational way, which serves the need to punish international crimes yet respects the essential importance of the right to a fair trial. The cases of the Tribunal have made great strides in explaining the doctrines which govern this process, as they exist in customary international law.[43]

There are three particular developments in the law governing the responsibility of individuals for crimes committed by others which I would like to discuss.

The first is 'Joint Criminal Enterprise', or 'JCE'. Of any doctrine established by the Tribunal, this has been the most controversial.[44] Yet it has also been consistently upheld by other international or hybrid courts

---

42 See *Prosecutor v Duško Tadić (Tadić)*, Case No IT-94-1-A, Judgement, 15 July 1999, para 186; *Sylvestre Gacumbitsi v the Prosecutor*, Case No ICTR-2001-64-A, Judgement, 7 July 2006, Separate Opinion of Judge Shahabuddeen, para 43.

43 See eg *Prosecutor v Milan Milutinović et al. (Milutinović et al.)*, Case No IT-99-37-AR72, Decision on Dragoljub Ojdanić's Motion Challenging Jurisdiction – Joint Criminal Enterprise, 21 May 2003, para 21.

44 As a very limited sample of writings on JCE, see eg Schomburg, W, 'Jurisprudence on JCE – revisiting a never ending story,' 2010, available at http://www.brandeis.edu/ethics/pdfs/internationaljustice/Schomburg1.pdf (accessed 16 December 2013); Cassese, A, 'The proper limits of responsibility under the doctrine of Joint Criminal Enterprise,' (2007) 5 *Journal of International Criminal Justice* 109; Ambos, K, 'Joint Criminal Enterprise and command responsibility,' (2007) 5 *Journal of International Criminal Justice* 159; Badar, ME, 'Just convict everyone! Joint perpetration: from *Tadić* to *Stakić* and back again,' (2006) 6 *International Criminal Law Review* 293; Danner, AM, & Martinez, JS, 'Guilty

and tribunals such as the ICTR (Rwanda),[45] the SCSL (Sierra Leone),[46] the ECCC (Cambodia),[47] and the STL (Lebanon).[48]

In simple terms, the JCE doctrine explains that a person who joins with others to commit a common criminal plan – and therefore intends the planned crimes – does not have to achieve every part of that criminal plan by themselves. All they have to do is make a 'significant contribution' to the plan with the necessary intent.[49] This idea is not new. National legal systems have had their own doctrines to achieve a similar result for many years.[50] And likewise in the *Tadić* case, when the concept of JCE was first explained, the Judges of the Tribunal emphasized the links with cases dating back to the Second World War.[51] There is no doubt, as the *Tadić* Appeals Chamber declared, that JCE exists in customary international law.[52] And as the ECCC in Cambodia has ruled more recently, it has existed in some form since at least 1975.[53]

---

associations: Joint Criminal Enterprise, command responsibility and the development of International Criminal Law,' (2005) 93 *California Law Review* 75; Powles, S, 'Joint Criminal Enterprise: criminal liability by prosecutorial ingenuity and judicial creativity,' (2004) 2 *Journal of International Criminal Justice* 606.

45 See eg *Prosecutor v Edouard Karemera et al.*, Case Nos ICTR-98-44-AR72.5, ICTR-98-44-AR72.6, Decision on Jurisdictional Appeals: Joint Criminal Enterprise, 12 April 2006, paras 13, 16.

46 See eg *Prosecutor v Issa Hassan Sesay et al.*, Case No SCSL-04-15-A, Judgment, 26 October 2009, para 283.

47 See eg Case No.002/19-09-2007-ECCC/OCIJ (PTC38), Decision on the Appeals against the Co-Investigative Judges Orders on Joint Criminal Enterprise (JCE), 20 May 2010, paras 50–89, especially paras 73, 83, 88; Case No 002/19-09-2007-ECCC/TC, Decision on the Applicability of Joint Criminal Enterprise, 12 September 2011, para 38.

48 See eg Case NoSTL-11-01/I, Interlocutory Decision on the Applicable Law: Terrorism, Conspiracy, Homicide, Perpetration, Cumulative Charging, 16 February 2011, paras 236–252, 264, *especially* para 236.

49 See eg *Prosecutor v Momcilo Krajišnik (Krajišnik)*, Case No IT-00-39-A, Judgement, 17 March 2009, paras 215, 675; *Prosecutor v Radoslav Brđanin (Brđanin)*, Case No IT-99-36-A, Judgement, 3 April 2007, para 430.

50 See eg *Tadić*, above n42, para 224.

51 See eg ibid., paras 195–219.

52 See eg ibid, para 220 ('the notion of common design as a form of accomplice liability is firmly established in customary international law'). *See further Milutinović et al.*, above n43.

53 See eg Case No 002/19-09-2007-ECCC/OCIJ (PTC38), Decision on the Appeals against the Co-Investigative Judges Orders on Joint Criminal Enterprise (JCE), 20 May 2010, paras 46, 69, 83 (holding that JCE I and JCE II were recognized in customary international law in 1975, but not JCE III).

Although the basic idea sounds simple, JCE is a highly effective tool for charging and prosecuting international crimes. This is because it is flexible enough to accommodate the complex structures by which many international crimes are committed. For example, since the days of *Tadić*, the ICTY's Appeals Chamber has recognized an 'extended' form of JCE which covers crimes which were not part of the plan yet were 'foreseeable' as a consequence of the plan.[54] In other words, crimes which were not intended by the JCE member, but which were known to be a possible further consequence of their contribution to the JCE.[55] This aspect of JCE doctrine recognizes the significant likelihood that international crimes, once started, will escalate – and that the leadership should be accountable for that. A classic example from many of our cases is where JCE members agree on a plan to violently deport persons of a certain ethnicity – but additional crimes such as murder were committed in the execution of that plan. In this example, the JCE member would not only be responsible for the deportation which they had planned but also for the murder, which they foresaw as a possible consequence of their plan.

Likewise, the ICTY has recognized that the way in which an influential or powerful person may contribute to a JCE lies in their use of other people as 'tools'.[56] So, a General who joins a JCE may not go out and commit a murder himself. But he may well instruct the forces under his command to do so, or to lend practical assistance to those who do. More recent cases (such as *Brđanin*, *Martić* and *Krajišnik*) reflect that it is not always easy to determine what it means to 'use' another person[57] – sometimes, there is a direct order; other times, it may be necessary to draw inferences from the circumstances.

Second, the ICTY has also clarified that an individual may commit a crime, or contribute to the commission of a crime, through an omission as well as a positive act.[58] The cases at the ICTY have underlined, quite rightly, that an omission is only punishable when it is proven that the

---

54 See eg *Tadić*, above n42, paras 220, 227–8.

55 See *Prosecutor v Radovan Karadžić*, Case No IT-95-5/18-AR72.4, Decision on Prosecution's Motion Appealing Trial Chamber's Decision on JCE III Foreseeability, 25 June 2009, para 18.

56 *See Brđanin*, above n49, paras 362, 391–2, 404–414, especially 414.

57 See eg *Brđanin*, ibid, paras 410–413, 430; *Prosecutor v Milan Martić*, Case No IT-95-11-A, Judgement, 8 October 2008, paras 168–169, 182–215; *Krajišnik*, above n49, paras 225–226, 235–84.

58 See *Tadić*, above n42, para 188; *Prosecutor v Tihomir Blaškić (Blaškić)*, Case No IT-95-14-A, Judgement, 29 July 2004, paras 47, 663; *Prosecutor v Stanislav Galić*, Case No IT-98-29-A, Judgement, 30 November 2006, para 175; *Brđanin*, above n49, para 274;

accused had a duty to act, the ability to act and they failed in that duty.[59] Omission liability is important since many international crimes reflect not only the bad acts of a few but also the failings of those in positions of power, whether through cowardice or malice. These failings may not always be the only factor leading to a crime – but even where they only facilitate it, with knowledge of the consequences, then there should be accountability.

In the *Mrkšić* case, the ICTY Appeals Chamber confirmed this very principle. It considered that a military officer with custody of prisoners of war has a positive duty to assure themselves that those prisoners will be safe if they are transferred to the custody of another person.[60] If the military officer fails in that duty, knowing of the likelihood that those prisoners will be murdered, then the officer aids and abets those murders.[61] This judgment, which clarifies long-established principles of international humanitarian law and criminal law, is an excellent example of how a court can not only make law practical and accessible, but also how by so doing it can materially increase the protection afforded to the victims of armed conflict.

Related to the idea of omissions is the concept of superior responsibility. For more than 80 years, international law has recognized that a military commander bears some sort of criminal responsibility for the conduct of the troops under their command. Landmark cases after the Second World War – such as the *High Command* and *Hostages* cases at Nuremberg,[62] and the *Yamashita* case at the US Supreme Court[63] – established the skeleton of this form of responsibility. But at the Tribunal,

---

[59] See *Prosecutor v Naser Orić (Orić)*, Case No IT-03-68-A, Judgement, 3 July 2008, para 43; *Prosecutor v Mile Mrkšić and Veselin Šljivančanin (Mrkšić and Šljivančanin)*, Case No IT-95-13/1-A, Judgment, 5 May 2009, para 81.

[60] Ibid., paras 69–74.

[61] Ibid, paras 81–103. *But see Prosecutor v Veselin Šljivančanin*, Case No IT-95-13/1-R.1, Review Judgment, 8 December 2010, para 32 (reversing Šljivančanin's conviction for aiding and abetting murder by omission on the basis of fresh evidence).

[62] See *Trial of Wilhelm von Leeb and Thirteen Others*, Trials of War Criminals before the Nuremberg Military Tribunals under Control Council Law No 10, vol XI (Washington DC: US Government Printing Office, 1950), Judgment, pp 462–697; *Trial of Wilhelm List and Others*, Trials of War Criminals before the Nuremberg Military Tribunals under Control Council Law No 10, Vol XI (Washington DC: US Government Printing Office, 1950), Judgment, pp 1230–319.

[63] See *In re Yamashita*, 327 US 1 (1946). *See also Trial of General Tomoyuki Yamashita*, US Military Commission (Manila), 7 December 1945, Law

where jurisdiction to punish superiors for their failure to prevent or punish the crimes of their subordinates is expressly included in our Statute,[64] flesh has been added to the bones. In particular, our cases have set 'effective control' as the touchstone for proving a superior–subordinate relationship.[65] They have underlined that, although a superior need not intend their subordinates' crimes, they must either know of them or have reason to know of them.[66] That standard is more than mere negligence.[67] And they have confirmed that superior responsibility is not just a matter for military commanders but is equally applicable to civilian leaders, provided that the superior-subordinate relationship is proven.[68] Mere political influence is not enough.[69]

The importance of superior responsibility cannot be overstated. An ICRC study called 'The roots of behaviour in war', based on a survey of some 15,000 civilians and combatants in 15 war zones, concluded that the single most important step to promote compliance with the law of war is influence over the people who are in charge.[70] Criminal liability for superiors' failure to ensure that compliance sends a very clear message. Yet it must be acknowledged that, although we have frequently charged superior responsibility at the ICTY, the number of convictions we have obtained has been relatively low.[71] This is partly because where

---

Reports of Trials of War Criminals, Selected and Prepared by UN War Crimes Commission, Vol IV (London: His Majesty's Stationery Office, 1948), pp 1–37.

64 ICTY Statute, as amended, September 2009, Art 7(3).

65 See eg *Prosecutor v Zejnil Delalić et al. (Delalić et al.)*, Case No IT-96-21-A, Judgement, 20 February 2001, paras 196–7; *Prosecutor v Sefer Halilović (Halilović)*, Case No IT-01-48-A, Judgement, 16 October 2007, para 59; *Orić*, above n59, paras 91–2.

66 See *Delalić et al.*, ibid, paras 222, 228–39, 241.

67 See *Blaškić*, above n58, paras 62–4. See also *Delalić et al.*, ibid, para 226.

68 See *Delalić et al.*, ibid, paras 195–6, 240. *But see further Prosecutor v Ignace Bagilishema*, Case No ICTR-95-1A-A, Judgement (Reasons), 3 July 2002, paras 50–5.

69 See *Delalić et al.*, ibid, paras 257–66.

70 See Muñoz-Rojas, D, & Frésard, J, 'The roots of behaviour in war: understanding and prevent IHL violations,' (March 2004) 86(853) *International Review of the Red Cross* 189 at 204 ('For the ICRC and other humanitarian organizations, the main thing is not to persuade combatants that they must behave in a different way, or to win them over personally, but rather to influence the people who have an ascendancy over them').

71 See eg *Prosecutor v Jadranko Prlić et al. (Prlić et al.)*, Case No IT-04-74-T, Judgement, 29 May 2013, vol 4, paras 1245–52 (convicting Ćorić pursuant to superior responsibility); *Prosecutor v Momčilo Perišić*, Case No

a person is found responsible both on the basis of their own criminal contribution but also as a superior, it is the practice of the Tribunal to enter convictions only for the former.[72] In this scenario, their additional superior responsibility should instead be taken into account in sentencing.[73] But the lower conviction rate may also be explained by the difficulties of proving elements such as effective control in factual circumstances that are often chaotic or hard to identify with structures of control from everyday life.

B. Elaborating Crimes, Such as Offences of Sexual and Gender-based Violence

In addition to modes of liability, the other major area in which the ICTY has clarified the law is in the definition of the elements of international crimes themselves. The important issue of sexual and gender based violence is just one area in which the ICTY has clarified the law. In so

---

IT-04-81-A, Judgement, 28 February 2013, paras 119–20 (reversing conviction pursuant to superior responsibility); *Prosecutor v Ante Gotovina and Mladen Markač*, Case No IT-06-90-A, Judgement, 16 November 2012, paras 136, 157 (declining, by majority, to enter convictions pursuant to superior responsibility as an alternate mode of liability); *Popović et al.*, above n40, paras 2107, 2110 (convicting Borovčanin and Pandurević pursuant to superior responsibility); *Prosecutor v Ljube Boškoski and Johan Tarčulovski*, Case No IT-04-82-A, Judgement, 19 May 2010, paras 224–73 (upholding Boškoski's acquittal pursuant to superior responsibility); *Prosecutor v Dragomir Milošević*, Case No IT-98-29/1-A, Judgement, 12 November 2009, para 282 (entering convictions pursuant to superior responsibility as an alternate mode of liability); *Prosecutor v Rasim Delić*, Case No IT-04-83-T, Judgement, 15 September 2008, para 557 (convicting Delić pursuant to superior responsibility); *Orić*, above n59, paras 77–8, 180–1 (reversing conviction pursuant to superior responsibility); *Prosecutor v Enver Hadžihasanović and Amir Kubura*, Case No IT-01-47-A, Judgement, 22 April 2008, paras 155, 164, 231–2, 272 (reversing in part Hadžihasanović and Kubura's convictions pursuant to superior responsibility); *Halilović*, above n65, paras 198–217 (upholding acquittal pursuant to superior responsibility); *Prosecutor v Pavle Strugar*, Case No IT-01-42-T, Judgement, 31 January 2005, para 446 (convicting Strugar pursuant to superior responsibility); *Blaškić*, above n58, Disposition (reversing in part convictions pursuant to superior responsibility); *Delalić et al.*, above n65, paras 214, 312–14 (upholding Mučić's conviction pursuant to superior responsibility and Delić's acquittal pursuant to superior responsibility).

72 *Blaškić*, above n58, para 91. See eg *Đorđević*, above n40, para 2195.

73 See *Blaškić*, above n58, para 91. *See further* ICTR, *Ephrem Setako v the Prosecutor*, Case No ICTR-04-81-A, Judgement, 28 September 2011, paras 266, 268.

doing, it has also contributed to an important re-evaluation of the role that gender plays in international crime.

Crimes of sexual violence, both as war crimes and crimes against humanity, have been part of international criminal law for decades. Yet cases at the ICTY, as well as those at the ICTR, have seen the jurisprudence develop rapidly and place the prohibition of sexual and gender-based violence on a sounder footing. Landmark judgements include *Furundžija* (which provided an international definition of rape and recognized that rape can amount to an act of genocide);[74] the '*Čelebići*' trial (which confirmed that rape qualifies as a form of torture);[75] and *Kunarac* (which considered sexual enslavement and rape as crimes against humanity).[76] Various cases at the Tribunal have also imposed convictions for sexual violence committed against men.[77] The Tribunal's work in prosecuting crimes of sexual violence is important because these crimes are often seen as 'opportunistic' or 'side effects' of conflict. Yet the cases have come to show that sexual violence is in fact used as a tool of ethnic cleansing and may play a central role in that criminal process.

V. INTERNATIONAL JUSTICE IS A COOPERATIVE PROJECT

The rule of law does not mean the rule of lawyers.[78] It is also crucial to recall the various ways in which international criminal justice requires

---

[74] *Prosecutor v Anto Furundžija*, Case No IT-95-17/1-T, Judgement, 10 December 1998, paras 164–86.

[75] *Prosecutor v Zejnil Delalić et al. (Čelebići)*, Case No IT-96-21-T, Judgement, 16 November 1998, paras 475–96.

[76] *Prosecutor v Dragoljub Kunarac et al.*, Case Nos IT-96-23-T and IT-96-23/1-T, Judgement, 22 February 2001, paras 436–64, 515–543.

[77] See eg *Prosecutor v Duško Tadić*, Case No IT-94-1-T, Opinion and Judgement, 7 May 1997, paras 198, 206, 237, 242, 726; *Čelebići*, paras 1062–6, 1072; *Prosecutor v Stevan Todorović*, Case No IT-95-9/1-S, Sentencing Judgement, 31 July 2001, paras 37–40, 64, 66, 113; *Prosecutor v Milan Simić*, Case No IT-95-9/2-S, Sentencing Judgement, 17 October 2002, paras 4, 11, 54, 63; *Prosecutor v Ranko Češić*, Case No IT-95-10/1-S, Sentencing Judgement, 11 March 2004, paras 13–14, 35–6, 52–4, 107.

[78] See Gleeson, M, 'Courts and the Rule of Law', lecture at Melbourne University, 7 November 2001, available at http://www.hcourt.gov.au/assets/publications/speeches/former-justices/gleesoncj/cj_ruleoflaw.htm (accessed on 12 December 2013) ('the rule of law does not necessitate an ever-expanding role for

organizations such as the ICTY to work with a range of other actors and through means other than litigation.

The need for international criminal courts and tribunals to have a good relationship with the international community is obvious. In order for international criminal justice to be effective *in* the courtroom, it requires cooperation *out* of the courtroom with states and those who govern them. Only states have the power to deliver much of the support which a court or tribunal needs to function. So, it means finding a way to work with political organs and politicians in order to obtain state assistance. And therefore it means that international courts and tribunals sometimes need to work by negotiation and consensus. The experience of the ICTY demonstrates the paradox that the rule of law is rarely secured simply by the *force* of law. Instead, it often depends on the *voluntary* cooperation of the community which the rule of law serves and protects. This is especially true when confronting states or individuals seeking to obstruct legal proceedings.

The experience of the ICTY has shown a number of areas in which we depended on state assistance to meet our objectives. These considerations will be common to most international court and tribunals and point the way to the expertise and policy which needs to be set in order to further enhance the rule of law. Furthermore, difficulties in achieving state cooperation often mean evidentiary difficulties which have real effects on the progress of trials. Defence teams, not unreasonably, will attempt to take advantage of any reasonable doubts that may arise from the issues surrounding independent access to evidence.

A. Conduct of Investigations, Access to Documents, etc

The first challenge faced by an international prosecutor is limited or no access to the crime scene. It seems obvious that when atrocities are committed, it is important to get people on the ground immediately to secure crimes scenes and to safeguard critical evidence. But identifying, collecting and preserving evidence in conflict zones is fraught with problems. When the ICTY was established, access was limited, particularly in the Republika Srpska, where many of the crimes we were investigating were committed. There were no security services available to accompany ICTY investigators in the field or to secure crime scenes on our behalf. At that time UNPROFOR was present, but apart from

---

the courts and the legal profession in the affairs of governments and citizens. And the rule of law does not mean rule by lawyers').

providing security within Sarajevo and some other areas, they could do little to protect themselves, let alone a civilian tribunal. So when the Srebrenica genocide was committed in July 1995, there was no infrastructure in place to secure the crime scenes. It was 12 months before investigators were able to access the sites to carry out exhumations and collect other evidence. As we now know, delayed access enabled the Bosnian Serbs to remove the bodies from primary graves and relocate them to secondary graves in a bid to cover up the crimes.[79] The scattered remains of Srebrenica victims are still being recovered from graves today.

Access to documentary evidence was also problematic. It was not until December 1997 that we were able to do our first search and seizure mission into Prijedor, one of the municipalities where thousands of Bosnian Muslims were brutally killed and detained in life-threatening conditions in 1992. The situation was much more difficult in Croatia and Serbia. Without the ability to use a regular search warrant, it took ten years to get hold of documentation from those governments. Both states invoked sovereignty and stated in no uncertain terms that the ICTY had no right to the documents. The ICTY had to negotiate, in most instances, with many of the same people who were in power during the conflict, including perpetrators of crimes or their superiors. To this day, access to archives remains an open issue. Although the ICTY's 'Chapter VII' powers as an organ of the UN Security Council means that it can issue binding orders to states, including for the production of documents, such powers are only to be used in the last resort.[80] They are not an alternative to cooperative endeavours.

States in the region in which crimes were committed are not the only states with which the ICTY must have dealings and with which it must act with sensitivity. For example, other states are frequently conflicted when it comes to sharing information garnered from domestic intelligence services. Although they may wish to assist the ICTY's mandate, they may naturally be reluctant to reveal the methods by which they acquire information for the purpose of protecting their national interests or endangering their sources. While the situation has improved, intelligence sharing remains a problematic and sensitive issue. Even where we get information, restrictions are often placed on its use, affecting our

---

79 See *Blagojević and Jokić*, above n40, paras 380–390, *especially* para 382; *Popović et al*, above n40, paras 600–6.

80 See *Prosecutor v Tihomir Blaškić*, Case No IT-95-14-AR108*bis*, Judgement on the Request of the Republic of Croatia for Review of the Decision of Trial Chamber II of 18 July 1997, 29 October 1997, para 31.

ability to disclose the information or to call witnesses who can provide vital evidence.[81]

An international prosecutor may also face difficulty accessing witnesses, especially 'insider' witnesses who were involved in groups relevant to particular crimes and who may have vital information about the links between perpetrators on the ground and the authorities behind the crimes. In the early days at the ICTY, interviews were often monitored by local authorities and reports were sent back to those in power, hardly the circumstances under which useful and truthful evidence can be elicited. Witness interference has been another significant challenge. For example, it was so widespread and had such an impact on the *Haradinaj* trial that the Appeals Chamber ordered a retrial – the prosecution had simply been unable to secure the testimony of some witnesses, who had cited fear as the main reason for not testifying.[82] The Tribunal also suspended the *Šešelj* trial in 2009 over fears that witnesses were being intimidated.[83] Šešelj has also been convicted of contempt three times now for revealing the names of protected witnesses.[84]

In general, we must be particularly conscious of the difficulties surrounding witness protection in conflict zones. Inadequate financial, human and technical resources mean that witness protection programmes are never as comprehensive as one would wish. It is also very hard to keep investigations confidential and discreet when all one's movements are accompanied by a security detail. Equally, in attempting to protect witnesses, we have to avoid creating too many incentives, which may provide a basis for challenging their credibility when they testify.

---

[81] See ICTY, Rules of Procedure and Evidence, Rule 70.

[82] *Prosecutor v Ramush Haradinaj et al.*, Case No IT-04-84-A, Judgement, 19 July 2010, para 50.

[83] *Prosecutor v Vojislav Šešelj*, Case No IT-03-67-T, Decision on Prosecution Motion for Adjournment with Dissenting Opinion of Judge Antonetti, 11 February 2009.

[84] See *Prosecutor v Vojislav Šešelj,* Case No IT-03-67-R77, Public Edited Version of 'Judgement on Allegations of Contempt' Issued on 24 July 2009, 24 July 2009 (sentenced to 15 months); *Prosecutor v Vojislav Šešelj*, Case No IT-03-67-R77.3, Public Redacted Version of 'Judgement' issued on 31 October 2011, 31 October 2011 (sentenced to 18 months); *In the Matter of Vojislav Šešelj*, Case No IT-03-67-R77.4, Public Redacted Version of Judgement issued on 28 June 2012, 28 June 2012 (sentenced to 24 months).

B. The Challenge of Securing Arrests and Cooperation

Problems of access have an obvious relevance to the challenge of arresting indictees. In general, international tribunals, even those mandated by the Security Council like the ICTY, have problems arresting indictees. The ICTR has made considerable progress but still has nine indictees at large.[85] It is a serious problem for the ICC, with at least eight indictees still believed to be at large.[86] Not only does the ICC have limited access to the territories it is investigating but the most prominent – and possibly the most protected – fugitive is the sitting President of Sudan, who remains in power.[87] For political reasons, some states – including parties to the Rome Statute – have permitted him to travel to their territory without fear of arrest.[88] Similarly, the Special Tribunal for

---

85 See MICT, 'Searching for the Fugitives,' available at http://www.unmict.org/searching-for-fugitives.html (accessed 11 December 2013).

86 See Amnesty International, Fugitives from International Justice, available at http://demandjusticenow.org/fugitives/ (accessed 11 December 2013) (listing Bosco Ntaganda, Joseph Kony, President Omar Al Bashir, Vincent Otti, Dominic Ongwen, Ahmad Harun, Aly Kushayb, Okot Odhiambo, Abdel Raheem Muhammad Hussein). In 2013, Bosco Ntaganda surrendered to the ICC.

87 See *Prosecutor v Omar Hassan Ahmad Al Bashir*, Case No ICC-02/05-01/09, Warrant of Arrest for Omar Hassan Ahmad Al Bashir, 4 March 2009; *Prosecutor v Omar Hassan Ahmad Al Bashir*, Case No ICC-02/05-01/09, Second Warrant of Arrest for Omar Hassan Ahmad Al Bashir, 12 July 2010.

88 These states parties appear to include Kenya, Chad, Djibouti, and Malawi. *See Prosecutor v Omar Hassan Ahmad Al Bashir*, Case No ICC-02/05-01/09, Decision informing the UN Security Council and the Assembly of the States Parties to the Rome Statute about Omar Al-Bashir's Presence in the Territory of the Republic of Kenya, 27 August 2010; *Prosecutor v Omar Hassan Ahmad Al Bashir*, Case No ICC-02/05-01/09, Decision informing the UN Security Council and the Assembly of the States Parties to the Rome Statute about Omar Al-Bashir's Recent Visit to the Republic of Chad, 27 August 2010; *Prosecutor v Omar Hassah Ahmad Al Bashir*, Case No ICC-02/05-01/09, Urgent Decision requesting observations from the Republic of Kenya, 25 October 2010; *Prosecutor v Omar Hassah Ahmad Al Bashir*, Case No ICC-02/05-01/09, Demande de coopération et d'informations adressée à la République Centrafricaine, 1 December 2010; *Prosecutor v Omar Hassan Ahmad Al Bashir*, Case No ICC-02/05-01/09, Decision informing the UN Security Council and the Assembly of the States Parties to the Rome Statute about Omar Al-Bashir's Recent Visit to Djibouti, 12 May 2011; *Prosecutor v Omar Hassan Ahmad Al Bashir*, Case No ICC-02/05-01/09, Decision requesting observations about Omar Al-Bashir's recent visit to the Republic of Chad, 18 August 2011; *Prosecutor v Omar Hassan Ahmad Al Bashir*, Case NoICC-02/05-01/09, Decision requesting observations about Omar Al-Bashir's Recent Visit to Malawi, 19 October 2011; *Prosecutor v Omar*

Lebanon has been unable to secure the arrest of any indictees and is likely to conduct their first significant trial *in absentia*.[89]

At the ICTY, we indicted 161 accused and none remains a fugitive today.[90] But it was not without difficulty and frustration. Executing arrest warrants was particularly problematic in our early years. The ICTY had no police force of its own, and the role of peacekeepers was limited. We were dependent on the states of the former Yugoslavia to cooperate by arresting and handing over fugitives. But arrests were not carried out because there was a lack of political will to do so – and not only at the national level but also at the international level. Many indicted war criminals are still seen as heroes in their own communities.

C. Incentives for State Cooperation – The Experience of the ICTY

If we recognize that arresting indictees is particularly difficult, and that the ICTY has been successful in achieving this, then we must ask what made the ICTY's experience different. While we are all used to the idea

---

Hassan Ahmad Al Bashir, Case No ICC-02/05-01/09, Decision Pursuant to Article 87(7) of the Rome Statute on the Failure by the Republic of Malawi to Comply with the Cooperation Requests Issued by the Court with Respect to the Arrest and Surrender of Omar Hassan Ahmad Al Bashir, 12 December 2011; *Prosecutor v Omar Hassan Ahmad Al Bashir*, Case No ICC-02/05-01/09, Decision Pursuant to Article 87(7) of the Rome Statute on the refusal of the Republic of Chad to comply with the cooperation requests issued by the Court with respect to the arrest and surrender of Omar Hassan Ahmad Al Bashir, 13 December 2011; *Prosecutor v Omar Hassan Ahmad Al Bashir*, Case No ICC-02/05-01/09, Decision Requesting Observations on Omar Al-Bashir's Visit to the Republic of Chad, 22 February 2013; *Prosecutor v Omar Hassan Ahmad Al Bashir*, Case No ICC-02/05-01/09, Decision on the Non-Compliance of the Republic of Chad with the Cooperation Requests Issued by the Court Regarding the Arrest and Surrender of Omar Hassan Ahmad Al-Bashir, 26 March 2013. *See also Prosecutor v Omar Hassan Ahmad Al Bashir*, Case No ICC-02/05-01/09, Decision Regarding Omar Al-Bashir's Visit to the Federal Republic of Nigeria, 15 July 2013; *Prosecutor v Omar Hassan Ahmad Al Bashir*, Case No ICC-02/05-01/09, Decision on the Cooperation of the Federal Republic of Nigeria Regarding Omar Al-Bashir's Arrest and Surrender to the Court, 5 September 2013 (noting that President Al Bashir was on the territory of Nigeria but that he departed 'suddenly' while 'officials' were 'considering the necessary steps to be taken in respect of his visit in line with Nigeria's international obligations').

89 See *Prosecutor v Salim Jamil Ayyash et al.*, Case No STL-11-01/I/TC, Decision to Hold Trial *In Absentia*, 1 February 2012.

90 See ICTY, The Fugitives, available at http://www.icty.org/sid/10010 (accessed 11 December 2013). *See also* ICTY, Infographic: ICTY Facts & Figures, available at http://www.icty.org/sid/11186 (accessed 5 December 2013).

that justice must not be influenced by politics, we have to accept that politics is still a factor which impacts many of the practicalities of the rule of law. Although the particular means by which the ICTY could secure state cooperation were specific to the circumstances of the former Yugoslavia, the approach is transferable to other international courts and tribunals. The political conditions applicable to situations over which they have jurisdiction may be complex and challenging – but the ICTY's experience tells us that we have to begin, at the very least, by recognizing that it is a political problem.

Arguably, the single most important factor in securing cooperation for the arrest of the last ICTY fugitives was the diplomatic pressure applied to the states concerned by other members of the international community. This pressure was concerted and clearly linked not only to potential sanctions but also to incentives. The ICTY was able to mobilize this pressure not only by deft conduct of its affairs but also as a result of the legitimacy conferred by its role in championing the rule of law in the former Yugoslavia.

Sanctions and incentives were effectively blended by the policies of 'conditionality' imposed on Serbia and Croatia by the European Union (EU) and the United States (US). These were vital to generating a change of political attitude, and securing the arrests of the fugitives. First, in 2001 the US Congress placed conditions on aid to Serbia, requiring the US President to certify that Serbia was cooperating with the ICTY.[91] Second, in 2002, the EU made membership conditional on full cooperation with the ICTY,[92] which created powerful pressure. At each and every step of the EU accession process, the state's level of cooperation with the ICTY was evaluated. And this evaluation was based on ICTY assessments provided to the EU and to the Security Council. When progress was considered insufficient, the EU did not shy away from taking tough decisions. They postponed accession talks with Croatia in March 2005 and with Serbia in 2006, for example.

It is my strong belief that, without EU and US conditionality, many fugitives – and in particular Karadžić, Mladić and Hadžić – would still be at large. That said, to ensure the success of the conditionality policy,

---

[91] See eg Erlanger, S, US Makes Arrest of Milosevic a Condition of Aid to Belgrade, *NY Times*, 10 March 2001; Congressional Research Service, Report for Congress, Woehrel, S, *Conditions on US Aid to Serbia*, 7 January 2008, available at https://www.fas.org/sgp/crs/row/RS21686.pdf (accessed 12 December 2013), 1.

[92] See eg Bull EU 1/2-2003, Pt. 1.6.102; Bull EU 6-2004, Pt I.7.31; European Commission 2004 Annual Report [2004] COM (2004) 202/2.

political action had to be coupled with investigations on the ground. We could not direct local authorities in their investigations as to the whereabouts of fugitives, but we could facilitate results by being present. Our tracking unit, and often the chief of investigations, were on the ground, asking questions and requiring information about the progress of the local investigation. The information we obtained informed the assessments provided to the EU member states and the Security Council.[93] Based on this information, the absence of concrete results could be

[93] See eg ICTY, Address of Serge Brammertz, Prosecutor of the International Criminal Tribunal for the Former Yugoslavia, to the Security Council, 4 June 2008, available at http://www.icty.org//x/file/Press/Statements%20and%20Speeches/Prosecutor/080604_proc_brammertz_un_sc.pdf (accessed 12 December 2013); ICTY, Address of Serge Brammertz, Prosecutor of the International Criminal Tribunal for the Former Yugoslavia, to the United Nations Security Council, 12 December 2008, available at http://www.icty.org//x/file/Press/Statements%20and%20Speeches/Prosecutor/081212_proc_brammertz_un_sc.pdf (accessed 12 December 2013); ICTY, Address of Serge Brammertz, Prosecutor of the International Criminal Tribunal for the Former Yugoslavia, to the Security Council, 4 June 2009, available at http://www.icty.org//x/file/Press/Statements%20and%20Speeches/Prosecutor/090604_proc_brammertz_un_sc.pdf (accessed 12 December 2013); ICTY, Address of Serge Brammertz, Prosecutor of the International Criminal Tribunal for the Former Yugoslavia, to the Security Council, 3 December 2009, available at http://www.icty.org/x/file/Press/Statements%20and%20Speeches/Prosecutor/091203_proc_brammertz_un_sc.pdf (accessed 12 December 2013); ICTY, Address of Serge Brammertz, Prosecutor of the International Criminal Tribunal for the Former Yugoslavia, to the Security Council, 18 June 2010, available at http://www.icty.org/x/file/Press/Statements%20and%20Speeches/Prosecutor/100618_proc_brammertz_un_sc_en.pdf (accessed 12 December 2013); ICTY, Address of Serge Brammertz, Prosecutor, International Criminal Tribunal for the Former Yugoslavia, to the United Nations Security Council, 6 December 2010, available at http://www.icty.org/x/file/Press/Statements%20and%20Speeches/Prosecutor/101206_proc_brammertz_un_sc_en.pdf (accessed 12 December 2013); ICTY, Address of Serge Brammertz, Prosecutor of the International Criminal Tribunal for the Former Yugoslavia, to the Security Council, 6 June 2011, available at http://www.icty.org/x/file/Press/Statements%20and%20Speeches/Prosecutor/110606_proc_brammertz_un_sc_en.pdf (accessed 12 December 2013); ICTY, Address of Serge Brammertz, Prosecutor, International Criminal Tribunal for the Former Yugoslavia, to the United Nations Security Council, 7 December 2011, available at http://www.icty.org/x/file/Press/Statements%20and%20Speeches/Prosecutor/111207_proc_brammertz_un_sc_en.pdf (accessed 12 December 2013); ICTY, Address of Serge Brammertz, Prosecutor, International Criminal Tribunal for the Former Yugoslavia, to the United Nations Security Council, 7 June 2012, available at http://www.icty.org/x/file/Press/Statements%20and%20Speeches/Prosecutor/120607_proc_brammertz_un_sc_en.pdf (accessed 12 December 2013).

criticized, shortcomings in the search methods for tracking fugitives identified, and remedies proposed.

Looking to the future, we can see that the next generation of international courts and tribunals, like the ICC, will continue to need state assistance in order to carry out their mandates. But there is cause for optimism that this is achievable, with effort and political will. Some recent measures taken by the US show that the ICC can forge effective collaborations even outside the framework of its states parties to address areas of mutual interest.[94] One good example is the recent inclusion of five ICC fugitives, including Joseph Kony and the recently arrested Bosco Ntaganda, in the US State Department's 'Rewards for Justice' programme.[95] Both the ICTY and ICTR have benefited in the past from inclusion in this programme, but it was only this year that the US Congress authorized its extension to include the ICC.[96] More can still be done, however.

---

[94] ICC, Statement on Behalf of the United States of America by Ambassador-at-Large Stephen J Rapp, 12th Session of the Assembly of States Parties to the Rome Statute of the International Criminal Court, 21 November 2013, available at http://www.icc-cpi.int/iccdocs/asp_docs/ASP12/GenDeba/ICC-ASP12-GenDeba-USA-ENG.pdf (accessed 11 December 2013):

> In the past year we have attempted, through our outreach, diplomacy, and support, to contribute to this work in a manner that furthers our own abiding interest in justice and the rule of law. Let me provide a few examples to be more concrete. [...] This year US military advisors supported militaries from the AU Regional Task Force, who moved closer to apprehending top Lord's Resistance Army (LRA) commanders [...] And in January 2013, President Obama signed legislation expanding the War Crimes Rewards Program, enabling the United States to offer rewards [...] for information leading to the arrest of ICC fugitives [...] The United States also played a key role in the surrender of Bosco Ntaganda to the ICC in March of this year.

[95] See US Department of State, 'Fugitives from Justice,' available at http://www.state.gov/j/gcj/wcrp/c56848.htm (accessed 11 December 2013) (offering rewards up to US $5 million for information leading to the arrest, transfer or conviction of Joseph Kony, Dominic Ongwen, Okot Odhiambo, Jean Bosco Ntaganda and Sylvestre Mudacumura).

[96] See US Department of State, 'President Obama signing legislation expanding the War Crimes Rewards Program,' available at http://www.state.gov/j/gcj/wcrp/index.htm (accessed 11 December 2013).

VI. COOPERATION BETWEEN INTERNATIONAL AND NATIONAL PROCEEDINGS

Finally, international criminal courts and tribunals are not only obliged to work with states in order to support international trials. They may also be obliged to work with states, and to assist them, in order to re-establish the rule of law and ensure that the accountability project continues. At the ICTY, for example, although we have tried a significant number of cases, many perpetrators are yet to face justice. However, we are a temporary institution, now well advanced in our completion strategy. Our doors will close before the end of the decade. As part of our mandate to end impunity, and to ensure a comprehensive and balanced approach to transitional justice, it has always been incumbent upon us to assist the states of the former Yugoslavia in their own endeavours to create accountability for crimes.

We have done this in three distinct ways.

A. ICTY Support for National Prosecutions

First, the ICTY – and especially the prosecution – provides practical support for investigations and prosecutions in national proceedings. This support can take many forms, including through information sharing, training, and capacity building.

While accountability for war crimes was vigorously opposed at the ICTY's inception, pressure imposed through discussions and reports to the Security Council led to strengthened relations with local authorities. This meant that local courts were eventually established to prosecute conflict-related crimes. Once the Security Council mandated the ICTY's completion strategy, we began transferring cases and investigative materials to authorities, facilitated by a 'transition team'. This was an area in which the EU played a big role by financially supporting capacity-building projects as part of the EU enlargement process. One such project was an initiative known as the 'Rules of the road' project to assist and advise domestic prosecutors in evaluating cases for possible national prosecution.

At the ICTY, we also support domestic investigations and prosecutions through the liaison prosecutors and the young professional programme, again made possible with financial support from the EU. We have a regular rotation of interns from the former Yugoslavia who assist us with our cases and three liaison prosecutors from Bosnia and Herzegovina, Croatia and Serbia, who work with us in The Hague on local cases. The liaison prosecutors benefit from on-the-job training, help national prosecutors access our database of some nine million documents and have a unique opportunity to consult with in-house experts on their cases. Physically bringing the three prosecutors together in The Hague also encourages their collaboration on regional issues concerning war crimes prosecutions. This was impossible to imagine ten years ago.

B. Transfer of Cases to National Courts (Rule 11*bis* and 'Category 2')

Second, although the ICTY has the right of 'first refusal' over cases concerning crimes in the former Yugoslavia – 'primacy' jurisdiction[97] – we also have provision for returning suitable (usually lower-level) cases back for prosecution before national courts. There are two main ways in which we do this.

One way is through a process known as Rule 11*bis*, which we use to transfer ICTY indictees for national prosecution.[98] Since the ICTY has already asserted jurisdiction over these individuals by indicting them, this process requires judicial authorization.[99] It has been used in eight cases involving 13 persons.[100] Not only does Rule 11*bis* allow ICTY resources to be prioritized on higher-level cases (which may be more suitable for international trial), it also feeds into the ICTY's positive complementarity. Not least, since transferred cases concern individuals who have come within the ICTY's jurisdiction, the transfer back for national prosecution

---

97 ICTY Statute, as amended, September 2009, Art 9(2).

98 ICTY Rules of Procedure and Evidence, Rule 11*bis*.

99 See ICTY Rules of Procedure and Evidence, Rule 11*bis*(A):

> After an indictment has been confirmed and prior to the commencement of trial [...] the President may appoint a bench of three permanent Judges selected from the Trial Chambers (hereinafter referred to as the 'Referral Bench'), which solely and exclusively shall determine whether the case should be referred to the authorities of a State.

100 See *Prosecutor v Radovan Stanković*, Case No IT-96-23/2-PT; *Prosecutor v Rahim Ademi and Mirko Norac*, Case No IT-04-78-PT; *Prosecutor v Gojko Janković*, Case No IT-96-23/2-PT; *Prosecutor v Željko Mejakić et al.*, Case No IT-02-65-PT; *Prosecutor v Paško Ljubičić*, Case No 00-41-PT; *Prosecutor v Mitar Rašević and Savo Todović*, Case No IT-97-25/1-PT; *Prosecutor v Vladimir Kovačević*, Case No IT-01-42/2-I; *Prosecutor v Milorad Trbić*, Case No IT-05-88/1-PT. *But see also Prosecutor v Milan Lukić and Sredoje Lukić*, Case No IT-98-32/1-AR11*bis*.1, Decision on Milan Lukić's Appeal Regarding Referral, 11 July 2007.

is contingent upon international monitoring of the fairness of the trial.[101] Rule 11*bis* cases thus provide some measure of 'quality control' of national proceedings, supplementing the assistance and support which the ICTY otherwise may provide.

We have also transferred 13 open case-files involving 38 suspects from the ICTY back to authorities in Bosnia and Herzegovina for investigation and potential prosecution. These are cases for which we did not seek ICTY indictments but do believe there may be a case to answer. This kind of transfer is important because it complies with the rule of law principle that due process should take place where the facts appear to require it. Yet these open cases also pose a challenge since they require both international and national authorities to take a risk: to trust in the adequacy and effectiveness of national proceedings, and to live up to that trust. The Prosecutor's Office of Bosnia and Herzegovina is making progress with these open cases, and has so far issued indictments in seven out of 13. However, we continue to encourage the Prosecutor's Office either to prosecute the remaining six cases or to close them if the evidence is insufficient.[102]

C. Outreach

Finally, another way in which the ICTY has sought to promote the rule of law, as well as to address the lack of political will for cooperation, is

---

[101] See ICTY Rules of Procedure and Evidence, Rule 11*bis*(B) (power to order referral 'after being satisfied that the accused will receive a fair trial and that the death penalty will not be imposed or carried out'), (D)(iv) ('the Prosecutor may send observers to monitor the proceedings in the national courts'), (F) ('At any time after an order has been issued pursuant to this Rule and before the accused is found guilty or acquitted by a national court, the Referral Bench may, at the request of the Prosecutor and upon having given to the State authorities concerned the opportunity to be heard, revoke the order'). See eg *Prosecutor v Milorad Trbić*, Case No IT-05-88/1-PT, Decision on Referral of Case under Rule 11*bis*, 27 April 2007, paras 45–46:

> the reports provided to the Bench [...] will also set forth concerns relating to the defence of the accused and any other issues of general importance for the realization of a fair trial [...] [I]f a given case is not being satisfactorily prosecuted or tried, the Bench maintains the power [...] to revoke the referral.

[102] ICTY, Address of Serge Brammertz, Prosecutor, International Criminal Tribunal for the Former Yugoslavia, to the United Nations Security Council, 5 December 2013, p 2, available at http://www.icty.org/x/file/Press/Statements%20and%20Speeches/Prosecutor/131205_proc_brammertz_un_sc_en.pdf (accessed 12 December 2013).

through outreach to the communities whose interests we seek to protect. Our experience has shown that international prosecutions do not automatically lead to acceptance of wrongdoing and reconciliation at the local level. As practitioners of international justice, we have a problem if we cannot explain to the victims and perpetrators what we are doing. By reaching local communities and convincing them that criminal justice is viable and necessary, we may help to generate public pressure on politicians that make a pro-prosecution policy more politically viable come election time.

This is one area in which we have only been partially successful, for a number of reasons which are not unique to the ICTY. We are far away from the conflict area, mostly working in a different language and in a different legal system.[103] The judgments are long and complicated,[104] and are therefore difficult if not impossible for many non-lawyers to understand. The expectations of victims are also, at times, impossible to meet. As a result, public opinion in the Balkans concerning the ICTY is wide-ranging. Our outreach has also not always been able to curb that section of the public who see indicted war criminals as war heroes. When Karadžić and Mladić were indicted, they were prevented from playing a role in the Dayton peace negotiations and were precluded from holding public positions. But they were given standing ovations in football stadiums. Notwithstanding damning video and other evidence against them and the successful prosecution of their close war-time associates, surveys show that 50 per cent of Serbs believe Ratko Mladić and Radovan Karadžić are not responsible for the crimes for which they are charged.[105] An OSCE survey showed that 66 per cent of the Serbian population thinks the establishment of the ICTY was unnecessary – but, on the other hand, that 90 per cent of the Serbian population has not read

---

[103] See ICTY Statute, as amended, September 2009, Arts 1–5 (the Tribunal has jurisdiction over 'serious violations of international humanitarian law' including genocide, crimes against humanity, grave breaches of the Geneva Conventions, violations of the laws or customs of war), 31 (the seat of the Tribunal shall be at The Hague), 33 (the working languages of the Tribunal shall be English and French).

[104] See eg *Prosecutor v Jovica Stanišić and Franko Simatović*, Case No IT-03-69-T, Judgement, 30 May 2013 (two volumes; 2,445 paragraphs); *Prlić et al.*, above n71 (six volumes; more than 6,388 paragraphs); *Prosecutor v Mićo Stanišić and Stojan Župljanin*, Case No IT-08-91-T, Judgement, 27 March 2013 (three volumes; 5,554 paragraphs).

[105] Organization for Security and Cooperation in Europe, Survey, Attitudes towards war crimes issues, ICTY and the national judiciary, October 2011, available at http://www.osce.org/serbia/90422 (accessed 20 January 2014).

an ICTY judgement and 62 per cent do not follow proceedings at the ICTY.[106] In such circumstances, it is not compelling for politicians in the region to adopt a policy of cooperation.

On the flipside, the lack of political will and nationalistic rhetoric can impact negatively upon public opinion. State officials continue to glorify illegal wartime conduct and question the impartiality of the ICTY's judgments. For example, while we had seen progress in Serbia with the election of a cooperative government and the arrest of Mladić and Hadžić, this was more recently undermined by the statement by the new Serbian President, Tomislav Nikolić, denying the Srebrenica genocide.[107] As previously discussed, President Nikolić also recently disputed the work of the ICTY at the UN General Assembly.[108] The President of the Republika Srpksa entity of Bosnia similarly made such denials that the Srebrenica killings constituted genocide.[109] When Biljana Plavšić, a former President of the Republika Srpska entity, completed her sentence for persecution of non-Serbs in Bosnia,[110] she was returned to Belgrade on a private Republika Srpska government plane and received like a hero.[111]

---

[106] Organization for Security and Cooperation in Europe, Survey, attitudes towards war crimes issues, ICTY and the national judiciary, October 2011, available at http://www.osce.org/serbia/90422 (accessed 20 January 2014).

[107] See eg ICTY, Press Release, Completion Strategy Report: Prosecutor Brammertz's Address before the Security Council, 7 June 2012, available at http://www.icty.org/sid/10984 (accessed 11 December 2013) ('recent comments made by the newly elected President of Serbia who denied that genocide occurred in Srebrenica in July 1995 are not acceptable').

[108] See above n28.

[109] See Institute for War & Peace Reporting, Halimović, D, 'Anxieties raised by Bosnian Serb premier's recent refusal to acknowledge the scale of the Srebrenica atrocity,' TRI Issue 663, 1 October 2010, available at http://iwpr.net/report-news/genocide-denial-concern-bosnia (accessed 11 December 2013). *But see* Institute for War & Peace Reporting, Bjelajac, M, 'Bosnian Serb leader opportunistic or committed nationalist?' TRI Issue 731, 2 March 2012, available at http://iwpr.net/report-news/bosnian-serb-leader-opportunistic-or-committed-nationalist (accessed 11 December 2013).

[110] See *Prosecutor v Biljana Plavšić*, Case Nos IT-00-39&40/1-S, Sentencing Judgement, 27 February 2003 (sentencing Plavšić to 11 years' imprisonment for participation in the persecution of non-Serbs in 37 municipalities of Bosnia and Herzegovina, to which she pleaded guilty, including through murder, rape, torture and mistreatment of men, women and children in approximately 400 detention facilities).

[111] See eg Institute for War & Peace Reporting, Martinović, I, 'Outcry at Plavšić's welcome,' TRI Issue 622, 4 November 2009, available at http://iwpr.net/

Lack of political will and limited local support is a challenge that future courts and tribunals and the international community must embrace. While some situations before the ICC were voluntarily submitted to its jurisdiction,[112] it may face even greater problems when the Prosecutor initiates an investigation *proprio motu*[113] or situations are referred by the Security Council.[114] For example, how can the ICC provide outreach to the Sudanese community when it is unable to enter the country? Are partnerships with local organizations enough? Willingness to cooperate and submit to a Tribunal's jurisdiction can also change. We saw initial domestic support for the STL wane with the shift in political power in Lebanon.[115] International prosecutions must be accompanied from the outset by a carefully devised and adequately funded outreach programme if we are to truly translate international justice into reconciliation.

VII. CONCLUSION

Having shared some of the ICTY's experiences, three points offer themselves in conclusion.

First, international criminal justice must always be a part of our efforts to promote and sustain the rule of law – but it will not be sufficient, by itself, to make the law's protection truly universal. The international accountability of leaders is not a substitute for engagement with local societies, local fears and local needs. This is an area where the ICTY's

---

report-news/outcry-plavsics-belgrade-welcome (accessed 11 December 2013). Other figures, such as Momčilo Krajišnik, have also been popularly received after completing their sentences: *see* Jukić, EM, BIRN, 'Bosnian Serbs welcome home freed wartime politician,' 2 September 2013, available at http://www.balkaninsight.com/en/article/pale-prepares-to-welcome-momcilo-krajisnik (accessed 11 December 2013); *Krajišnik*, above n49.

[112] For example, the situations in Uganda, the Democratic Republic of the Congo, the Central African Republic, Côte d'Ivoire and Mali.

[113] See ICC Statute, Art 15. See further *Situation in the Republic of Kenya*, Case No ICC-01/09, Decision Pursuant to Article 15 of the Rome Statute on the Authorization of an Investigation into the Situation in the Republic of Kenya, 31 March 2010.

[114] For example, the situations in Darfur (Sudan) and Libya were referred to the ICC by the UN Security Council. *See* SC Res 1593 (31 March 2005), UN Doc S/RES/1593; SC Res 1970 (26 February 2011), UN Doc S/RES/1970.

[115] See eg *Prosecutor v Salim Ayyash et al.*, Decision on the Defence Challenges, above n26, paras 9–12.

experience is particularly relevant. We have found that one of the most important factors in addressing the potential 'impunity gap' between international and national proceedings is simply the investment of time. Yet an investment of this kind may be a particular challenge for the ICC, from which the international community frequently demands swift results and which may be obliged to take on new situations at short notice.

Second, the international community needs an integrated approach to addressing rule of law issues. Both states and international organizations, including UN bodies, need to cooperate and coordinate with one another. Peace-building missions must include a rule of law component, as an essential foundation for the society they seek to repair. And the international investigation and prosecution of crimes has to be matched by capacity building to restore local justice systems.

Third, although the international community has a vital role to play, it is a mistake to think that it can do so purely in a 'top down' way. Even when international action has the strongest moral and legal mandate, it is most effective when it benefits from the concerted assistance and goodwill of states. It has to be smart, as well as righteous.

10. The Iran-United States Claims Tribunal and its contribution to international law

Hans van Houtte and Barbara Concolino

I. INTRODUCTION: HISTORIC BACKGROUND

The Iran-United States Claims Tribunal (IUSCT or the Tribunal) is one of the oldest international tribunals in The Hague. The Tribunal was established in 1981, as one of the measures to resolve the 1979 crisis between Iran and the US. To fully understand the circumstances that brought about its creation, however, it is necessary to go back in time to the 1950s.

Before embarking on a short historical journey, it is important to mention the geopolitical context. Iran's geographic position south of the Soviet Union, the presence of spread of communism and its oil reserves, made Iran strategically, politically and economically important.

Following the Second World War, Iran had close links with the West, in particular with Great Britain. Iran's oil industry was controlled by the British-owned Anglo-Iranian Oil Company (AIOC) and the British had significant influence over Iran's internal affairs. In 1953, following the 1951 nationalization of Iran's oil industry and a series of unsuccessful attempts to find an agreement between Iran and the United Kingdom (UK) on a new oil agreement or on the kind of compensation the UK would be entitled to,[1] the Iranian Prime Minister Mohammad Mosaddegh was overthrown in a *coup d'état* orchestrated by the UK and the United

[1] The UK, on 26 May 1951, brought *The Anglo-Iran Oil Company* Case before the International Court of Justice (ICJ), which, however, in its Judgment of 22 July 1952 on Iran's preliminary objection, declared that it lacked jurisdiction. See ICJ Reports 1952, 93.

States (US), in collaboration with Mosaddegh's domestic opponents.[2] Mohammad Reza Shah himself supported the *coup* and, after a brief exile in Italy, he returned to power until he was overthrown by the Islamic Revolution in 1979.

The 1953 *coup* is historically considered a turning point. From Iran's internal prospective, it marks the turn of the Shah's reign from a constitutional monarchy to a dictatorship.[3] From an external prospective, it marks the beginning of the US' increasing influence and close relationship with Iran. The internal and external prospective are closely connected and they are among the factors that lead to the 1979 Islamic Revolution.

Throughout the 1950s, US aid in the form of financial aid and military grants was crucial to Iran. Even though the rapid increase in oil revenue in the 1960s made Iran increasingly independent from foreign aid, the Shah was determined to transform Iran into an industrialized nation in a

---

[2] The 1953 *coup* has been described as 'a product of the close collaboration between Mosaddeq's domestic as well as foreign opponents, even though the role of foreign governments, especially the United States, in organizing and financing it was indispensable', see H Katouzian, *The Persians: Ancient, Mediaeval and Modern Iran* (hereinafter 'The Persians') (New Haven and London, Yale University Press, 2009) at 252. For a comprehensive account of the 1953 *coup* see MJ Gasiorowski, 'The 1953 Coup d'État Against Mossaddeq', in MJ Gasiorowski and M Byrne (eds), *Mohammed Mosaddeq and the 1953 Coup in Iran* (Syracuse, Syracuse University Press, 2004) at 227 ff.

The relevance of the 1953 *coup* was emphasized during the hostage crisis in a letter dated 9 December 1979 from the Iranian Government to the Registrar of the ICJ with respect to the US 29 November 1979 application to the Court. The Iranian Government claimed that the question submitted by the US was:

> a marginal and secondary aspect of an overall problem, one such that it cannot be studied separately, and which involves, *inter alia,* more than 25 years of continual interference by the United States in the internal affairs of Iran, the shameless exploitation of our country, and numerous crimes perpetrated against the Iranian people, contrary to and in conflict with all international and humanitarian norms' and specifically referred to 'the crimes perpetrated in Iran by the American Government, in particular the *coup d'état* of 1953 stirred up and carried out by the CIA, the overthrow of the lawful national government of Dr. Mossadegh, the restoration of the Shah and of his régime which was under the control of American interests … .

United States Diplomatic and Consular Staff in Tehran, Judgment of 24 May 1980, ICJ Reports 1980, 3, para 35.

[3] H Katouzian, above n2 at 231 and 253.

short period of time[4] and, in these aspirations, he looked to the US as a model of industrial excellence and sought American technology, equipment, advisers and investments. The Shah's relationship with the US became particularly strong during Nixon's and Ford's presidencies. In the 1970s, increasing oil revenue attracted foreign investment in Iran. The Shah spent large portions of Iran's oil income on military equipment purchased from the US[5] and on infrastructure projects such as road construction, factory modernization and communication systems. Many American companies were involved in these projects and opened offices in Iran. As a result, during the 1970s, thousands of American citizens were living in Iran.

Increasing wealth and modernization, however, did not prevent increasing social discontent. The Shah's absolute dictatorship after the 1963 revolt,[6] widespread violations of human rights, rampant inflation, and the perception among many Iranians that the Shah was in the pocket of the West, and in particular of the US, led to more and more social discontent.

From the beginning of 1978 more and more demonstrations were seen in Iran. Between September and December 1978 massive demonstrations were organized and large strikes, involving virtually every profession, became frequent. People were demanding the fall of the Shah and called for the leadership of the exiled Ayatollah Khomeini, the lifelong opponent of the Shah.

The situation became increasingly difficult for foreigners. Anti-Western feelings were growing among the Iranian population; as a result,

---

[4] In 1963 the Shah launched a six-point reform programme called the White Revolution which included land reform, nationalization of woods and forests, women's suffrage, creation of literacy corps to combat illiteracy, industrial profit sharing, and denationalization of some state industries. See H Katouzian, ibid at 280 ff.

[5] Most military procurement was purchased directly from the US Department of Defense through its Foreign Military Sale (FMS) Program; however, also American manufactures sold military equipment and services to Iran.

[6] The 1963 revolt has been described as a 'rehearsal for the revolutionary uprising a decade and a half later'. G Sick, *All Fall Down. American's Tragic Encounter with Iran* (hereinafter 'All Fall Down') (New York, Random House, 1985) at 10. The key figure of the revolt had been the Ayatollah Khomeini who strongly criticized the Shah's reforms and the Shah himself. Demonstrations chanting anti-Shah and pro-Khomeini slogans were violently suppressed. Khomeini was arrested, and later exiled to Turkey. He then went first to Iraq and then to Paris, from where, in 1979 he returned to Iran.

by the end of 1978, most American businesses had to suspend their activities and many expatriate employees had left Iran.

In January 1979 the Shah, who some years earlier had been diagnosed with cancer, left Iran. On 1 February 1979, Ayatollah Khomeini returned from exile and, on 11 February 1979, he declared the victory of the Islamic Revolution and established a new provisional government. In a referendum held on 31 March 1979 the vast majority of Iranians voted for the establishment of the Islamic Republic of Iran. Between spring and summer 1979 the new provisional government began instituting numerous reforms that were seriously restrictive of foreign companies' business activities: in June 1979, banks and insurance companies were nationalized;[7] at the same time, the Government started a de facto nationalization of the oil and gas industries which culminated in the Single Article Act Concerning the Nationalization of the Oil Industry of Iran of 8 January 1980.[8] Simultaneously, the Islamic Revolutionary Courts began expropriating the property of American and other foreign corporations,[9] several

---

[7] On 7 June 1979, all banks in Iran were nationalized by the Banks Nationalization Law: see, *Faith Lita Khosrowshahi, Susanne P Khosrowshahi, Marcene P Khosrowshahi, Kevin Kayvan Khosrowshahi, and Cameron Kamran Khosrowshahi v The Government of the Islamic Republic of Iran, The Ministry of Industries and Mines, The Alborz Investment Corporation, The Kbc Company, and The Development and Investment Bank of Iran*, Award No 558-178-2 (30 June 1994), in 30 Iran-US CTR 76 at 96, para 61. On 25 June 1979, all insurance companies operating in Iran were proclaimed nationalized by the Law of Nationalization of Insurance Corporations: see, *American International Group, Inc And American Life Insurance Company v Islamic Republic of Iran and Central Insurance of Iran (Bimeh Markazi Iran)*, Award No 93-2-3 (19 Dec 1983) in 4 Iran-US CTR 96 at 98.

[8] The Tribunal, in its Award No 310-56-3 (14 July 1987) in *Amoco International Finance Corporation v The Government of the Islamic Republic of Iran, National Iranian Oil Company, National Petrochemical Company and Kharg Chemical Company Limited*, in 15 Iran-US CTR 189, recognized that the expropriation which took place in that case was the outcome of a lengthy process which was complete only on 24 December 1980 but started more than 20 months before (para 132), therefore well before the Single Article Act Concerning the Nationalization of the Oil Industry was approved in January 1980.

[9] See *Aram Sabet, Karim Sabet, Reja Sabet v The Islamic Republic of Iran, Bonyad-E-Mostazafan*, Award No 593-815/816/817-2 (30 June 1999), in 35 Iran-US CTR 3 at 31, para 95; and *Gulf Associates, Inc. v The Islamic Republic of Iran, Zamzam Bottling Company, Mina Glass Co, Radio and Television Corporation of Iran, Iran Industrial Credit Bank (Bank Sanaye), Bank Melli, Bank of Tehran, Bank Sepah*, Award No 594-385-2 (7 October 1999), in 35 Iran-US CTR 45 at 68, para 78.

confiscating laws were enacted, and various Iranian governmental agencies cancelled their contracts with American companies.[10]

In October 1979, the Shah was admitted to the US for medical treatment. On 4 November 1979 Iranian student protestors, who later described themselves as 'Muslim Student Followers of the Imam's Policy', invaded the US Embassy in Tehran, seized the Embassy personnel, and demanded the US return the Shah and his assets back to Iran. It was not the first time that the US Embassy had been attacked. On 14 February 1979, a similar incident had occurred but the quick intervention of the newly established provisional government assured a prompt release of the Embassy.[11] This time, however, the events took a different course of action. Despite several requests for assistance from the Embassy and from Washington, no attempt was made by the Iranian Government to clear the Embassy premises, to rescue the people held hostage, or to persuade the students to terminate their actions against the Embassy. In a series of messages in the following days the Iranian Foreign Minister, Mr. Yadzi, and the Ayatollah Khomeini expressly endorsed the actions of the students. In a decree dated 17 November 1979, the Ayatollah Khomeini asserted that the US Embassy in Iran was 'a centre of espionage and conspiracy', that 'those people who hatched plots against [their] Islamic movement in that place d[id] not enjoy international diplomatic respect' and asked for the return of the deposed Shah and of his property to Iran.[12] Khomeini asked for the release of women and back office staff if it was proven that they did not spy. After this statement some of the hostages were released but 52 remained seized.

The International Court of Justice (ICJ), in its judgment of 24 May 1980, though considering the actions of the students not initially attributable to the Iranian Government, concluded that:

---

10 See NA Combs, 'Carter, Reagan, and Khomeini: Presidential Transitions and International Law', 52 *Hastings LJ* 303 at 314.

11 In a letter of March 1979 to the US Ambassador, the Prime Minister of the provisional government, Dr Bazargan, expressed regrets for the attack on the Embassy, and stated that arrangements had been made to prevent any repetition of such incidents. Interestingly, before February 1979, the US Ambassador in Tehran had been ordered to ship all reference files to Washington. After the 14 February attack, when the Embassy was reconstituted, those files were shipped back to Tehran. See G Sick, above n6 at 190–1. This suggests that, even after the Shah was admitted to the US, the US did not expect that events could take such a course.

12 *United States Diplomatic and Consular Staff in Tehran,* Judgment of 24 May 1980, ICJ Reports 1980, para 73.

> [t]he approval given to these facts by the Ayatollah Khomeini and other organs of the Iranian State, and the decision to perpetuate them, translated continuing occupation of the Embassy and detention of the hostages into acts of that State. The militants, authors of the invasion and jailers of the hostages, had now become agents of the Iranian State for whose acts the State itself was internationally responsible.[13]

Once President Carter realized that the American citizens would not be quickly released, he began to impose sanctions on Iran. On 8 November 1979, the US halted shipments of military spare parts ordered by Iran. On 10 November, steps were taken to identify all Iranian students in the US who were not in compliance with the terms of their entry visas and to commence deportation proceedings against those who were in violation of applicable immigration laws and regulations. On 12 November, President Carter blocked all oil purchases from Iran for delivery in the US. Finally, on 14 November 1979, believing that the Government of Iran was about to withdraw all Iranian funds from US banks, the President issued Executive Order No 12,170, which blocked the transfer of Iranian governmental assets subject to the jurisdiction of the US or in the possession or control of persons subject to the jurisdiction of the US. The US Department of the Treasury subsequently issued a series of 'Iranian Assets Control Regulations' implementing Executive Order No 12,170.[14] As a result, more than US $12 billion was blocked.

After Executive Order No 12,170 was issued, hundreds of American individuals and companies that had suffered losses in Iran rushed to the US courts bringing breach of contract and expropriation claims and often seeking judicial attachments of frozen Iranian property in the US.

On 7 April 1980 the US Government announced new measures, including the break of diplomatic relations with the Government of Iran. During the night of 24–25 April 1980, the US set in motion an unsuccessful operation within Iranian territory to rescue the hostages; the operation was terminated for equipment failure.

In the fall of 1980, Iran and the US begun to negotiate, through the Government of Algeria, to resolve the crisis. In a Resolution dated 2 November 1980, the Majlis, the Iranian Parliament, indicated four

---

13 Ibid., para 74. The US had filed an application with the ICJ on 29 November 1979. The Court, in its Judgment of 24 May 1980, concluded that Iran was responsible under international law for the violation of several obligations owed to the US under both conventional and customary international law (para 95).

14 See *United States Diplomatic and Consular Staff in Tehran, Judgment,* ICJ Reports 1980, 3, para 30, and Combs, above n10 at 316.

conditions for resolving the crisis: the non-intervention of the US in Iran's internal affairs; the lifting of the block on the Iranian assets; the cancellation of the claims against Iran; and the return of the wealth of the former Shah to Iran. The US found that the Resolution was acceptable as the basis for ending the crisis, but it made clear that claims could be removed from US courts only by the establishment of an alternative arrangement to ensure their settlement.

On 19 January 1981, the Government of Algeria recorded the mutual commitments of the parties in two declarations (the Algiers Declarations): the General Declaration[15] and the Claims Settlement Declaration.[16] On 20 January 1981, the 52 US citizens were released after 444 days.

II. THE ALGIERS DECLARATIONS

The General Declaration records the central commitments of the parties. While Iran would bring about the release of the 52 American citizens, the US would: (i) pledge not to intervene directly or indirectly, politically or militarily, in Iran's internal affairs (para 1); (ii) assist Iran in returning the assets of the former Shah and of any close relative of the Shah back to Iran (paras 12–16); (iii) restore, within the framework of and pursuant to the provisions of the two Declarations, Iran's financial position, in so far as possible, to that which existed prior to 14 November 1979 (General Principle A); (iv) terminate all legal proceedings in US courts involving claims of US persons and institutions against Iran and its state enterprises, nullify all attachments and judgments obtained therein, prohibit all further litigation based on such claims, and bring about the termination of such claims through binding arbitration (General Principle B).

By the time the detained US nationals were released, some 450 law suits against Iran were pending in US courts, with approximately $4 billion of Iranian assets the subject of prejudgment attachments. The Claims Settlement Declaration establishes the IUSCT as the mechanism for bringing about the termination of these legal proceedings and underlying claims through binding third-party arbitration. The Tribunal

---

15 Declaration of the Government of the Democratic and Popular Republic of Algeria (hereinafter General Declaration), 19 January 1981.

16 Declaration of the Government of the Democratic and Popular Republic of Algeria Concerning the Settlement of Claims by the Government of the United States of America and the Government of the Islamic Republic of Iran (hereinafter Claims Settlement Declaration), 19 January 1981.

has jurisdiction over claims and counterclaims of nationals of the US against Iran and of nationals of Iran against the US arising out of debts, contracts, expropriations or other measures affecting property rights (Article II). Article VII(2) of the Claims Settlement Declaration provides that: 'Claims referred to the arbitration Tribunal shall, as of the date of filing of such claims with the Tribunal, be considered excluded from the jurisdiction of the courts of Iran, or of the United States, or of any other court.'

President Reagan, who was sworn in the day after the Algiers Declarations were approved, on 24 February 1981 issued Executive Order No 12,294 which required US courts to suspend all claims which may be presented to the IUSCT under the terms of the Claims Settlement Declaration. Several claimants in US courts challenged the constitutionality of the Algiers Declarations but, on 2 July 1981, the US Supreme Court upheld the constitutionality of the Executive Orders implementing the Algiers Declarations.[17]

Hostage-related claims were left outside the framework of the Tribunal. Notably, in the General Declaration the US undertook to bar and preclude the prosecution against Iran of any pending of future claims of US nationals arising out of 'the seizure of the 52 United States nationals on November 4, 1979, [and] their subsequent detention' (para 11).

The Tribunal has also jurisdiction over official claims of the US and Iran against each other arising out of contractual arrangements between them for the purchase and sale of goods and services and on disputes over the interpretation or performance of any provision of General Declaration.

The General Declaration also provided for the establishment of an Escrow Account and a Security Account (paras 2–7). The financial arrangements for the implementation of these provisions were recorded in several technical agreements between the Federal Reserve Bank of New York, acting as fiscal agent of the US, Bank Markazi Iran, the Banque Centrale d'Algérie acting as Escrow Agent, Bank of England, De Nederlandsche Bank NV, and the NV Settlement Bank of the Netherlands. The Security Account was established for the purpose of securing payment of claims against Iran in accordance with the Claims Settlement Declaration. In the General Declaration Iran has agreed to maintain the Security Account at the minimum balance of US $500 million (para 7).[18]

---

[17] See *Dames and Moore v Regan*, 453 US 654 S Ct 2972 (1981).

[18] The technical arrangements for establishing the Escrow Account provided for the transfer of the amount of $7,955 billion held by the Federal Reserve Bank

III. THE IRAN-US CLAIMS TRIBUNAL

After the release of the hostages on 20 January 1980 and the implementation of financial arrangements, the next step was the creation of the Tribunal.

Article VI of the Claims Settlement Declaration provides that '[t]he seat of the Tribunal shall be The Hague, The Netherlands, or any other place agreed by Iran and the United States'. There is no official record as to the reasons why the negotiators of the Algiers Declarations chose The Netherlands. One of the reasons may be that The Netherlands, during the crisis, had remained on cordial terms with both countries and was geographically well placed between Iran and the US. Moreover, The Hague was the home of the Permanent Court of Arbitration (PCA), the Secretary-General of which was to be given important functions with respect to the Tribunal under the Arbitration Rules of the UN Commission on International Trade Law (UNCITRAL). The Netherlands had also a solid arbitration tradition, and it was a party to the 1958 UN Convention on the Recognition and Enforcement of Foreign Arbitral Award (New York Convention) whose father, Pieter Sanders, was a Dutch national.

On 1 July 1981, the Tribunal held its first meeting in the Peace Palace in The Hague and in April 1982, it moved to its own premises. The Tribunal consists of nine Members: three Members are appointed by each government (the six party-appointed arbitrators) and the remaining three Members (the third-country arbitrators) are appointed by the six party-appointed Members by mutual agreement. If the party-appointed arbitrators fail to agree, the third-country Members are appointed by an 'Appointing Authority' agreed by the parties. If the parties fail to agree on the Appointing Authority, the Tribunal Rules empower the Secretary-General of the PCA to designate the Appointing Authority. One of the third-country Members acts as the president of the Tribunal.

---

of New York and foreign branches of US banks in an escrow account held by the Banque Centrale d'Algérie. Upon the transfer of this amount Iran would release 52 US nationals detained in Iran. Upon certification that the US citizens had safely departed from Iran, the Algerian Central Bank would transfer US $3,667 billion to the Federal Reserve Bank of New York to pay agreed debts owed to certain US banks. US $1,418 billion would be retained in the escrow account for the purpose of paying the amount claimed by US banks but disputed by Iran. The remaining amount (approximately US $2,870 billion) would be transferred to Bank Markazi Iran.

Claims may be decided by the Full Tribunal (the nine Members together) or by a Chamber, a panel of three members of the Tribunal (one Iranian, one American and one third country). By presidential order, three Chambers were established, and cases were distributed to Chambers by lot. The Full Tribunal decides all disputes between the two governments concerning the interpretation of and compliance with the Algiers Declarations, as well as important questions referred to it by the Chambers.

Claims before the Tribunal were to be filed within one year after the adoption of the declarations or six months after the date the President was appointed, whichever was later, with the exception of claims between the two governments concerning the interpretation or performance of any provision of that General Declaration for which no deadline applies. In total 3,953 claims were filed with the Tribunal's Registry, of which 961 were 'large claims' for more than $250,000 presented directly by individuals or corporations against the government, 2,884 were 'small claims' for less than $250,000 presented by the governments on behalf of the individual claimants, 75 were contractual claims of one government against the other (designated by the Tribunal as 'B' cases), and 33 were disputes between the two governments concerning the interpretation or performance of the Declarations (designated by the Tribunal as 'A' cases).

To deal expeditiously with thc 'small claims', a number of those claims were selected for priority treatment in the expectation that decisions on those claims would offer guidance with respect to cases with similar factual and legal issues. After some 400 of these cases had been decided, settled or withdrawn, Iran and the US agreed on a lump sum settlement of all but two of the remaining claims.[19] Private settlement has also been encouraged from the beginning, therefore many awards have been awarded on agreed terms.

Today all of the Chamber cases are terminated and 16 of the Full Tribunal cases are still pending. Even if this number seems relatively small, if compared with the number of cases decided by the Tribunal, these are the biggest and politically most delicate cases.

The expenses of the Tribunal are borne equally by the two governments and the official languages of the Tribunal are Farsi and English. Each government has designated an agent at the seat of the Tribunal to represent it to the Tribunal and to receive notices or other communications directed to it or its nationals in connection with proceedings before the Tribunal.

---

[19] See Award No 483-Claims of less than US $250,000/86/B38/B76/B77-FT, 25 Iran-US CTR 327.

The Tribunal is a provisional institution. When it was established in 1981, no one predicted that it would last for 32 years. Today the Tribunal comprises approximately 50 staff members, including two co-registrars, legal advisers, secretaries, translators and staff in the administration. Two Exchange of Letters between the President of the Tribunal and the Dutch Ministry of Foreign Affairs specify the privileges and immunities of the Tribunal, its Members and the staff. These include inviolability of the Tribunal's premises, archives, communication and correspondence, immunity of its properties and assets, immunity from judicial process and attachment and other fiscal privileges.

IV. CONTRIBUTION TO INTERNATIONAL LAW

A. The Hague: Judicial Capital of the World

In 1981, when the IUSCT was established, the 'Judicial The Hague' as we know it today was a sleeping beauty. The only two judicial institutions at the time were the ICJ, which had an average of one case every three years and the PCA, which had no activity at all. The IUSCT brought hundreds of cases to be decided and hundreds of lawyers and experts to The Hague. It was against this scenario that in 1993 Boutros Boutros Ghali, at the time Secretary-General of the UN, indicated in his Report to the Security Council pursuant to paragraph 2 of the Security Council Resolution 808 (1993) that he believed that the seat of the International Criminal Tribunal for the Former Yugoslavia (ICTY) should be The Hague.[20]

Suddenly the judicial The Hague became busy again and started its second life. As we all know, after the ICTY, other international tribunals also came to The Hague: the International, the Special Tribunal for Lebanon, the Appeals Chamber of the International Criminal Tribunal for Rwanda and the Special Court for Sierra Leone's trial of Charles Taylor. The Hague today also hosts the Organization for the Prohibition of Chemical Weapons and European Agencies such as Eurojust and Europol.

There is no doubt that today The Hague has well deserved the title of 'Legal Capital of the World'.

[20] Report of the Secretary-General pursuant to paragraph 2 of the Security Council Resolution 808 (1993), S/25703, 3 May 1993, paras 131–132.

B. Development of International Arbitration

1. The UNCITRAL Rules

Before 1981 there were few arbitration cases involving states. With its hundreds of cases, the Tribunal put arbitration with states to the forefront.

The Claims Settlement Declaration provides that the Tribunal shall conduct its business in accordance with the arbitration rules of the UNCITRAL (hereinafter UNCITRAL Rules), as modified by the Tribunal or by the two governments. Despite the possibility of modifying the UNCITRAL Rules, the Tribunal has not made many significant modifications.[21]

The UNCITRAL was established in 1966 in Vienna as a subsidiary body of the General Assembly of the UN.[22] The UNCITRAL Rules were adopted in 1976 as a procedural framework for non-institutional arbitration, therefore, when the Tribunal was established in 1981, they had not been widely tested. There were only few procedures adopting them and they were not frequently included in arbitration clauses. The Tribunal was the first significant arbitral institution to apply the UNCITRAL Rules. Suddenly hundreds of lawyers had to familiarize themselves with these Rules and, as a consequence, they became well known and highly respectable. Nowadays they are often referred to in investment contracts, investments treaties, and BITs (bilateral investment treaties); reference to the UNCITRAL Rules is also included in the Energy Charter Treaty[23] and in the NAFTA (North American Free Trade Agreement),[24] and they are also popular for commercial disputes between business companies.

---

[21] The Tribunal Rules of Procedures (hereinafter Tribunal Rules) were adopted on 3 May 1983. Most modifications of the UNCITRAL Rules were directed at adjusting the rules and facilitating their application to the specific situation of the Tribunal. One of the few significant modifications will be illustrated infra para (B). For an overview of the modifications see, KH Böckstiegel, 'Applying the UNCITRAL Rules: The Experience of the Iran-United States Claims Tribunal', (1986) 4 *International Tax & Business Lawyer* 266 at 267 ff.

[22] See UN General Assembly's resolution 2205 (XXI) of 17 December 1966 (Annex I).

[23] According to Article 26 of the Energy Treaty Charter, one of the options available to an investor who chooses to bring a dispute under the Charter to arbitration is to submit the dispute to 'a sole arbitrator or an ad hoc arbitration tribunal established under the rules of the United Nations Commission on International Trade Law (UNCITRAL)' (Art 26(4)(b)).

[24] Article 1120 (Chapter 11) of the NAFTA provides that a disputing investor may submit the claim to arbitration under the UNCITRAL Arbitration Rules.

A significant role in the increasing popularity of the UNCITRAL Rules has been played by the Tribunal's jurisprudence. Contrary to the general rule prevailing at the time, and to some extent still today, under which arbitral awards shall be confidential, the Tribunal's awards are published.[25] Therefore, the Tribunal's cases have provided a wealth of jurisprudence on the scope and application of the UNCITRAL Rules and have ultimately contributed to their knowledge and acceptance.

Some of the issues on which the Tribunal has provided several precedents include: the exchange of written pleadings between the parties,[26] witnesses' statements[27] and party witnesses,[28] evidentiary issues

---

25 While Article 32(5) of the UNCITRAL Rules provides that 'award may be made public only with consent of both parties', the Tribunal has reversed the rule as follows:

> All awards and other decisions shall be made available to the public, except that upon the request of one or more arbitrating parties, the arbitral tribunal may determine that it will not make the entire award or other decision public, but will make public only portions thereof from which the identity of the parties, other identifying facts and trade or military secrets have been deleted.

The Tribunal's decisions and awards are published by the Lauterpacht Centre for International Law in the Iran-US Claims Tribunal Report (Iran-US CTR). So far 38 volumes have been published. The Tribunal's awards are also available on the Tribunal's webpage: www.iusct.net.

26 The UNCITRAL Rules on statement of claim (Art 18), statement of defense (Art 19), amendments to claim or defence (Art 20), and further written statements (Art 22) have not been the subject of substantive modifications. Article 22, which was adopted unchanged provides that:

> [t]he arbitral tribunal shall decide which further written statements, in addition to the statement of claim and the statement of defence, shall be required from the parties or may be presented by them and shall fix the periods of time for communicating such statements.

The Tribunal's practice has consistently provided for four rounds of pleadings, with the last two submissions filed simultaneously.

27 Article 25(5) of the UNCITRAL Rules, which was left unchanged by the Tribunal Rules, provides that '[e]vidence of witnesses may also be presented in the form of written statements signed by them'. Böckstiegel, one of the former Presidents of the Tribunal, noted that 'in order to avoid devoting precious hearing time to the examination of oral witnesses, the Tribunal urges parties to file evidence in the form of affidavits where possible'. See Böckstiegel, above n21 at 270.

28 In its practice the Tribunal created a distinction between 'independent' witnesses and 'party' witnesses. For the latter category, which include for instance claimants' spouse and children or executive or senior officers of a corporate claimant, the Tribunal usually has not applied the provisions of Art 25

concerning lost documents, the shifting of the burden of proof,[29] discovery and adverse inferences,[30] interim measures to preserve goods or forbid parallel proceedings[31] and dissenting and concurring opinions.

---

of the Tribunal Rules (and its note thereof) with respect to the prior notification and solemn declaration to be made before the testimony. See G Aldrich, *The Jurisprudence of the Iran-United States Claims Tribunal* (Oxford, Clarendon Press; New York, Oxford University Press, 1996) at 347–9.

[29] The Tribunal has adopted a flexible approach with respect to evidentiary issues taking into consideration the circumstances of each case. The Tribunal, for instance, in some cases, took into consideration the difficulties that some claimants experienced in collecting evidence when, at the time of the Islamic Revolution, they were forced to rush out of Iran without having the opportunity to take the relevant documents with them. The issue was addressed in a memorandum dated 17 February 1988 from the late Professor Virally, at the time Chairman of Chamber III incorporated in *W Jack Buckamier v The Islamic Republic of Iran, Isiran/Army, Tehran Redevelopment Corporation, Bank Mellat, Hejrat Branch (formerly Iran-Arab Bank)*, Award No 528-941-3 (6 March 1992), in 28 Iran-US CTR 53 at 74, para 67. In some cases, prima facie evidence was considered sufficient to satisfy the Claimant's initial burden of proof. The Tribunal has also considered, in establishing whether a party had met its burden of proof, whether the party had access to confirming or rebutting evidence and failed to provide it. See DD Caron, LM Caplan and M Pellonpää, *The UNCITRAL Arbitration Rules. A Commentary* (Oxford and New York, Oxford University Press, 2006) at 570.

[30] Article 24(3) of the Tribunal's Rules provides that '[a]t any time during the arbitral proceedings the arbitral tribunal may require the parties to produce documents, exhibits or other evidence within such a period of time as the tribunal shall determine'. The Tribunal has not made use of this provision extensively and, in case of failure of a party to produce the requested evidence, has been reluctant to draw the inference that such evidence would have been unfavorable to the non-producing party. See SA Backer and MD Davis, *The UNCITRAL Arbitration Rules in Practice. The Experience of the Iran-United States Claims Tribunal* (Boston, 1992) at 113–14.

[31] Article 26(1) of the Tribunal Rules, which reflects the text of the UNCITRAL Rules, provides that at the request of either party, 'the arbitral tribunal may take any interim measures it deems necessary in respect of the subject-matter of the dispute, including measures for the conservation of the goods forming the subject-matter in dispute, such as ordering their deposit with a third person or the sale of perishable goods'. While the Tribunal has sometimes applied Art 26, it has more often invoked its 'inherent power to issue such orders as may be necessary to conserve the respective rights of the parties and to ensure that this Tribunal's jurisdiction and authority are made fully effective', especially in cases of parallel proceedings before the Tribunal and in national courts (see *E-Systems, Inc v The Islamic Republic of Iran, Bank Melli Iran*, Award No ITM 13-388-FT (4 February 1982), in 2 Iran-US CTR 51).

2. Specific procedural features proper to state-to-state arbitration

(i) The 'Mosk' Rule One noteworthy change to the UNCITRAL Rules appears in Article 13(5) of the Tribunal's Rules, which provides that 'after the effective date of a member's resignation he shall continue to serve as a member of the Tribunal with respect to all cases in which he had participated in a hearing on the merits, and for that purpose shall be considered a member of the Tribunal instead of the person who replaces him'. The rule is based on similar provisions in the Statutes of the ICJ and the European Court of Human Rights (ECtHR) and was introduced in March 1984, and unofficially named after the arbitrator whose departure sparked the debate. It applies whenever a resigning member has participated in a hearing on the merits and the case remains unresolved after the effective date of his or her resignation. The rule intended to ensure an orderly processing of cases and avoid repetition of hearings. Despite the language of the provision, the rule, obviously, cannot be enforced if an arbitrator is unwilling to serve.

While the Mosk Rule is a fundamental rule to safeguard the efficient conduct of the proceedings, its application to bifurcated proceedings may not serve that purpose. The Tribunal, in some cases, has rendered partial awards, sometimes postponing the final resolution of the cases to many years after the partial award was rendered. In those cases, a completely new panel may sit to render the final award. While this situation is far from ideal, applying the Mosk Rule to these cases would not only be of little benefit, but often unfeasible.

(ii) Equal-time rule Article 15(1) of the Tribunal Rules provides that the 'tribunal may conduct the arbitration in such manner as it considers appropriate, provided that the parties are treated with equality …'. With respect to the parties' filings, the Tribunal has applied the equal-time rule rather strictly, giving to the respondent exactly the same time – in terms of years, months and days – that it had taken the claimant to file its submission.

While this rule is rather common – the ICJ, for example, applies the same rule – it has proven to be not very efficient with respect to state-to-state claims. These claims, though not very numerous, are the most complicated, politically sensitive and often involve billions of US dollars. It is therefore not surprising that the claimant often took several years before filing its first brief and the respondent has taken advantage of the equal time to file its response. In several cases, both parties have often sought many requests of extension of the deadline to submit their briefs, and the Tribunal has been reluctant in denying such requests.

It may therefore take more than a decade for the Tribunal to go through its docket of pending cases – unless, of course, the parties decide to settle the remaining claims. Although this may raise concerns in terms of judicial efficiency, one should not forget the political importance of the Tribunal.

(iii) Sampling As mentioned earlier, in its early years, the Tribunal, faced with almost 3,000 small claims, adopted a sampling procedure and selected a number of cases for preliminary consideration in the hope that the resolution of these cases would offer guidance for the resolution of cases presenting similar legal and factual issues. This approach has been followed by the UN Compensation Commission (UNCC) and was considered, though ultimately not adopted, by the Eritrea-Ethiopia Claims Commission (EECC).

(iv) Finality of awards Article 32(2) of the Tribunal's Rules provides that awards shall be final and binding on the parties. The rules do not provide for exception to the finality of the awards in case of newly discovered documents which would have changed the outcome of the award if known when it was rendered or in cases of serious procedural irregularities or forged documents or fraud on the Tribunal.

In commercial arbitration, local arbitration laws may provide for grounds of revision within a certain amount of time after an award is rendered. Other international courts or settlement mechanisms, such as the ICJ, the ICSID (International Centre for the Settlement of Investment Disputes), the ECtHR, and the ITLOS (International Tribunal for the Law of the Sea), have specific provisions on revision.[32]

The Tribunal has been requested several times to revise a previous decision. While the Tribunal has never granted such requests, it has not always been consistent on whether the Tribunal may have an inherent power to revise its own decisions.

Some years ago, the Full Tribunal was seized again with a request for revision alleging serious procedural irregularities. The Full Tribunal noted that while courts and tribunals which permit revision of awards have express provisions in their rules of procedures to that effect, when the Tribunal, in consultation with the parties, modified the UNCITRAL Rules, neither the Tribunal nor the two state parties considered the

---

[32] See Art 61 of the Statute of the ICJ, Art 51 of the Convention on the Settlement of Investment Disputes Between States and Nationals of Other States, Rule 80 of the Rules of the ECtHR, and Art 127 of the ITLOS, Rules of the Tribunal.

remedy of revision of awards. The Tribunal concluded, unanimously, that because the parties may modify the Tribunal's rules to empower the Tribunal to revise final and binding awards, the Tribunal was not prepared to hold that it had an inherent power to do so.

3. Expertise spread

The Tribunal played also a fundamental role in the acquisition and spreading of know-how and expertise in the field of claims resolution. The Members of the Tribunal had important roles in other institutions, including the Commission for Real Property Claims of Displaced Persons and Refugees (CRPC), the Claims Resolution Tribunal (CRT) for dormant accounts in Switzerland, the UNCC and the EECC. The latter, notably, included among its five Members, two former US Agents to the Tribunal, one Member of the Tribunal and a commissioner who later became, and still is, the President of the Tribunal. Many of the legal advisers, after serving with the Tribunal, went to practice arbitration or joined academia.

C. Contribution to the *Lex Mercatoria*

As mentioned earlier, prior to the 1979 Revolution, Iran and the US were close allies. For years Iran had purchased vast quantities of military and non-military equipment from the US and hundreds of American companies were involved in a variety of large-scale projects which included oil drilling, roads contraction, communication systems and industrial complexes.

The Revolution abruptly ended all commercial relations. As a consequence, many American claimants brought to the Tribunal hundreds of contract claims, and the Tribunal had the opportunity to decide on a number of issues, including claims for payment, formation, validity and interpretation of contracts, breach of contracts and damages.

The Claims Settlement Declaration and the Tribunal Rules afford the Tribunal a wide margin of discretion in choosing the applicable law to resolve its cases. Indeed, Article V of the Claims Settlement Declaration and Article 33(1) of the Tribunal Rules share the same language and provide that the Tribunal:

> shall decide all cases on the basis of respect for law, applying such choice of law rules and principles of commercial and international law as the Tribunal determines to be applicable, taking into account relevant usages of the trade, contract provisions and changed circumstances.

The Tribunal, in its jurisprudence, has been reluctant to apply either Iranian or American domestic law, even when the contract at issue indicated such a choice of law. Rather, the Tribunal, when a contract did not provide adequate rules to resolve the dispute, has resorted to general principles of commercial law. The Tribunal's many decisions on commercial claims have not only strengthened its effectiveness as a public international disputes resolution mechanism, but also have provided it with numerous opportunities to expound on general principles of transnational commercial law,[33] otherwise known as *lex mercatoria*.

It is obviously impossible within the limited framework of this chapter to analyse in more details all the relevant contributions that the Tribunal has made to principles of commercial law. We will therefore confine my analysis to three principles, namely, *force majeure*, unjust enrichment, and estoppel.

1. *Force majeure*

The Tribunal has dealt extensively with the concept of *force majeure*.[34] Considering the events that brought about the constitution of the Tribunal, it is not surprising that both parties have often invoked *force majeure* as an excuse for non-performance of their contractual obligations. The Tribunal has applied *force majeure* as a general principle of law and in many cases has held that *force majeure* conditions existed in Iran during the Islamic Revolution and in the months thereafter. Equally, the Tribunal considered that the events following the seizure of the US Embassy in Tehran and the economic sanctions imposed as a result on Iran by the US also constituted *force majeure*. In these cases, the Tribunal held that the performance of the relevant obligation was suspended and the non-performance by the affected party was excused.

A considerable problem that the Tribunal had to deal with was the situation of prolonged *force majeure*. In several cases the Tribunal concluded that the prolonged existence of a situation of *force majeure* may lead to the termination of the contract by reason of frustration or impossibility of performance. In these cases the Tribunal held that losses must 'lie where they fall', subject to the Tribunal's discretion to allocate equitably such losses in proportion to the extent that the contract was performed.

---

33 See M Brunetti, 'The *Lex Mercatoria* in Practice: The Experience of the Iran-United States Claims Tribunal' (2002) 18 *Arbitration International* 355.

34 For a detailed account of the Tribunal's jurisprudence on *force majeure*, see M Brunetti, ibid., 359–67.

Particularly interesting in this field is the case of Iran's property in the US that could not be sent back to Iran because of lack of export licence. The Tribunal consistently held that the refusal of the US, after 14 November 1979, to issue licences to export Iran's goods created a situation of *force majeure*. This is clearly an example of prolonged *force majeure* as economic sanctions against Iran are still in place today. The continuing storage of Iran's property in the US gives rise to several issues, including storage costs, and the deterioration and depreciation of the property. While the ultimate solution may be to consider the contract terminated and sell the property, it may prove difficult to decide at what point this should happen and whether and how losses should be allocated.

2. Unjust enrichment and *quantum meruit*

The Tribunal has applied the concept of unjust enrichment as a 'last resort' when compensation could not be awarded based on other theories of recovery, and not awarding any compensation would be inequitable.[35] The Tribunal has considered both unjust enrichment and *quantum meruit* as general principles of law.

While the application of the theories of unjust enrichment and *quantum meruit* may not present particular difficulties, the determination of the value may be challenging. This is particularly true in cases where, for instance, a certain work was only partially performed.

3. Estoppel

The Tribunal, in adjudging contract claims, has often given relevance to the parties' conduct throughout the contract. Specifically, even in cases of formally invalid contracts, the Tribunal has considered the later conduct of the parties executing the contract as an element to uphold the validity of the contract. For example, in the *Shifflette* case, the respondent challenged the existence of an enforceable contract for teaching services between the claimant and an Iranian University because, inter alia, the University regulations did not recognize oral agreements. The Tribunal concluded that because the claimant had worked for about two weeks and the University accepted his service, the respondent 'was estopped from invoking invalidity of the agreement on merely formal grounds'.[36]

---

35 Ibid., 368–73.

36 *Stephen G Shifflette, a Claim of less than U.S. $250,000 presented by the United States of America v the Islamic Republic of Iran*, Award No 423-10645-1 (12 June 1989), in 22 Iran-US CTR 111 at 115, para 18.

D. Contribution to International Law

In 2007, Christopher S Gibson and Christopher R Drahozal published a book entitled: *The Iran-U.S. Claims Tribunal At 25: The Cases Everyone Needs To Know For Investor-State & International Arbitration*. The two authors also conducted a study in 2006 which shows that 44.7 per cent of ICSID awards that reached the merits cited Tribunal precedent, most commonly an award but occasionally the Claims Settlement Declaration, the Tribunal Rules of Procedure, or a secondary source discussing Tribunal cases.[37] According to the same study, in NAFTA cases, 73.5 per cent of party submissions on the merits, and 45 per cent of submissions limited to jurisdiction, cite at least one (but often more) Tribunal case.[38]

The decisions that are cited more often deal with the following subjects:

(a) Nationality: the Tribunal dealt with several issues concerning nationality. A crucial one in the Tribunal's jurisprudence has been the issue of dual nationals, which is also relevant for the applicability of investment treaties to investors with dual nationality. While the Claims Settlement Declaration defines the term 'national' of Iran or of the US (Article VII),[39] the question of dual nationals remained open. In its decision in Case No A18, the Tribunal interpreted the Claims Settlement Declaration to give it jurisdiction over the claims of dual nationals against one state party, where the

---

[37] CS Gibson and CR Drahozal, 'Iran-United States Claims Tribunal Precedent in Investor-State Arbitration' (2006) 23(6) *Journal of International Arbitration* 521 at 540.

[38] Ibid., 542. According to the study, 'the number of different Tribunal precedents cited was substantially greater in memorials dealing with the merits (4.4 different citations per memorial) than in memorials limited to jurisdictional issues (1.4 different citations per memorial)'.

[39] Article VII of the Claims Settlement Declaration:

> 1. A 'national' of Iran or of the United States, as the case may be, means (a) a natural person who is a citizen of Iran or the United States; and (b) a corporation or other legal entity which is organized under the laws of Iran or the United States or any of its states or territories, the District of Columbia or the Commonwealth of Puerto Rico, if, collectively, natural persons who are citizens of such country hold, directly or indirectly, an interest in such corporation or entity equivalent to fifty per cent or more of its capital stock.

dual national's 'dominant and effective nationality' was that of the other state party.[40]

Another complex issue was the one of nationality of companies – equally relevant for the applicability of investment treaties. While the Claims Settlement Declaration expressly addresses the issue of the nationality of corporations and other legal entities, the criteria are not always easily applicable in cases of large traded corporations with thousands of shareholders or in cases of joint ventures. The Tribunal, in applying the test based on capital stock ownership, has given directions as to the requirements to prove corporate nationality with reference to the circumstances of specific cases.[41]

(b) Attribution: the jurisprudence of the Tribunal has been considered an important source with respect to the issue of state liability for actions of their agencies, instrumentalities and subdivisions. While the Claims Settlement Declaration defines Iran as 'the Government of Iran, any political subdivision of Iran, and any agency, instrumentality, or entity controlled by the Government of Iran or any political subdivision thereof', the Tribunal, in several cases, had to deal with the attribution to Iran of acts of entities not officially controlled by Iran such as revolutionary guards, universities or charitable foundation.[42]

(c) Expropriation: the Tribunal was the first international arbitral institution in a great number of years to deal with a substantial number of cases on expropriation. Its role was thus fundamental in updating the law on expropriation.

Article II (1) of the Claims Settlement Declaration grants the Tribunal the authority to resolve claims arising out of 'expropriations or other measures affecting property rights'. The reference to *other measures affecting property rights* suggests that not only formal acts of expropriation would be within the subject matter jurisdiction of the Tribunal, but also other measures constituting indirect or creeping expropriation. In some cases the Tribunal

[40] Decision No DEC 32-A18-FT (6 April 1984), in 5 Iran-US CTR 251. The Tribunal relied heavily on the *Nottebohm* decision by the ICJ (*Liechtenstein v Guatemala*) ICJ Reports (1955) 4.

[41] For more information on the Tribunal's jurisprudence in this field, see G Aldrich, above n28 at 47 ff.

[42] For more information on the Tribunal's jurisprudence in this field, see CN Brower and JD Brueschke, *The Iran-United States Claims Tribunal* (The Hague, Nijhoff, 1998) at 442 ff.

awarded compensation for measures affecting property rights while finding that they did not amount to expropriation.[43]

As for the standard of compensation, the US' view was crystallized in a 1938 famous letter from US Secretary of State Cordell Hull to the Mexican Government asking Mexico for 'prompt, adequate and effective' compensation for the expropriated land of US nationals. Ten years earlier in the *Chorzow Case*, the Permanent Court of International Justice held that expropriation required 'the just price of what was expropriated', measured by 'the value of the undertaking at the moment of dispossession'.[44] The Tribunal's awards have taken into consideration different concepts, such as fair market value, going concern value and discounted cash flow, and have applied them depending on the circumstances of the cases, eg whether it was dealing with a lawful or unlawful expropriation or with other measures affecting property rights.[45]

V. CONCLUSION

The Tribunal was intended to settle all disputes within a few years; not to last for over 30 years. However, '*Ce n'est que le provisoire qui dure.*' The Tribunal has settled 3,844 claims from persons or companies against Iran or the US and 92 claims from one of these states against the other. In doing so, it has taken away another source of tension between two countries whose recent relations have been tense. The circumstance that the claims concern events of 30 years ago and that the parties' submissions with regard to these claims are purely factual and legal – and not political – makes the Tribunal one of the few places where Iran and the US are engaged in dialogue and interaction. Thus, the Tribunal has also a diplomatic function as a place of encounter between Iran and the US.

The Tribunal has shown the way to many post-war settlement mechanisms, which have been installed in the last decades. The UNCC, the EECC, the Dormant Accounts Tribunal, the Bosnian Commission for Real Property Claims and many other bodies are tributary to the IUSCT, which explored the modalities to allow private claims against states to be

---

43 G Aldrich, above n28 at 173.

44 *Case Concerning the Factory at Chorzow (Merits)*, Permanent Court of International Justice, Judgment of 13 September 1928, No 13, Series A – No 17, p 47.

45 For more details on the jurisprudence of the Tribunal, see G Aldrich, above n28 at 218 ff.

brought before an international tribunal.[46] Moreover, the Tribunal has developed important principles of international law and arbitration law, which are of general use.

46 Eg S Murphy, W Kidane and T Snider, *Litigating War-Mass Civil Injury and the Eritrea-Ethiopia Claims Commission* (Oxford 2013) at 44.

11. The Special Tribunal for Lebanon and the rule of law

Daniel Fransen

Indicators such as access to justice, effectiveness and efficiency, integrity, transparency and accountability are well accepted in democratic societies with a strong rule of law tradition. Governments, international organisations and civil society play an integral role in safeguarding it. When governments fall short of their responsibility and civil society or the media are unable to sufficiently influence or denounce government practices, the international community may have a duty to act in the most grievous of situations. At least this is the position that has been largely argued.

In those circumstances, the responsibility to uphold the rule of law may rise to the international level. The creation of international criminal tribunals, such as the Special Tribunal for Lebanon (STL) with jurisdiction over the most heinous crimes, may be considered acceptable in such contexts.

To be clear, as a general rule, the establishment of ad hoc international criminal tribunals with jurisdiction over offences committed within the territorial boundaries of a sovereign State is an anomaly. Crimes should normally be investigated and tried in the country where they have been committed, by the local authorities and judiciary of that State. It is in the interest of the citizens of that State, the victims and the accused that this be so. It is only in exceptional circumstances that the international community should intervene and take over the responsibility of a State to investigate, prosecute and try. A weakening of the rule of law in a State where heinous crimes, such as terrorism, have 'contributed to the creation of a climate of insecurity and intimidation, which seriously affects the functioning of the country's political institutions as well as economic and social life',[1] may fall in the category of exceptional circumstances.

[1] Report of the Secretary-General pursuant to para 6 of Resolution 1644 (2005), UN Doc S/2006/176, 21 March 2006, para 13.

This is the context in which, seven years ago, the STL was established to investigate and try the alleged perpetrators of several terrorist attacks committed in Lebanon between 2004 and 2005. Like the other ad hoc tribunals that preceded it, the STL was designed to have an international character and to be based on the highest standards of criminal justice.[2] It was the first to address the distinct crime of terrorism which, in the circumstances, was seen as a threat to international peace and security. This jurisdiction *ratione materiae* is one of several unique attributes of the STL which will be explored in this chapter.

Now having had its mandate extended twice, the specific contribution of the STL to the rule of law can be analysed both on a domestic and international level in light of the overall judicial process which has so far only addressed one specific event while Lebanon underwent numerous destabilising terrorist attacks.[3] The STL was aimed at setting an example, not only by fighting against impunity for these specific acts of terror but also by upholding and, where appropriate, further developing the rule of law, no matter the challenges it encountered. Such a task can really only be met if the Tribunal's foundation lies on solid ground.

I. INTRODUCTORY REMARKS ON THE ESTABLISHMENT OF THE STL, THE CURRENT STAGE OF THE PROCEEDINGS AND THE RULE OF LAW

A. The Special Tribunal for Lebanon

On 14 February 2005, at around 13:00, a very large explosion struck in downtown Beirut, the capital of Lebanon. A bomb, strategically placed in an ordinary vehicle as alleged by the STL Prosecutor, detonated as a six-vehicle convoy of high-ranking officials was driving by. The explosion killed the former Lebanese Prime Minister, Rafiq Hariri, and 21

---

[2] UNSC Resolution 1757 (2007) adopted by the Security Council on 30 May 2007.

[3] Since the killing of former Prime Minister Rafiq Hariri in February 2005, a number of prominent Lebanese figures have been assassinated in terrorist attacks, including: politician Pierre Amine Gemayel (November 2006); politician Walid Eido (June 2007); politician Antoine Ghanem (September 2007); Major General François al-Hajj (December 2007); politician Saleh al Aridi (September 2008); the head of the intelligence branch of the Internal Security Forces Wissam al-Hassan (October 2013); former Minister Mohamad Chatah (December 2013).

other people. Many bystanders – 226 – were injured by the blast which left a crater at least ten metres wide and two metres deep. The explosion has been estimated as the equivalent of 2500 kg of TNT. The 14 February 2005 attack was not an isolated incident. A series of other killings and bombings occurred before and after that date.

The Lebanese population was moved by the incident as was the international community. The UN Security Council issued a statement calling the explosion a 'terrorist act [whose] implications constitute a threat to international peace and security'.[4] It also reaffirmed 'its profound commitment to the national unity and stability of Lebanon' and that its future should be decided by the Lebanese themselves 'free of intimidation and foreign interference, and warning in this regard that attempts to undermine the stability of Lebanon will not be tolerated'.[5] It declared itself convinced that 'it is unacceptable in principle that anyone anywhere should escape accountability for an act of terrorism for any reason, including because of his own obstruction of the investigation or failure to cooperate in good faith'.[6] Finally, it called on the Lebanese government to bring to justice the perpetrators, organisers and sponsors of the attack.

To assist in this endeavour, the UN Secretary-General commissioned a fact-finding mission that was sent to Beirut 11 days after the explosion – a very swift response – to enquire into the causes, circumstances and consequences of the attack.[7] This mission worked in close cooperation with the Lebanese authorities. Of interest perhaps, is that the head of the mission noted in his report of 24 March 2005 a certain lack of commitment in the local investigation of the crime. As a result, a Commission – the UN International Independent Investigation Commission (Commission) – was established by the UN Security Council in April 2005.[8]

These attacks, among other things, prompted the government of Lebanon to approach the UN on 13 December 2005 with a request to

---

[4] UNSC Resolution 1636 (2005), Preambular para 19.

[5] Ibid., para 15.

[6] Ibid., para 18.

[7] See generally, Report of the Fact-finding Mission to Lebanon Inquiring into the Causes, Circumstances and Consequences of the Assassination of former Prime Minister Rafik Hariri, UN Doc S/2005/203, 24 March 2005.

[8] See UNSC Resolution 1595 (2005).

create an independent tribunal of 'an international character'.[9] The request was made a day after the assassination of M Gebran Tueni, a prominent journalist, killed by way of a bomb placed in a car parked along the route taken the day of the Hariri attack, the same alleged modus operandi as 14 February 2005 attack. Two days later, the UN Security Council acknowledged the request and authorised the Secretary-General to assist the government of Lebanon in identifying the nature and scope of its request.[10] This process culminated in the signing of an Agreement by the government of Lebanon and the UN for the establishment of the Tribunal, to which its Statute is attached.[11] However, owing to domestic institutional impediments, ie the speaker of the Lebanese parliament refused to convene parliamentarians to hold a vote, the Lebanese authorities were unable to ratify the Agreement. The Lebanese government then sent a petition signed by a majority of members of parliament to the UN Secretary-General requesting that the UN Security Council create the Tribunal nonetheless. In light of this situation, and on the basis of the coercive powers conferred upon it under Chapter VII of the UN Charter, the UN Security Council adopted Resolution 1757 (2007) on 30 May 2007, bringing into force the provisions of the Agreement and the Statute.

This process thus led to the establishment of the Special Tribunal for Lebanon which opened on 1 March 2009 in Leidschendam, in The Netherlands. It was the first – and so far only – hybrid (in terms of composition of judiciary) tribunal of an international character with jurisdiction over the crime of terrorism. This jurisdiction is limited in time and in scope. It covers the 14 February 2005 attack and any connected incidents committed between 1 October 2004 and 12 December 2005. At the time, the Commission had identified 20 attacks in its reports and had reached the conclusion that they were neither disparate nor unconnected to the 14 February 2005 attack.[12] The Tribunal can also

---

[9] See Letter dated 13 December 2005 from the Chargé d'affaires a.i. of the Permanent Mission of Lebanon to the United Nations addressed to the Secretary-General, UN Doc S/2005/783, 13 December 2005.

[10] UNSC Resolution 1644 (2005), para 6.

[11] See Agreement between the United Nations and the Lebanese Republic on the establishment of a Special Tribunal for Lebanon; Statute of the Special Tribunal for Lebanon (annexed to Report of the Secretary-General on the establishment of a Special Tribunal for Lebanon, UN Doc S/2006/893, 15 November 2006).

[12] 11th Report of the International Independent Investigation Commission, 10 December 2008, para 34.

be seised of other connected cases which are in nature and gravity similar to the 14 February 2005 attack, not falling within the specified time period, but only with the consent of the Security Council. Indeed, as stated by the UN Secretary-General 'singling out for prosecution the assassination of Rafiq Hariri, while disregarding a score of other connected attacks could cast a serious doubt on the objectivity and impartiality of the tribunal and lead to the perception of selective justice'.[13]

The establishment of the STL has been criticised by many, including the defence for the accused before the Tribunal who have alleged that it was created illegally and violated Lebanese sovereignty. Their main argument was that the Agreement annexed to Security Council Resolution 1757 had not validly entered into force in Lebanon. In 2012, the Trial Chamber of the STL determined that Security Council Resolution 1757 was the sole basis for establishing the Tribunal.[14] This determination was endorsed by the Appeals Chamber.[15] As a result, Lebanon's obligations under the draft Agreement stemmed from Lebanon's own obligation under Article 25 of the UN Charter to abide by Security Council's resolution and from the preamble to its Constitution.

B. The Current Stage of the Proceedings

To date, five persons have been charged with respect to the 14 February 2005 attack. The initial indictment, targeting four accused and which enumerates the crimes, was confirmed by the Pre-trial Judge on 28 June 2011.[16]

The trial started on 16 January 2014 after the completion of the pre-trial phase during which arrest warrants against each accused went unexecuted, the indictment was amended several times and over 60 victims were admitted to participate in the proceedings. An initial trial date of 25 March 2013 was vacated upon a defence request because

---

[13] Report of the Secretary-General on the Establishment of a Special Tribunal for Lebanon (S/2006/893), 15 November 2006.

[14] STL, *Prosecutor v. Ayyash et al.*, STL-11-01/PT/TC, Decision on the Defence Challenges to the Jurisdiction and Legality of the Tribunal, 27 July 2012, para 45 and following.

[15] STL, *Prosecutor v. Ayyash et al.*, STL-11-01/PT/AC/AR90.1, Decision on the Defence Appeals Against the Trial Chamber's 'Decision on the Defence Challenges to the Jurisdiction and Legality of the Tribunal', 24 October 2012.

[16] STL, *Prosecutor v. Ayyash et al.*, STL-11-01/I, Decision Relating to the Examination of the Indictment of 10 June 2011 Issued Against Mr Salim Jamil Ayyash, Mr Mustafa Amine Badreddine, Mr Hussein Hassan Oneissi and Mr Assad Hassan Sabra, 28 June 2011.

prosecution disclosure had not been completed.[17] Later in 2013, while the pre-trial phase of the case against the four accused was ongoing, the prosecutor seised the Pre-trial Judge of a motion to confirm an indictment against a fifth accused with respect to the same 14 February 2005 attack. That indictment was confirmed on 31 July 2013.[18] Five months later, the prosecution requested that the two cases be joined. This was done by the Trial Chamber on 11 February 2014[19] and caused the trial, which had started mid-January 2014, to be adjourned for some months to allow the defence for the fifth accused to prepare.

C. The Rule of Law

There is no single agreed upon definition or interpretation of the 'rule of law'. The phrase has been widely used by politicians, judges and academics. In fact, in the minds of some, the concept of the rule of law remains 'exceedingly elusive', or perhaps more alarmingly, according to one political theorist,[20] 'the phrase has become meaningless thanks to ideological abuse and general over-use'.

I would rather advocate that the rule of law has in the past had specific and important meanings. Today, it is best understood by appreciating its specific elements; many of which are cited, in general terms, in various modern day definitions. The Secretary-General of the UN, for example, has defined the rule of law as:

> a principle of governance in which all persons, institutions and entities, … , including the State itself, are accountable to laws that are publicly promulgated, equally enforced and independently adjudicated, and which are consistent with international human rights norms and standards. It requires, as well, measures to ensure adherence to the principles of supremacy of law, equality before the law, accountability to the law, fairness in the application of the law,

---

[17] STL, *Prosecutor v. Ayyash et al.*, Case No STL-11-01/PT/PTJ, Decision Relating to the Defence Motion to Vacate the Date for the Start of Trial, 21 February 2013.

[18] STL, *Prosecutor v. Merhi*, Case No STL-13-04/I/PTJ, Public Redacted Version of the 'Decision Relating to the Examination of the Indictment of 5 June 2013 Issued Against Mr Hassan Habib Merhi' dated 31 July 2013, 11 October 2013.

[19] STL, *Prosecutor v. Ayyash et al.*, Case No. STL-11-01/T/TC, Decision on Trial Management and Reasons for Decision on Joinder, 25 February 2014.

[20] Judith N Shklar, *Political Thought & Political Thinkers, ed* Stanley Hoffmann (University of Chicago Press, 1998) 21.

> separation of powers, participation in decision-making, legal certainty, avoidance of arbitrariness and procedural and legal transparency.[21]

This definition refers to many important normative, procedural and institutional principles which over time have been defined, debated and, in some cases, thoroughly adjudicated by a large number of domestic jurisdictions. This has led to the maturing of specific rule of law indicators which are commonly used by, among others, the UN in the assessment of State practices.

II. THE STL'S FEATURES AND THE RULE OF LAW

A. The Different Organs of the Tribunal

To be credible, the establishment of an international body must start with the creation of a solid institutional and structural framework. At the STL, this is composed of four independent organs: the Office of the Prosecutor (OTP), the Defence Office, the Chambers and the Registry. This chapter will refer to the first three organs and only focus on some key or novel elements.

1. The Office of the Prosecutor

The OTP is responsible for the investigation and prosecution of the crimes falling within the Tribunal's jurisdiction. The Prosecutor acts independently and must not seek or receive instruction from any government or other source (see Article 11 of the Statute). The office carries out its functions not solely in its capacity as a party to the proceedings, but also as a judicial organ that shall assist the Tribunal in establishing the truth and protect the interest of the victims and witnesses pursuant to Rule 55 (C) of the Rules of Procedure and Evidence (Rules or RPE). These characteristics are no different from those of the Office of the Prosecutor at the other international criminal tribunals, although the STL's Statute is the only one to explicitly mention them.

Rather the distinctive feature of the STL OTP resides in the scope of its investigative powers. The statutes of other international tribunals generally lay out a broad investigative mandate and refer to certain categories of crimes: war crimes, crimes against humanity, genocide. The

---

[21] Report of the UN Secretary-General, *The Rule of Law and Transitional Justice in Conflict and Post-Conflict Societies*, UN Doc S/2004/616, 23 August 2004, para 6.

Prosecutor may select cases whose facts he or she regards as falling under one or more of those categories and then attempt to identify those responsible.

The STL Statute, on the other hand, limits the Tribunal's jurisdiction to a set of facts: the killing of the former Prime Minister Hariri and 21 other persons, as well as additional attacks connected with that killing under Articles 1 and 11(1) of the Statute. The Prosecutor must determine whether those facts can be characterised, under Lebanese law, as (i) 'acts of terrorism', (ii) 'crimes and offences against life and personal integrity', (iii) crime of 'illicit association', (iv) crime of conspiracy (complot), or (v) crime of 'failure to report crimes and offences' (see Article 2 of the Statute). In that sense, the investigative powers of the Prosecutor replicate more closely those found in domestic jurisdictions, where a set of facts leads to a complaint and an investigation. The STL Prosecutor's role is much more focused and less discretionary.

2. The Defence Office

This independent office does not fall under the authority of the Registry as in other international criminal tribunals (see Articles 7 and 13 of the Statute). The establishment of this autonomous organ was aimed at redressing the imbalance often observed in adversarial systems between the prosecution and the accused; the former generally being well-equipped and capable of counting on numerous competent investigators and prosecutors, the latter often being at a disadvantage with regard to manpower and equipment. Thus, the Defence Office serves to strengthen the principle of equality of arms.[22]

When defining the parameters of this office, two options were available: first, it could be assigned the comprehensive task of providing legal representation to the accused, or it could be confined to providing assistance to appointed defence counsel. The latter option was chosen, for it better ensured the neutrality and impartiality of the Defence Office while protecting the right of each accused to choose his counsel and strategy. The roles of the Defence Office and defence counsel are consequently separate and distinct. Defence counsel represent the accused and the Defence Office supports the efforts of these counsel. However, pursuant to Article 13(2) of the Statute and Rule 57(F) of the Rules, the Defence Office 'shall have a right of audience in relation to

---

22 Rules of Procedure and Evidence – Explanatory memorandum by the Tribunal's President, April 2012, 10.

matters of general interest to Defence teams, the fairness of the proceedings or the rights of a suspect or accused'. For instance, before the assignment of defence counsel, the Defence Office has taken an active role with respect to issues related to the absent and unrepresented accused. This has created some friction about the role and function of the Defence Office.

In its support role, the Head of the Defence Office 'may seek co-operation [...] from any State, entity or person to assist with the defence of suspects and accused before the Tribunal' pursuant to Rule 15 of the Rules. This is an important aspect of the work of the Defence Office as it is not uncommon for accused persons or their legal counsel to encounter resistance from domestic authorities when seeking cooperation. The intervention of the Head of the Defence Office may prove critical in these instances.

It is in fact for that reason that the Defence Office independently negotiated an agreement on cooperation with the Minister of Justice of Lebanon aimed at authorising Defence investigations to conduct their work on Lebanese territory.[23] These types of investigations were completely foreign to Lebanese officials who are accustomed to the Romano-Germanic tradition for the investigation of crime. Under this tradition, lawyers are not permitted to conduct investigations themselves. Such conduct can lead to disciplinary action or even criminal sanctions. Conversely, the STL's procedures empower defence counsel by recognising their need to conduct confidential investigations, including finding and questioning their own witnesses wherever they may be. Technically, under the aforementioned agreement, defence counsel are no longer limited by the Romano-Germanic rules when investigating in Lebanon. Without successfully addressing this issue, the proceedings before the Tribunal could have been brought to a complete standstill. This same agreement ensures that requests for cooperation emanating from defence counsel are actioned separately from those submitted by the prosecutor.

3. The Pre-trial Judge or *juge de la mise en état*

There appears to be no adequate English translation for the term *juge de la mise en état*. Pre-trial Judge does not cut it. This is perhaps not surprising, as the role of this judge does not exist in Anglo-Saxon legal traditions nor does it exist as such at other international tribunals. In that

[23] Memorandum of Understanding between the Government of the Lebanese Republic and the Defence Office on the modalities of their cooperation, 28 July 2010.

regard, the concept of the Pre-trial Judge is a novelty in international criminal justice.

In terms of background, this novelty is the result of various experiences at other international criminal tribunals where procedures have been excessively long and trial judges have had little authority to intervene. Something needed to be done. The appointment of a Pre-trial Judge with extended powers over the preparation of the trial seemed quite a natural idea, especially given the fact that Lebanon already recognises the role of juges d'instruction or investigative judges.

However, under normal circumstances, the Pre-trial Judge does not conduct investigations nor does he take responsibility for them. The Pre-trial Judge is not a juge d'instruction's alter ego, nor is he a prosecutor. He is not part of the Trial or the Appeals Chamber either. He will not rule on the admissibility of evidence at trial nor participate in the rendering of the verdict. He stands alone, between the participants and the Trial Chamber. Thanks to this unique position, and in order to ensure a fair and expeditious trial, he may intervene in the case to resolve practical issues or rule on procedural matters without jeopardising or tainting the judicial process. This gives the Pre-trial Judge a lot of freedom in his functions.

To illustrate, the Pre-trial Judge may summon and hear witnesses or request a State to do so under Rules 77, 78, 79 and 88 of the Rules, as well as search for or seise probative materials under Rule 77(B) of the Rules. He may furthermore, under certain conditions, act like a juge d'instruction and gather important incriminating and exculpatory evidence himself that the parties have not been able to obtain under Rule 92 of the Rules. This approach can also be less invasive. The Pre-trial Judge may simply intervene in or support a party's request for cooperation under Rule 20 of the Rules.

For instance, five motions – pertaining to 119 requests for assistance – were presented to the Pre-trial Judge by defence counsel during the pre-trial phase to hold the Lebanese government to its obligation to cooperate with the Tribunal. The Pre-trial Judge deemed his intervention to be necessary in order to ensure the fairness of the proceedings, especially in light of the fact that defence counsel are currently unable to obtain instructions from their clients, who are all at large. So, on 11 February 2013, the Pre-trial Judge invited Lebanese officials to reply to the various cooperation requests of the defence.[24] This invitation equated more or less to an order. In case of

---

24 STL, *Prosecutor v. Ayyash et al.*, STL-11-01/PT/PTJ, Decision on the Defence Request Seeking to Obtain the Cooperation of Lebanon, 11 February 2013.

non-compliance, it is possible to bring the matter before the Security Council under Rule 20(C) of the Rules. Unfortunately, the cooperation issues were not solved during the pre-trial phase of the proceedings and were brought before the Trial Chamber as part of the residual issues that were transferred with the case file by the Pre-trial Judge.

4. An active role of the judges of the Trial Chamber

The Trial Chamber can shorten the duration of examinations and cross-examinations or summon witnesses and experts who have not been called to give evidence by the parties. These powers are not specific to the STL.

However, Trial Chamber judges have a wide range of specific powers enabling them to conduct expeditious and fair proceedings. For example, under Rule 145(A) they can examine witnesses themselves before the parties have done so. This presupposes that the Trial Chamber has been provided with the complete case file (*dossier de la cause*) to familiarise itself with the evidence collected, as well as any potential legal and factual problems. Despite the fact that the Trial Chamber had been provided with the case file in October 2013, just before the start of the trial, it has to date not used this power thereby reverting to the same practices as seen before other international criminal tribunals.

The debate regarding this more active role of the judges, in particular with regard to accessing the dossier before evidence is presented at trial by the parties, is real. It stems from the different legal traditions, ie common law and civil law. On the one hand, it is part of the adversarial system that judges know as little as possible about the case before the trial. That way, they can assess the evidence with fresh and independent eyes. On the other hand, judges coming from the inquisitorial system like to study the case before trial and actively lead and direct the proceedings.

5. Independence and separation of powers

(i) Independence When setting up the STL, its independence was a natural prerequisite. Indeed, an important aspect of the rule of law is that judicial decisions be made by a court which is independent of any influence or pressure and can be seen as such. Therefore, the potential for political influence/interference needed to be considered.

The Tribunal's Statute was clearly drafted with 'independence' in mind. It describes the required qualifications of judges and specifies that they are to be independent in the performance of their functions and are not to accept or seek instructions from any government or any other source under Article 9 of the Statute.

The appointment of the judges followed a rigorous process involving a selection panel of two international judges and a representative of the UN Secretary-General. Still, it is sometimes alleged that political forces play, improperly so, a role in this process. After all, the judges are ultimately appointed by the UN Secretary-General who is the head of a political body. But the following combination of factors makes it very difficult for anyone to cause the Tribunal to deviate from its responsibility to act independently. As a preliminary matter, judges are usually very keen on differentiating themselves from the organ which appointed them. They fiercely protect their independence and often make a point of judging free of any political influences.

The Chambers' composition is also interesting in that regard. There exists a mix of experience, legal cultures (as already mentioned, common law vs civil law) and nationalities (no two judges come from the same jurisdiction, except for the Lebanese judges who, within each chamber, represent a minority). This mix is an effective way of safeguarding against political influences or attempts to corrupt the decision-making process.

The stable status of judges is also important. Judges are nominated for three years and cannot be removed during that time. Their tenure can, however, be renewed.

Another issue that comes up from time to time when examining the independence of international tribunals is that of monetary considerations. The Republic of Lebanon is required to contribute 49 per cent of the Tribunal's total budget. The other 51 per cent comes from donor States. It could be argued that this situation calls the judicial independence of the Tribunal into question.

However, the Agreement between the UN and Lebanon stipulates that 'should voluntary contributions be insufficient for the Tribunal to implement its mandate, the Secretary-General and the Security Council shall explore alternate means of financing the Tribunal'. Given this option, it is highly unlikely that say Lebanon, by itself, could influence the course of justice by withholding its mandatory contributions. This is especially in light of the support of a fair amount of other States which recognise that there is far too much at stake to let financial considerations detract from fighting terrorism. This support is certainly reassuring; still, a more consistent financial scheme (not solely reliant on donations) would be quite welcome, not only to guarantee stability for the Tribunal's activities but also to ease staff members' worries as has been seen in the last few years with Lebanon's yearly contribution being delayed, except in 2012 – although always forthcoming in the end.

However, financial considerations can also be invoked to shorten the timelines of proceedings. No State intends to contribute to ad hoc international tribunals forever. These are, after all, temporary institutions, created to judge specific facts or crimes which occurred within a determined period of time. The international community expects results quickly. There is no doubt that expedition benefits all interested, including the accused and victims. Swift justice, however, can never justify breaches of the principle of the rule of law. Judges must be wary not to sacrifice fairness in favour of expediency due to financial considerations.

(ii) Separation of power and law-making process A second point concerns the separation of powers. A clear separation of the legislative, executive and judicial powers of government is also critical in upholding the rule of law, in that it protects against, among other things, abuse or a lack of accountability. This separation is even more important in the context of – what one may call – aggressive legislative reform by governments in matters of terrorism. While the legislative branch enacts these reforms, the judiciary must have the authority to assess their legality.

In the context of international criminal tribunals, there appears to be a slight anomaly. Judges at such tribunals are called upon to adopt the RPE which will govern the proceedings before them. It is during the plenary sessions that the RPE are discussed and drafted or amended by the judges. The RPE of the STL contain 202 provisions and have already been modified eight times within the last six years.

Realistically speaking, if not entirely justified from a rule of law point of view, the drafting of one's own rules is explained by the temporary nature of many international criminal tribunals, their limited resources, their novel structure or jurisdictional scope and the need for expediency, to name just a few arguments. In contrast, at International Criminal Court (ICC) – the world's only permanent international criminal tribunal – the RPE are drafted and approved by the ICC Assembly of States Parties, not its judges.

Whether or not this is entirely convincing, the high degree of scrutiny to which the STL is subjected is certainly a factor that keeps the judges' legislative power in check. Unlike domestic legislation and decisions, which can arguably remain 'buried' within their jurisdiction, the STL's every move makes the front page of Lebanese newspapers and/or becomes the subject of worldwide academic and media attention. In addition, even if the judge's plenary meetings are held in closed sessions, as they are, a summary of the accepted amendments and key rejected amendments is made available to the public. There is a great deal of accountability that flows from the public's interest in these tribunals. This power should not be underestimated.

Nevertheless, one could reflect upon the idea of creating, perhaps within the UN system, an organ with consultative or supervisory powers over the rules adopted by international tribunals.

Another apparent anomaly related to the separation of powers may reside in the fact that judges are asked to rule on the legality of the institutions of which they are part. Indeed, at the STL the defence raised, *in limine litis*, two questions before the Trial Chamber. The defence asked: what is the legal basis that authorised the creation of the Special Tribunal for Lebanon? And, if such a basis exists, what authority did the Tribunal possess to review the legality of its own creation? These questions stirred up some passionate debates; although the same questions have also been previously raised before all ad hoc tribunals.

The first question stirred up mostly political questions. People wanted to know whether Lebanon played a legal role in the establishment of the Tribunal. On 27 July 2012, the Trial Chamber ruled that the Tribunal was created solely by the Security Council's Resolution.[25] As may be recalled, the Agreement between the UN and Lebanon to create the Tribunal was never properly domestically ratified by Lebanese legislative authorities. In that context, the Security Council chose to enforce not the Agreement itself but the provisions of the Agreement. This meant that the Tribunal had been created unilaterally by the Security Council through a Resolution passed under Chapter VII of the UN Charter. As a result, Lebanon complies with its obligations under the Agreement, not because this agreement is binding per se but because, like other UN member States, it has the obligation to abide by all Chapter VII Security Council Resolutions as per Article 25 of the UN Charter.

A second question was debated before the Trial Chamber: would the Tribunal follow the path of the International Criminal Tribunal for the former Yugoslavia (ICTY) in the Tadić case;[26] a landmark decision which recognised the Tribunal's inherent jurisdiction to review the validity of a Security Council decision which created it – the *Kompetenz-Kompetenz* principle. At the STL, the Trial Chamber went down a perhaps more unexpected route. It departed from the Tadić case and rejected the notion

---

[25] STL, *Prosecutor v. Ayyash et al.*, STL-11-01/PT/TC, Decision on the Defence Challenges to the Jurisdiction and Legality of the Tribunal, 27 July 2012, para. 46.

[26] ICTY, *Prosecutor v. Tadić*, IT-94-1-AR72, Decision on the Defence Motion for Interlocutory Appeal on Jurisdiction, 2 October 1995.

that a Tribunal, created by a Security Council Resolution, has the power to review the legality of its own creation.[27]

However, the Trial Chamber found a very limited power of review under international human rights law, which guarantees every accused the right to be tried by 'a tribunal established by law'. The Trial Chamber proceeded with a two-pronged analysis of the question: first it examined whether the Security Council had the formal authority to create a tribunal and concluded that it did under the UN Charter. Then, in line with previous decisions by international tribunals and the case law of the European Court of Human Rights (ECtHR), the Trial Chamber examined whether the laws governing the Tribunal guaranteed the basic rights of the accused. It found that the Statute and Rules of the Tribunal did not infringe the rights of the accused, or at least that it was possible for the Tribunal to conduct proceedings and issue decisions which would not infringe these rights. The STL Appeals Chamber held by a majority that it lacked authority to investigate the legality of its creation and confirmed the Trial Chamber's decision on 24 October 2012.[28]

This decision could be seen as a backwards step with respect to the power of review of international criminal tribunals created by the Security Council. It could also be seen as an encouragement for the implementation of a true mechanism of control over the powers of the Security Council and other UN organs.

B. The Applicable Law

1. Lebanese criminal law

Without a doubt, one of the key elements of the rule of law is that legislation should not be ambiguous.

As aforementioned, the STL is the first tribunal of an international character to have jurisdiction over the crime of terrorism. At present, a universally accepted definition of this offence does not exist. Other tribunals (such as the ICTY and the Special Court for Sierra Leone (SCSL)) have dealt with the crime of terror under the umbrella of war

---

[27] STL, *Prosecutor v. Ayyash et al.*, STL-11-01/PT/TC, Decision on the Defence Challenges to the Jurisdiction and Legality of the Tribunal, 27 July 2012, para 55.

[28] STL, *Prosecutor v. Ayyash et al.*, STL-11-01/PT/AC/AR90.1, Decision on the Defence Appeals Against the Trial Chamber's 'Decision on the Defence Challenges to the Jurisdiction and Legality of the Tribunal', 24 October 2012.

crimes, not as an isolated offence.[29] The ICC Statute does not include this offence, primarily because States could not agree on a definition, in which case it was better to not include it at all. In this context, the question arose as to whether the STL could have a substantive impact in the elaboration of a universal definition of terrorism.

Article 2(a) of the Statute of the Tribunal states that the provisions of the Lebanese Criminal Code relating to the prosecution and punishment of acts of terrorism are to apply. Thus, the Statute makes a direct reference to domestic Lebanese law. In fact, the STL is the first international criminal tribunal with the mandate to exclusively apply domestic law to the substantive crimes falling under its jurisdiction.

In terms of procedural law, the situation is completely different owing to the Tribunal's international character. The Secretary-General discussed this character in these terms:

> [T]he constitutive instruments of the special tribunal in both form and substance evidence its international character. The legal basis for the establishment of the special tribunal is an international agreement between the United Nations and a Member State; its composition is mixed with a substantial international component; its standards of justice, including principles of due process of law, are those applicable in all international or United Nations-based criminal jurisdictions; its rules of procedure and evidence are to be inspired, in part, by reference materials reflecting the highest standards of international criminal procedure.[30]

These references to international law are in contrast, to some extent, with the Statute's specific reference to domestic Lebanese law. This situation led many to conclude that ambiguity existed as to the law governing the STL and prompted the Pre-trial judge to invoke Rule 68(G) of the RPE. This rule, created by the judges for such circumstances in November 2010, allows the Pre-trial Judge to immediately seise the Appeals Chambers with critical legal questions which, if left unanswered, may have a significant impact on the rest of the proceedings.

After having received the indictment from the prosecutor, the Pre-trial Judge submitted to the Appeals Chamber the following preliminary questions, inter alia: based on the international nature and mandate of the STL, in what circumstances should the Tribunal apply Lebanese law,

---

[29] See, ICTY, *Prosecutor v. Galić*, IT-98-29-A, Appeal Judgment, 30 November 2006, paras 79–98; SCSL, *Prosecutor v. Fofana and Kondewa*. SCSL-04-14-T, Trial Judgment, 2 August 2007, paras 167–75.

[30] Report of the Secretary-General on the Establishment of a Special Tribunal for Lebanon, UN Doc S/2006/893, 15 November 2006, para 7.

international law or both international and domestic law? In case of conflict between the two regimes, which is to prevail?

Without any guidance, the parties and the Trial Chamber would be left 'speculating' about what law(s) to apply. A final decision on this matter by the Appeals Chamber during the appellate phase of the case and near the end of the Tribunal's life – which could have overruled the trial judgment's interpretation of the applicable law – would have been devastating. Much time, energy and resources would have been spent in vain, not to mention the stress imposed on the accused, witnesses and victims during that time.

After hearing both the Prosecutor and the Defence Office, on 16 February 2011 the Appeals Chamber rendered its decision on this matter.[31]

The Appeals Chamber ruled that the Tribunal should apply the Lebanese domestic definition of the crime of terrorism, interpreted in consonance with international conventional and customary law that is binding on Lebanon. In other words, Lebanese law is to prevail but international law may supplement Lebanese law for interpretation purposes. The Appeals Chamber took two sets of rules into account: the Arab Convention on the Suppression of Terrorism (to which Lebanon was a party) and customary international law on terrorism in time of peace, applicable to all States.

With regard to the Lebanese crimes, such as homicide, attempted homicide and conspiracy, the Appeals Chamber ruled that solely domestic law should apply. However for the modes of liability, such as aiding and abetting a crime, both Lebanese law and international law are relevant. Where a conflict arises between the two, the body of law that leads to a result more favourable to the accused is to prevail.

This decision provided sufficient clarity for the Tribunal going forward, but, in addition to the other decisions and final judgment of the Tribunal, will it create an impetus for the elaboration of a universally accepted definition of the crime of terrorism or, less ambitiously, will it set the path towards such an endeavour? Only time will tell.

If it does, the impact of the Tribunal should not stop there. Its innovative approach to, for instance, witness protection is also worth adopting.

---

[31] STL, Case No STL-11-01/I/AC/R176*bis*, Interlocutory Decision on the Applicable Law: Terrorism, Conspiracy, Homicide, Perpetration, Cumulative Charging, 16 February 2011.

2. The specificities of terrorism

Terrorism, as already mentioned, is a difficult crime to investigate and prosecute, in part because of the need to rely on intelligence and witnesses who are reluctant to testify in these types of cases. Given this reality, the RPE authorise the use of special procedures without which the truth surrounding terrorist attacks may never be revealed such as the possibility of not disclosing the identity of particular witnesses. From a defence perspective, this measure clearly limits the accused's rights to a full defence. This infringement must therefore be minimal and fairly balanced with the opposing need to protect information that otherwise would not be available.

Thus Rule 93 of the RPE allows witnesses to give testimony anonymously, while still ensuring the accused's right to confront the allegations made against him or her and cross-examine these witnesses. This is the procedure: when a party considers that there is a serious risk to the life or physical or mental well-being of a witness or a family member of a witness and that the regular protective measures do not suffice, it may request that the Pre-trial Judge hear the witness anonymously. Such a request can also be made for national security considerations.

To safeguard the rights of the accused in these situations, parties may ask questions of the witness but only via the Pre-trial Judge. The Pre-trial Judge then draws up a transcript of the witness's answers, taking care to redact the information that might allow the witness to be identified, and gives his opinion as to the veracity of the statement. To ensure additional protection to the accused's rights, Rule 159(D) of the RPE provides that a conviction cannot be based solely, or to a decisive extent, on a statement of an anonymous witness.

As unusual as this procedure may seem, it is not completely novel and has been admitted by the ECtHR. The STL adopted it partly on account of some judge's experience in their domestic jurisdiction, which shows how domestic practices can influence procedural rules at the international level.

Another special regime concerns the protection of sensitive information, such as information coming from intelligence services. The RPE limit the disclosure of this type of information under certain conditions, and can be subject to compensatory measures (see Rules 117 and 118 of the RPE).

These regimes are 'special' with respect to admissibility of evidence before the STL.

3. Admission of written evidence

The RPE assume that the normal way of presenting evidence at the Tribunal would be through witnesses who are called to testify in Court under Rule 150 of the RPE. This provides the accused (and victims) with the opportunity to examine and cross-examine them fully.

In certain circumstances, judges may allow the presentation of evidence by other means, such as in written form, if the evidence has probative value and the right of the accused to a fair trial is not jeopardised.

The RPE create distinct categories of written evidence – a distinction largely based on the experience of the other international criminal tribunals.

The first category includes documents, other than written statements, like a letter, an intercept transcript or the minutes of a meeting. Such documents may be admitted into evidence pursuant to Rule 154 of the RPE if they have probative value.

The second category is of written statements and transcripts of testimonies given in previous proceedings which are admissible in lieu of oral testimony only if they do not relate to individual acts or conduct of the accused as charged in the indictment under Rule 155 of the RPE. This Rule has one exception: when the witness who provided the written statement or has previously testified, is in court and is prepared to be cross-examined. In that case, pursuant to Rule 156 of the RPE, the statement can be used to prove the individual acts or conduct of the accused, unless the other party objects to it.

Lastly, if a witness is unavailable due to his or her death or for some other compelling reason, judges have the discretion to admit that witness' statement pursuant to Rule 158 of the RPE. They will then assess the reliability of the statement according to the circumstances.

C. Other Main Features

1. Trial *in absentia*

In a number of civil law countries, including Lebanon, trials in absentia are permitted. The case law of the ECtHR and the UN Human Rights Committee has repeatedly emphasised that trials in absentia are consistent with the principles of fair justice provided that a set of safeguards for the accused are employed.[32]

---

[32] Rules of Procedure and Evidence – Explanatory memorandum by the Tribunal's President, April 2012, 19.

In contrast, such trials are criticised and strongly opposed in some common law systems, in particular where the right of the accused to attend trial is enshrined in the constitution, like in the US. Where a system is based on an adversarial model, ie a 'duel' between parties, it would seem necessary to have the accused present during examination and cross-examination in order to instruct his or her counsel.[33] Having said that, some common law countries, such as the UK, are opening the door to trials without the accused after a plea of not guilty in pre-trial proceedings, and where he or she has later absconded. In 2002, the House of Lords permitted proceeding to a trial in absentia from the beginning of the trial, when the accused absconded after being released on bail.[34]

Other arguments against these types of trials often relate to political trials. Trials in absentia are often used by dictatorial regimes to try and condemn, and hence ostracise, political opponents exiled abroad.

Based on such considerations, generally speaking, trials in absentia are not popular in public opinion.

At the international level, trials in absentia were contemplated in the Charter of the Nuremberg Tribunal. Such a trial was indeed held in the case of Martin Bormann; indicating that trials in absentia were, at least in the post-World War II period, considered acceptable at the international level. This is not to say that some countries, common law countries especially, did not have mixed feelings about the process. In fact, two of the States behind the Nuremberg Charter, namely the US and the UK, only grudgingly accepted these types of trials.[35]

Other than the Nuremberg Tribunal, no other international criminal tribunal has proceeded in absentia.

So, the question remains: are trials in absentia to be encouraged? Is the STL setting an unwelcome precedent?

There is of course no simple or unified answer to this question. Certainly in praesentia trials should be preferred and in absentia trials should be the exception and not be held unless, as the aforementioned human rights bodies have stated, a set of safeguards for the accused are employed. However, there are a number of valid reasons for holding a trial in absentia.

---

33 Ibid.

34 *See*, House of Lords: *R v Jones (On Appeal from the Court of Appeal (Criminal Division)),* 22 February 2002, [2002] UKHL 5.

35 Rules of Procedure and Evidence – Explanatory memorandum by the Tribunal's President, April 2012, p. 19.

Justice delayed, is justice denied. If legal redress is available for a party that has suffered some injury, but is not forthcoming in a timely fashion, it is effectively the same as having no redress at all. In that spirit, more and more, victims of crimes are being given due consideration in fora where the focus has nearly exclusively been on the accused. At the STL, for instance, participating victims are granted standing before the Tribunal. Such victims may never experience a sense of justice where the accused have absconded (as is the case here), unless a trial is held in their absence.

Of course, trials in absentia are not held only to satisfy the victims. There is also a public interest in seeing that justice be done within reasonable time limits notwithstanding the voluntary or non-voluntary absence of the accused.

Even the accused benefit from having his or her case heard as closely in time to the date of the crime; the passage of time affects the quality of evidence, whether that evidence is incriminating or exculpatory. No one profits from witnesses's memories fading over time or worse, being contaminated through post-event information and experiences.

Putting aside these considerations, the STL may conduct trials in absentia when an accused has expressly waived in writing his right to be present, has not been handed over by a State, or has absconded or otherwise cannot be located. If the accused appears during or after the in absentia proceedings, he may ask for a retrial (see Section 6 of the RPE).

After the confirmation of the indictment against four accused on 28 June 2011,[36] many steps were taken with a view to ensuring their participation in the proceedings. The Pre-trial Judge issued arrest warrants and asked the Lebanese authorities to execute these warrants as well as notify the accused of the indictment against them. After that, the Pre-trial Judge issued international arrest warrants through Interpol. In the absence of any arrest, the names, aliases and other personal information, including photographs of the accused as well as the charges laid against them were made public. In addition, the President of the Tribunal made a public announcement inviting the accused to appear before the Tribunal, either in person or by video-link. They were encouraged to appoint counsel to represent them. The President also ordered the authorities of Lebanon to take all reasonable steps to provide notification to the public of the existence of the indictment and to call upon the accused to surrender to the Tribunal. And finally, the text of an

---

[36] STL, *Prosecutor v. Ayyash et al.*, see note 16.

advertisement notifying the public of the identity of the accused and of the charges laid against them was published in Lebanese media.

All these steps were unsuccessful. Therefore, in accordance with Rule 105bis of the RPE, the Pre-trial Judge invited the Trial Chamber to start proceedings in absentia. After hearing the Prosecutor and the Defence Office, and having carefully reviewed the aforementioned steps, the Trial Chamber ruled in favour of a trial in absentia on 1 February 2012.[37] A similar process was undertaken with respect to the subsequent accused person whose case was then joined to the main case.[38]

After that decision, the first action taken by the Pre-trial Judge was to ensure the protection of the rights of the absent accused by requesting the Head of the Defence Office to assign a defence counsel to each of them. The case then entered the pre-trial. This gave way to requests from alleged victims to participate in the proceedings, which is an important aspect of the rule of law.

2. Victims participating in the proceedings[39]

One of the elements of the rule of law is the right of equal access to justice for all, including members of vulnerable groups. This raises the question of victims' rights in criminal proceedings. In this regard, the Statute of the STL stipulates a very important place for the victims in its proceedings, although not quite as important as that reserved for so-called parties civiles in Lebanon and other civil law countries. The victims may present their 'views and concerns' before the STL at various stages of the proceedings under Rule 87 of the RPE. They are given extensive procedural rights and powers. These include the right to receive documents and probative materials, be a witness or call witnesses, tender evidence, as well as, under the control of the Trial Chamber, examine or cross-examine witnesses and file motions and briefs. They may also participate at the appeal stage subject to the authorisation of the Appeals Chamber. However, they are not vested with the right to appeal against a judgment. Victims can also play a significant role in sentencing proceedings by assisting the Trial Chamber in assessing the personal impact of the crimes on them.

---

37 STL, *Prosecutor v. Ayyash et al.*, STL-11-01/I/TC, Decision to Hold Trial *In Absentia*, 1 February 2012.

38 *See*, STL, *Prosecutor v. Merhi*, STL-13-04/I/TC, Decision to Hold Trial *In Absentia*, 20 December 2013.

39 See, Rules of Procedure and Evidence – Explanatory memorandum by the Tribunal's President, April 2012, 7–10.

This extensive right of victims to participate is of course not without limitations. The Pre-trial Judge must first determine who is a victim and at what stage of the proceedings a victim may participate: at the stage of investigations, at the pre-trial phase or at the stage of trial proceedings?

Regarding the first question, it was decided that the notion of 'victim' must be defined rather narrowly so as to include only those persons who have suffered material, physical or mental harm as a direct result of an attack within the jurisdiction of the Tribunal (see Rule 2 of the RPE). Legal persons, as well as individuals who may have suffered indirect harm, are thus excluded. Also, victims who wish to participate in the proceedings must be authorised by the Pre-trial Judge before they can do so pursuant to Rule 87 of the RPE.

As regard the second question, the stage at which participation is allowed, it was decided that this was possible only after the confirmation of the indictment. This decision is consistent with the aims of (i) avoiding confusion that might somehow hamper the actions of the Prosecutor, and (ii) preventing possible undue delay.

In addition, the Pre-trial Judge decides how to group victims wishing to participate in the proceedings. Only after such a decision is reached can the registrar designate counsel to represent them.

Of particular importance is the fact that the Statute rules out the possibility of victims claiming compensation, leaving matters of reparation to national courts. To help facilitate this, the Tribunal provides any person identified as a victim in a final judgment with a certified copy of the judgment.

To date, 70 victims out of 84 applicants have been authorised to take part in the proceedings. They have been united under one group and are represented by a single counsel together with support staff. A number of decisions have been issued by the Pre-trial Judge on the modalities of their participation in the proceedings.

One of these decisions concerned the question of the anonymity of the victims. Indeed, the Legal Representative of the Victims requested that certain victims remain anonymous. On 19 December 2012, the Pre-trial Judge ruled against the total anonymity of victims vis-à-vis the parties, contrary to the current practice at the ICC.[40] The STL Rules do not provide for such a measure but more fundamentally, the Pre-trial Judge considered that, as a matter of principle, anonymity cannot be granted to

---

[40] STL, *Prosecutor v. Ayyash et al.*, STL-11-01/PT/PTJ, Decision on the Legal Representative of Victims' First, Second and Third Motions for Protective Measures for Victims Participating in the Proceedings, 19 December 2012.

victims participating in the proceedings. Indeed, how can the accused be denied the right to know the identity of a victim who is granted the right to call or cross-examine witnesses, tender evidence, file submissions or participate in an appeal? Furthermore, where a victim is found to have suffered harm resulting from an act for which the accused is held criminally responsible and then proceeds against the accused for compensation, the latter should be entitled to know the identity of the claimant. The matter was brought before the Appeals Chamber which ultimately confirmed the approach taken by the Pre-trial Judge.[41] In this respect, the Chamber handed down a landmark decision, since there is no definitive ruling on the question by the ICC Appeals Chamber.

Having addressed the participation of victims, the role of the accused at his or her trial should also be discussed before dealing with the importance of gaining the confidence of various communities if the STL is to make a significant difference.

3. Role of the accused during the proceedings

The accused is expected to play an active part in his or her trial. Pursuant to Rule 144 of the RPE, he or she may decide to appear as a witness in his or her own defence, in which case an oath is taken and the accused must answer questions put by the Chamber and the parties. But, and this is a novelty, the accused may choose, on the other hand, to limit his or her intervention by making one or more statements, without taking an oath and without any obligation to answer questions. Of course, this remains theoretical at this stage, since the accused are all at large.

Furthermore, in an effort to encourage the accused to participate in the proceedings, the RPE allow the accused to take part in his or her trial through counsel or by video-conferencing. Although not ideal, this alternative measure is a realistic approach given the context of the case before the Tribunal, and the Lebanese environment.

D. Confidence in the Tribunal: Transparency, Outreach and Legacy

A Tribunal such as the STL can only be effective or successful in its mandate if it can gain and maintain the confidence of the people it attempts to serve, ie the Lebanese people, and more broadly the international community. This is not a small or easy task. Scepticism,

---

41 STL, *Prosecutor v. Ayyash et al.*, STL-11-01/PT/AC/AR126.3, Decision on Appeal by Legal Representative of Victims Against Pre-trial Judge's Decision on Protective Measures, 10 April 2013.

political agendas, fear, distance between the Tribunal and the people, to name just a few factors, can easily taint the views of various observers.

Distance is perhaps the biggest obstacle to reaching out to the targeted population. The Tribunal dispenses justice thousands of kilometres away from where the acts have been committed. This distance can certainly cause a sense of disconnect between the Lebanese population and the decision-makers at the Tribunal. Non-Lebanese judges from the Tribunal have visited Beirut with a view to better understand Lebanese society, the political environment and the crimes allegedly committed, and to fill in – what some may call – the knowledge gap. This gap was noticeable at the ICTY where none of the judges came from the area under its jurisdiction. At the STL, the presence of Lebanese judges makes up for the potential lack of understanding of the other international judges regarding the country and its history.

More generally, the STL has adopted various methods to further bring together the Tribunal and the Lebanese and international community. For instance, it has a comprehensive outreach and legacy programme to which many STL heads of organs, even the judges, contribute. The primary role of this programme is to explain to the Lebanese the purpose, role and functioning of the Tribunal and to address misperceptions about the Tribunal's work.

Outreach is a new concept for judges coming from domestic systems, where they are expected to issue judgments but never comment on them or the work leading to their issuance. They generally do not bother with the public's reaction to their judgments. They are more concerned with rendering justice fairly. Here, the rule of no comment also applies. However, judges cannot disregard completely the wider impact of their decisions. This is not to say that they should adapt their decisions to the circumstances, but simply that they need to be particularly transparent. In that regard their work is followed closely by the Public Affairs Section.

The Public Affairs Section of the Tribunal is the first point of contact for external communications with journalists and the general public, principally in Lebanon and the broader Middle East. It has developed a comprehensive method for reaching out to the various segments of society through the Tribunal's website, a number of social media tools such as YouTube, Twitter and Facebook and more traditional forms of interaction with journalists.

A majority of the Tribunal's written decisions are publicly available through its website and are available in three languages, Arabic, English and French. Judges are extremely conscious of the need to disseminate their decisions as well as to give access to the proceedings. The goal is to concretely bring justice to the people. This type of transparency also holds the judges accountable for their decisions, which in turn allows the people to decide for themselves on the credibility of the process.

Some proceedings must nonetheless be conducted in closed session. One of the particularities of this Tribunal is the potential risk to people's security. Terrorism at the scale of the attack being investigated, prosecuted and tried implies managing high-security threats. The threats can be directed towards the Tribunal, but ultimately they are most likely to be directed towards the witnesses and victims. Appropriate security measures and a stable environment are obviously very important.

III. CONCLUSION

This chapter has highlighted some particular features of the Special Tribunal for Lebanon, which will, hopefully, tend to advance the rule of law in Lebanon, the region and internationally, be it features related to judicial independence and the active role of judges in the proceedings, the creation of an autonomous and independent Defence Office, the clarity of the law, procedural innovations with respect to the singular nature of terrorism, the participation of victims, or the protection of the rights of the accused in proceedings in absentia. The 14 February 2005 incident is surely the most notorious terrorist attack in Lebanon's recent history, although by no means an isolated one. Many, if not all, of these crimes remain unsolved and unpunished. The referral of the 14 February 2005 terrorist attack to the UN could be viewed as an implicit recognition of Lebanon's limited capacity to uphold the rule of law ie to deal adequately with this act and other connected events. There is no doubt that investigating, prosecuting and trying terrorism cases represent monumental challenges for any State, let alone the State where alleged terrorist groups have purportedly infiltrated society, are highly organised and have extraordinary means. Significant resources, specialised expertise and a strong rule of law culture are fundamental components for successful terrorism investigations, prosecutions and trials. The referral by Lebanese authorities should in fact be seen as a sincere attempt by them at that time to bring those responsible for terrorism to account, if not through their own institutions, then through that of an independent international body like the STL. According to the International Center for Transitional Justice's latest report on Lebanon, the STL is the first significant attempt to pursue accountability for political violence in Lebanon for a limited number of crimes.[42] Albeit significant, this attempt is indeed limited by the STL's narrow jurisdiction.

The establishment of the STL may also be the first step towards a permanent terrorism tribunal, which could be a strong signal from the international community demonstrating its determination to combat this phenomenon. As recent events in the Middle East and Europe show, the scourge of terrorism remains as prevalent as ever. Such a potential contribution by the STL also implies the need for it to be accepted and be seen as a credible institution at the international level of course, among regional actors in the Middle East, but also and especially by the Lebanese population. It is only by meeting this last condition that the Tribunal will be able to fulfil its mandate, which is to strengthen justice and the rule of law in Lebanon and, let us hope, peace and security as well.

42 Failing to deal with the past: the cost to Lebanon, ICTJ, January 2014.

PART V

Epilogue

12. Epilogue: Curb, channel and coordinate: The constitutionalisation of international courts and tribunals

Andreas Follesdal

The growth in number and caseload of international courts and tribunals (ICs) over the last 35 years is striking. Consider: in 1980, only three of the nine ICs presented in this volume existed.[1] Some scholars link the surge to the fall of the Berlin Wall and the hopes of that event for a new international legal order. The contributions in this volume elaborate in fascinating ways both the potential and the pitfalls of this cascade of ICs.

They were set up to promote multifarious objectives, without much attention to the risks of fragmentation within and among them, their potential for 'hollowing out' the sovereignty of their creators, or the new risks they created.[2] No surprise that concerns have blossomed about the legitimacy of these ICs, singly and as a 'global judiciary' as they multiply, come of age and gain institutional interests and momentum. Jointly, they have become so powerful and autonomous that they cannot be reined in – nor explained nor assessed – simply as the creators of their masters. Yet many of them still appear unable to meet the – possibly unrealistic – aspirations of their creators and other 'compliance communities'.[3]

---

[1] ICJ (1945); ECJ (1952); ECtHR (1959, but became a permanent court only in 1998); Lebanon (2009); ICC (1998 (Statute adopted), 2002 (started functioning)); US-Iran Claims Tribunal (1981); ICTY (1993); ITLOS (1996); Appellate body of WTO (1995).

[2] A von Bogdandy and I Venzke, 'On the Functions of International Courts: An Appraisal in Light of Their Burgeoning Public Authority' (2013) 26 *Leiden Journal of International Law* 49–72 and A Follesdal and S Hix, 'Why There Is a Democratic Deficit in the EU: A Response to Majone and Moravcsik' (2006) 44 *Journal of Common Market Studies* 533–62.

[3] X Dai, *International Institutions and National Policies* (Cambridge, Cambridge University Press, 2007) and K Alter, *The New Terrain of International Law: International Courts in International Politics* (Princeton, Princeton University Press, 2013).

From the vantage point of normative political philosophy the preceding chapters offer several lessons and further research questions of how to assess and promote the legitimacy of these ICs. The following comments identify some of these.

Section I identifies some of the hitherto understudied arenas where the authors remind us that the perceived legitimacy of the ICs matters if they are to secure their various objectives.

Section II addresses one central standard of legitimacy: the content of the concept of the rule of law, which remains contested both as an objective of ICs, and as a requirement on their operation. I stipulate that two central underlying values justify several if not all rule of law norms: non-domination and stable legitimate expectations. Respect for human rights is a further substantive value which many but not all contributors include in the concept.

I then consider two main challenges to the legitimacy of ICs from rule of law standards. One is the possible fragmentation and the legal uncertainty that may ensue. Section III thus summarizes the chapters' insights about the alleged fragmentation wrought by so many ICs. Section IV considers some further challenges to the objectives and performance of ICs by these rule of law standards. Their multiple objectives require that the judges and arbitrators enjoy a wide berth of discretion in interpretation and adjudication – which raise the risk that states and individuals become subject to domination by the ICs themselves. Individuals may end up not living under the rule of law but under the rule of international lawyers.

The following two sections gather several possible strands of responses to these fears. Section V elaborates how the power of ICs is constrained by their complex interrelationship with domestic authorities. Some such interdependence may be assessed by a further popular standard of legitimacy in addition to the rule of law, namely *subsidiarity*. This concept is often invoked in international law, explicitly so for the European Union[4] and in debates concerning the European Convention on Human Rights.[5] The section explores how several features of the authority of ICs presented by the authors may be explained and perhaps assessed by some standard of subsidiarity, to reduce the risks wrought by the ICs themselves. Appeals to subsidiarity may not so much lay issues to

---

[4] *Treaty of Lisbon Amending the Treaty of European Union and the Treaty Establishing the European Community* (Adopted 13 December 2007, in Force 1 December 2009) [2007] *Official Journal of the European Union C306/1*.

[5] Council of Europe, *Protocol No 15 Amending the Convention on Fundamental Freedoms* 2013.

rest as stimulate more structured and systematic arguments concerning the legitimacy of ICs. Section VI considers several ways to regulate the discretion of the ICs to reduce the risks of fragmentation and domination, garnered from the contributions of this volume, establish more curbs on the international courts, and guide and coordinate them better; in short: increased legitimacy of international courts requires their constitutionalisation.

I. WHY LEGITIMACY MATTERS

How do the contributions in this volume elucidate questions about the legitimate authority of ICs? An influential tradition maintains that the core issue of legitimate authority is why a judgment by an IC gives other actors a reason to act differently than they would, even imposing on them a moral obligation to do so.[6] When actors such as domestic courts regard an IC as a *legitimate* authority, they are *somewhat* more likely to comply or defer, be it because they are socialized to do so;[7] or due to their 'capacity to be moved for moral reasons'.[8] Several scholars have noted that the range of actors possibly affected by ICs is wide: there are many important 'compliance communities' including domestic civil society and other ICs.[9]

Contributions in this volume remind us that much of the impact of ICs – intended or not – depends on compliance communities often overlooked, far beyond states who must decide to change their legislation or policies eg in response to the WTO dispute settlement system.[10]

If ITLOS, ECtHR and other ICs succeed in specifying legal norms[11] or in redefining concepts such as the ICTY's definition of 'joint criminal

---

[6] J Raz, 'The Problem of Authority: Revisiting the Service Conception' (2006) 90 *Minnesota Law Review* 1003–44.

[7] I Hurd, *After Anarchy. Legitimacy and Power in the United Nations Security Council* (Princeton, Princeton University Press, 2007).

[8] A Buchanan and R O Keohane, 'The Legitimacy of Global Governance Institutions' (2006) 20 *Ethics and International Affairs* 405–37 at 409.

[9] Dai, above n3 and K Alter, 'The New Terrain of International Law: Courts, Politics, Rights' in K Alter (ed.), *The New Terrain of International Law: International Courts in International Politics* (Princeton University Press, 2013).

[10] P Van den Bossche, 'The Appellate Body of the World Trade Organization' in the present volume.

[11] P Gautier, 'The Contribution of the International Tribunal for the Law of the Sea to the Rule of Law' and P Lemmens, 'The Contribution of the European Court of Human Rights to the Rule of Law', both in the present volume.

enterprise' or gender based violence,[12] this is due to a wide range of private and public actors who accept the authority of these ICs in this regard. ICs that seek to bolster the domestic rule of law through training and capacity building must likewise do so not by sanctions but by voluntary acceptance by domestic audiences. Likewise, if ICs are to succeed in ambitious objectives such as *halting* crimes – as the UN Security Council sought with the ICTY[13] – or to combat terrorism at large as is hoped with the STL[14] – this requires the voluntary cooperation of local communities to generate public pressure on politicians at large – as well as regional actors and the international community at large.

In general, then, the manifold objectives of ICs force us to look very broadly to identify the important actors who must be convinced that the IC is indeed legitimate. This leads us to two further issues: what standards are relevant for such assessments of legitimacy, and what are the 'functions' or 'objectives' of ICs?

II. THE CONTESTED CONCEPT OF THE RULE OF LAW

A central standard of legitimacy is that which is the focus of this volume: the rule of law. The content of this concept is contested, even among the authors represented here. Discussions of the rule of law in domestic settings typically include several norms or values. Thus Lon Fuller listed eight desiderata of the 'inner morality of law', including general applicability, promulgation, non-retroactivity, clarity, consistency, within human capability, *stare decisis*, and congruence.[15] Lord Bingham offers a somewhat different list, including that the law must apply to all equally, it must be accessible and intelligible, clear and predictable; resolve disputes concerning legal rights and liabilities fairly, according to law rather than discretion; and public officials must act reasonably and subject to law in their exercise of the powers of their offices. Moreover, the law must afford adequate protection to fundamental human rights;

---

[12] S Brammertz, 'International Criminal Justice and the Rule of Law: the Experience of the ICTY' in the present volume.

[13] Ibid.

[14] D Fransen, 'The Special Tribunal for Lebanon and the Rule of Law' in the present volume.

[15] L L Fuller, *The Morality of Law* (New Haven, Yale University Press, 1964).

and nation states must generally comply with international law.[16] The UN Secretary-General provides yet another list.[17]

It is interesting in its own right to address the differences and to what extent there is a common set of norms among such helpful definitions. For our purposes – the legitimacy of ICs – two main issues may suffice: which underlying values might justify such various norms; and which values may merit our attention regardless of whether they are to be included among 'rule of law' values.

I submit that several of the nominated norms – though not all – may be justified on the basis of two interests of individuals: our interest in non-domination and in predictability.

The interest in non-domination is to enjoy 'protection from the arbitrary use of political authority and coercive power',[18] cf 'to protect the individual against arbitrary action'.[19] Such protection is especially important domestically against rulers and governments, as mentioned by several of the present authors, even finding expression in norms requiring 'equality of arms'.[20] The same interest also justifies norms that require impartial, rule-guided conflict resolution by peaceful means, to reduce the risk of domination among private actors. For our purposes, ICs may enhance non-domination by guarantees and protections of individuals against infringements by their state.[21]

The second interest concerns our ability to make longer term plans in pursuit of our various interests with some expectation of success – in particular, to be able to rely on general compliance with legal rules.[22] This interest supports such norms as legality and non-retroactivity and may justify the use of precedents in some cases – as well as the contribution ICs can play in ensuring implementation by states with their

---

[16] T Bingham, 'The Rule of Law' (2007) *Cambridge Law Journal* 67–85 cf Brammertz, above n12.

[17] Secretary-General, United Nations, 'The Rule of Law and Transitional Justice in Conflict and Post-Conflict Societies' (2004) *UN Doc. S/2004/616* para 6 cf Fransen, above n14.

[18] P Pettit, *Republicanism: A Theory of Freedom and Government* (Oxford, Clarendon Press, 1997).

[19] Lemmens, above n11.

[20] P Couvreur, 'The International Court of Justice' in the present volume; Fransen, above n14 cf J Waldron, 'Are Sovereigns Entitled to the Benefit of the International Rule of Law?' (2011) 22 *European Journal of International Law* 315–43 at 323.

[21] Couvreur, ibid.

[22] cf J Raz, 'The Rule of Law and Its Virtue' in *The Authority of Law* (Oxford, Oxford University Press, 1979) 210–32.

international legal obligations,[23] and in clarifying existing provisions – eg as expressed in DSU Art 3.2.[24]

A striking divergence of views concerning the concept of the rule of law is how expansive it should be. In particular, does the rule of law require respect for human rights? Divergent views are found even at the United Nations: some statements hold that human rights and the rule of law are *separate* norms:

> human rights, the rule of law and democracy are interlinked and mutually reinforcing and that they belong to the universal and indivisible core values and principles of the United Nations.[25]

Other statements suggest that respect for human rights is *part of* the rule of law, defined as:

> a principle of governance in which all persons, institutions and entities, … , including the State itself, are accountable to laws that are publicly promulgated, equally enforced and independently adjudicated, *and which are consistent with international human rights norms and standards*[26] (my emphasis).

I submit that this disagreement, whilst important, need not be settled for our purpose here which is rather to identify which norms – possibly *beyond* the rule of law – are appropriate standards to assess the legitimacy of ICs. Respect for human rights, somehow defined, is included by many authors as such a standard – separate or not from the rule of law.

Let us now bring these standards to bear on the ICs as presented in this volume. The next sections consider two of several concerns which stand out to this reader: various forms of fragmentation within and among the ICs which may foster legal uncertainty and responses to such risks; and the risks that ICs themselves may become sources of domination.

---

23 Couvreur, above n20.

24 Van den Bossche, above n10.

25 General Assembly of the United Nations. 'Resolution on the Rule of Law at the National and International Levels' (2012) *A/RES/67/97*, cf K Chan and J Wouters, 'Constructing the International Criminal Court's Rule of Law Identity' in the present volume.

26 Secretary General 2004, above n17 at para 6; cited by Fransen, above n14.

III. FRAGMENTATION WITHIN AND AMONG ICS

Concerns about the fragmentation of international law have flourished over the last decade.[27] ICs might be suspected of giving rise to at least two forms of worrisome fragmentation, which in turn create risks that they will subject individuals and other actors to domination.

First, several ICs have multiple objectives, which may sometimes conflict. Such a multiplicity requires the judges to exercise more discretion in interpreting the treaty, especially when they are forced to 'balance' partially conflicting objectives – such as human rights courts which must both provide individual justice and specify general human rights standards;[28] or the ICC which should hold perpetrators accountable *and* build local judicial capacity *whilst* maintaining rule of law standards.[29] Different judges may even reasonably weigh the objectives differently, thus Chan and Wouters note that domestic judges in hybrid tribunals may be more concerned with domestic capacity building than their international colleagues on the bench. With the broader scope of such discretion comes a risk that individuals, private parties and states become subject to the arbitrary will of the judges of ICs. One response is to strengthen procedural requirements of ICs, eg by requiring reasoned opinions and constraints such as precedents. Note, however, that the interpretive practices of different ICs differ, perhaps for good reason. Thus the Appellate Body of the WTO stays closer to the words of the treaty, rather than more (dynamic) interpretations based on the object and purpose of the treaty. This, argues Van den Bossche, helps explain the perceived high legitimacy of the Appellate body. The ECtHR, on the other hand, has a quite different interpretative policy – possibly for good reasons.

Secondly, with more ICs, there is a risk that they will yield conflicting judgments. Their jurisdiction may come to overlap either due to overlooked possibilities when drafting the treaties or as a result of their dynamic interpretation by the ICs themselves. Several authors in this volume note such possibilities,[30] but they have strikingly different

[27] M Koskenniemi, 'Fragmentation of International Law: Difficulties Arising from the Diversification and Expansion of International Law' in *International Law Commission, Study Group on Fragmentation* (2006).

[28] Lemmens, above n11.

[29] Chan and Wouters, above n25.

[30] A A C Trindade, 'An Overview of the Contribution of International Tribunals to the rule of law' in the present volume, above n11.

prognoses. Thus Trindade claims to observe a trend toward harmonization among the ICs:

> Each international tribunal operates in the ambit of its own jurisdiction, but all undertake in harmony their *common mission* of imparting justice; ... distinct trends of protection of the human person ... *converge*, rather than conflict with each other, at normative, hermeneutic and operational levels.

While the evidence of such a harmonization is scant, Gautier claims that some fears of fragmentation have been overstated at least with regard to the various courts and tribunals for dispute settlements permitted by the Convention on the Law of the Sea Part XV Art 280.[31] Judicial practice did not yield such fragmentation.

Various authors in this volume can be read as contributing to a taxonomy of mechanisms which deflect or reduce such risks of fragmentation, and thus bolster predictability and hence the rule of law. We turn to survey such suggestions below, after considering another threat to the rule of law wrought by ICs, due to their many objectives. This raises the risks of domination by these courts themselves.

IV. THE OBJECTIVES OF ICS

The multiplicity of objectives of ICs merits particular attention from the perspective of developing appropriate standards of legitimacy. Many scholars have insisted that the states seldom only intended ICs to resolve disputes but often had further objectives. Whether the ICs contribute toward these intended objectives seems highly relevant for whether they merit deference. Furthermore, other effects of ICs beyond those stated in their treaties affect our assessment of the performance of the ICs. Such functions include, inter alia:

> four dimensions of effectiveness that have engendered debates among scholars or received insufficient scrutiny. The first dimension, *case-specific effectiveness*, evaluates whether the litigants to a specific dispute change their behavior following an IC ruling, an issue closely linked to compliance with IC judgments. The second variant, *erga omnes effectiveness*, assesses whether IC decisions have systemic precedential effects that influence the behavior of all states subject to a tribunal's jurisdiction. The third approach, *embeddedness effectiveness*, evaluates the extent to which ICs anchor their judgments in

---

[31] United Nations, '*United Nations Convention on the Law of the Sea*' (1982).

> domestic legal orders, enabling national actors to remedy potential treaty violations at home and avoid the need for international litigation. The fourth type, *norm-development effectiveness*, considers how IC decisions contribute to building a coherent body of international jurisprudence[32] (my emphasis).

Karen Alter also argues that ICs perform several roles:

> Old-style ICs were primarily inter-state dispute settlement bodies with jurisdiction to adjudicate disputes and access rules that allowed only states to initiate binding litigation. New-style ICs have more extensive mandates that can include jurisdiction to rule on state compliance with international law and jurisdiction to review the legal validity of state and international legislation and administrative acts.[33]

Against this backdrop, it is illuminating to consider the wide range of values various compliance communities expect ICs to promote. The broad set of high expectations suggests that many ICs will fail in the eyes of many beholders, at the risk of reducing their perceived legitimacy and hence support among crucial actors. Moreover, the breadth of tasks indicates that we must be wary of generalizing the purposes or goals of ICs, and therefore also wary of recommending general strategies for improving their performance.

ICs discussed in this volume are – with the exception of the international criminal court and tribunals – generally engaged in *dispute resolution*. But many are also expected to engage in several other objectives mentioned by Helfer or Alter – and beyond.

Several ICs engage in – and are even expected to – increase *predictability*, including the predictability of UN organs.[34] This is one of the two values underlying rule of law norms. ICs promote this objective in several ways. The judgments and advisory opinions[35] of many but not all ICs are expected to establish *precedents*[36] and this is especially likely when judgments or awards are made public rather than remain confidential. A further important way that ICs provide more predictability is when they interpret and *clarify* the law, be it the European Convention on

32 L Helfer, 'The Effectiveness of International Adjudicators' in K Alter, C Romano and Y Shany (eds), *Oxford Handbook of International Adjudication* (Oxford, Oxford University Press, 2013).

33 Alter, above n9.

34 Trindade, above n30.

35 Ibid.

36 H van Houtte and B Concolino, 'The Iran-United States Claims Tribunal and its Contribution to International Law' in the present volume.

Human Rights,[37] the ICTY,[38] by defining terrorism,[39] or of DSU Art 3.2.[40] ICs may also contribute by *disseminating* existing rules – such as when the IUSCT was the first to apply the UNCITRAL rules.[41] Often ICs must also engage in law making or *norm development*;[42] or in norm *specification*, eg when the ICJ must determine which rules of international law apply to delimit the continental shelf.[43]

A striking aspect of the ICs brought out in this volume is the breadth of objectives they pursue, both as a whole and by individual ICs. The objectives range from those of mutual material interest, such as those regulating trade[44] to others that are mainly 'other regarding' – ie aimed at the protection of the interests of non-citizens. The latter include cases where the Rome Statute requires *every* state to hold those engaged in international crimes responsible, and the creation of the special tribunal for Lebanon.[45]

An important general tendency among ICs is that many of them have several, often conflicting, objectives. Thus the ECtHR must both provide individual relief *and* set general human rights standards.[46] The Court of Justice of the EU must both incorporate international law and ensure compliance with fundamental rights – leading to conflicts such as *Kadi*.[47] Several of the ICs must generally balance rule of law standards with considerations of practicality and political realism.[48]

Indeed, some ICs have a perplexing number of objectives: the ICTY's task is to *reassert* the rule of law, to redress crimes, and even to halt them – and to contribute to local capacity building – and to restore and maintain peace.[49] No wonder that some of these ICs are criticized as ineffective: there are clearly intractable tensions between ensuring retributive and restorative justice in addition to forward-looking objectives of rule of law promotion.

---

37 Lemmens, above n11.

38 Brammertz, above n12.

39 Fransen, above n14.

40 Van den Bossche, above n10.

41 Van Houtte and Concolino, above n36.

42 Trindade, above n30 and Lemmens, above n11.

43 Gautier, above n11.

44 Van den Bossche, above n10.

45 Fransen, above n14.

46 Lemmens, above n11.

47 K Lenaerts, 'The Court of Justice as the Guarantor of the Rule of Law within the European Union' in the present volume.

48 Brammertz, above n12.

49 Ibid.

With the plethora of objectives come several challenges we still have not addressed properly. One set of issues concern the mandates and structures of ICs required to manage such goal conflicts in constructive and responsible ways, eg by exemption clauses or priority rules. Another set of issues relate to how the judges and arbitrators should exercise their discretion responsibly when pursuing such baskets of objectives, eg when selecting some cases – and not others – in order to guide the resolution of yet other cases.[50] Chan and Wouters point to a third set of issues in the intersection between the institutional and the professional: in hybrid courts, we should expect that domestic and international judges are likely to give higher priorities to the varying objectives – eg to domestic capacity building rather than combating impunity – so how should such hybrid courts be composed, and how should they operate?

One implication of this multiplicity of objectives is that the ICs must enjoy wide discretion in 'balancing' the various values and aims. Thus certainty and consistency becomes more difficult with multiple objectives for any single IC or several ICs.[51] Indeed, with wide discretion comes the risk of abuse of such authority and hence a concern that the ICs may become new sources of domination. Thus, the fragmentation and multiplicity of objectives of ICs are profound challenges to the rule of law. There are at least two aspects of ICs that may still reduce such risks. The ICs are not unchecked powers: to the contrary, their impact is typically indirect, in complex modes of interaction with domestic authorities as well as other international bodies. Secondly, there are several features which reduce the scope of unchecked – ie arbitrary – discretion by the ICs.

V. THE INTERACTION BETWEEN ICS AND DOMESTIC AUTHORITIES

An important point to consider when understanding and assessing the roles and risks of ICs is how different ICs interact with domestic judiciaries and other authorities in a complex multilevel legal and political order. There are several ways of dividing the labour between ICs and domestic authorities, many guided albeit vaguely by some conception of subsidiarity. These serve to reduce the risk of domination by the

---

50 Van Houtte and Concolino, above n36.

51 Chan and Wouters, above n25.

ICs – but possibly at the cost of increasing the risk of domination by domestic authorities.

The IC may serve as the court of last resort if domestic courts *cannot* resolve the issues. Thus, the WTO is regarded as a last resort and prefers parties to settle without adjudication[52] – though even then agreements will occur 'in the shadow' of the WTO bodies. Likewise, the rules of composition to the Iran-United States Claims Tribunal illustrate how carefully states seek to maintain sufficient loyalty while ensuring sufficient independence from each party.[53]

Alternatively, ICs should intervene only when domestic courts *will not* do so, raising important challenges to develop trigger criteria.[54]

The task of the IC may also be 'positive complementarity': to enhance or empower the domestic judiciary or the democratically accountable bodies, as the ICTY and the ECtHR should.

The IC's authority may also be limited as regards how specific its judgment should be, again possibly by appeals to subsidiarity. Thus ITLOS specifies damages in detail[55] while the ECtHR often leaves it to the domestic authorities to decide how to best avoid future violations.[56]

Several contributions illustrate how the relationship between domestic authorities and ICs is dynamic. The ad hoc criminal tribunals' failure in building local capacity led to the establishment of hybrid criminal tribunals.[57] Likewise, Van den Bossche's account of the WTO Appellate body underscores that states learned from GATT that they needed to relinquish somewhat more veto power so as to render WTO settlements compulsory, and to allow the conclusions of the IC to become legally binding even against opposition by some states. Furthermore, the Appellate body has been very cautious in its interpretation, resulting in broad support. However, once established, judicial activism might increase.

The appeals to subsidiarity thus do not settle once and for all how authority should be allocated and used between the states and the ICs. Indeed, several of the ICs canvassed in this volume point to another ambiguity in appeals to subsidiarity: Who are the ultimate units of concern? Much international law has assumed 'state-centric' conceptions of subsidiarity.[58] However, several historical traditions of subsidiarity –

---

52 Van den Bossche, above n10.
53 Van Houtte and Concolino, above n36.
54 Chan and Wouters, above n25.
55 Gautier, above n11.
56 Lemmens, above n11.
57 Chan and Wouters, above n25.
58 Follesdal, above n1.

from which international law has borrowed the term – are person-centred: it is the interests of individuals, not of states, which should determine where to allocate authority. These two different vantage points have interestingly different implications for some ICs, for instance as regards the role of international human rights courts. Interestingly, the presentation of the WTO Appellate body suggests that it is companies or industries rather than states who push to develop this IC. In some such cases, it may appear that it is the perceived interests of corporations, rather than of states, which explain – if not justify – the relationship between domestic authorities and ICs. One preliminary conclusion is that appeals to subsidiarity may not so much lay these important issues to rest, but rather stimulate more structured and systematic arguments concerning the legitimacy of ICs.

VI. REDUCING RISKS OF FRAGMENTATION AND ARBITRARY DISCRETION

We finally consider ways to reduce fragmentation among ICs and reduce the risk that they will abuse their discretion. First, there are several modes of 'jurisprudential cross-fertilization'. Several authors point out that endeavours of coordination already exist,[59] but these are insufficient – and some create risks of their own.

- *Judicial dialogues* among the tribunals in the form of meetings do occur and should perhaps be institutionalized,[60] thus argues Slaughter.[61]
- ICs' *advisory opinions* reduce the risk of conflicting judgements.[62]
- ICs already borrow interpretations of concepts, such as 'joint criminal enterprise' or redefining crimes against humanity or terrorism to include gender based violence as laid out by the ICTY has 'migrated' to other international and hybrid courts and tribunals.[63]

One of the problems of these practices is that they do not reduce the risk of domination *by* the ICs. To the contrary: some may fear that such

---

59 Trindade, above n30.
60 Ibid.
61 A M Slaughter, *A New World Order* (Princeton, Princeton University Press, 2004).
62 Trindade, above n30 and Couvreur, above n20.
63 Brammertz, above n12.

networks of international judges and arbitrators increase their influence at the cost of other public authorities and individuals – thus detrimental to democratically accountable modes of governance.

A second way to reduce fragmentation, which can also reduce the scope of discretion judges enjoy, could be to establish principles for settling precisely such uncertainties.[64] Chan and Wouters do not provide examples, but three illustrations of ways to channel or guide the judges of ICs might be in order: Some might argue that international human rights treaties should override other treaty obligations in times of conflict to increase predictability and perhaps normative legitimacy. There is no evidence of such a primacy of human rights currently,[65] but the point is here rather that this may be a defensible objective, and possibly a standard of legitimacy for the set of ICs as a whole. A second example is drawn from GATT, which includes exemption clauses (Art XX) that permit regulations of trade to protect public morals or human health. Such exemptions could be laid out in a wide range of treaties, and include, inter alia, certain human rights norms or other international norms of high priority.[66] A third strategy could be to require that ICs may not interpret their treaties as 'self-contained', but instead require them to engage in systematic interpretation – in particular human rights treaties or environmental treaties.[67]

---

[64] Chan and Wouters, above n25.

[65] J Vidmar, 'Norm Conflict and Hierarchy in International Law: Towards a Vertical International Legal System?' in E de Wet and J Vidmar (eds), *Hierarchy in International Law: The Place of Human Rights* (Oxford, Oxford University Press, 2012) 13.

[66] M Wu, 'Free Trade and the Protection of Public Morals: An Analysis of the Newly Emerging Public Morals Clause Doctrine' (2008) 33 *The Yale Journal of International Law* 215–51; M J Trebilcock and R L Howse, 'Trade Policy and Labour Standards' (2005) 14 *Minnesota Journal of Global Trade* 261.

[67] S H Cleveland, 'Human Rights Sanctions and International Trade: A Theory of Compatibility' (2002) *Journal of International Economic Law* 5; J Dine, *Companies, International Trade and Human Rights* (Cambridge, Cambridge University Press, 2005); H Keller, 'Codes of Conduct and Their Implementation' in R Wolfrum and V Roben (eds), *Legitimacy in International Law* (Heidelberg, Springer, 2008) 219–98; cf N Lavranos, 'Towards a "Solange"-Method between International Courts and Tribunals?' in Y Shany and T Broude (eds), *The Shifting Allocation of Authority in International Law* (Oxford, Hart Publishing, 2008).

VII. CONCLUSION

The above philosophical reflections have drawn on the learned preceding chapters to indicate some general lessons concerning the legitimacy of ICs. They have focussed largely on the contributions by ICs to rule of law standards – but also threats wrought by ICs to these very same values: of non-domination and stable legitimate expectations. Fragmentation within and among ICs, and their multiple objectives, require that the judges and arbitrators enjoy a wide berth of discretion in interpretation and adjudication – which raises the risk that states and individuals become subject to domination by the ICs themselves. The contributions in this volume have indicated several responses worth pursuing further to alleviate these fears. The complex, differing and dynamic relationships between ICs and domestic and other international authorities may help blunt risks of abuse of their power – at the cost of less effective ICs. Finally, several authors have pointed to ways to check and guide the discretion of the ICs to reduce the risks of fragmentation and domination. Such checks, guides and coordination among bodies in complex interdependence are typical contributions from a constitution which considers the complex, interdependent set of institutions as a whole. A conclusion to be drawn from the insights in previous chapters is thus that increased legitimacy of international courts requires perspectives and measures of constitutionalisation. Promote rule of law standards by better checks on the international courts, and channel and coordinate them better. If we want other actors to regard the judgments of ICs as reasons for action, these two paths of exploration seem worthwhile starting points.

Index